NEW COMMENTARY

ON

ACTS OF APOSTLES

BY

J. W. McGARVEY, A. M.

VOLUME 1

THE STANDARD PUBLISHING FOUNDATION

CINCINNATI, OHIO

2783

Printed in U. S. A.

PREFACE.

The composition of my first commentary on Acts was begun when I was about thirty years of age, and the work was published about four years later. The greater part of the writing was done amid the distractions of the first two years of our civil war, and the volume was issued in the autumn of 1863, when men's thoughts were turned away from religion to the events of the mighty struggle. The publication of a commentary under such circumstances was considered so hazardous, that it was not undertaken until the demand for it was tested by a call for subscribers in advance. The response to this call was unexpectedly encouraging, and the volume was issued in the inexpensive form which it has since retained.

The sale of the old work, though never very large, has been continuous from the time of its publication till the present hour ; and the author has received from time to time most gratifying assurances of the good it has done, both in furnishing needed instruction to many young preachers, and in teaching many other earnest souls "the way of the Lord more perfectly." Encouraged by these assurances, yet becoming more and more conscious every year of the defects of the work, I have felt a very keen desire to bring it to a higher state of excellence before my life-work is done. I would be ungrateful indeed were I not very thankful now for the kind providence which has prolonged my life, and given me the strength to accomplish in some degree this desire of my heart.

During the twenty-nine years that have intervened, I flatter myself that I have become far better fitted to write a commentary on this precious book ; for I have not only experienced the mental growth which is common to men of studious habits, but during twenty-seven of those years I have annually given instruction on every verse of the book to the senior class in the College of the Bible. Within the same time questions of vital importance, pertaining both to the trustworthiness of this narrative, and through it to the foundations of the faith itself, have been imported from the rationalistic schools of Germany, and have sprung up in our own country and Great Britain, which were unknown to me thirty years ago. These questions must of necessity be discussed in a commentary on Acts that shall be suited to the wants of present day students. In seeking to meet these new issues, the friends of the Bible have been not less industrious than its foes have been in presenting them, and the result is an extensive literature not in existence when my first commentary was printed. Not only so, but the life-long labors of Tischendorf and Tregelles on the Greek text have been completed, as well as those of Westcott and Hort which were then but fairly begun, and we now have for the first time since the early centuries of our era a corrected text in which to read these invaluable writings. The Revised Version has also come to my relief, saving me the necessity of correcting my own revision of the Authorized Version which was the basis of my former work.

In making use of all these new and better facilities, I have produced a work which is much more than a new and improved edition of my first commentary, and which I am constrained to style my New Commentary on Acts. It is new in almost everything except the form. As regards this, I have found the old form, which enables one to read the book, not as you read a dictionary, but continuously as you do other books, so advantageous in many respects, that I have retained it with slight modifications. My advanced age, and the many calls of duty which seem to claim the remnant of my active life, remind me that this is most probably the last effort that I shall make to improve a work which many of my friends have represented as the most useful of all my writings ; and I now commit this labor of my hands and brain to the fate that awaits it in the form in which it will outlive me in this world. The Lord, in whose service I have written it, will deal with it according to its merits.

THE AUTHOR.

Lexington, Ky., 1892.

INTRODUCTION.

I. Acts of Apostles is a much neglected book. It was so in the days of Chrysostom, who lived in the fifth century, and who says: "There are many who do not even know that this book is in existence, or who can state the name of the author."[1] It is so to the present time; and thousands go to other books of the Bible to find that which is the distinctive teaching of this. The reason is to be found in the fact that before the time of Chrysostom the church had departed from its distinctive teaching, and that to this day they have not returned to it. It was a painful consciousness of this fact which led the present writer, more than thirty years ago, to undertake a popular commentary on the book; and, although it is not now so much neglected as formerly, it still needs to be brought more prominently before the attention of this age. The fresh attention which has been given to it within our own generation, is mainly a result of attacks made upon its credibility by rationalists; and this may prove the providential means of calling men back to that clear understanding of its teachings, and that faithful observance of them, which characterized the primitive church.

II. THE TITLE, "The Acts of the Apostles," is misleading: it leads the uninitiated reader to suppose that it treats of all or nearly all the acts of all the apostles; whereas it actually treats of only a few acts of any of them, and of almost none of the acts of the majority.

---

[1] Homily on Acts I.

By omitting the two definite articles we obtain the title, Acts of Apostles, which answers well to the contents, representing some of the acts of some of the apostles, without pointing to the number of either. This is the very title which the book bears in one of the two oldest existing MSS. (B), while in the other (the Sinaitic) it is styled simply, Acts. The title was doubtless given after the book left the hands of its author; for the writers of that age were not accustomed to giving titles to their books; but it would be difficult to invent a better title than the one which we have adopted.

III. Its Author. This book comes to us without an external expression of its authorship; but in its opening sentence it is addressed to one Theophilus, and it claims to be from the pen of one who had written a previous treatise concerning the career of Jesus, addressed to the same person. This previous treatise is our third Gospel, and it is credited to Luke. This claim of a common authorship is confirmed by the uniformity of style which pervades the two books.[1] All the evidence, therefore, which tends to prove that Luke wrote our third Gospel has equal force in proof that he wrote the book of Acts. While unbelieving writers in general deny that he wrote either, all admit that the same author wrote both.

In the course of the writing we learn, from the use of the pronoun " we " in connection with large sections of the narrative,[2] that the author claims to have been a

---

[1] " Not fewer than fifty words are common to the two books that are not found elsewhere in the New Testament " (Plumptre, *Int.* I.).

[2] Beginning with chap. xvi. 11, when Paul was first at Troas, it occurs at short intervals in the narrative to the end.

traveling companion of the apostle Paul during a large part of his ministry, and to have been with him during his first imprisonment in Rome.[1] These indications point exclusively to him whom Paul styles " Luke the beloved physician;" for he was with Paul in the Roman imprisonment, as appears from salutations sent by him in the epistles to the Colossians, and to Philemon, both written in that imprisonment; and the author is distinguished in Acts from all the other habitual companions of Paul. He is thus distinguished in the account of the company which started with Paul on his last journey to Jerusalem (xx. 4–6); for there Sopater, Aristarchus, Secundus, Gaius, Timothy, Tychicus, and Trophimus, are mentioned as going before Paul to Troas, and there waiting for " us," meaning the writer and Paul. As then the writer was none of these, and yet he journeyed with Paul on this visit to Jerusalem, and thence to Rome, we can identify him with no other than Luke. True, some others besides Luke were with Paul when the two epistles just mentioned were written, but none of these journeyed with Paul as did the author.[2]

The internal evidence of the authorship of any written document has a presumption in its favor, like that in favor of a deed or a will when found in proper form; and it stands good before the bar of law and of reason until it is set aside by stronger evidence from external sources. In order to set aside this evidence that Luke is the author of Acts, we should find some writer competent to testify, who contradicts it. Not only so, but, as the book was certainly written by somebody, the

---

[1] Acts xxviii. 16.

[2] The persons named are Aristarchus, Jesus called Justus, Mark, Epaphras, Luke, Demas (Col. iv. 10–14; Philemon, 23, 24).

question of authorship lies between Luke and some other writer; and the adverse testimony, to be conclu- sive, should name that other writer. But it is not pre- tended that such evidence is in existence. Not only is the book not credited by name to any other known author, but it is not pretended that there is any ex- ternal evidence that Luke is not its author. On the contrary, the two earliest writers of antiquity whose works have been preserved, and who mention this book by name, declare that Luke is its author. One of these is Irenæus, who was born in the vicinity of Smyrna in the first half of the second century, became an elder in the church of Lyons, France, in the year 170, and died about the close of that century. In his boyhood he knew Polycarp, who was acquainted with several of the apostles, and therefore he could not well be mistaken in regard to this matter.[1] The other is the author of the Muratorian Canon, written about the same time, who makes the same statement.[2] Such evidence in regard to the authorship of any book of a secular kind would not be doubted by any scholar; for in reality there is less evidence than this for the authorship of almost every secular book of antiquity.

Such being the internal evidence, and the earliest external evidence of the origin of the book, we find, as we should expect to find, traces of its existence all through the period intervening between the time of its composition and the days of the authors just mentioned.

---

[1] *Against Heresies*, iii. 14, 1.

[2] The words are, "The acts of all the apostles are written in one book, Luke relates the events of which he was an eye wit- ness to Theophilus." The statement is inaccurate, but it is ex- plicit as to the authorship.

Going backward from the latter date, Acts is found in the two translations of the New Testament made about the year 150, one of them into the Latin language, and the other into the Syriac. The former, the old Latin version, circulated in the Roman province of Africa, and the latter, the Peshito Syriac, in Syria, north of Palestine. That the book was thus translated shows that it had previously existed in Greek long enough to be credited to an inspired source, and this at a time when old men in the churches remembered far back into the days of the apostles. We find, also, that Polycarp, above mentioned as a contemporary of the apostles, makes quotations from Acts.[1] This chain of evidence is too strong to be broken. It has withstood the strain of unbelieving attacks in all the past, and it will doubtless continue to do so in all the future.

IV. THE AUTHOR'S SOURCES OF INFORMATION. While the use of the first person in the passages in which it occurs proves that the author was present in the scenes therein described, it does not imply that he was present in these alone. He may have spoken of Paul's company in the third person when he was himself present. When he was present his source of information was of course his own personal observation, and this covers not only the so-called "we" passages, but, in all probability, some others. For nearly all the rest, including the account of Stephen's speech and martyrdom, he had Paul as an informant; and concerning those events with which Paul had no connection, he had opportunity to converse with those who had—with Philip,

---

[1] In the first chapter of his epistle to the Philippians, he quotes from Peter's sermon on Pentecost the words, "whom God raised from the dead, having loosed the bands of hades."

for instance, concerning the latter's labors in Samaria and Philistia; and with Peter and James the Lord's brother, for all in which they participated. The fact that some Hebraisms characterize his earlier chapters has led some scholars to suppose that he employed written documents to some extent, and this is not at all improbable. We must not forget, also, that he almost certainly enjoyed the miraculous gift of the Holy Spirit through the imposition of apostolic hands; and this, while it may not have superseded the necessity for careful inquiry, must have guided him in his selections, and guarded him against accepting misinformation.

V. Its Credibility. The question of the credibility of the book is resolved by the nature of the subject matter into two—its credibility, first, as to the facts recorded; and second, as to the speeches reported. The former rests upon three substantial grounds. In the first place, the book comes to us from a writer possessed of the first degree of credibility according to the canons of historical criticism; that is, he was a contemporary of the events which he records, and, to the extent that he was not an eye-witness of them, he obtained them from those who were. Such a writer, unimpreached, possesses the highest degree of credibility known to secular history. In the second place, the events which he records correspond in many important particulars with the statements of other competent writers of the age in which he lived, and whose creeds and nationalities were hostile to his own. This adds greatly to the force of the evidence based on the ground first mentioned. In the third place, the book contains many points of incidental agreement with the acknowledged epistles of the apostle Paul, which can not be accounted for except on the supposition that he and Paul both give a truthful account of these events. For a somewhat elaborate exhibition of the specifications under the last two heads, the reader is referred to Paley's Horæ Paulinæ, the great masterpiece on the subject, and to the author's Evidences of Christianity, Part Third, which presents some points of the evidence omitted by Paley. The principle ground on which the credibility of Acts has been called in question is undoubtedly the fact that it contains so many accounts of miracles; but this objection is urged only by rationalists, who reject all such accounts, wherever found, without deeming them worthy of investigation. All special objections, based on particular passages in the book, will be noticed in the course of the commentary.

As to the speeches in Acts, it has been urged that, in the absence of any method of short-hand writing, it was impossible to preserve them as they were delivered; and it has been charged that certain characteristics of Luke's style of writing which they contain prove that he composed them and put them into the mouths of the supposed speakers. But these two objections are met by the consideration in regard to the first, that all of these speeches are obviously only epitomes of the originals, very greatly abbreviated, such as could be remembered and reported by the speakers, or even by their hearers; and that, as respects the marks of Luke's peculiar style, they can be accounted for partly by the part which he took in the abbreviation of them, and partly by the fact that some of them, having been delivered in Aramaic, were translated by Luke, and thus received the impress of his style. Furthermore, it has been clearly demonstrated by scholars who have taken the pains to search into the phraseology of these speeches, and to compare them with the epistles of the speakers, that in the speeches of every speaker who has left epistles there are found some of the characteristics of his own style.[1] In reality, then, the speeches have precisely the characteristics which we should expect them to have if they originated and came to us as the narrative requires us to suppose.

VI. Its Divisions. Like all other early historians, Luke goes through his narrative from beginning to end without a mark or note to indicate the divisions of his subject; but while there is nothing addressed to the eye for the purpose of marking the divisions, they are made, and they are unmistakable. No one can read the book through without observing two great divisions, the first of which might be styled a general history of the church up to the death of Herod (xii. 23–25); and the second, extending thence to the end of the book, might be styled an account of the labors of the apostle Paul. Consequently, many writers treat the book as being divided only into these two parts. But each of these contains divisions which are sufficiently distinguished from one another, and of sufficient length to be also styled parts. The career of Paul, for instance, is divided into the account of his preaching tours among the Gentiles, from his being set apart to this work (xiii. 1–3), till his last visit to Jerusalem at the close of his third tour (xxi. 16); and the account of his five years of imprisonment, which occupies the remainder of the book. The general history, too, is divided into two very distinct parts, the first of which, ending with viii. 4, treats exclusively of the

---

[1] Numerous specifications are given in Alford's Introduction to Acts, Sec. II., and Canon Cook's Introduction to Acts in the Speaker's Commentary, Sec. 8.

Jerusalem church, and the remainder, from viii. 5 to xii.
25, of the spread of the gospel in Judea, Samaria, and
surrounding countries.   I prefer, therefore, a distribution
into four parts, according to these four large divisions
made by the author.

Each of these parts is subdivided into sections,
treating each of a special topic under the general head.
These should be distinguished by the chapters in our
printed New Testaments, and they would be if the
division into chapters had been made on scientific principles; but as the chapters are arbitrary, frequently
severing natural sections, and thus leading to confusion,
I have distributed the text into its natural sections, and
have employed the chapter divisions only for convenience of reference.   I have also, for the purpose of ex-
hibiting more clearly still to the eye of the reader the
author's divisions of his subject matter, separated the
text into paragraphs, and appended to each its proper
heading.   These divisions, with their headings and sub-
headings, are really parts of the commentary, as they
help to exhibit to the reader the author's plan; and a
careful study of them in connection with the remarks
made on the details of the narrative, will enable the
student to form a much higher opinion than he is otherwise apt to do of the author's literary skill.

VII. ITS DESIGN.   Between believing scholars and
rationalists there is a radical difference in regard to the
chief purpose for which the book of Acts was written.
F. C. Baur, in common with all his followers of the
Tübingen school, assumes that Peter was the leader of
those Judaizers who were in continuous antagonism with
Paul, the other apostles being also in full sympathy with
Peter; that this antagonism was unremitting throughout

the lives of the apostles; and that Acts was written about the close of the first century, or a little later, for the deliberate purpose of making it appear that no such antagonism had ever existed. Baur says: " We are thus obliged to think that the immediate object for which Acts was written was to draw a parallel between the two apostles, in which Peter should appear in Pauline, and Paul in a Petrine character. Even in respect to the deeds and the fortunes of the two men, we find a remarkable agreement. There is no kind of miracle ascribed to Peter in the first part of the work which does not find its counterpart in the second. It is even more striking to observe how in the doctrine of their discourses, and in their mode of action as apostles, they not only agree with each other, but appear to have actually changed parts."[1] This view of the author's design makes the book entirely untruthful, and a sufficient refutation of it is found in what we have said above as to its authorship and its credibility. We may add here, that the parallel between Paul and Peter, which really exists, fails to support the theory, because it is fully accounted for on the supposition that the whole story is truthful. If Peter and Paul had the power to heal diseases, they must have healed such diseases as they found among the people, and therefore they must have healed some of the same kinds of diseases. If they preached the same gospel, they must have given utterance to many of the same ideas, especially if they preached, as they must have done, to many persons in the same state of mind and needing the same instruction. If they were persecuted, they must have suffered alike the afflictions which men commonly visit on those whom

---

[1] *Church History,* i. 133.

they persecute; and if they were guided by the same Spirit, they must have agreed with each other. Both the theory, then, and the reasoning by which it is supported, are fanciful and false.

While believers must of necessity reject the radical theory just stated, they differ very much among themselves as to the chief design of the writer. Opinions on this point are almost as numerous as commentators. We shall not attempt to name them: it is sufficient to say that they nearly all involve the mistake of failing to distinguish between what the author has done, and the design for which he did it. What he has done is to write a very brief account of the origin and progress of the church in Jerusalem, until its dispersion under the persecution which arose about Stephen; of the men and methods by which churches were then established in surrounding districts, including the baptism of Gentiles; of Paul's preaching tours among the districts of Asia Minor, Macedonia and Greece, including the origin and partial settlement of a controversy in regard to the relation of Gentile converts to the law of Moses; and finally, of Paul's imprisonment, which began in Jerusalem, and was terminated in Rome. This is what he has done; and his purpose in doing it is to be ascertained by an inspection of the subject matter which he has introduced into the different parts of his narrative. Doubtless, like other historians, he had more than one purpose in view, one of which may be regarded as chief, and the others as subordinate; and we are to distinguish these by the relative amount of attention which he has given to each. That must be the chief purpose to which the most space is devoted, and to which the statements on other matters sustain a subordinate relation. Now much the greater part of the book consists in detailed accounts of conversions to Christ, and of unsuccessful attempts at the same. If we extract from the book all accounts of this kind, together with the facts and incidents preparatory to and consequent upon each, we shall have exhausted almost entirely the contents of the book. The first chapter shows us how the apostles were prepared for the work of converting men; the second gives the account of converting the three thousand; the third recounts the conversion of many others, followed by the arrest and trial of Peter and John in consequence of these conversions; the persecutions in the next four chapters all grew out of opposition to these conversions; the eighth, ninth and tenth chapters are devoted to the conversions of the Samaritans, the eunuch, Saul of Tarsus, and Cornelius; the eleventh, mainly to the establishment of the church in Antioch by the baptism of Jews and Gentiles there; the twelfth is an episode, showing the benevolence of the new converts, and another persecution in Jerusalem; the thirteenth and fourteenth give the sermons and conversions on Paul's tour with Barnabas; the fifteenth describes the controversy on circumcision which grew out of the conversions on Paul's first tour; the sixteenth gives mainly the incidents leading to and immediately connected with the conversions of Lydia and the Philippian jailer; the seventeenth, the conversions in Thessalonica and Bœrea, followed by a nearly fruitless effort to the same end in Athens; the eighteenth, the conversions in Corinth, occupying a year and a half; the nineteenth, the many conversions followed by persecution in Ephesus; the twentieth, Paul's last journey to Jerusalem, followed by his arrest and his futile attempts to convert the mob in

Jerusalem, Felix, Festus, and Agrippa; and his journey
to Rome, where he attempts in vain to convert the
leaders of the unbelieving Jews in that city. Undoubtedly, then, the writer's chief design was to set forth to
his readers a multitude of cases of conversion under the
labors of apostles and apostolic men, so that we may
know how this work, the main work for which Jesus
died and the apostles were commissioned, was accomplished. The cases recorded represent all the different
grades of human society, from idolatrous peasants up to
priests, proconsuls and kings. They represent all the
degrees of intellectual and religious culture; all the
common occupations of life; and all the countries and
languages of the then known world; thus showing the
adaptation of the one system of life and salvation to all
the inhabitants of the earth.

The history of a case of conversion embraces two
distinct classes of facts; first, the agencies and instrumentalities employed in effecting it; and second, the
changes wrought in the subject of it. In the pursuit of
his main design, therefore, the author was led to desig-
nate specifically all these agencies, instrumentalities, and
changes. He does so that his readers may know what
agents are employed, and how they work; what instrumentalities are used, and how they are applied; and
what changes take place in a Scriptural conversion.
Men are taught more successfully and moved more easily
by example than by precept; and in accordance with
this well known characteristic of our nature, many religious teachers depend much more, in their efforts at the
conversion of sinners, on well told "experiences," than
on the direct preaching of the word. This method was
anticipated by the Lord in giving us the book of Acts.

The cases herein recorded have this superiority over all that now occur, in that they were directed by infallible teaching, and that they were selected by infallible wisdom from among the thousands which had occurred, because of their peculiar fitness for a place in the inspired record. If, then, modern conversions accord with these, they must be right; if they do not, they must be to that extent wrong. The man who proposes to guide others in the way of salvation is in duty bound to guide them by these models; and the man who supposes himself to be a genuine convert to Christ may test his experience by comparing it with these.

If it be asked, why may we not as well take as our model the conversions which occurred under the old dispensations, or under the personal ministry of Jesus, the answer is, that we do not live under the law of Moses, or under the personal ministry of Jesus, but under the ministry of the Holy Spirit. Forasmuch as Jesus, just previous to his ascension, committed all the affairs of his kingdom on earth into the hands of twelve men, to be guided by the Holy Spirit, who descended shortly after he ascended, all that we can know of the present terms of pardon must be learned through the teaching and the example of these men. If the conditions of pardon, therefore, under any preceding dispensation, differ in any particular from those laid down and exemplified in Acts, in all the points of difference we are bound by the latter and released from the former. To study the book of Acts aright is to study it with supreme reference to this subject; and for this reason this topic is never lost sight of in the following pages.

If this book has been neglected in the past, it has been neglected most of all, as we have intimated above, in reference to this its most distinctive teaching. Through ignorance of this, thousands of evangelists are accustomed to referring sinners for instruction on the subject of conversion more frequently to the book of Psalms, than to Acts of Apostles. It is therefore a demand of this age, an intensely missionary age, that we understand better this one book of all in the Bible which is devoted to this transcendently important subject.

The principal agent in bringing about these conversions, and in directing all the labors of the apostles, was the Holy Spirit; and it is undoubtedly a secondary, if not a coördinate purpose of the author, to show how this divine power was exerted in compliance with the oft repeated promise of our Lord. The book has its starting point in the apostolic commission (i. 2) ; but the apostles were instructed not to begin their appointed work until the Holy Spirit should come upon them (i. 4); and so the main body of the book opens with an account of the descent of the Spirit, and from beginning to end it sets forth the labors of the apostles and evangelists as being constantly directed by the Spirit who dwelt within them. Our Lord had said to his disciples, before his departure, " It is expedient for you that I go away : for if I go not away the Advocate will not come to you ; but if I go, I will send him to you " (Jno. xvi. 7). " I have yet many things to say unto you, but ye can not bear them now. Howbeit when he, the Spirit of truth, is come, he shall guide you into all the truth " (*ib.* 22, 23). The account of the departure of the first of these heavenly guides is found in the introduction to Acts (i. 9–11), and the body of the book sets forth the promised work of the second. If, then, we may properly style the combined accounts of the four evangelists the Gospel of

Christ, we may with equal propriety, as Plumptre suggests,[1] style Acts the Gospel of the Holy Spirit.

In carrying out his main purpose in regard to conversions and the guidance of the Holy Spirit, it was necessary for Luke to make selections from the multitudinous
events which occurred in the thirty years covered by his
narrative, and the plan on which these selections were
made brings to view another of his subordinate designs.
He evidently designed to set forth the labors of Paul
more fully than those of all other men ; probably because,
while they would serve his main purpose as well, he at
the same time had a better personal acquaintance with
them. But to set these forth alone would have been to
present them without their historical connection in the
past, and consequently he was constrained to begin with
those events which preceded Paul's ministry and prepared the way for it. As Peter was the leader in all
these preceding events, it was but natural that he should
figure most prominently in that part of the narrative ;
and inasmuch as there were many Judaizers at the time
of the composition of the book, who were busily propa-
gating the report that Paul's teaching was in some respects
antagonistic to that of Peter, it was a wise expedient to
refute this false and injurious report by selecting such actions and words of the two as would prove their perfect
agreement. This further accounts for that phase of the
narrative mentioned above which has been seized upon
by rationalists as a ground for denying the credibility of
the book.

When we inquire into the special character of the
selections made in connection with Peter's work, we discover another subordinate design, that of giving in brief

---

[1] Handy Commentary, *Introduction*, IV.

the fortunes of the mother church in Jerusalem, and then the secondary agencies by which the gospel was carried to the peoples living adjacent to Palestine. At the same time, both in this part and in that with Paul as the central figure, the writer accomplishes another very important purpose, that of setting forth the apostolic method of organizing the individual congregations of the believers. Other subordinate purposes might be pointed out if we were disposed to exhaust this topic; but these are sufficient to show that the author's plan was systematic, well studied, and far-reaching. No book in the Bible gives finer proofs of a thorough forecasting of its method and matter with reference to the purposes in the mind of the writer.

VIII. Its Date. F. C. Baur, and all the rationalists of the Tübingen school, fix the composition of the Book of Acts at a date too late for Luke to have been its author. For this they have no reason except the demands of their theory respecting the design of the author, which we have briefly stated above (VII).; but as the theory is unquestionably false, the conclusion based on it is unworthy of serious consideration. Some writers who are more conservative, but who are to some extent under rationalistic influence, date it not earlier than A. D. 70.[1] The controlling reason for assigning it this late date is the assumed fact that Luke's gospel was written after the fall of Jerusalem; and the ground of this assumption is the further assumption that the prediction of the destruction of Jerusalem, quoted from Jesus in xxi. 20–25, was written after the event. But as such assumptions can have no weight at all with men

---

[1] Meyer, *Introduction*, Sec. III.; Lechler, *Introduction*, Sec. II.; Weiss, *Life of Christ*, i. 88.

who believe in the reality of miraculous prediction, we are justified in laying aside without further notice the conclusion which is based upon it.

Conservative writers in general, guided by the indications found in the book itself, unite in assigning it the date of the last circumstance mentioned in it.[1] This circumstance is the continuance of Paul's imprisonment in Rome for "two whole years." That the narrative here closes without telling the reader whether Paul was liberated or put to death, is held to be conclusive proof that neither had taken place when the last word of the book was written. This proof is greatly strengthened when we consider it in connection with the course of the narrative in the last four chapters. In chapter xxv., the writer gives the account of Paul's appeal to Cæsar, which broke off his trial before Festus, and which led to all the subsequent proceedings. It was in consequence of this appeal that Festus, being puzzled as to what report he should send to the Emperor with the prisoner, brought his case to the attention of Agrippa, and also brought Paul himself before this young king (xxv. 12, 26, 27). He was sent upon the voyage described in the twenty-seventh chapter in compliance with the law governing the right of appeal; he was cheered when life was despaired of in the storm by the divine message, "Fear not, Paul; thou must stand before Cæsar" (xxvii. 24); his appeal to Cæsar was the topic of the first conversation which he held with the Jews in the city of Rome (xxviii. 17–19); and he was kept in prison two whole years awaiting his trial. Now, if his trial before Cæsar had taken place when this book was completed, whether

---

[1] Gloag, *Int.*, Sec. V.; Canon Cook, Speaker's Commentary, *Int. to Acts*, Sec. X.: Aiford, *Int.*, Sec. IV.: Hackett, *Int.*, Sec. V.

it resulted in acquittal or conviction, it is unaccountable that the book was closed without a word on the subject. This would have been, not a mere omission like many others which we know to have occurred in the course of the narrative—the omission of matters the mention of which was not required by the historical context—but the omission of the culminating fact to which a long series of events previously mentioned led forward, and concerning which the writer had deliberately awakened the curiosity of his reader. It would be like a drama in which the deepest interest in the sequel of the plot is excited, but which closes just at the point when the sequel would have been the next and the last thing to be witnessed. Or, more pointedly still, it would be like the story of a noted trial, which would give the arrest of the prisoner, his transportation from a distant country to the place of trial, the incidents of a long imprisonment leading up to the very day of the trial, and then closing without a word about the trial itself. Such a narrative was never written, unless it were some fictitious story thus closing for the very purpose of tantalizing its readers. Such a close to a serious and truthful history is unheard of. Our only rational inference, then, is that Luke wrote the last sentence of this book just at the close of the two whole years which he mentions, and before Paul's case had yet been adjudged by the emperor.

An attempt has been made to break the force of this reasoning by supposing that Luke may have intended to write another book, and that, as he left the account of the ascension of Jesus incomplete at the close of his Gospel, and then completed it by giving other particulars in the beginning of Acts, so he intended to do with the account of Paul's trial.[1] But there is not the least foundation for the supposition that Luke had any such intention. It is invented to explain a fact which admits of explanation without it. Moreover, the supposed case is not a parallel; for in Luke's Gospel he did mention the ascension, of which he gave a fuller account in his next book; but here he says not a word about the result of Paul's trial, although he could have done so in a single line. He disposes of the death of the apostle James in seven words in the Greek (xii. 2), and he could certainly have added that many to tell us that Paul was acquitted, or that he was convicted; and then, if he had another book in contemplation, he could have reserved for it a fuller account.

It is proper to say, before we leave this subject, that Irenæus, who wrote in the latter half of the second century, says that Luke wrote his Gospel after the death of the apostles Peter and Paul;[2] but the internal evidence adduced above outweights this traditional evidence, and it acquires a still greater weight when we consider that on this supposition the author not only omitted to tell the result of Paul's appeal to Cæsar, but also failed to mention two events immediately connected with his story, which were the most alarming and distressing of all the calamities that befell the apostolic church, the execution in Rome of these two prominent apostles.

IX. Its Chronology. With the exception of some sections in Part Second, in which the author starts from the dispersion of the Jerusalem church to follow the preacher or preachers who carried the gospel to a

---

[1] Meyer, Int., Sec. III., following several rationalistic German critics.

[2] Against Heresies, iii. 1.

certain district, and then returns to the same point to follow another, all the matter in Acts is arranged in chronological order, and yet the author gives no connected notes of time from which we can make out either the whole time occupied by the events, or the time covered by any one part of the book except the last. In this last part he is explicit as to time, stating that Paul was arrested in Jerusalem at a feast of Pentecost; that he was held in prison from that time two years till the accession of Festus; that in the following autumn he was sent by Festus to Rome, reaching that city in the spring following; and that he remained a prisoner in Rome two whole years.[1] Thus we have nearly five years occupied with this portion of the history, and as it is a well established fact that Festus was sent to Judea in the year 60,[2] we see that Paul's arrest two years previous was at Pentecost 58; that his departure to Rome was in the fall of 60; that he reached Rome in the spring of 61; and that the narrative closes in the spring of 63. As the epistles entitled Ephesians, Colossians, Philemon and Philippians, were written during this imprisonment,[3] they bear date 61–62.

If we start from Paul's arrest in Jerusalem, Pentecost 58, and count backward, we can go a certain distance by the light of Luke's statements alone, and still farther by the aid of Paul's. On the journey by which he reached Rome he spent at Philippi the preceding days of

---

[1] Acts xx. 16, *cf.* xxiv. 27; xxvii. 1; 9; xxviii. 11-16; 30.

[2] This I think is clearly established by the evidence in Conybeare and Howson, Appendix II., note (C), against the views of Meyer, *Int. to Acts*, Sec. IV.

[3] Eph. iii. 1; iv. 1; Phil. i. 12, 13; iv. 22; Col. iv. 10, 18; Philemon 1, 9, 10, 23.

unleavened bread (xx. 6), and he came thither directly from Greece, where he had remained three months (xx. 1–6). These must have been the three winter months, as they were followed by the trip to Philippi in the early spring. Here, then, we have reached the winter of 57-58; and as Romans was written on the eve of leaving Greece on the same journey (Rom. xv. 25, 26, *cf.* Acts xxiv. 17), its date is the beginning of 58. Galatians shows internal evidence of having been written about the same time.[1]

As Paul went directly from Macedonia into Greece, he must have spent the autumn in the former country; and as he tells the Corinthians that he intended to abide in Ephesus till Pentecost, and spend at Corinth the next winter, he must also have spent the summer in Macedonia (I. Cor. xvi. 5–8). This was the summer of 57, and as he wrote Second Corinthians in Macedonia (II. Cor. i. 12; vii. 5), this must be the date of that epistle. But he wrote First Corinthians in Ephesus not long before Pentecost the same year (I. Cor. xvi. 8), and consequently this is the date of that epistle, and it is also the year in which his labors in Ephesus ended. He had been there two years and three months (xix. 8–10), and therefore he commenced his work there in the beginning of 54. From this point backward we have no connecting figures, but we can feel our way by conjecture a short distance with a good degree of probability. As Paul, on his last homeward journey to Antioch left an appointment at Ephesus, and left there Priscilla and

---

[1] This is seen in the sameness of subject matter making up the principal argument of the two epistles, that is, justification by faith, together with Paul's allusion (Gal. i. 6) to the shortness of time since he had been in Galatia, a little over three years.

Aquila with the purpose of thus securing their aid on his return (xviii. 19–21), it is almost certain that on his return he passed very rapidly over the districts lying between Antioch and Ephesus, giving to the journey much less than a year. If so, he commenced his third tour in 53, having closed his second tour about the middle, or in the first half of that year. But in closing the second tour he came direct from Corinth, a journey of a week or two ; and in Corinth he had stayed eighteen months (xviii. 11). This takes us back to about the beginning of the year 52, or late in 51, for the beginning of his labors in Corinth. About this time he wrote the two epistles to the Thessalonians.[1] If, now, we allow a little less than two years for the events of the second tour as far as to Corinth, we fix the beginning of that tour early in 50 ; and as that tour was begun almost immediately after the conference in Jerusalem on circumcision, we fix the beginning of the year 50 as the probable date of that event.

At this point some of Paul's figures come to our assistance. He states in Galatians (i. 18) that three years after his conversion he went from Damascus to Jerusalem, and that after fourteen years (ii. 1) he went there again with Barnabas to the conference. Now if these two periods are to be understood as consecutive,

---

[1] This is ascertained by comparing what is said of the arrival of Timothy and Silas in Corinth, Acts xviii. 5, with I. Thess. iii. 3–6, which shows that Timothy had been sent back to Thessalonica from Athens, and had returned to Paul at Corinth when the first epistle was written ; and the sameness of the condition of the Thessalonian church, together with the continued presence of Silas with Paul, who was not with him after he left Corinth, shows that Second Thessalonians was written soon afterward. See II. Thess. 1–4.

making it seventeen years from his conversion to the
conference, the conference could not have been in 50
without throwing Paul's conversion into 33, the year
previous to the founding of the church.[1] But if we

---

[1] The majority of chronologists date the death of our Lord and
the founding of the church in the year 33; but I am constrained,
after much reflection, to believe that it occurred in 34. Jesus was
baptized, according to Luke (iii. 24), when he was about thirty
years of age, and consequently he entered almost immediately
upon his thirty-first year. If he died in his thirty-third year, his
ministry can have lasted only a little over two years. Our only
means of ascertaining how long it lasted is by observing the number of passovers that occurred during his ministry according to
the statements of John, the only writer who pays attention to this
matter. The one mentioned in the second chapter of John is the
first of these, and it probably occurred nearly or quite six months
after the baptism of Jesus. If the feast mentioned, but not
named, in v. 1 was a passover, the whole time of the ministry
from the first passover was three years; for he certainly passed
the time of one other mentioned in vi. 4, which would make two
years, and he lived till the next, mentioned in xii. 1, which
makes three years. The only debatable question, if we rely upon
John's testimony, is as to whether the feast of v. 1 was a passover, or some other feast. If we argue that it can not be a passover because John calls it a mere feast without naming it, we
may as well argue from the same fact that it can not have been
the feast of pentecost, or that of tabernacles, or that of dedication; for he names all three of these feasts in other places. But
it must have been one of the four, for the Jews had no others.
If it was either the pentecost, the tabernacles, or the dedication
following the supposed passover, this would make no difference as
to the whole length of the ministry; for we would have the passover in question passed by in silence, and the space between the
passover of chap. ii. and that of chap. vi. would still be two
whole years. The supposition adopted by those who make the
whole ministry last but two years after the first passover is, that
the feast of v. 1 was the feast of dedication following next after the
passover of chap. ii. But this requires a forced interpretation of
the remark of Jesus to his disciples in John iv. 35: "Say ye not,
There are yet four months, and then cometh the harvest?"

count the three years and the fourteen as both beginning from his conversion, which best agrees with the argument of the first chapter of Galatians, then fourteen years back from 50 fixes his conversion in the year 36, the second year after the founding of the church, and this is quite harmonious with the course of events in the first eight chapters of Acts.

With Paul's conversion in 36 as a new starting point, his first visit to Jerusalem thereafter, three years later, and his departure to Tarsus, are fixed in 39, and the labors of Philip in Samaria, together with his baptism of the eunuch, in the interval between 36 and 39.[1]

Next in advance of these figures we have a date fixed by Josephus. From him we learn that Agrippa died in 44,[2] and this was while Barnabas and Paul were

---

The natural implication in this question is that at the time it was propounded the next harvest was four months in the future; and as the harvest in Palestine begins late in April, the remark was made in the last of December, or the first of January. If so, the feast of dedication for that year was most probably already past, for it occurred on the fifteenth of the tenth month, which was never later than the fifth of our January, nor earlier than the fifth of December. Even if that was one of the years in which this feast fell late in our calendar, it is scarcely possible that it was the feast of John v. 1; for if it was, Jesus made this journey into Galilee only to return immediately to Jerusalem, and this in the dead of winter. For these reasons I think that the feast of v. 1 was a passover, and that therefore the ministry of Jesus lasted more than three years, and terminated in the year 34.

[1] By describing these labors between his account of the dispersion of the church and the return of Paul to Jerusalem, Luke evidently means that they occurred in this interval.

[2] He informs us (Ant. xix.; iv. 4, *cf.* v. 1; viii. 2) that soon after Claudius came to the throne he gave to Agrippa all the dominions of his grandfather Herod, and that Agrippa reigned over this enlarged kingdom three years. But Claudius came to

engaged in their visit of charity to the churches in Judea
(xi. 29; xii. 25). But previous to starting on this visit,
these two brethren had spent a whole year in Antioch
(xi. 26), and this fixes both the arrival of Paul in that
city in the year 43, and the duration of his stay in Syria
and Cilicia from 39 to 43, a period of about four years.
During this period occurred the labors of Peter recorded
in the ninth and tenth chapters of Acts, and the founding of the Antioch church. We can trace the chronology
of these with a good degree of probability. We are
told that after Paul was sent away from Jerusalem the
church throughout Judea, Samaria and Galilee had peace,
and that Peter went " throughout all parts," meaning all
parts of these three districts, until he finally came down
to Lydda, whence he was called to Joppa; and that
there he tarried " many days" (ix. 32–43). Now it
would appear quite unreasonable to suppose that all these
labors and journeys of Peter occupied less than one year,
and it is more probable that they occupied two. If we
adopt the former estimate, his call from Joppa to Cæsarea
to baptize the Gentiles was in the year 40; and if the
latter, it was in 41. The latter has been adopted as the
correct date by the majority of commentators. It can
not be far from correct; and it shows that the apostles
continued to confine their preaching to the circumcised
for seven years, from 34 to 41.

The date of founding the church of Antioch can be
approximated by a similar calculation. As soon as the
brethren in Jerusalem heard of the baptism of Greeks
there, they sent Barnabas thither (xi. 22). This can not
have been many weeks after the event, and Barnabas re-

---

the throne A. D. 41, and therefore Agrippa's death, three years
later, must have been in 44.

mained there apparently but a short time before he went to Tarsus, and brought Paul to Antioch. But this last event, as we have seen above, was in 43; and consequently the founding of the church could not have been earlier than some time in 42. Thus we see that the baptism of Greeks in Antioch was begun some months after the baptism of the house of Cornelius, just as the course of the narrative in Acts would naturally lead us to suppose.

The results obtained by this zigzag line of research, the only kind of line which our detached figures permit us to follow, may be arranged for convenience in the following form, an interrogation point being placed after those dates which depend largely on conjecture:

1. The first Pentecost, May 34.

2. The dispersion of the Jerusalem church, and the conversion of Saul, 36.

3. The return of Paul to Jerusalem after his conversion, 39.

4. Philip's labors in Samaria, and the baptism of the eunuch, between 36 and 39.

5. The baptism of the house of Cornelius, 41?

6. Founding the Antioch church, 42?

7. First labors of Barnabas and Saul together in Antioch, 43.

8. Barnabas and Saul sent to Judea with alms, death of James, imprisonment of Peter, and death of Herod, 44.

9. The conference on circumcision, 50?

10. Paul's first tour among the Gentiles, between 44 and 50, five years lacking a stay in Antioch before he started, and a stay in Antioch just before the conference. The tour probably occupied nearly four years.

11. Paul's second tour, 50 to 53, including eighteen months, near about half the time, in Corinth. There he wrote I. and II. Thessalonians.

12. Paul's third tour, 53–58, including two years and three months in Ephesus, his longest stay in any one place. On this tour he wrote I. and II. Corinthians in 57, and Galatians and Romans in the beginning of 58.

13. From 58 to 63, his imprisonment, beginning in Jerusalem in 58, continuing in Cæsarea from 58 to 60, on the voyage to Rome from the fall of 60 to the spring of 61, and in Rome from 61 to 63. In the last two years, the writing of Ephesians, Colossians, Philemon, Philippians, and also Hebrews, if he wrote the last at all (Heb. xiii. 18, 19).

Meyer, in his Commentary on Acts (Introduction), gives a table presenting the chronologies of thirty-three authors, ancient and modern, including only one of the many English authors who have written on the subject. No two of these fully agree with each other, yet so nearly do they all approximate agreement that very few of them differ more than two years at any one point from the figures given above. This is therefore a sufficiently near approach to the exact truth in the case to answer all practical purposes, especially as Luke shows by his almost total disregard of chronology that he did not base upon it the value of his facts.

X. LITERATURE. It would be easy to copy a list of all the books, ancient and modern, which have been written for the elucidation of Acts ; but I think it sufficient here to name those which I have found most useful in my own studies.

When I wrote my old commentary, I had constantly in hand only Bloomfield's, Olshausen's and Hackett's commentaries on the original text, and the popular commentaries of J. A. Alexander, Albert Barnes, and a few of the older English works which are now obsolete. I also made constant use of Conybeare and Howson's Life and Epistles of Paul, which was then a new work, and, being the first of its kind, was like a fresh revelation to all who had never studied Acts in the light of Paul's Epistles.

In preparing the present commentary, I have had the additional assistance of the following works:

1. COMMENTARIES: Alford's, Meyer's, Gloag's, Lechler's (in Lange's Bible Work), Jacobson's (in Speaker's Commentary), Plumptre's (a volume of the Handy Commentary), Stokes' (a volume of Expositor's Bible), and Lumby's (a volume of the Cambridge Bible for Schools and Colleges). Of these, I have found Meyer's the most elaborate and instructive in grammatical exegesis; while Alford's and Plumptre's have proved the most helpful in other particulars.

2. LIVES OF PAUL. Farrar's Life and Works of Paul has vivified the picture drawn with so much precision by Conybeare and Howson, while the infidel works of C. F. Baur and Ernest Renan, have been of service in pointing out the approaches of the enemy, so that we may guard the student more securely against him.

3. OTHER WORKS. I have found a similar utility to that last mentioned, in the infidel work of Baur on the History of the Christian Church in the first three Centuries, in Zeller's work on Acts, and in the anonymous English work entitled Supernatural Religion.

In addition to the information derived from such books as I have mentioned, I also made the tour of

Palestine in the year 1879, and visited points of Biblical interest in Asia Minor and Greece. I traveled more extensively in Palestine, and saw more of its out-of-the-way places, than any other American with whose writings I am acquainted; and I did so for the distinct purpose of better qualifying myself to speak and to write on such topics as are illuminated by an exact knowledge of the country.

COMMENTARY ON ACTS.

PART FIRST.

THE ORIGIN, PROGRESS, AND DISPERSION OF THE CHURCH IN JERUSALEM.

(*I. 1—VIII. 4.*)

SEC. I.—INTRODUCTORY STATEMENTS.

(I. 1-26.) *Extensive Research*

1. THE STARTING POINT OF THE NARRATIVE.

Vv. 1, 2. Luke fixes the starting point of this narrative on the day in which his account of Jesus terminated: (1) The former treatise I made, O Theophilus, concerning all that Jesus began[1] both to do and to teach, (2) until the day in which, having given commandment through the Holy Spirit unto the apostles whom he had chosen, he was taken up.[2] This is the proper starting point chronologically, because the present treatise is a continuation of the history begun in the former; and

---

[1] "Began both to do and teach" is an idiomatic expression in which "began" is superfluous in English. We would say, *both did and taught*. For other examples of this idiom, see Mark vi. 2; xiii. 5; Luke iii. 8; xi. 29; xiii. 25; xiv. 9, 29; John xiii. 5. It is a mistake to suppose that there is an allusion in this expression to the personal acts and teaching of Christ as a mere beginning of that which he continued to do and teach after his ascension.

[2] In this rendering of verse 2 the exact order of the clauses in the Greek is followed, and the connection between the day of the

1

the commandment given "on the day in which he was taken up," which can be no other than the Apostolic Commission, is the proper starting point logically, because from it the apostles derived their authority for the acts about to be recorded. During the personal ministry of Jesus, he authorized no one to preach him as the Christ; on the contrary, he forbade his apostles to do so.[1] He was doubtless moved to this by consideration of their inadequate conceptions of the Messiahship, their misunderstanding of the nature of his kingdom, and their imperfect apprehension of much that he had taught them. They were as yet incapable of setting forth his claims correctly. On the night of the betrayal he informed them that in a short time the Holy Spirit would be given to them to guide them into all the truth, and that then this restriction would be removed. Finally, "on the day in which he was taken up," he said, as Luke had written before, "Thus it is written, that the Christ should suffer, and rise again from the dead the third day; and that repentance and remission of sins should be preached in his name unto all the nations, beginning from Jerusalem;"[2] and as Mark had written, "Go ye into all the world, and preach the gospel to the whole creation. He that believeth and is baptized shall be saved; but he that disbelieveth shall be condemned."[3] We shall find that this commission is the key to the whole narrative before us; that the acts

---

ascension and the commandment given on that day is expressed as in the original. At the same time the words "after that" used in A. V. and R. V., but not represented by corresponding words in the original, are avoided, and the participle, ἐντειλάμενος, has its proper rendering.

[1] Matt. xvi. 20; xvii. 9.   [2] Luke xxiv. 46, 47.   [3] Mark xvi. 15, 16.

of the apostles here recorded are the counterpart of its terms, and the best exposition of its meaning.

VER. 3. As the apostles are soon to appear in the narrative testifying to the resurrection of Jesus, our author next gives a compendious statement of their qualifications for this testimony : (3) **to whom he also showed himself alive after his passion by many proofs, appearing unto them by the space of forty days, and speaking the things concerning the kingdom of God :** In the concluding chapter of the former narrative a number of these proofs had been given, and they are not here repeated. We learn here, however, a fact not there related, that the time from the resurrection to the ascension was forty days. This statement has been treated by unfriendly critics as an after-thought on Luke's part, it being held that in his former narrative he represents Jesus as ascending to heaven on the same day on which he arose from the dead.[1] The truth is, that in the former account he describes an interview which occurred on the day of the resurrection, and one on the day of the ascension, without noting the fact that there was an interval between them;[2] while here he distinctly states that there was an interval of forty days. The latter statement serves the purpose of an explanation ; but it is not a contradiction.

Vv. 4, 5. To account for the delay of the apostles in Jerusalem after receiving their commission, and also to fix more definitely the time at which they were to begin their work, the historian next quotes a part of the conversation which took place on the day of the ascension : (4) **and being assembled together with them, he charged them not to depart from Jerusalem, but**

---

[1] Renan, *Apostles,* 20; Meyer *in loco.* [2] Luke **xxiv.** 43, 44–51.

to wait for the promise of the Father, which, said he, ye
heard from me: (5) for John indeed baptized with water;
but ye shall be baptized in the Holy Spirit not many
days hence. This commandment has been mistaken by
commentators for the command referred to above (2);
but, as we have seen, that commandment is the commission, while this is but a limitation of the commission
as to its time and place of beginning. The " promise of
the Father," which they had heard from him, is the
promise of the Holy Spirit which he had made them on
the night of the betrayal.[1] On the meaning of the expression, " baptized in the Holy Spirit," see forward
under ii. 4. The allusion to John's baptism was probably suggested by the well remembered remark of John:
" I indeed baptize you with water; but there cometh he
that is mightier than I, the latchet of whose shoes I am
not worthy to unloose: he shall baptize you in the
Holy Spirit and in fire" (Luke iii. 16).

2. THE FINAL PROMISE OF THE HOLY SPIRIT, 6–8.

VER. 6. When Jesus died, all hope that he would
set up the expected kingdom expired for a time; but
since his resurrection he had spoken much to the disciples concerning the kingdom (verse 3), and he had
said, as reported by Matthew, " All authority hath been
given unto me in heaven and on earth" (xxviii. 18);
and from such remarks the apostles had begun to believe
that the kingdom which he had failed to establish before
his death he would yet establish after his resurrection.
Luke reveals this revival of hope by his next statement: (6) They therefore, when they were come together, asked him, saying, Lord, dost thou at this time

---

[1] John xiv. 26; xv. 26, 27; xvi. 12, 13.

restore the kingdom to Israel ? The form of the question, "restore the kingdom to Israel," shows that they
still retained their former misconception, that Christ's
kingdom was to be a restoration of the old kingdom of
David, and not a new and different institution. The
question also shows unmistakably that his kingdom had
not yet been inaugurated ; for if it had been, it is inconceivable that these men, who were its chief executive
officers on earth, knew nothing of the fact; and it is
equally inconceivable that, if it had been, Jesus would
not have promptly corrected so egregious a blunder on
the part of the disciples. Nothing, indeed, but a misconception almost as gross as that of the twelve concerning
the nature of the kingdom could have originated the
thought entertained by some in modern times, that
Christ's kingdom had been set up previous to this time.
All the arguments in support of this idea, and all the
interpretations of special passages in its favor, plausible
as they may be, are set aside by the one decisive consideration, that this kingdom could not be inaugurated
until the King was crowned in heaven. This occurred
after the ascension,[1] and his first administrative act on
earth was that of sending the Holy Spirit upon the
apostles on the next Pentecost.[2]

Vv. 7, 8. We now take up the answer to the question which we have just considered : (7) **And he said to
them, It is not for you to know times and seasons,
which the Father hath set within his own authority.
(8) But ye shall receive power, when the Holy Spirit is
come upon you : and ye shall be my witnesses both in
Jerusalem, and in all Judea and Samaria, and unto the
uttermost part of the earth.** The answer suggests that

---

[1] Phil. ii. 8–11 ; Heb. ii. 9.   [2] Acts ii. 32, 33.

the times and seasons of God's purposes are kept more
in reserve than the purposes themselves; and this is in
harmony with the known characteristic of prophecy,
that it deals more in facts and the succession of events
than in dates or definite periods. It was not important
for them to know the time at which the kingdom would
be established; but it was all-important that they should
receive the power necessary to the part which they were
to take in its inception and progress; so the answer is
concerned chiefly with the latter. The power promised,
and their work as witnesses, are so connected together
as to indicate that the power to be effective witnesses is
meant. This, as we learn from the testimony which
they afterward gave, was not merely to tell what they
had seen and heard, which they could have done by
their unaided powers; but it included ability to recall
all that he had said to them in his years of ministry;
and to testify as to his exaltation in heaven, his will
concerning all spiritual affairs on earth, and his future
dealings with both men and angels. This power was to
be conferred as he had previously promised,[1] and as he
now once more assures them, by the Holy Spirit which
they were to receive "not many days hence." The
order of localities in which he tells them to bear witness
was not the result of partiality for the Jews and Samaritans over the Gentiles; nor yet was it merely to fulfill
the prediction that thus it must be; for it had been predicted because there were good reasons that it should
be so. One reason, suggested by the commentators in
general, for beginning in Jerusalem, was that he might
be vindicated in the same city in which he was condemned; but the controlling reason was doubtless this:

---

[1] Luke xxiv. 48.

the most devout portion of the Jewish people, that
portion which had been most favorably impressed by
the preparatory preaching of John and Jesus, were
always collected in Jerusalem at the great annual festivals, and hence a beginning could be made there with
greater success than elsewhere. Next to these, the inhabitants of the rural districts of Judea were best prepared by the previous preaching; then the Samaritans,
who had seen some of the miracles of Jesus; and last
of all, the Gentiles. Thus the rule of success was made
their guide from place to place, and it became the
custom, even in heathen lands, to preach "first to the
Jew, and then to the Gentile." The result justified the
rule, for the most signal triumph which the gospel ever
achieved was in Jerusalem, and the most successful approach to the Gentiles in every country was through
the Jewish synagogue.

3. THE ASCENSION OF JESUS, 9–11.

VER. 9. Having now completed his brief account
of the last interview between Jesus and his disciples,
Luke says: (9) **And when he had said these things, as
they were looking, he was taken up; and a cloud received him out of their sight.** We learn from Luke's
former account of the ascension, to which this is a supplement, that Jesus was in the act of blessing them with
uplifted hands, when he was parted from them and
borne aloft into heaven.[1] The cloud formed a back-
ground which rendered the outline of his person very
distinct while in view, and suddenly shut him off from
view as he entered its bosom. Thus all the circumstances of this most fitting departure are calculated to

---

[1] Luke xxiv. 50, 51.

preclude the suspicion of deception, or of optical illusion.

It has been urged by some skeptical writers that the silence of Matthew and John in reference to the ascension, who were eye-witnesses of it if it really occurred, while it is mentioned only by Luke and Mark, who were not present, is ground for suspicion that the latter derived their information from impure sources. That the testimony of Mark and Luke, however, is credible, is made apparent to all who believe in the resurrection of Jesus by simply inquiring, What became of the body after it was raised? Even if none of the historians had described the ascension, we should still conclude that at some time and in some manner it did take place. It should be observed, too, that while John does not mention it, he quotes a conversation between Jesus and Mary Magdalene which implies it. He said to her, "Touch me not; for I am not yet ascended to my Father."[1] Perhaps it was omitted by Matthew and John because they both close their narratives with scenes in Galilee, far removed from Jerusalem; and mentioned by Mark and Luke because they conclude the previous part of their narratives in Jerusalem and on the day the ascension took place. Thus the association of thought, which so often governs insertions and omissions, may have had its natural influence on them. Finally, as to Luke, there was a special reason why he should mention it, found in the fact that the speeches and discussions which he is about to record had constant reference to Christ ascended and glorified, and it was most fitting that his introduction should mention the fact of the ascension.

---

[1] John xx. 17.

Vv. 10, 11. Not only the ascension of Jesus to heaven, but also his future coming to judgment, was to be a prominent topic in the coming narrative, hence the introduction here of another fact which Luke had omitted in his former account: (10) And while they were looking steadfastly into heaven as he went, behold, two men stood by them in white apparel; (11) who also said, Ye men of Galilee, why stand ye looking into heaven? This Jesus, who was received up from you into heaven, shall so come in like manner as ye beheld him going into heaven. The sudden coming, the appearance, and the words of these "two men in white," combined to show that they were angels, as the author would have us to believe. They state not merely that Jesus shall come again, but that he shall come in like manner as the apostles had seen him go; that is, visibly and bodily.

4. The Waiting in Jerusalem, 12–14.

Ver. 12. At the rebuke of the angels the disciples withdrew their gaze from the cloud, and left the spot: (12) Then returned they unto Jerusalem from the mount called Olivet, which is nigh unto Jerusalem, a sabbath day's journey off. The ascension took place near Bethany,[1] which was nearly two miles from Jerusalem,[2] and on the eastern slope of the mount. It is the nearer side of the mount, or rather the summit of it, which is a Sabbath day's journey, or seven-eighths of a mile from the city. We learn from Luke's former narrative that they returned to Jerusalem "with great joy;"[3] their sorrow at parting from the Lord being turned into joy at the thought of meeting him again.

---

[1] Luke xxiv. 50.   [2] John xi. 18.   [3] Luke xxiv. 52.

VER. 13. (13) And when they were come in, they went up into the upper chamber, where they were abiding; both Peter and John and James and Andrew, Philip and Thomas, Bartholomew and Matthew, James the son of Alphæus, and Simon the Zealot, and Judas the son of James. This fresh enumeration of the eleven very appropriately finds place here, because it shows that all of those to whom the commission was given were at their post, ready to begin their appointed work, and waiting only for the promised power from on high.

VER. 14. The manner in which these men spent the time of their waiting, an interval of ten days,[1] was such as we should expect: (14) These all with one accord continued steadfastly in prayer, with the women, and Mary the mother of Jesus, and with his brethren. The place of this prayer and supplication was not chiefly the "upper chamber were they were abiding," but the temple; for we learn from Luke's former narrative that they "were continually in the temple blessing God."[2] This is the last time that the mother of Jesus appears in New Testament history. The fact that she had returned with the disciples to Jerusalem, and remained with them instead of resuming her residence in Nazareth, indicates that John was faithful to the dying request of Jesus, and was caring for her as his own mother, though his natural mother was still living.[3] Though the prominence here given to her name shows that she was regarded with great respect by the apostles, yet the manner in which Luke speaks of her shows that he had no thought

---

[1] From the "morrow a ter the Sabbath" of the passover week until Pentecost was fifty days (Lev. xxiii. 15, 16), and forty of these had passed when the ascension took place.

[2] Luke xxiv. 53. [3] Matt. xxvii. 56.

of the homage that was to be paid her in later ages by
an idolatrous church.   Those styled "the women," who
were also in this company of worshipers, were those who
had come with Jesus from Galilee;[1] and they are mentioned in this informal way because they would be remembered by one who, like Theophilus, had read the
former treatise.   They, too, had returned from their
Galilee homes to await with the twelve the coming
"promise of the Father."   The fact that the brethren
of Jesus were of the company is proof that a great
change had come over them since their divine brother
had closed his labors in Galilee: for then they did not
believe in him,[2] but now they do, and they are closely
identified with the apostles.   What special evidence had
brought about this change, or just when it had taken
place, we have no means of ascertaining.

5. The Place of Judas Filled, 15–26.

Vv. 15–19. The next incident is introduced in these
terms: **(15) And in these days Peter stood up in the
midst of the brethren, and said, (and there was a multitude of persons gathered together, about a hundred and
twenty, (16) Brethren, it was needful that the Scriptures should be fulfilled, which the Holy Spirit spoke
before by the mouth of David concerning Judas, who
was guide to them who took Jesus. (17) For he was
numbered among us, and received his portion in this
ministry. (18) (Now this man obtained a field with the
reward of his iniquity; and falling headlong, he burst
asunder in the midst, and all his bowels gushed out.
(19) And it became known to all the dwellers at Jerusalem; insomuch that in their language that field was**

---

[1] Luke xxiii. 49.   [2] John vii. 1–5.

called Akeldama, that is, The field of blood.)   The parenthetical statement that the number together was about
one hundred and twenty, is not to be understood as
meaning that these were all the disciples Jesus then had,
but only those then and there assembled; for Paul says
that Jesus was seen after his resurrection by more than
five hundred brethren at once.[1]   The hundred and
twenty were probably all who at that time resided in
Jerusalem.

The latter part of the parenthesis which describes
the fate of Judas is unquestionably the language of
Luke, and it is so closely connected with the former
part as to indicate the same authorship for both.   The
certainty that it is Luke's arises from the use of the expression, "their language;" whereas Peter would have
said, "our language;" and from the translating of the
Hebrew word Akeldama into Greek, which Peter would
not have done in addressing, as he did, an audience of
Hebrews.   The parenthesis was inserted to make intelligible to Luke's readers Peter's allusions to Judas,
which, though perfectly intelligible without the parenthesis to Peter's hearers, would not be to Luke's readers.

But while this parenthesis serves very well its obvious purpose, it presents three points of apparent conflict with Matthew's account of the fate of Judas.   First,
it says that he fell headlong and burst asunder, whereas
Matthew says that he hung himself; second, it represents him as obtaining a field with the reward of iniquity, whereas Matthew represents the chief priests as
buying the field with the same money; third, it derives
the name Akeldama from the circumstance of Judas
having fallen there and burst asunder, whereas Matthew

---

[1] I. Cor. xv. 6.

derives it from the circumstance that the field was bought with the blood money.[1] As to the first, the two accounts are in perfect harmony : for if he hung himself, he was either taken down, or he fell ; and Luke says he fell. If he fell and burst asunder, he must have fallen a considerable distance ; or when he fell his abdomen must have been in a somewhat decayed condition ; or both may have been true. His hanging himself, and remaining suspended till he fell, supplies both conditions, and fully accounts for his bursting asunder. Furthermore, if we attempt to account for his bursting asunder on any other hypothesis, we find it very difficult to imagine one that is adequate. The two accounts, then, are not only harmonious, but Luke's is supported by Matthew's. As to the second point, if Judas returned the money as described by Matthew, and if the priests bought with it the potter's field, then that field was really the property of Judas, and could have been claimed by his heirs ; for it was bought with money that belonged to him ; and it could be truthfully said by Luke that Judas obtained the field. Thirdly, if the field was bought with the blood money, or if Judas fell there and burst asunder, the field could have derived its name from either circumstance, and much more might it have derived it from both. The probability is that the piece of land had been rendered comparatively worthless by the excavations which the potter had made in search of potter's clay ; and when, in addition to this, it was found spattered with the contents of the putrefied bowels of a traitor who had hung himself there, it was so horrible a place that the owner was glad to sell it for a trifle, and this enabled the priests to buy it for the thirty

---

[1] Matt. xxvii. 3–8.

pieces of silver, amounting probably to about sixteen dollars. No other piece of land large enough for a small burying ground could have been purchased near the wall of Jerusalem for so small a sum. It was intended for the burial of foreigners too poor to afford a rock-hewn sepulcher. The poor, whether Jews or Gentiles, were buried in the ground.

VER. 20. The historian now resumes the report of Peter's speech, which he had interrupted with a parenthesis. In the remarks already quoted, Peter had based the action which he was about to propose on a prediction uttered by David, and he had stated, as the ground of the application about to be made, the fact that Judas had been numbered with them, and had " received his portion in this ministry." He now quotes the prediction alluded to : (20) For it is written in the book of Psalms, Let his habitation be made desolate, and let no man dwell therein : and, His office[1] let another take. These two passages, the former from Psalm lxix. 25, and the latter from Psalm cix. 8, have no specific reference to Judas in their original context. They occur in the midst of curses pronounced, not by David, but, as Peter

---

[1] The word ἐπισκοπὴν, here rendered " office " in the R. V., and "bishoprick " in the A. V., is quoted from the Septuagint, and its exact etymological equivalent in English is *overseership* What particular kind of overseership is meant in the Psalm from which it is quoted, the context there does not indicate; but that it had not in the days of the Psalmist the meaning now attached to the word bishoprick in English, is absolutely certain, for no such office then existed. In the absence of definite knowledge as to the overseership originally referred to, it is probable that the generic term office is here the best representative of the word, especially as it is so rendered in the Psalm from which the quotation is made. See more on the N. T. use of the word, under xx. 28.

explicitly states, by the Holy Spirit through the mouth of David (16), concerning wicked men in general who persecute the servants of God. But if it be proper that the habitations of such men in general should be made desolate, and that any office they held should be given to others, it was preëminently so in the case of Judas; and it was proper to say that these words were written of him as one among many. This was unquestionably Peter's meaning, for he could see as plainly as we can the general aim of the denunciation.

Vv. 21, 22. It is of some moment to observe here that the question on which Peter is discoursing is not the original appointment of an apostle, but the selection of a man to succeed an apostle. The qualifications, therefore, which are declared necessary to an election are those which must be possessed by any one who aspires to be a successor to an apostle. He states them in the next sentence: (21) **Of the men therefore who have companied with us all the time that the Lord Jesus went in and went out among us,** (22) **beginning from the baptism of John, unto the day that he was received up from us, of these must one become a witness with us of his resurrection.** There being no other instance in the New Testament of the selection of a successor to an apostle, this is our only scriptural guide on the subject; and we must conclude that all those who have since claimed to be successors to the apostles, but were not with the Lord in his personal ministry, lack an essential qualification for the office. The obvious reason for confining the choice to such as had been with the apostles from the beginning is that only such would be thoroughly competent witnesses of the identity of Jesus when they saw him after his resurrection. Thus Peter, like Paul in his first epistle to the Corinthians (ix. 1), makes it an essential characteristic of an apostle that he be a witness of the resurrection of Jesus.

Vv. 23–26. (23) And they put forward two, Joseph called Barsabas, who was surnamed Justus, and Matthias. (24) And they prayed, and said, Thou Lord, who knowest the hearts of all men, show of these two the one whom thou hast chosen, (25) to take the place in this ministry and apostleship, from which Judas fell away, that he might go to his own place. (26) And they gave lots for them; and the lot fell upon Matthias; and he was numbered with the eleven apostles.

It should be observed that the disciples did not themselves select Matthias, but, having first put forward the two persons between whom the choice was to be made, they prayed the Lord to show which one *he* had chosen, and then they cast lots, understanding that the one on whom the lot fell was the Lord's choice. This shows that they believed in a providence of God so especial that it includes, in the things that it determines, even the casting of lots—of all things apparently the most accidental. If it be inquired why they confined the Lord's choice to two persons, the obvious answer is, that these were the only two who possessed all of the qualifications laid down by Peter.

The prayer offered on this occasion is a model of its kind. The petitioners had a single object for which they bowed before the Lord, and to the proper presentation of this they confine their words. They do not repeat a thought, nor do they elaborate one beyond the point of perspicuity. Their petition having reference to the spiritual as well as the intellectual qualifications of two persons, they most appropriately address the Lord as καρδιογνῶστα, *the heart knower.* They do not pray, Show us which thou *wilt* choose, or *dost* choose; as though there was need of reflection with the Lord ; but, " show of these two the one whom thou hast chosen." They describe the office which they desire the Lord to fill, as " the place in this ministry and apostleship from which Judas fell away, that he might go to his own place." He had been in a place of which he had proved unworthy, and now they have no hesitation in saying that he has gone to his *own* place, the place to which hypocrites go after death. So brief a prayer on so important an occasion would in this voluble age be scarcely regarded as a prayer at all ; and one expressing so plainly the fate of a dead man would be regarded as uncharitable ; for who dares to hint, at this day, that any dead sinner has gone to his own place ?

Forasmuch as this transaction occurred before the inspiration of the apostles, and forasmuch as Peter bases his authority for it, not on any command of Jesus, but on what some critics regard as irrelevant citations from the Psalms, it has been held by some that it was totally unauthorized, and that Matthias was not therefore a real apostle. But the statement of Luke, " he was numbered with the eleven apostles," was written long after the inspiration of the twelve, and it expresses their final judgment in the case. Moreover, from this time on the company of the apostles is styled no longer " the eleven," but " the twelve," [1] indicating that from the time of the appointment Matthias was held to be one of the number. Let it be observed, too, that Peter's omission to cite the authority of Jesus for the appointment is by no means proof that they did not have his authority.

---

[1] Chap. ii. 14; vi. 2.

Among the things concerning the kingdom of which he had spoken during the forty days (3), this may have been one, for aught we know; and Peter may have omitted to mention it because it was already well known to all the disciples, while they had failed to observe the predictions which also made it proper. Finally, the promise that the twelve apostles should sit on twelve thrones, judging the twelve tribes,[1] required that the vacant place be filled; and even this may have been spoken of on some previous occasion, and was therefore omitted now. Paul's apostolate was a special one to the Gentiles.

The author has now completed his introductory statements. He has shown that his narrative starts from the commission given on the day of the ascension; that the apostles were assured on that day of a speedy baptism in the Holy Spirit, which would give them full power to testify for Jesus; that they witnessed his ascension to heaven whence he was to send the promised Spirit; that the original eleven were all at their post after the ascension, awaiting the promise; and that they had filled the vacant place of the traitor with a suitable successor. All was now in readiness, and the next section of the story opens with the advent of the expected Spirit.

---

[1] Matt. xix. 28.

SEC. II. — THE CHURCH IN JERUSALEM ES-TABLISHED.

(II. 1–47).

1. THE APOSTLES ARE FILLED WITH THE HOLY SPIRIT, 1–4.

Vv. 1–4. The author now enters upon the main body of his work by describing the promised advent of the Holy Spirit : (1) **And when the day of Pentecost was now come, they were all together in one place.** (2) **And suddenly there came from heaven a sound as of the rush-ing of a mighty wind, and it filled all the house where they were sitting.** (3) **And there appeared unto them tongues parting asunder, like as of fire ; and it sat upon each one of them.** (4) **And they were all filled with the Holy Spirit, and began to speak with other tongues, as the Spirit gave them utterance.**

The day of Pentecost was the fiftieth day after the sabbath of the passover week ; and as the count com-menced on the day after the sabbath, it also ended on the same day of the week, or our Sunday.[1] On account of

---

[1] The commentators in general, misled by Josephus, represent the fifty days as being counted from "the second day of unleav-ened bread, which is the sixteenth day of the month" (Ant. iii. 10. 5). If this were correct, the first of the fifty, and consequently the last, might fall on any day of the week. But the enacting clause in the law reads as follows : "And ye shall count unto you from the morrow after the sabbath, from the day that ye brought the sheaf of the wave offering ; seven sabbaths shall there be complete : even unto the morrow after the seventh sabbath shall ye number fifty days; and ye shall offer a new meal offering unto the Lord" (Lev. xxiii. 15, 16.) This language is not easily mis-understood ; for if even in the first clause, the words "from the morrow after the sabbath" could be construed as meaning from

the seven weeks which intervened between it and the passover sabbath, it was called in the Old Testament "the feast of weeks;"[1] on account of the wheat harvest having occurred in that interval, it was called "the feast of harvest;"[2] and on account of the offering peculiar to it, it was called "the day of first fruits."[3] But after the Greek language become known in Palestine, in consequence of Alexander's conquest of Asia, it acquired the name Pentecost (fiftieth), because it was the fiftieth day. It was celebrated, according to the Mosaic ritual, by the special service of offering the first fruits of the wheat harvest in the form of two loaves of bread.[4] This was one of the three annual festivals at which all of the male Jews were required to be present. The condemnation and death of Jesus had occurred during one of these,

the morrow after the first day of unleavened bread, the latter part of the sentence precludes such a construction; for the count was to be "unto the morrow after the *seventh sabbath*," and the word sabbath here unquestionably means a weekly sabbath; and if the fiftieth day was the morrow after a weekly sabbath, then the first must also have been the morrow after a weekly sabbath. That it was is further proved by the terms of the law, fixing the day of offering the sheaf of the wave offering: "And he shall wave the sheaf before the Lord, to be accepted for you: on the morrow after the sabbath the priest shall wave it" (Lev. xxiii. 11.) The first day of unleavened bread, although in it "no servile work" was to be done, is never called a sabbath. As to the testimony of Josephus on the subject, we must remember that, although he claims to have been of priestly ancestry, he was never consecrated as a priest, he wrote his antiquities many years after the fall of the temple and the cessation of its solemnities, and he depended for his knowledge of such topics on his readings of the Old Testament, in which he had no advantage over modern scholars. He has here, as in many other places, misinterpreted the text.

[1] Deut. xvi. 10.   [2] Ex. xxiii. 16.   [3] Num. xxviii. 26.   [4] Lev. xxiii. 15–21; Num. xxviii. 26–31.

and the next was most appropriately chosen as the occasion for his vindication, and for the inauguration of his kingdom on earth. The day was also appropriate from its being the day of the week on which he arose from the dead.

The persons thus assembled together and filled with the Holy Spirit were not, as many have supposed, the one hundred and twenty disciples mentioned in a parenthesis in the previous chapter, but the twelve apostles. This is made certain by the grammatical connection between the first verse of this chapter and the last of the preceding. Taken together they read as follows: "And they gave lots for them, and the lot fell upon Matthias; and he was numbered with the eleven apostles. And when the day of Pentecost was now come, they were all together in one place."[1]

The house in which the apostles were sitting when the Spirit came upon them was not the upper chamber in which they were abiding, but some apartment of the temple; for, as we learn from Luke's former treatise, the apostles during these days of waiting were "contin-

---

[1] The supposition first advanced by Chrysostom, and adopted very generally by more recent commentators, that all the one hundred and twenty were included, and the view advanced in modern times (see Alford *in loco*), that all the disciples of Jesus who had come to the feast were included, are entirely without support in the context; and the only plausible reason given for either is the universal language employed in the quotation made below from Joel: "I will pour out my Spirit upon all flesh; and your sons and daughters shall prophesy, and your young men shall see visions, and your old men shall dream dreams," etc. But it is obvious at a glance that these words were not all fulfilled on that occasion. Nobody then present was seeing visions, or dreaming dreams. There was here only the beginning of a fulfillment which afterward was extended until all was done which Joel predicted.

ually in the temple praising God;" that is, continually there through the hours in which the temple was open. The upper chamber was their place of lodging.[1]

The firelike and forked tongues which were visible above the heads of the apostles were symbols of the audible tongues in which they immediately began to speak; and they added much to the splendor of the scene, which soon riveted the attention of the gathering throng. The statement that the tongues "appeared to them" is not intended to exclude as witnesses of it those who were drawn together, but it points to the fact that the apostles were alone when the phenomenon first made its appearance.

When the apostles were filled with the Holy Spirit, and began to speak as the Spirit gave them utterance, the promise of a baptism in the Holy Spirit and of power from on high was fulfilled. The power took effect on their minds, and its presence was manifested outwardly by their speaking in languages which they had never learned.[2] The inner and mental miracle was demon-

---

[1] In opposition to this conclusion, Alford says: "Certainly Luke would not have used this word ('all the house') of a chamber in the temple, or of the temple itself, without further explanation." (See also Meyer *in loco*). But explanation sufficient had already been given by the statement that the apostles were "continually in the temple;" and, although Alford says that this statement can not apply here, he gives no good reason for the assertion, and we insist that it can and does. An upper room in a private house could not possibly have afforded space for the assembly which witnessed this phenomenon; while one of the many apartments in the temple court, with one side open to the whole area of the court, would have been perfectly suited to the occasion.

[2] In regard to the author's meaning here, the following emphatic statement of Alford is to be heartily adopted: "There can be no question in any unprejudiced mind, that the fact which

strated by the outward and physical. The promise, "It shall not be ye that speak, but the Spirit of my Father that speaketh in you," was fulfilled in its most literal sense; for the very words which they uttered were supplied to them immediately by the Spirit. They were not anxious how or what they should say, neither did they premeditate. It was literally given them in that hour what they should speak. Such power had never before been bestowed on men. It was the baptism in the Holy Spirit; not of their bodies, like John's baptism in water, but of their spirits. It was not a literal baptism, for this act is not to be affirmed of the connection between spirit and spirit; but the word baptism is used metaphorically. As the body, when baptized in water, is sunk beneath its surface and completely overwhelmed, so their spirits were completely under the control of the Holy Spirit, their very words being his and not theirs. The metaphor is justified by the absolute power which the divine Spirit exerted upon their spirits. Such is not the case with the ordinary influences of the

---

this narrative sets before us is that the disciples began to *speak in various languages, viz: the languages of the nations below enumerated, and perhaps others.* All attempts to evade this are connected with some forcing of the text, or some far-fetched and indefensible explanation." To admit with Meyer (Com. *in loco*), that this is the author's meaning, and then to say, "The sudden communication of a facility of speaking foreign languages is neither logically possible nor psychologically and morally conceivable," is not only to deny the reliability of the author, and thus to throw discredit on all of his accounts of miracles, but it is to deny that the Spirit can act miraculously upon the minds of men. The reader who is curious to know the many preposterous attempts which have been made to explain away this miracle, will find a sufficient account of them in Meyer's Commentary on this passage.

Spirit, consequently these are not styled baptisms in the Spirit.[1]

2. THE EFFECT ON THE MULTITUDE, 5–13.

Vv. 5–13. If we attempt to conceive some method by which the miraculous inspiration of a company of men could be immediately demonstrated to an audience, we shall doubtless be at a loss to think of any other than the one employed on this occasion—that of speaking intelligibly the wonderful works of God in a variety of tongues unknown to the speakers. This shows the appropriateness of the particular miracle here wrought, and even the necessity for it in order to the immediate conviction of the hearers. Such an exhibition could be available for its purpose only in the presence of persons acquainted with the languages spoken; but the present occasion supplied this condition, and to this the author next addresses himself: (5) Now there were dwelling at Jerusalem Jews, devout men, from every nation under heaven. (6) And when this sound was heard, the multitude came together, and were confounded, because that every man heard them speaking in his own language. (7) And they were all amazed, and marveled, saying, Are not all these who speak Galileans? (8) And how hear we every man in our own language, wherein we were born? (9) Parthians and Medes and Elamites, and the dwellers in Mesopotamia, in Judea and Cappadocia, (10) in Pontus and Asia, in Phrygia and Pamphylia, in Egypt and the parts of Libya about Cyrene, and sojourners from Rome, (11) both Jews and proselytes, Cretans and Arabians, we do hear them speaking in our own tongues the mighty works of God. (12) And

---

[1] See further remarks on this subject under chap. x. 44–46.

they were all amazed, and were perplexed, saying to one another, What meaneth this?   (13) But others mocking said, They are filled with new wine.

The native tongues of these Jews were those of the countries enumerated in which they were born; yet all, or nearly all of them, had been taught by their parents the home dialect of Judea; for such was the custom of the Jews of that age. This enabled them to understand the tongues spoken by the apostles, and to know the reality of the miracle. Such a miracle had never before been witnessed, and the author exhausts his vocabulary in the attempt to describe its effect on the hearers. He says, "They were confounded," "they were amazed," "they marveled," "they were perplexed," and they said to one another, "What meaneth this?" On this question their thoughts centered when they had time to think; and it shows that they recognized the miraculous nature of the phenomenon, but could not determine what it meant; that is, for what purpose the miracle was wrought. As yet they knew nothing of the men who were speaking, except that they were Galileans. Their question, however, was the very one which the miracle was designed to call forth, and the speech which followed furnished the answer.

The mockers who said, "They are filled with new wine," were irreverent men, who either did not understand more than one of the tongues spoken, and so mistook the rest for nonsense; or were so excessively irreverent as to mock at that which filled all others with amazement. Their mockery received due notice in the speech which followed.

3. Peter's Sermon, 14–40.

I.

INTRODUCTION: THE MIRACLE EXPLAINED, 14–21.

Vv. 14–21. (14) But Peter standing up with the eleven, lifted up his voice, and spake forth unto them, saying, Ye men of Judea, and all ye that dwell in Jerusalem, be this known unto you, and give ear unto my words. (15) For these are not drunken as ye suppose; seeing it is but the third hour of the day; (16) but this is that which hath been spoken by the prophet Joel;

(17) And it shall come to pass in the last days, saith God,
 I will pour forth of[1] my Spirit upon all flesh:
 And your sons and your daughters shall prophesy,
 And your young men shall see visions,
 And your old men shall dream dreams:
(18) Yea, and on my servants and on my handmaidens in
  those days
 Will I pour out my Spirit; and they shall prophesy.
(19) And I will show my wonders in the heaven above,
 And signs on the earth beneath;

---

[1] The use that has been made of the expression "pour forth" in connection with the controversy on baptism (Alexander on Acts *in loco*) is a specimen of partisan zeal which is worthy of notice only because it is made to figure in discussions on the subject by men of little discrimination. It is used figuratively for the sending of the Holy Spirit, for it can not be used literally of a person. The mission of the Spirit thus designated, and the baptism in the Spirit, are two distinct conceptions, and the term in which the former is expressed can have no possible bearing on the meaning of the term by which the latter is expressed. Moreover, the term baptism is also used figuratively in this connection. It expresses the power which the Spirit exerted over the minds of the apostles after he entered into them; while the term pour forth ($\dot{\epsilon}\kappa\chi\epsilon\hat{\omega}$) expresses the act of Christ in sending the Spirit from heaven.

Blood, and fire, and vapor of smoke:

(20) The sun shall be turned into darkness,
And the moon into blood,
Before the day of the Lord come,
The great and notable day:

(21) And it shall be, that whosoever shall call upon the name of the Lord shall be saved.

Peter had heard what the mockers said, and although it came from only a few, he spoke of it as though it expressed the sentiment of the multitude. This had the advantage of avoiding a personal issue with those who had made the remark, while it was calculated to excite for it the disgust of those who had taken the matter seriously. His answer was not a complete refutation of the charge, for men might be intoxicated at any hour of the day; but the early hour made it highly improbable that they were under the influence of wine, while the rest of his discourse was relied upon to demonstrate the falsity of the charge.

The first part of the citation from Joel, verses 17, 18, are used by Peter to answer the question of the multitude, "What meaneth this?" and the answer was conclusive. If he had ascribed the speaking in tongues to the ingenuity of himself and his fellows, or to any other than divine power, his hearers could not have accepted his explanation; for they knewthat only divine power could enable men thus to speak. When, therefore, he ascribed it to the Spirit of God, they could but see that he was right; and when he cited the passage from the prophet which was obviously fulfilled before their eyes, they could but see that the miracle was predetermined in the mind of God. They could see, too, that the prediction involved much more than they were then witnessing; for it contemplated an outpouring of the Holy Spirit, not only on the men then before them, but on "all flesh," such as would cause men and women to prophesy, to see visions, and to dream dreams. All but the first was yet to be fulfilled, but all was fulfilled in the course of the events which the author is about to record. By "all flesh" is obviously meant, not every human being, but persons of all nationalities.

The remainder of the quotation from Joel, verses 19, 20, has no bearing on Peter's argument, but was probably made in order to complete the connection of that which his argument demanded. The great and notable day to which it refers has been variously understood; some referring it to the destruction of Jerusalem, some to the day of judgment, and some even to the day of Pentecost itself. The fact that in connection with it the promise is made, "Whosoever shall call on the name of the Lord shall be saved," seems to identify it with the day of judgment; for the terrors of that day alone will be escaped by calling on the name of the Lord. We are not to understand that the mere act of calling on the name of the Lord will save, but such prayer to the Lord as accompanies the faith and the obedience without which all prayer is vain.

Thus far in his discourse Peter has confined himself to the proof of the inspiration of himself and his companions. This was a necessary preparation for what is to follow, for his hearers could in this way alone be prepared to receive with implicit confidence what he had to say of Jesus. Had he closed his discourse at this point, they would have been convinced (that is, the thoughtful portion of them) that they were listening to an inspired man; but they would have learned no more about Jesus,

or about salvation through him, that they knew before.
But now the introduction of the discourse is completed;
the way is paved for the presentation of the principal
theme, and he proceeds at once to announce the proposition for which all that he had said was but introductory.

II.

JESUS PROCLAIMED AS CHRIST AND LORD, 22-32.

(a). HIS RESURRECTION DECLARED, 22-24.

Vv. 22-24. It is impossible for us, at this distance of
space and time, to realize, except in a faint degree, the
effect on minds so wrought up of the next announcement
made by Peter : **(22) Ye men of Israel, hear these words :
Jesus of Nazareth, a man approved of God to you by
mighty works and wonders and signs,**[1] **which God did by
him in the midst of you, even as ye yourselves know ;
(23) him, being delivered by the determinate counsel and
foreknowledge of God, ye by the hands of lawless**[2] **men
did crucify and slay : (24) whom God raised up, having
loosed the pangs**[3] **of death : because it was not possible**

---

[1] By the three terms, mighty works ($\delta v v \acute{a} \mu \epsilon \iota \varsigma$), wonders ($\tau \acute{\epsilon} \rho a \tau a$),
and signs ($\sigma \eta \mu \epsilon \acute{\iota} a$), Peter does not mean three classes of actions, but
he uses the three terms to describe the same phenomena. He
means the miracles of Jesus, which were mighty works, or
powers, because wrought by the immediate power of God ; wonders, because they excited wonder in those who witnessed them ;
signs, because they signified God's approval of what Jesus taught
in connection with them.

[2] The original, $\dot{a} v \acute{o} \mu o \iota$, means in this place, as is indicated in the
margin of the R. V., not men who are violators of the law, but
men who are not under the law, i. e., Gentiles, cf. I. Cor. ix. 21.

[3] In the expression, "loosed the pangs of death," $\tau \grave{a} \varsigma \, \dot{\omega} \delta \hat{\imath} v a \varsigma \, \tau o \hat{v}$
$\theta a v \acute{a} \tau o v$, the pangs of dying are figuratively regarded as bonds
which hold the victim of death in confinement until they are
loosed. Both terms are used figuratively, and it is not Peter's

that he should be held by it. Filled with amazement as the hearers already were, by a visible and audible manifestation of the Spirit of God, they now see that the whole of this amazing phenomenon is subservient to the name of that Nazarene whom they had despised and crucified. This conviction is forced upon them in a sentence packed with a series of facts calculated to make them reel and stagger as under a rapid succession of heavy blows. In one breath they are reminded of the wonderful miracles and signs which Jesus had wrought among them ; they are charged with knowing this to be true ; they are informed that it was in accordance with God's preordained purpose that he was delivered into their power, and not through his own impotence ; and they are boldly told that God had raised him from the dead, it being impossible that such a being as he should be permanently held down among the dead. Never did mortal lips announce in so brief a space so many facts of import so terrific to the hearers. We might challenge the world to find a parallel to it in the speeches of her orators, or the songs of her poets. There is not such a thunderbolt in all the burdens of the prophets of Israel, or among the voices which echo through the Apocalypse. It is the first public announcement to the world of a risen and glorified Redeemer.

(b). THE RESURRECTION OF THE CHRIST PREDICTED BY DAVID, 25–31.

Vv. 25–28. Two of the facts stated in this announcement required proof ; the others required none. That Jesus had been approved of God to them by miracles,

---

purpose to intimate that Jesus suffered any pangs after dying. But for another view of the meaning, see Alford and Meyer.

and that they had by the hands of the lawless Romans
put him to death, were facts well known to the auditors;
but that Jesus had been delivered up to them in accordance with a predetermined purpose of God, was news to
them; and that God had raised him from the dead they
did not believe; both these latter statements, therefore,
needed proof, and Peter proceeds to give the proof in a
way both formal and conclusive. He cites first a passage in which David had very clearly predicted a resurrection of some one from the dead, speaking in the first
person, as if he meant himself: (25) For David[1] says
concerning him,

> I beheld the Lord always before my face;
> For he is on my right hand, that I should not be
>   moved:
> (26) Therefore my heart was glad, and my tongue re-
>   joiced:
> Moreover my flesh also shall dwell in hope:
> (27) Because thou wilt not leave my soul in hades,
> Neither wilt thou give thy Holy One to see corrup-
>   tion.
> (28) Thou madest known to me the ways of life;
> Thou shalt make me full of gladness with thy
>   countenance.

Only so much of this quotation as refers to the resurrection suits the special purpose of the apostle, the
preceding portion (verses 25, 26) serving to connectedly
introduce it. The words, "Thou wilt not leave my soul

---

[1] To deny that David wrote Psalm xvi., which is here quoted by
Peter (Meyer *in loco*, and rationalists in general), is to deny that
he was speaking by inspiration, and therefore it is to deny the
historic truthfulness of the preceding account of the Holy Spirit's
work in him and the other apostles.

in hades," assert a return of the soul from the disembodied state;[1] while the words, "Neither wilt thou give thy Holy One to see corruption," assert that the body would be reanimated by the return of the soul, before corruption would set in. The added words, "Thou madest known to me the ways of life; thou shalt make me full of gladness with thy countenance," refer first to the knowledge of this subject imparted previous to death, and secondly to the gladness of the one raised from the dead when beholding the countenance of God. That this passage predicts the resurrection of some person from the dead previous to the corruption of his body, is undeniable; and the only question between Peter and his hearers was, of whom does David speak? As he uses the first person, and therefore appears to speak of himself, it was necessary for Peter, in order to make out his argument, to show that he refers to some other person, and that person the Christ. This he proceeds to do.

Vv. 29-31. (29) **Brethren, I may say to you freely of the patriarch David, that he both died and was buried, and his tomb is with us unto this day.** (30) **Being therefore a prophet, and knowing that God had sworn with an oath to him, that of the fruit of his loins he would set one upon his throne;** (31) **he foreseeing this,**

---

[1] Hades is a Greek word transferred into English because our language has no native word to exactly represent it. It is compounded of ἀ privative and ἰδεῖν, to see, and means literally *the unseen;* but in usage it is applied exclusively to the unseen abode of disembodied human spirits. If we had no other proof of this meaning, our text, combined with Peter's comment, verse 31 below, would make it clear. While the body of Jesus was in the tomb, his soul was in hades, and yet it was in Paradise, as we learn from his declaration to the dying robber (Luke xxiii. 43). This shows that to the righteous hades is a place of enjoyment.

spake of the resurrection of Christ, that neither was he
left in hades, nor did his flesh see corruption.   It was
well known to the Jews, as it now is to all interpreters
of the prophetic Psalms, that David habitually speaks in
the first person when prophesying of the Christ; and in
any given case, if it is made clear that he does not speak
of himself, the conclusion is that he speaks of the Christ.
This is the force of Peter's argument, and it proved to
his Jewish hearers that which he set out to prove, that
the Christ, according to a predetermined and expressed
purpose of God, was to suffer death, and to arise again
speedily from the dead.   It also corrected their conception of an earthly reign of the Christ, and showed them
that he was to sit on David's throne after his resurrection, and not before his death.

(c). *THE RESURRECTION OF JESUS ATTESTED BY THE
TWELVE, 32.*

VER. 32. Thus far in his argument the speaker has
proved that the Christ was to be delivered up to death,
and that he was to arise from the dead to sit on his
throne; but he has yet to prove that this was true of
Jesus.   This he now proves by the testimony of himself
and the eleven standing with him : (32) **This Jesus did
God raise up, whereof we all are witnesses.**   It is probable that this is only the substance of what he said on
this point, and that he went into the details of the testimony.   As the witnesses were personally unknown to
the multitude, their testimony as mere men could have
had but little weight with their hearers; but they spoke
as men filled with the Spirit of God, and this to men of
Jewish education was a sufficient guarantee that what
they said was certainly true.   Consequently, the fact

now established by this testimony, taken in connection with that just learned from the Psalm, that the Christ was to suffer and rise from the dead as Jesus had suffered and risen, proved beyond a doubt that Jesus was the Christ. So it must have appeared to every thoughtful hearer.

(d). *JESUS EXALTED TO THE THRONE OF GOD, 33–35.*

VER. 33. In order to sustain the proposition that the Christ was to be thus raised that he might sit on David's throne (verses 30, 31), it was necessary for Peter to trace his progress beyond the resurrection, and show that he had actually been exalted to a throne. This he does in these words : **(33) Being therefore by the right hand of God exalted, and having received of the Father the promise of the Holy Spirit, he hath poured forth this which ye see and hear.** His proof is not the fact recited in the introductory chapter of Acts, that he and his companions had seen Jesus ascend into heaven ; for this would have been unavailing, seeing that their eyes followed him no farther than the cloud which received him out of their sight ; but it is that which his hearers were witnessing with their own eyes and ears, the fact that he and his companions were speaking as the Holy Spirit gave them utterance, while the tongues of flame sat upon their heads. In saying that Jesus had been exalted by the right hand of God, Peter spoke that which neither he nor any other mortal could know except by direct revelation ; but as the direct revelation was manifested before the people, it was clear that the testimony given was that of the Holy Spirit himself, who had just descended from heaven where the exaltation had taken place. Here was testimony which no sane man among the Jews could think of calling in question.

Vv. 34, 35. One more point established, not in further proof that Jesus had been exalted, but to show that this which was now proved concerning him was predicted of the Christ, and this inimitable argument will be completed : (34) **For David**[1] **ascended not into the heavens : but he saith himself,**

> **The Lord said unto my Lord, sit thou on my right hand,**

Till I make thine enemies the footstool of thy feet. The Pharisees themselves admitted that in this passage David referred to the Christ ; and they had been much perplexed in consequence of this admission in a memorable conversation with Jesus ;[2] but Peter, taking nothing for granted, guards the application, as he had done that of the previous quotation from David, by remarking that David himself had not ascended to heaven, and therefore he could not in these words be speaking of himself. This admitted, the only alternative was, as in the other instance, that he referred to the Christ ; for certainly David would call no other his Lord.

---

[1] In here quoting Psalm cx. as having been written by David, Peter by the Holy Spirit follows the example of Jesus, who did the same, and who also declares that David said this "in the Spirit" (Matt. xxii. 43, 44). This explicit testimony to the Davidic authorship of that Psalm can not be set aside by claiming that it was, in the lips either of Jesus or Peter, a mere accommodation to an incorrect opinion then current among the Jews; for the argument in both instances turns upon the fact that David was the writer, and it is fallacious if this is not a fact. Neither can it be regarded as a mistake on the part of either Jesus or Peter; for this would be to accuse them of fallacious reasoning based on premises assumed in ignorance. It would be a denial of supernatural knowledge on the part of Jesus, and of inspiration on the part of Peter.

[2] Matt. xxii. 43, 44.

(e). THE LOGICAL CONCLUSION, 36.

VER. 36. Having now established by incontestable evidence the two statements made in his opening announcement which needed proof; first, that Jesus had been delivered to his enemies by the determinate counsel and foreknowledge of God; and second, that God had raised him from the dead; and having gone beyond his first announcement by proving that God had also exalted him, and caused him to sit at his own right hand in heaven, Peter now announces his final conclusion in these confident and startling terms: **(36) Let all the house of Israel therefore know assuredly, that God hath made him both Lord and Christ, this Jesus whom ye crucified.** He had made him Lord by causing him to sit on God's own throne, to rule over angels and men; and he had made him Christ by causing him to sit on the throne of David according to the promise. It was God's throne, because it was the throne of universal dominion; and it was David's throne, because it was the lineal descent from David which made Jesus the rightful king. From this conclusion the Jewish hearers of Peter learned that, contrary to their previous conception, the promised Christ was to sit, not on an earthly throne, however glorious, but on the throne of the universe.

III.

THE PEOPLE EXHORTED TO SAVE THEMSELVES, 37-40.

VER. 37. As we have already observed, up to the moment at which Peter arose to address the audience, although the baptism of the Holy Spirit had occurred, and its effects on the subjects of it had been witnessed, no change had taken place in the minds of the people in reference to Jesus, nor did they experience any emotion except amazement and confusion. The desired change in reference to Christ was not effected till Peter spoke; and all the power to effect it which resided in the baptism in the Spirit was brought to bear through the words which the Spirit caused Peter to speak. The first visible effect is described in these words: **(37) Now when they heard this, they were pricked in their heart, and said unto Peter and the rest of the apostles, Brethren, what shall we do?** In this exclamation they tacitly confessed their belief of what Peter had preached; and the statement that they were pierced to the heart shows that they felt keenly the remorse which the facts they now believed were intended to inspire. Since Peter began to speak a change has taken place in both their convictions and their feelings. They now believe that Jesus is the Christ, and they are pierced to the heart with the thought that they have murdered him. All this effect Luke traces, as we see it must be traced, to what they had heard: "Now when they *heard* this they were pricked in the heart." This exemplifies Paul's teaching,— that "faith comes by hearing; and hearing by the word of Christ."[1]

VER. 38. The question, "What shall we do?" had reference to the escape of these guilty men from the consequences of their crime; and although the idea of salvation from their sins in general could scarcely yet have had a place in their minds, the real force of their question would be well expressed by the full inquiry, What shall we do to be saved? This is the first time under the reign of Christ that this momentous question was propounded, and the first time of course that it received an answer. Whatever may have been the proper answer

---

[1] Rom. x. 14–17.

under any previous dispensation, or on any previous day in the world's history, the answer given by Peter on this day of Pentecost, the day in which the reign of Christ on earth began, is the true and infallible answer for all such inquirers in all subsequent time. (38) **And Peter said to them, Repent**[1] **ye, and be baptized every one of you in the name of Jesus Christ for**[2] **the remission of sins; and ye shall receive the gift of the Holy Spirit.**

It should be observed that in this answer to the question, what shall we do? they are told to do two things; first, to repent; and second, to be baptized in the name of Jesus Christ. If Peter had stopped here, the people would have learned their immediate duty, and we also would have learned that the immediate duty of men pricked in the heart by a sense of guilt is to repent and be baptized; we would also know that this is what we are to do to be delivered from our guilt. But Peter did not stop with the two commands; he saw fit to state specifically the blessings which would follow compliance with them. The people were told to repent and be baptized " for the remission of sins." This is only stating more specifically what would have been understood from connecting the question with its answer, as we have just stated. It makes it doubly certain that

---

[1] That these persons were commanded to repent after they had been "pricked in the heart" by the power of the Spirit through the truth preached, and were so penetrated with a sense of guilt as to cry out, "Brethren, what shall we do?" shows plainly that repentance is not mere sorrow for sin, but a change which follows after it. For a further definition of it, see the note under chap. iii. 19.

[2] For a justification of this departure from the R. V., and for a full statement of the connection between baptism and the remission of sins, see Excursus A.

remission of sins follows baptism, and is therefore to be expected by the baptized. This is equally true if the correct rendering be, as in R. V., "unto remission of sins," for if we are baptized "unto" remission, remission follows baptism, and baptism brings us to it. Remission of sins, forgiveness of sins, and pardon, are synonymous terms, and they express the chief want of the human soul in its most favorable earthly circumstances. The rebel against God's government, though he lay down his arms and become a loyal subject, can have no hope without pardon for the past; and after being pardoned, while he is humbly struggling in the service of God, he knows himself still guilty of shortcomings by which he must fail of the final reward unless he is pardoned again and again. The question as to the conditions of pardon, therefore, divides itself into two; one having reference to the hitherto unpardoned sinner, and the other to the saint who may have fallen into sin. It was the former class who propounded the question to Peter, and it is to them alone that his answer applies.

The second blessing promised on condition of repentance and baptism, is the "gift of the Holy Spirit." By this is not meant that miraculous gift which had just been bestowed upon the apostles; for we know from the subsequent history that this gift was not bestowed on all who repented and were baptized, but on only a few brethren of prominence in the several congregations. The expression means the Holy Spirit as a gift; and the reference is to that indwelling of the Holy Spirit by which we bring forth the fruits of the Spirit, and without which we are not of Christ. Of this promise Peter speaks more fully in the next sentence of his sermon.

Ver. 39. (39) **For to you is the promise, and to your children, and to all that are afar off, even unto as many as the Lord our God shall call unto him.** As this is a conditional promise, conditioned on repentance and baptism, the children mentioned can be no others than those who repent and are baptized. This promise can not therefore be understood of infant children. Moreover, the promise is to those whom the Lord shall "call unto him," and he calls only those who can hear and believe. We may remark that the universality of this promise, while very plain to us who read it in the light of subsequent revelations, was understood by Peter and the other apostles to include the Gentiles only as they might be circumcised. This is an instance among many in which inspired men, while speaking the words which the Spirit gave them, did not themselves adequately apprehend their import.

Ver. 40. In concluding his report of Peter's sermon, the author indirectly informs us that he has given only an epitome of it: (40) **And with many other words he testified, and exhorted them, saying, Save yourselves from this crooked generation.** The term "testified" refers to the argumentative part of the discourse; and the term "exhorted" to the hortatory part. The latter naturally followed his statement of the conditions of pardon, and it is summed up in the words, "Save yourselves from this crooked generation." They were to save themselves by complying with the conditions of salvation just laid down; for salvation from sin is accomplished in the remission of sins;[1] and the reference

---

[1] "*Become saved from this* (the now living) *perverse generation away*, in separating from them by the μετάνοια and baptism."— Meyer. In opposition to this, Alford says: "The apostles' com-

to these conditions was too obvious to be misunderstood. This exhortation should have prevented any one from ever conceiving the idea so often expressed by modern revivalists, that a sinner can do nothing toward saving himself. While it is true that the sinner can do nothing in the way of procuring or meriting his own salvation, or of forgiving his own sins, he *must* do that which is prescribed as the method of accepting the salvation procured for him and offered to him. To this extent he saves himself. To be saved from that generation was to be saved from the fate awaiting that generation in the eternal world, as we may be saved from a sinking ship by escaping its fate.

If the reader will carefully review this discourse, with reference to its plan as a sermon, and the conduct of its line of argument, he will find that it complies with the rules of homiletics as strictly as though Peter had been trained in this modern science; and that its logic is faultless from beginning to end. This could not have been a result of Peter's education or training; for he had no previous instruction which could have qualified him for extemporaneous work of this character; but it must be ascribed to the guiding power of the Holy Spirit, giving him, according to the promise,[1] "a mouth

---

mand is improperly rendered in A. V., '*save yourselves.*' It is strictly passive—be saved—'let us save you,' 'let God by us save you.'" But the staggering effort which this ingenious interpreter makes to extract from the precept the meaning which he assigns to it, betrays the weakness of the attempt. The original word is in the imperative mood, σώθητε, and as it expresses the command, *Be saved*, it requires the act of saving to be done by the persons addressed, and it is, therefore, properly expressed by the terms, "save yourselves."

[1] Luke xxi. 15.

and wisdom which all his adversaries were not able to withstand or to gainsay."

4. Effect of the Sermon, and Progress of the Church, 41–47.

Ver. 41. The auditors who had been so pierced to the heart as to cry out, "Brethren, what shall we do?" were happily surprised to find the terms of pardon so easy; and they acted with becoming promptness: (41) They then that received his word were baptized; and there were added to them in that day about three thousand souls. They received his word in the sense that they believed it to be true, and adopted it as their rule of action.

Times without number it has been urged, and as often refuted, that three thousand men could not have been baptized (immersed) during the remainder of that day, and with the supply of water accessible in Jerusalem. It is true that there is no running stream in the vicinity of the city, and there never has been, suitable for the purpose; but from a time long prior to the birth of Jesus the city has been supplied with artificial pools in which the ordinance could be administered even to such a multitude. At the present day, the only one of these which remains entirely suitable for the purpose, and which has been so used in modern times by missionaries, is the pool of Siloam, situated in the valley immediately south of the temple enclosure. It is fifty feet long, has an average width of about sixteen feet, and is walled up with masonry to a height of about eighteen feet. At its southwestern corner, where the wall does not rise so high, a flight of stone steps, four feet wide, leads down to the bottom of it. The water comes in at the northern end, being conducted by an underground conduit from the Virgin's Pool, a perennial spring, and it escapes at the opposite end through two orifices, one at the bottom, and the other some three or four feet above the bottom. When the former is closed, as it usually is, the water stands at the depth most suitable for baptism.

The pool now called Upper Gihon, situated about half a mile due west from the Joppa gate, is at present the next most suitable place. It is three hundred and sixteen feet long, two hundred and eighteen wide, and has an average depth of about twenty feet. It is supplied by surface drainage, and is now seldom full. It was supplied with broad steps at every corner, descending to the bottom, now in a state of dilapidation; and when the water was at a suitable depth it afforded facilities for baptizing such a multitude as were baptized on Pentecost. But the most suitable of all the ancient pools is the one now called Lower Gihon by Europeans, but called the Pool of the Sultan, on account of its size, by the natives. It was formed by constructing an immense dam across the valley which lies under the western wall of Mount Zion, to retain the water flowing through the valley, and another wall, five hundred and ninety-two feet higher up the valley, to hold back the earth at that end. The sides and bottom of this pool consist of the shelving rock of the valley, and this, on the side next to the city, lies in ledges from two to three feet thick, with an exposed surface in many places from eight to ten feet wide. On these ledges, at any depth of the water, a large number of administrators could stand, many more than the twelve apostles, and baptize at one time without interfering with one another. The plastering on the lower dam of the pool was three and a half inches thick :

but it is now broken off to such an extent that the water freely pours through, and the pool is empty in the dry season; but when this dam was in a good state of preservation no one accustomed to baptizing would think of resorting to any other place about the city. Indeed, it is seldom that a better baptistery can be found anywhere. Since a knowledge of these facilities for baptizing in ancient Jerusalem has been spread abroad by the writings of explorers within our own generation, it has become inexcusable in any person of intelligence to raise the objection which we have been considering.

As to the question of time for the baptism of so many, any one who will make the mathematical calculation, without which it is idle to offer the objection, can see that there was the greatest abundance of time. Peter's sermon began at nine o'clock, and we may safely suppose that the proceedings at the temple closed as early as noon. This allows six hours for the baptizing to be completed that day, as the text asserts. It is very deliberate work for an administrator to baptize one person in a minute; and if he stands at one spot, as is often the case when a large number are to be baptized, and has the candidates to come and go in a continuous line, the work can be done in half this time. But, at the rate of sixty to the hour, twelve men could baptize seven hundred and twenty in one hour, and three thousand in four hours and a quarter. This simple calculation shows how idle the objection is, and it proves that those who urge it have never given the subject proper consideration.

Not satisfied with the two objections to the immersion of the three thousand which we have now disposed of, many affusionists insist that "access to the reservoirs, most precious to the population of a large city, would not have been allowed to such a multitude."[1]   This objection betrays ignorance of the design of these pools, and of the use which is made of them.   Even at this day, when water is far more scarce than in ancient times, they are freely used as swim pools, and their water is never employed for drinking or culinary purposes. Baptizing in them did not reduce the quantity or impair the quality of the water for any of the purposes for which it was used.   The multitude who heard Peter could resort to them for baptism with precisely the same freedom with which believers now resort to streams and pools in the vicinity of any of our American cities or villages.   It is to be hoped that the day has come when this objection will be heard no more from men of average intelligence.[2]

Before leaving this verse, we should observe that two distinct steps were taken by the three thousand : they were baptized, and then, as a distinct process, they were added to the previous number of the believers.   The adding doubtless consisted in some form of public recognition, by which they were acknowledged as members of the church.   As the form is not specified, it is not authoritative ; and believers are now free to adopt any form which appears appropriate and in harmony with the simplicity of the gospel.

VER. 42. These young disciples having now been baptized on the same day in which they first became be-

---

[1] The Bishop of Chester, (Speaker's Com. *in loco*).

[2] And yet, in the volume of The Expositors' Bible on Acts, the author, G. T. Stokes, D. D., makes this statement: "On the day of Pentecost it was clearly impossible to immerse three thousand persons in the city of Jerusalem" (p. 143).   We may charitably suppose that the author has never made himself acquainted with the water supply of Jerusalem.

lievers, had many subordinate objects of faith to become acquainted with, and many duties yet unknown in which to be instructed. In giving an account of these matters Luke is far more brief, adhering strictly to the chief purpose of his narrative, that of giving the process and means of conversion, rather than those of edification and instruction. He closes this section of the history with a brief notice of the order established in the new church, first mentioning their acts of public worship : (42) **And they continued steadfastly in the apostles' teaching and fellowship, in the breaking of bread, and the prayers.** The apostles were as yet the only teachers, and in teaching the disciples they were executing the part of their commission which required them to teach those whom they baptized all things which Jesus had commanded.[1] The command which made it their duty to teach made it also the duty of the disciples to learn from them, and to abide by their teaching; and that they did both is affirmed in saying, "They continued steadfastly in the apostles' teaching."

The fellowship in which they continued was their joint participation in religious privileges. The original term, κοινωνία, is sometimes used for contributions made for the poor;[2] but while this is one of the ways in which fellowship is manifested, the word is not usually restricted to this sense. It usually occurs in such connections as the following : "Ye were called into the fellowship of his Son Jesus Christ;" "the favor of our Lord Jesus Christ, the love of God, and the fellowship of the Holy Spirit be with you;" "and truly our fellowship is with the Father, and with his Son Jesus Christ;"[3] "we have

---

[1] Matt. xxviii. 19, 20. [2] Rom. xv. 26; II. Cor. ix. 13. [3] I. Cor. i. 9; II. Cor. xiii. 14; I. Jno. i. 3, 7.

fellowship with one another." We have fellowship with God, because we are made partakers of the divine nature as we escape the corruption which is in the world through lust. We have fellowship with his Son, because of the sympathies which his life and sufferings have established between him and us; and with the Holy Spirit, because we partake of the strength and enlightenment which he imparts, and because he dwells in us. We have fellowship with one another, because of mutual participation in one another's affection and good offices. The term is also used with reference to the Lord's supper: "The cup of blessing which we bless, is it not the fellowship of the blood of Christ? the loaf which we break, is it not the fellowship of the body of Christ?"[1] This fellowship is our joint participation in the benefits of Christ's broken body and shed blood. In all these particulars the first disciples continued steadfastly in the fellowship.

The breaking of bread and the prayers, in which they also steadfastly continued, are the breaking of the emblematic loaf, or the observance of the Lord's supper, and the public prayers in the congregation. The frequency with which the loaf was broken is not here intimated; but it was doubtless the same weekly observance of this ordinance which we afterward find in existence in distant congregations.[2] This, as well as the number and character of the prayers offered at the meetings, was so well known to Theophilus that it was needless to give the details.

VER. 43. Next to this brief notice of the public service of the church, we have a glance at the effect of the scenes just described on the surrounding community:

---

[1] I. Cor. x. 16.   [2] Acts xx. 17; I. Cor. x . 20.

(43) **And fear came upon every soul: and many wonders and signs were done by the apostles.** This fear was not that which partakes of aversion; for we learn below (47) that many were daily added to the church. It was that solemn awe which miracles naturally inspire, mingled with profound reverence for a community universally characterized by holy living.

Vv. 44, 45. We are next introduced to a remarkable exhibition of the fellowship previously mentioned: (44) **And all that believed were together, and had all things common; and they sold their possessions and goods, (45) and parted them to all, according as any man had need.** This conduct was in marked contrast with the neglect of the poor which was then common among the Jews, in violation of their own law, and which was universal among the Gentiles. Nothing like it had ever been seen on earth before. For a fuller account of it, see the remarks under chap. iv. 32, below.

Vv. 46, 47. The further history of the church for a short time is condensed into this brief statement: (46) **And day by day, continuing steadfastly with one accord in the temple, and breaking bread at home, they did take their food with gladness and singleness of heart, (47) praising God, and having favor with all the people. And the Lord added to them day by day those that were being saved.** This shows plainly that the temple was the daily meeting place of the church. Its courts were open at all times; all Jews had as free access to them as to the streets of the city; and even Gentiles had free access to the outer court, which was called on this account the Court of the Gentiles.[1] No other place inside

---

[1] See more as to their use of the temple, under chap. iii. 11; v. 12, 20, 25, 42.

the city walls could have afforded room for the assemblage of such multitudes.

The breaking of bread mentioned here is not the same as that mentioned above at verse 42; for here the reference is to bread for food, as is seen in the qualifying clause, "they did take their food with gladness and singleness of heart." That they had "favor with all the people," was a natural consequence of the admirable lives which they led. The priests and scribes had received such a shock by the sudden rise of the church that they were not yet prepared for open opposition to it.

The statement that "the Lord added to them day by day those that were being saved," means that there were daily additions to the church, and that those daily added were daily being saved. The last expression does not mean that they were merely in the way of salvation; but that they were saved. They were saved in the sense in which Peter had exhorted those on Pentecost to "save themselves." The word save means to make safe; and a man is made safe from all his past sins when they are forgiven. He can be saved from them in no other way. In this sense those daily added were saved. Paul uses the word in the same sense when he says: "According to his mercy he saved us through the washing of regeneration and the renewing of the Holy Spirit" (Titus iii. 5). The fact that it was the saved who were added to the church, justifies the conclusion that only those who are saved, or whose sins are forgiven, are entitled to church membership. It condemns the practice of receiving persons into the church "as a means of grace," that is, as a means of seeking pardon; and it also condemns the reception of infants who are incapable as yet of complying with the conditions on which pardon is offered.

SEC. III. — PROGRESS OF THE CHURCH, AND ITS FIRST PERSECUTION.

III. 1—IV 31.

1. A Lame Man Healed by Peter, III. 1–11.

Vv. 1–10. Thus far the labors of the apostles had met with uninterrupted and most astonishing success. Now we are introduced to a series of conflicts, in which success and apparent defeat alternate in the history of the Jerusalem church. The temple is still the place of meeting, and it becomes the place of conflict. (1) Now Peter and John were going up into the temple at the hour of prayer, being the ninth hour. (2) And a certain man that was lame from his mother's womb was carried, whom they laid daily at the door of the temple which is called Beautiful, to ask alms of them that entered into the temple; (3) who seeing Peter and John about to go into the temple, asked to receive an alms. (4) And Peter, fastening his eyes upon him, with John, said, Look on us. (5) And he gave heed to them, expecting to receive something from them. (6) But Peter said, Silver and gold have I none; but what I have, that I give unto thee. In the name of Jesus Christ of Nazareth, walk. (7) And he took him by the right hand, and raised him up; and immediately his feet and his ankle bones received strength. (8) And leaping up, he stood, and began to walk; and he entered with them into the temple, walking, leaping, and praising God. (9) And

all the people saw him leaping and praising God : (10)
and they took knowledge of him, that it was he who sat
for alms at the Beautiful Gate of the temple : and they
were filled with wonder and amazement at that which
had happened to him. This miracle is one of the many
signs and wonders mentioned before in chap. ii. 43, as
being wrought from day to day by the apostles ; and it
is selected for particular mention because of the consequences which followed it. The circumstances attending
it were calculated to make it attract unusual attention.
The Beautiful Gate was doubtless the favorite passway
into the temple court ; and as the subject of this cure was
laid there every day, he became well known to all who
frequented the temple. The natural curiosity of the
benevolent concerning the afflictions of those to whom
they minister had also led to the general knowledge that
he had been a cripple from his birth. Furthermore, the
time of the cure was when a multitude of pious people
were just entering the temple for evening prayer, at the
hour of evening incense,[1] and they could but notice the
leaping and shouting of the man who was healed. As
they witnessed his ecstasy, and saw him clinging to Peter
and John, no one needed to ask the meaning of his conduct, for all saw at once that he had been healed by the
apostles, and all stood gazing in amazement, forgetting
the prayers for which they had come together.

VER. 11. It was probably the intention of Peter and
John to go with the people into the Jewish court, and

---

[1] The hours of burning incense in the temple were the third
and the ninth ; and we learn from the example of the people at
the time of Zacharias' vision (Luke i. 10) that it was the custom
of devout persons in the city to assemble about the temple and
pray while the incense was burning.

engage with them in prayer while the incense was burning in the temple, but the conduct of the cripple and that
of the people combined brought about a different course.
(11) **And as he held Peter and John, all the people ran
together unto them into the porch that is called Solemon's,
greatly wondering.** The structure that is here called a
" porch," was a colonnade constructed along the inner
face of the enclosing wall of the outer court. It consisted, according to Josephus, of rows of stone columns
twenty-seven feet high, with a roof of cedar resting on
them and on the wall, so as to constitute a covered portico, with its inner side open toward the temple. On the
eastern side of the court there were two rows of these
columns, making that portico sixty feet deep and as long
as the wall, which Josephus estimates at a furlong,
though its exact measurement to-day is fifteen hundred
and thirty feet. Across the southern end, which now
measures nine hundred and twenty-two feet, there were
four rows of columns, making three walks or passages
between them, each thirty feet deep, and consequently the
depth of this portico was ninety feet.[1] These immense
covered porticos, or cloisters, as Josephus calls them,
served as a protection from the sun in the summer, and
from the rain in the winter. They contained space sufficient for the great multitude of the disciples when
assembled in one mass; and also for many separate meetings of large numbers to listen to different preachers
speaking at the same time. All the twelve apostles
might be preaching in them at the same hour, each to a
large audience, and yet be far enough apart to avoid
confusion of sound. In which of these porticos the
present meeting was held we can not tell, because we are

---

[1] Josephus (Ant. xv. 3. 5).

not informed as to which was distinguished by the name "Solomon's," this being of course an honorary title.

2. PETER'S SECOND SERMON.

I.

INTRODUCTION: THE MIRACLE EXPLAINED, 12–16.

Vv. 12–15. The admiration of the multitude was directed toward Peter and John, and the former saw that they ascribed the cure rather to something extraordinary in them than to the power of their Master. He takes advantage of this circumstance, and devotes the introduction of his sermon to turning their thoughts into the right channel. (12) And when Peter saw it, he answered unto the people, Ye men of Israel, why marvel ye at this man? or why fasten ye your eyes on us, as though by our own power or godliness we had made him to walk? (13) The God of Abraham, and of Isaac, and of Jacob, the God of our fathers, hath glorified his servant Jesus; whom ye delivered up, and denied before the face of Pilate, when he had determined to release him. (14) But ye denied the Holy and Righteous One, and asked for a murderer to be granted unto you, and killed the author [1]

---

[1] The word ἀρχηγός, here rendered *Prince* both in A. V. and R. V., can have this meaning only in the primary sense of *leader*. It also means author, or originator, and it is so rendered in R. V., in Heb. v. 9; xii. 2, "*author* of eternal salvation," "*author* and perfecter of our faith." In those places it could not be rendered prince. Its only two other occurrences in the N. T. are in this place and in a later speech of Peter, v. 31. In the last instance "*prince* and Saviour" is not so good a rendering as "*leader* and Saviour," because the mind is apt to associate with *prince* the conception of royalty, which is not suggested by the original word. There is the same objection to "prince" in the passage before us, and the further objection, that the expression, "prince of

of life; (15) whom God raised from the dead; whereof we are witnesses.

In this passage the apostle makes in substance the same announcement concerning Jesus with which he introduced the principal theme of his first discourse. The antithetical style adopted on this occasion gave his announcement a force even greater than before, if we consider it with reference to the effect on the consciences of his hearers. The fact that the God of their fathers had glorified Jesus is contrasted with the fact that they had delivered him up to die; their refusal to let him be released, with Pilate's desire to let him go; their rejection of one who was holy and just, with the demand that a murderer should be released to them; and the fact that they killed him, with the fact that he was the author of life. These four points of contrast form the steps of a climax. He whom the God of your fathers glorified, ye have delivered up to die. Your criminality in this is heightened by the consideration that when the heathen ruler of your nation pronounced him innocent, and proposed to release him, ye cried out against it. Even this does not express the enormity of your guilt, for ye yourselves knew him to be a man holy and just, and ye preferred the release of one whom ye knew to be a murderer. Finally, in murdering him ye put to death the very author of life itself, your own life, and the life of all men; and although ye put him to death, he has arisen from the dead. A grander climax, or a happier

---

life," conveys no distinct idea, and certainly not the correct idea. Peter is contrasting the act of killing Jesus with the fact that he is the *author* of life. For these reasons I have not hesitated to depart from the R. V. in this instance. See Thayer's Grimm; Meyer *in loco*, and Speaker's Com. *in loco*.

combination of climax and antithesis, is not found often, if at all, in literature. We have reason to believe (see below under verse 17) that the effect on the multitude was overwhelming. The facts set forth in it were undeniable, except the resurrection, and of this Peter declares himself and John to be witnesses.

VER. 16. By the preceding announcement Peter only in part introduced the theme of his discourse. He advanced as far as the resurrection, but he stopped short of the whole truth concerning the glorification of Jesus. He now completes his introduction, and at the same time demonstrates the reality of the resurrection and glorification of Jesus, by adding: (16) And by faith in his name hath his name made this man strong, whom ye behold and know: yea, the faith which is through him hath given him this perfect soundness in the presence of you all. Here is one of those repetitions common with extemporaneous speakers, intended to give greater emphasis to the principal thought, and at the same time to guard against a probable misunderstanding. Lest the peculiar use made of the name of Jesus should lead some of the excited multitude to think that there was some charm in the mere name, a mistake into which certain Jews in Ephesus afterward fell,[1] Peter is particular to say that it was by *faith* in his name that the miracle had been wrought. We must notice, too, that the faith which had effected the cure was not that of the cripple; for it is evident from the account of the cure (verses 4–8) that previous to it he had no faith at all. When Peter said to him, " Look on us," the man looked up, expecting to receive alms. And even when Peter told him in the name of Jesus Christ to walk, he made

---

[1] Acts xix. 13–17.

no attempt to move until Peter took him by the hand
and lifted him up.   He showed no faith either in Jesus,
or in the healing power of the apostles, until he found
himself able to stand and walk.   The faith, then, was that
of Peter; and this accords with what we learn in the
Gospels, that the working of a miracle by those possessed
of spiritual gifts was always dependent on their faith.
Peter was empowered to walk on the water; but when
his faith wavered he began to sink, and Jesus said, "O
thou of little faith, wherefore didst thou doubt?" [1]
When nine of the apostles on a memorable occasion,
tried to cast out a demon, and failed, Jesus explained
the failure by saying it was because of their little faith.[2]
It was only the "prayer of faith" which could heal the
sick.[3]

It may be well to observe here, that while faith was
necessary on the part of one to whom miraculous powers
had been imparted, in order to work any particular
miracle, no faith ever enabled one to work a miracle to
whom such powers had not been imparted. The notion,
therefore, which has existed in some minds from time to
time ever since the apostolic period, that if our faith
were strong enough we also could work miracles, has as
little foundation in Scripture as it has in experience.

II.

FORGIVENESS OF SINS OFFERED THROUGH CHRIST, 17-21.

Vv. 17, 18. At this point in the discourse there is a
marked change in Peter's tone and manner. He has
made a fearful arraignment of his hearers, exposing their
criminality in unsparing terms; but now he softens his
tone and extenuates their fault, influenced no doubt by a

---

[1] Matt. xiv. 31.   [2] Matt. xvii. 20.   [3] James v. 15.

perceptible expression of pain in their countenances. (17) And now, brethren, I know that in ignorance ye did it, as did also your rulers. (18) But the things which God foreshowed by the mouth of all the prophets, that his Christ should suffer, he thus fulfilled. That they acted in ignorance was an extenuation of their crime, but it did not render them innocent. The fact stated in connection with this, that in their mistreatment of Jesus God was fulfilling what he had declared through the prophets should be done, is not easily reconciled by human philosophy with the assertion of their guilt. Once before Peter had brought these two apparently conflicting facts, the sovereignty of God and the free agency of man, into juxtaposition, when he said, " Him, being delivered up by the determinate counsel and foreknowledge of God, ye by the hands of lawless men did crucify and slay." That God had predetermined the death of Jesus, can not be denied without contradicting both the prophets and the apostles ; and that those who slew him acted wickedly in doing what God had determined should be done, Peter affirms, and three thousand of the participants on Pentecost, together with many on this occasion, admitted it. If any man can frame a theory by which these two facts can be philosophically reconciled, we shall accept it if we can understand it; but unless both facts unaltered have a place in the theory, it must be rejected. In the mean time it is well to follow Peter's example, who lays the two facts side by side, appealing to the prophets for proof of the one, and to the consciences of his hearers for the proof of the other, and not seeming to realize that he has involved himself in the slightest difficulty. It is folly to climb where we are certain to fall.

Vv. 19–21. Having now demonstrated the resurrection and glorification of Jesus, together with the criminality of those who had condemned him, the apostle next offers forgiveness to his hearers on the terms prescribed in the commission. (19) Repent ye therefore, and turn again, that your sins may be blotted out, that so there may come seasons of refreshing from the presence of the Lord; (20) and that he may send the Christ who hath been appointed for you, even Jesus: (21) whom the heaven must receive until the times of the restoration of all things whereof God spake by the mouth of his holy prophets which have been since the world began. Here, as in his former statement of the conditions of pardon, the apostle makes no mention of faith; but, having labored from the beginning of his discourse to convince his hearers, his command to repent carries the assumption that they believed. A command based upon an argument, or upon testimony, always implies the sufficiency of the proof, and assumes that the hearer is convinced. Moreover, Peter knew that none would repent at his command who did not believe what he had said. In every view of the case, then, he proceeded naturally and safely in omitting the mention of faith.

In the command, "Repent and turn again," the word turn expresses something to be done subsequent to repentance, and something different from repentance; for there would be no propriety in adding the command, "Turn," if its meaning had already been expressed in the command, "Repent." In order to a proper understanding of the conditions of forgiveness here prescribed, we must determine the exact import of both these terms.

The most prevalent conception of repentance is godly sorrow for sin; but according to Paul, godly sorrow for sin stands related to repentance as cause to effect. "Godly sorrow," he says, "worketh repentance unto salvation, a repentance which bringeth no regret." He says further to the Corinthians: "Now I rejoice, not that ye were made sorry, but that ye were made sorry unto repentance."[1] These remarks show that it is godly sorrow that brings men to repentance; and the last implies that there may be sorrow for sin without repentance. The same distinction is implied in commanding those on Pentecost who were already "pricked in the heart" to repent. It is illustrated in the case of Judas, who experienced the most intense sorrow for sin; but instead of working repentance, it drove him to suicide.

The fact thus made clear, that repentance is a result of godly sorrow for sin, has led some critics to suppose and to teach, that repentance means reformation of life, seeing that this is a result of the sorrow in question.[2] But while reformation does result from sorrow for sin, the Scriptures furnish clear evidence that it is distinguished from repentance. Confounding the two terms would make the passage before us a piece of tautology; for when Peter says, "Repent and turn," the idea of reformation is involved in the word turn; and if repent meant to reform, then the command would be nothing more than reform, and reform. John the Baptist, in requiring the people to "bring forth fruits worthy of repentance," distinguished between repentance and the deeds of a reformed life, by referring to the latter as the fruits of the former. With him reformation is the fruit

---

[1] II. Cor. vii. 8–10.   [2] First propounded by Dr. George Campbell in his Notes on the Four Gospels.

of repentance, and not its equivalent. When Jesus speaks of repenting seven times a day, he certainly means something different from reformation; for this would require more time. Again, when Peter required those on Pentecost to repent and be baptized, if by repent he had meant reform, he would have given them time to reform before baptizing them, instead of baptizing them immediately. Finally, the original term is sometimes used in connection with such prepositions as are not suited to the idea of reformation. For instance, in II. Cor. xii. 21, it is said, " Many have not repented of the uncleanness and fornication and lasciviousness which they have committed." Men do not reform *of* their evil deeds; and the original preposition[1] in this case will not admit of a rendering that will suit the term reform.

Seeing now that repentance results from sorrow for sin, and leads to reformation of life, we can have no further difficulty in ascertaining what it is; for the only result of sorrow for sin which leads to reformation is a change of the will in reference to sin. The primary meaning of the Greek word ($\mu\varepsilon\tau\alpha\nuo\iota\alpha$) is a change of the mind; and in this sense it is used when it said that Esau " found no place for $\mu\varepsilon\tau\alpha\nuo\iota\alpha$, though he sought it carefully with tears." [2] What he sought was a change in his father's mind with reference to the blessing already bestowed on Jacob. Here the desired change was not a change from sin; for Isaac had committed no sin in conferring the blessing on Jacob; consequently, the word in this instance ought to be translated, not repentance, but change of mind. If the change of will designated by the word is not a result of sorrow for sin, but of some considerations of mere expediency, it is not the repent-

---

[1] It is $\dot{\varepsilon}\pi\iota$ with the dative.   [2] Heb. xii. 17.

ance required ; and if it stop short of reformation of life
on the part of the penitent, it falls short of the blessings
here promised by Peter. Repentance, then, fully defined, is a change of will caused by sorrow for sin, and
leading to a reformation of life. IMPORTANT !

We can now perceive more clearly than before that
in the command, " Repent and turn again," two distinct
changes are required, which occur in the order of the
words. In commenting on the latter as rendered in the
King James version, Mr. Barnes says : " This expression
(be converted) conveys an idea not at all to be found in
the original. It conveys the idea of passivity—be converted, as if they were to yield to some foreign influence
which they were now resisting. But the idea of being
passive in this is not conveyed by the original word.
The word properly means to turn—to return to a path
from which one has gone astray ; and then to turn away
from sins, or to forsake them."[1] This interpretation
was not disputed by competent scholars while the old
version was current, and now that the Revised Version
has stamped it with its authority, it will scarcely be disputed by any.[2] The term denotes a change of conduct.
But a change of conduct has a beginning ; and a person
is properly said to turn when he does the first act of the
better life. Now it so happens that one act was uniformly enjoined upon the penitent believer as the first
act of obedience to Christ ; that is, to be baptized. This
Peter's present hearers understood ; for it had been pro-

---

[1] Notes *in loco.*

[2] In this vision the terms *convert* and *converted* are not found,
the original word being everywhere translated *turn.* This better
rendering should promote a better understanding of an important
subject.

claimed from Pentecost onward, and they had seen it observed every day. When therefore they heard the command, "Repent and turn again," they could but understand that they were to turn by being baptized, thus entering upon a new and better life. Baptism was the turning act.

We may reach the same conclusion by another course of reasoning. The command, "Turn again," occupies the same position between repentance and remission of sins that the command, "Be baptized," does in Peter's former discourse. He then said, "Repent and be baptized for the remission of sins;" he now says, "Repent and turn, that your sins may be blotted out." We need scarcely remark that blotting out of sins is a mataphorical expression for their forgiveness, the forgiveness being compared to blotting out from a waxen tablet that which was written thereon. Now when Peter's hearers heard him command them to repent and turn for the same blessing for which he had formerly commanded them to repent and be baptized, they could but understand that the generic word turn was used with specific reference to baptism; and this, not because the two words mean the same, but because men turned by being baptized. This is the doctrine of the passage.

While the command to repent and turn again was for the primary purpose that their sins might be blotted out, two other consequences are mentioned as further inducements to compliance; first, "that so there may come seasons of refreshing from the presence of the Lord;" and second, "that he may send the Christ who hath been appointed for you, even Jesus." The "seasons of refreshing" are placed here where "the gift of the Holy Spirit" was placed in the first discourse, and the reference is to the refreshing of the soul effected by the joys of the Holy Spirit. The sending of Christ to them refers no doubt to his final coming; and it was dependent on their obedience, as we can know from later utterances, though Peter's hearers could not know it at the time, in the general way that a certain amount of work in the saving of men was to be accomplished before his coming. This is indicated by the qualifying remark, " whom the heaven must receive until the time of the restoration of all things whereof God spake by the mouth of his holy prophets since the world began." It is difficult to determine the exact meaning of the word restoration in this place; but it is limited by the expression, " all things whereof God spake by the Holy prophets," and consequently it consists in the fulfillment of the Old Testament predictions; and the remark gives assurance that Jesus will not return again till all these predictions shall have been fulfilled. It is quite common for those theorists who believe in the final salvation of all men to quote this passage improperly by omitting the last clause, quoting it, " the restoration of all things," and making it mean the restoration to primitive purity and happiness of all things and all men. This is to handle the word of God deceitfully.

III.

THESE THINGS MATTERS OF PREDICTION AND OF PROMISE, 22–26.

Vv. 22, 23. Whatever might be proved concerning the resurrection or glorification of Jesus, a Jew would not be prepared to accept him as the promised Messiah unless the proof contained evidence that the facts were subjects of prophecy. To this end, and also for the pur-

pose of warning his hearers against rejecting what they
had heard, Peter next introduces a well known prediction made by Moses: (22) **Moses indeed said, A prophet
shall the Lord God raise up unto you from among your
brethren, like unto me; to him shall ye hearken in all
things whatsoever he shall speak to you.** (23) **And it
shall be, that every soul which shall not hearken to
that prophet, shall be utterly destroyed from among the
people.** That Peter was right in applying this prediction
to Jesus, was perfectly obvious to all who believed what
he had previously said; for if what he had said of Jesus
was true, the likeness on which the application depended
was found in Jesus, and in no one else. Moses was
distinguished from all the other prophets in that he was
a deliverer and a lawgiver. The others were employed
in enforcing the law which Moses gave, but not in adding
to it, or setting any of it aside. Jesus, however, was like
Moses, in that he also came as a deliverer, proposing a
far more glorious deliverance than that effected by
Moses, and he also issued laws for a new government of
men. This proved that he alone was the prophet spoken
of by Moses, and it showed the audience that in obeying
Jesus they would be obeying Moses, while in rejecting
him they would incur the curse which Moses pronounced.

VER. 24. Not content with bringing to bear the
testimony of Moses, Peter adds to it the combined authority of all the prophets. (24) **Yea, and all the prophets from Samuel and them that follow after, as many as
have spoken, they also told of these days.** This declaration is to be understood only of those prophets whose
predictions are recorded in the Old Testament; for to
these alone could Peter appeal before his hearers. The

universal terms of the remark are used, as was common with Jewish speakers and writers, in only a general sense; for it can not be affirmed absolutely that all of the prophets had spoken explicitly "of these days;" but this was true of the prophets in general, and Peter dates the beginning of the series from Samuel, not because Samuel himself spoke of these days, but because the constant succession began with him. It is highly probable that in the actual delivery of the discourse, of which Luke has almost certainly given us only an epitome, as he did of the first discourse, Peter quoted many of these predictions, and made their application clear to his hearers. The argument of the discourse is now completed, and Jesus is once more proved to be the promised Messiah and the glorified Son of God.

Vv. 25, 26. Having completed his argument, Peter next makes an appeal to his hearers based on their veneration for the fathers of their nation, and for the covenant which they had inherited. (25) Ye are the sons of the prophets, and of the covenant which God made with your fathers, saying unto Abraham, And in thy seed shall all the families of the earth be blessed. (26) Unto you first God, having raised up his Servant, sent him to bless you, in turning away every one of you from his iniquities. This was a tender appeal to their national feelings, made more effective by the information that the blessing offered them in Christ was the very blessing contemplated in the well known promise to Abraham, and that to them first, because of their relation to the prophets and to Abraham, God had sent his risen Son to bless them before visiting the rest of mankind.

We here have an authoritative interpretation of the promise to Abraham. It is fulfilled, according to Peter, in turning living men away from their iniquities. Those only who turn away from their iniquities are the recipients of the promised blessing; and the fact that all the kindreds of the earth were to be blessed, does not affect this conclusion, except by extending its application to those among all kindreds who shall turn from their iniquities. To Peter's hearers this concluding remark not only conveyed this information, but it recalled the exhortation, "Turn again," by telling them that God had sent Jesus for the very purpose of turning them from iniquity.

For a cause which appears in the next paragraph of the narrative, this discourse of Peter was not brought to its conclusion. Doubtless, if he had been allowed to continue it, he would have closed with an exhortation to immediate obedience such as that which closed his first sermon.

3. PETER AND JOHN ARRESTED, iv. 1–4.

Vv. 1–3. Thus far the work of the apostles had gone on without interruption, and they probably began to imagine that the old enemies of their Lord were so completely paralyzed by the triumphs of the truth that they had lost all of their former zeal and courage. But just at this moment of hope and joy the calm was followed by a storm. (1) **And as they spake unto the people, the priests and the captain of the temple and the Sadducees came upon them, (2) being sore troubled because they taught the people, and proclaimed in Jesus the resurrection from the dead. (3) And they laid hands on them, and put them in ward unto the morrow: for it was now eventide.** This sudden disturbance of the interested audience by a body of armed men rushing through their midst and seizing Peter and John, was a very bold and startling movement on the part of the unbelievers.

At first thought we would have expected the Pharisees, the old persecutors of Jesus, to be the leaders in any persecution of his apostles; but here we see the Sadducees, who were comparatively indifferent to his pretensions, taking the lead; and it is explained by the fact that the apostles taught through Jesus the resurrection from the dead. While Jesus had taught the same doctrine, and on one occasion had maintained it against the Sadducees in special debate,[1] he had but seldom assailed either the doctrine or the practices of this party. But now the whole brunt of the preaching was in opposition to the denial by the Sadducees of the resurrection from the dead; and as for Caiaphas, the chief priest, who was a Sadducee, the preaching affected him still more seriously by accounting him a murderer. It was well calculated to arouse that party to violence. At the same time, although the Pharisees could by no means have looked upon the triumph of the apostles with indifference, even though their enemies were being discomfited by it, the doctrine of the resurrection was their own, and the only objection they had to the preaching was that the resurrection was proclaimed in the name of Jesus. They were as yet watching the course of things in amazement, unprepared for any decisive action. They had hated Jesus because he had assailed their traditions and exposed their hypocrisy; they had not yet learned to hate the apostles, because as yet the latter had not openly assailed them. The priests who assisted in this arrest may have been Sadducees, or they may have

---

[1] Matt. xxii. 23–33.

been instigated by the fact that this preaching of Peter, beginning that day at the hour of evening prayer, had diverted the minds of the people from the sacrifices and the customary prayers before the temple. The "captain of the temple," who led the party making the arrests, was the commander of the guard of Levites who always stood on duty at the gates and elsewhere, to keep order within the holy precincts.[1]

VER. 4. The people who had been listening to Peter must have been thrown into great excitement by the arrest, and the disciples present may have expected to see reënacted the murderous scenes which terminated the life of their Master; nevertheless, the words of Peter were not without a decided effect, for Luke says: (4) But many of them that heard the word believed; and the number of the men came to be about five thousand. True to the custom of Oriental nations even to the present day, the number of men alone is here given, the women not being counted. The whole number of believers of both sexes must have been largely in excess of these figures. The increase since the day of Pentecost must have been very rapid, for doubtless many of those baptized then must have departed to their distant homes, and still the increase had been more than two thousand, without counting women.

4. PETER'S DEFENSE BEFORE THE COUNCIL, 5–12.

Vv. 5, 6. The arrest having been made late in the afternoon (eventide, 3), further proceedings were postponed till the next day, and Peter and John had the

---

[1] They were first appointed under the name of porters by David (II. Chron. xxvi. 1–19). A plurality of them is alluded to in Luke xxii. ⟨

quiet of a night under guard for reflection and mutual encouragment ere they were brought to trial. (5) And it came to pass on the morrow, that their rulers and elders and scribes were gathered together in Jerusalem; (6) and Annas the high priest was there, and Caiaphas, and John, and Alexander, and as many as were of the kindred of the high priest. The men here called " rulers and elders and scribes " constituted the main body of the high court of the Jews, called the Sanhedrin. Annas, whom Luke both here and in his former narrative calls high priest, was the lawful high priest, but he had been deposed by Valerius Gratus, the predecessor of Pilate, and Caiaphas, his son-in-law, had been by the same unlawful procedure put in his place, so that while the latter was holding the office, the other was lawfully entitled to it, and was recognized as high priest by the people.[1] The John and Alexander mentioned were well known men of high authority, as the manner in which they are mentioned clearly indicates, but nothing more is now known of them. The assembly was called for the purpose of determining what should be done with Peter and John.

VER. 7. When the court was assembled the prisoners were brought in, and the cripple who had been healed, not willing that his benefactors should suffer without his presence and sympathy, boldly walked in and took position close to them. (7) And when they had set them in the midst, they inquired, By what power, or in what name, have ye done this ? This was not the first time that Peter and John had been in the presence of this august assembly. As they looked up into the faces of

---

[1] To represent this as a mistake on Luke's part, as do Meyer and others, is absurd.

their judges, and recognized many of them, they could but remember the morning when their Master stood there in bonds, while they stood in the court and looked on, full of fearful misgivings. The fall and the bitter tears of Peter on that occasion were now a warning and a strength to them both, while their position brought to mind some solemn words of Jesus which had never acquired a present value till now. "Beware of men: for they shall deliver you up to councils, and they will scourge you in their synagogues, and ye shall be brought before governors and kings for my sake, for a testimony to them and the Gentiles. But when they deliver you up, be not anxious how or what ye shall speak; for it shall be given you in that same hour what ye shall say. For it is not ye that speak, but the Spirit of your Father that speaketh in you."[1] Cheered by these promises, they now stood before their accusers and judges with a boldness which to the latter was altogether unaccountable.

The prisoners had been arrested and brought into court without a formal charge being brought against them, and the court was now dependent on what might be extorted from them for a ground of accusation. The question propounded is remarkable for its vagueness: "By what power, or by what name have ye done this?" Done what? might have been the answer. Done this preaching? or this miracle? or what? The question specified nothing, and the obvious reason is that there was no particular thing done by Peter and John on which they dared to fix attention, or on which they could base a charge of wrong doing. The chief priest cunningly framed an indefinite question, in the hope that

---

[1] Matt. x. 17–19.

the defendants, in their confusion, would furnish a
ground of accusation by speaking unguarded words.

Vv. 8–10. Cunningly devised as the question of the
council was, none could have served Peter a better purpose. It left him free to select as the subject of his
answer anything that he had done, and he chose, out of
all that he had done, that which was the most unwelcome
to his judges. He framed his answer, too, with a more
direct reference to the other terms of their question, than
they either desired or anticipated. (8) **Then Peter, filled
with the Holy Spirit, said unto them, (9) Ye rulers of
the people, and elders, if we this day are examined concerning a good deed done to an impotent man, by what
means this man is made whole; (10) be it known to you
all, and to all the people of Israel, that in the name of
Jesus Christ of Nazareth, whom ye crucified, whom God
raised from the dead, even in him does this man stand
before you whole.** This statement needed no proof, for
the judges could not deny, with the man standing before
them, that the miracle had been wrought; nor could
they with any plausibility ascribe the deed to any other
power or name than that claimed by him who performed
it. To deny that the power was divine, would have
been absurd in the estimation of all the people; and to
have rejected the explanation given by those through
whom the power was exerted, would have been not less
so. The answer, then, vindicated itself, and confounded
those who propounded the question.

Vv. 11, 12. Realizing the advantage which he had
now gained, Peter pushes it still farther by adding:
(11) **He is the stone which was set at naught by you
builders, which was made the head of the corner. (12)
And in none other is there salvation: for neither is there**

any other name under heaven, that is given among men, wherein we must be saved. Here, using the words of David,[1] he puts his judges and accusers in the ridiculous attitude of builders laying the foundation of a house, but rejecting the stone which was cut out for the corner, without which the foundation course could not be closed up, and no part of the wall could be built. Then, dropping the figure, he plainly declares that there is no salvation for man except in the name of the very Jesus whom they had crucified. This declaration is universal; and it shows that every human being who is saved at all will be saved in the name of Christ. If any who do not know him or believe in him are saved, still in some way their salvation will be in his name.

5. A Private Consultation, 13–17.

Vv. 13, 14. Instead of answering evasively, or timidly, as was expected of men in their social position when arraigned in such a presence, the apostles had unhesitatingly avowed the sentiments which they had been preaching, and on account of which they had been arrested, and it had the effect of silencing their accusers: (13) Now when they beheld the boldness of Peter and John, and had perceived that they were unlearned and ignorant men, they marveled, and they took knowledge of them that they had been with Jesus. (14) And seeing the man who was healed standing with them, they could say nothing against it. It was not till this moment, apparently, that the two apostles were recognized by the judges as former attendants of Jesus, though all perhaps had seen them with him repeatedly before his death, and John was a personal acquaintance of

[1] Psalm cxviii. 22, 23.

Caiaphas.[1] At the close of Peter's remarks there seems
to have been total silence for a time; for "they could
say nothing against it." Not one of them was ready to
contradict anything he had said, or to rebuke him for
saying it. Their embarrassment was painful.

Vv. 15, 16. The silence was broken by a proposal
that the prisoners be withdrawn. (15) **But when they
had commanded them to go aside out of the council, they
conferred among themselves, saying, (16) What shall
we do to these men? for that indeed a notable miracle
hath been wrought through them, is manifest to all who
dwell in Jerusalem; and we can not deny it.** This admission shows that in their public proceedings they had
been utterly hypocritical and heartless. How they could
now look one another in the face, is a moral puzzle.
Perhaps they did not; and certainly they could not have
allowed themselves to look up toward God.

Ver. 17. The motive which controlled them crops
out in the conclusion to which their deliberations brought
them: (17) **But that it spread no further among the
people, let us threaten them, that they speak henceforth
to no man in this name.** The man who made this proposal thought that he had solved a difficult problem, and
the others were too well pleased at finding a loophole of
escape from their present embarrassment, to forecast very
shrewdly the probable success of the measure. It was a
safe course, if not a very bold one, and as there was no
obstacle in the way except conscience, they did not hesitate to adopt it.

How Luke learned the particulars of this secret consultation, we are not informed; but it is not difficult to
imagine. Gamaliel, Saul's teacher, was probably present,

---

[1] John xviii. 15, 18.

and it is not unlikely that Saul himself was also there. Moreover, "a great company of the priests" afterward became obedient to the faith, and after they repented they would not hesitate to confess all of the villainy of their party.

6. More Preaching Forbidden, 18–22.

Ver. 18. The resolution was no sooner adopted than acted upon. (18) **And they called them, and charged them not to speak at all or teach in the name of Jesus.** This is the first time in the history of the church that preaching was forbidden; and now it was forbidden absolutely. If the apostles obey, not another word is to be spoken for Jesus in public or in private. We shudder to think of the consequences if that injunction had been obeyed.

Vv. 19, 20. The apostles, if at all solicitous for their personal safety, might have retired from the assembly in silence. (19) **But Peter and John answered and said to them, Whether it be right in the sight of God to hearken unto you rather than unto God, judge ye: (20) for we can not but speak the things which we saw and heard.** The first part of this answer was an appeal to the consciences of the judges, and the last part was a plain but modestly expressed avowal of the purpose to disregard their order. Silence might have been construed as giving assent; and the apostles were too candid to allow it to be thought for a moment that assent would be given.

Vv. 21, 22. It must have been a sore trial to the proud spirits of the Sanhedrin to brook such defiance from humble men like these ; but a desire to conciliate the people, mingled with a secret fear, perhaps, of doing violence to men possessed of such power, restrained their wrath. (21) **And they, when they had further threat-ened them, let them go, finding nothing how they might punish them, because of the people; for all men glorified God for that which was done. (22) For the man was more than forty years old, on whom this miracle of healing was wrought.** Whatever the people thought of the teaching of Peter, they could but admire and applaud the "good deed done to the impotent man;" and the fact that the latter was more than forty years of age, made him well known and an object of universal sym-pathy.

7. Report of the Two Apostles, and Prayer of the Twelve, 23–31.

Vv. 23–30. The apostles now retired in triumph from the assembly; but they were uninflated by their triumph as they had been undaunted in their danger. They seem to have attained to that lofty equipoise of faith and hope which enables men to maintain complete self-possession amid all the vicissitudes of life. The course which they immediately pursued is worthy of profound consideration. (23) **And being let go, they came to their own company, and reported all that the chief priests and elders had said to them. (24) And they, when they heard it, lifted up their voice to God with one accord, and said, O Lord, thou that didst make the heaven and the earth and the sea, and all that in them is: (25) who by the Holy Spirit, by the mouth of our father David thy servant,**[1] **didst say,**

---

[1] In this passage, contrary to the opinions of modern rational-ists, the apostles represent David as the author of the second Psalm, from which they quote, and they declare that God himself,

Why did the Gentiles rage,
And the peoples imagine vain things?
(26) The kings of the earth set themselves in array,
And the rulers were gathered together,
Against the Lord, and against his Anointed:
(27) for of a truth in this city against thy holy servant Jesus, whom thou didst anoint, both Herod and Pontius Pilate, with the Gentiles and the people of Israel (28) were gathered together to do whatsoever thy hand and thy counsel foreordained to come to pass. (29) And now, Lord, look upon their threatenings; and grant unto thy servants to speak thy word with all boldness, (30) while thou stretchest forth thy hand to heal; and that signs and wonders may be done through the name of thy holy servant Jesus.

In this prayer, as in all those recorded in the Bible, we find a propriety in each part, and a fitness in the whole, which are worthy of study and of imitation. On a former occasion the apostles had set before the Lord two persons between whom choice was to be made for the apostolic office, so they addressed God as the heart-knower;[1] but now they desire his protecting power, and their invocation is, "O Lord, thou that didst make the heaven and the earth and the sea, and all that in them is." Their petition is equally appropriate. They

---

by his Holy Spirit, spake these words by the mouth of David. Words could not be framed into a more explicit statement of both facts, and the truthfulness of the statement is attested not only by the authority of the inspired apostles, but by the manifest fulfillment of the predictions of the passage in the proceeding which they recite in the next division of the prayer. It is vain to say that these men did not understand higher criticism, for here they speak not as mere men, but as inspired men.

[1] Acts i. 24.

lay the foundation for it in the word of prophecy which the Lord himself had spoken, and which had now been fulfilled by Herod, Pilate, the people of Israel, and the Gentiles; and the petition is, first, "Behold their threatenings;" and second, "Grant unto thy servants to speak thy word with all boldness."

In these days of passion and war, when it is common for prayers to be filled with entreaties for victory over our enemies, and sometimes with maledictions upon those who are waging war against our supposed rights, it is quite refreshing to observe the tone of this apostolic prayer. These men were not in danger of losing some merely political power or privilege; but the dearest and most indisputable right they had on earth was denied them, and they were threatened with death if they did not relinquish it: yet in their prayer they manifest no vindictive or resentful spirit; but they pray in reference to their enemies only this, "Lord, behold their threatenings," while they leave the Lord without suggestion or request, to do as might appear good in his sight. By such prayers as are often uttered at the present time men seek to make God a partisan in all their angry contentions, as though he were nothing more than themselves.[20] In reference to their own work, the apostles pray only for boldness to continue it without regard to the threatenings of their enemies; and they intimate

---

[20] These thoughts were first written amid the din and confusion of our great civil war, when even devout men on both sides were beside themselves with the passions of the time. The composition of the first edition of this Commentary was once interrupted by the booming of cannon in the siege of Lexington, Mo., not many miles from the author's home in 1862, and once by the march and countermarch of contending armies through Lexington, Ky., where he lived in 1863.

how they expect this boldness to be given them by asking that the signs and wonders which had attested the
presence of God with them thus far, might continue to
attest it still. They had no thought of fear so long as
they had evidence of the divine presence and approval.

VER. 31. The prayer for boldness was answered at
once, but in a way not expected. (31) **And when they
had prayed, the place was shaken wherein they were
gathered together ; and they were all filled with the
Holy Spirit, and they spake the word of God with boldness.** The shaking of the house, attended by a conscious
renewal of the miraculous power of the Holy Spirit,
gave them the boldness for which they prayed, by
assuring them that God was still with them.

SEC. IV.—FURTHER PROGRESS OF THE CHURCH, AND A SECOND PERSECUTION.

(IV. 32—V. 42.)

1. UNITY AND LIBERALITY OF THE CHURCH, 32–37.

Vv. 32–35. After the preceding account of the first
persecution, Luke turns our attention once more to the
internal condition of the church. The religious life of
the disciples was now more developed than at the time
referred to in the close of the second chapter, and the
description enters more into details. (32) **And the multitude of them that believed were of one heart and soul :
and not one of them said that aught of the things that
he had was his own ; but they had all things common.
(33) And with great power gave the apostles their witness of the resurrection of the Lord Jesus : and great**

grace was upon them all. (34) For neither was there any among them that lacked: for as many as were possessors of lands or houses sold them, and brought the prices of the things that were sold, (35) and laid them at the apostles' feet; and distribution was made unto each, according as any one had need.

Considering the large number of persons in this congregation, and the variety of social relations from which they had been suddenly drawn together, it is truly remarkable, and well worthy of a place in the record, that they were "of one heart and soul." The unity for which the Saviour had prayed[1] was now enjoyed by the church, and witnessed by the world. The most surprising manifestation of it was seen in that complete subsidence of selfishness which led one and all to say that the things which he possessed were not his own, but the property of all. This was not the result of socialistic theorizing, or of rules laid down to govern all who sought admission into the new society; but it was the spontaneous expression of the love of God and man which had taken possession of every heart. Among the heathen nations of antiquity, systematic provision for the wants of the poor was unknown; and even among the Jews, whose laws made ample provisions for this unfortunate class, voluntary benevolence was greatly neglected. It was therefore a new thing under the sun to see many persons in a large community voluntarily selling houses and lands in order to supply the wants of the poor who were among them. It could not fail to have the effect which Luke traces to it in the words, "And with great power gave the apostles their witness of the resurrection of the Lord Jesus; and great grace was upon them all." The

---

[1] John xvii. 11, 20, 21.

fresh power was not in the testimony itself, which was a fixed quantity, the same at all times; but in its effect upon the people. Its effect was more powerful than before, because it was now backed up by such a life among those who accepted the testimony as could not have been seen or anticipated at the beginning. The "great grace" that was upon them all was not the grace of God, which had been upon them uniformly from the beginning: but the grace, more properly rendered, the favor of the people. It has been often observed since then that when unity and liberality prevail in a congregation the preaching has greater power because of its greater favor with the people; whereas, in the absence of unity and liberality, the most forcible preaching often fails of visible results.

This church was not at this time a commune, or a socialistic club, as many interpreters have fancied; for there was no uniform distribution of the property of all among the members; neither was the property of all held and administered by the apostles as a business committee. On the contrary, " distribution was made unto each as any one had need;" which shows that only the needy received anything, and that those who were not needy were the givers. This is further illustrated by the conduct of Ananias and Sapphira below (v. 1-4), and by the circumstances connected with the appointment of the seven to serve tables (vi. 1-3). It must not be supposed, either, that these disciples made a mistake in the matter of their benevolence, which they found it necessary afterward to correct by acting more rationally. This supposition can be adopted only by those who deny that the apostles were guided by the Holy Spirit in directing the affairs of the church, and who at the same

time fail to take into their minds an adequate conception
of Christian benevolence. In reality this church was
setting an example for all other churches in all time to
come, by showing that true Christian benevolence requires that we shall not let our brethren in the church
suffer for food, even if those of us who have houses and
lands can prevent it only by the sale of our possessions.
In other words, it teaches us to share the last crust with
our brother. We shall see hereafter that the church in
Antioch imitated quite closely this noble example (xi.
27–30).

VER. 36. Luke now brings forward an individual
instance of the liberality previously mentioned, which he
introduces no doubt on account of the subsequent prominence of the person. (36) **And Joseph, who by the
apostles was surnamed Barnabas (which is, being translated, Son of exhortation), a Levite, a man of Cyprus by
race, (37) having a field, sold it, and brought the money,
and laid it at the apostles' feet.** "Son of exhortation" is
a Hebraism for one noted as an exhorter. The name was
given to him on account of his superiority in hortatory
addresses. This is a power much rarer among public
speakers than logical or didactic force, and it has been
very highly prized throughout all the history of the
church. We shall see hereafter that it had much to do
with shaping the subsequent career of this excellent
man.

Inasmuch as the law of Moses made no appropriation
of lands for the tribe of Levi, but provided that it
should be supported by the tithes from the other tribes,
some surprise has been expressed that this Levite was
the owner of real estate. But it should be remembered
that the original allotment of certain lands to certain

tribes, and certain cities to the Levites, had been completely broken up by the Assyrian and Babylonian captivities, and had never been fully restored, for it was only remnants of some of the tribes which returned from captivity, and even they did not again settle within the old tribal limits. This state of things left the Levites to shift for themselves to a great extent, and there was no law, nor had there ever been, to prevent them from acquiring individual landed possessions. It is highly probable, too, though it is not asserted in the text, that Joseph's land was in Cyprus, which was his native country. In the expression, "a man of Cyprus by race," the term race is used, as it is in some other passages,[1] for the place of his ancestry, and not for his ancestral blood.

2. A Case of Discipline, v. 1–11.

Vv. 1, 2. Unfortunately for our race, every excellence in human character has its counterfeits, and the praise lavished on men of real benevolence prompts others at times to play the hypocrite by pretending to be more benevolent than they are. So it proved in the present instance: for the benevolence of the church, which was its noblest characteristic in the eyes of the world, became the occasion of the first piece of corruption among its members. **(1) But a certain man named Ananias, with Sapphira his wife, (2) sold a possession, and kept back part of the price, his wife also being privy to it, and brought a certain part and laid it at the apostles' feet.** The language implies what is distinctly avowed by the wife below, that this part was represented as the whole price of the possession. If we attempt to analyze the motive of the guilty pair, we shall find that

---

[1] Mark vii. 26; Acts xviii. 2, 24.

their act was a compromise between two unholy desires. The desire to have the praise of men, such as had been bestowed upon Barnabas and on some others, prompted the sale and the gift, while the love of money, which still held too strong a hold on them, prompted the retention of a part while they were pretending to give all. True benevolence seems to have had no part in moving them. But while they were undoubtedly governed by avarice in withholding a part, it was not, after all, an excess of avarice; for if this passion had been as strong in them as in many professors of the faith at the present day, they would not have sold the land at all. That they gave a large part, is proof that they were not sinners above all men in respect of love of money, and yet their fate is held up as a warning to all generations.

Vv. 3, 4. Never was a man, or an assembly of men, more astonished than were Ananias and the congregation in whose presence he had ostentatiously presented his gift, at that which followed: (4) But Peter said, Ananias, why hath Satan filled thy heart to lie to the Holy Spirit, and to keep back part of the price of the land? (4) While it remained, did it not remain thine own? and after it was sold, was it not in thy power? How is it that thou hast conceived this thing in thy heart? Thou hast not lied unto men, but unto God. In this heart-searching demand Peter brings together the power of Satan and the free agency of the tempted, just as he had in a former discourse the free agency of man and the sovereignty of God. He demands of Ananias, "Why hath Satan filled thy heart to lie to the Holy Spirit," and in the same breath, "Why hast thou conceived this thing in thy heart?" The existence and agency of the tempter are distinctly recognized, yet it is not Satan, but Ananias, who is rebuked, and he is rebuked for doing the very sin that Satan had done, showing that he is as guilty as though Satan had done nothing. The justice of this is manifest from the fact that Satan had no power over his heart without his coöperation. That he had rendered this coöperation, threw the responsibility on him.

Peter's knowledge of the attempt at deception was the result, not of human information, but of the insight miraculously imparted by the Holy Spirit. This conclusion is necessitated by the whole course of the narrative, as well as by the words of Peter concerning the Holy Spirit.

VER. 5. While the exposure of the hypocrisy of Ananias was a great surprise to the people present, they were not prepared, as probably Peter himself was not, for that which immediately ensued. (5) **And Ananias hearing these words fell down and gave up the spirit: and great fear came upon all that heard it.** There is no evidence that Peter had any will of his own in this sudden death. It seems to have been a sudden stroke of the divine will, the responsibility for which attached not to Peter as an officer of the church, but to God as the moral governor of men. The propriety of it may be appreciated if we suppose Ananias to have succeeded in his undertaking. His success would have been but temporary, for the fraud, like all other frauds, would have been detected sooner or later, and when detection came it would have brought with it a serious discount in the minds of the people on the powers of the Holy Spirit dwelling in the apostles. To learn that the Spirit could be deceived, would have undermined the whole fabric of apostolic authority, and might have overthrown

the faith of many, if not of all. The attempt brought on
a crisis of vital importance, and demanded such a vindication of the power of the Spirit as could be neither
mistaken nor forgotten. The immediate effect was precisely the effect desired: "great fear came upon the
whole church, and upon all who heard these things."

VER. 6. The scene was too awe-inspiring for lamentation, or for needless funeral ceremonies. As when
Nadab and Abihu fell dead at the door of the tabernacle,
with strange fire in their censers, there was no weeping
or delay.[1] (6) And the young men arose and wrapped
him round, and they carried him out and buried him.
This was an imitation of the burial of the two sons of
Aaron just mentioned; and as the latter was ordered by
Moses, the former was doubtless ordered by Peter. It
is scarcely conceivable that young men in the audience
would have felt at liberty to do anything, unless it would
be to go and tell the dead man's wife what had happened, if they had received no orders from the apostle.
So natural is this supposition, that the historian says
nothing as to the reason why the young men acted as
they did.

VER. 7. Sapphira was not present. (7) And it was
about the space of three hours after, when his wife, not
knowing what was done, came in. How she was kept
so long ignorant of the fate of her husband, we are not
informed, though it is a most extraordinary circumstance.
He had dropped dead in a public assembly, had been
carried forth for burial, and three hours had passed, yet
his wife came into the same assembly without a word
reaching her ear on the subject. Naturally, the first impulse of every one would have been to run at once and

---

[1] Lev. x. 1–7.

tell her the story, so that she could at least be present at her husband's burial. It is necessary to suppose here, as in case of the surprising act of the young men, some overruling authority; and it is not difficult to see that Peter himself, in order that the complicity of Sapphira in the crime might be fairly tested and exposed, commanded the disciples present to withhold the information from her.

Vv. 8–10. She came in prepared to act out in full the part agreed on between her and her husband. (8) And Peter said unto her, Tell me whether ye sold the land for so much. And she said, Yea, for so much. (9) But Peter said unto her, How is it that ye have agreed together to tempt the Spirit of the Lord? Behold, the feet of them who have buried thy husband are at the door, and they shall carry thee out. (10) And she fell down immediately at his feet, and gave up the spirit: and the young men came in and found her dead, and they carried her out and buried her by her husband. In her case Peter knew what was about to take place, and declared it; but there is no evidence that his own will was exerted in causing her death. We regard her death, like that of her husband, as a miracle wrought independently of the power lodged in the apostle; and it seems to have been so regarded by the authorities in Jerusalem; for when the apostles were afterward brought before them, no charge of murder was preferred, as might have been the case if the act had been understood differently.

In the question, " Why have ye agreed together to tempt the Spirit of the Lord?" Peter states the result of their agreement, and not the aim of it. The act was tempting the Spirit, in the sense of trying its power to detect the thoughts of men. If the guilty pair had been asked, beforehand, whether they thought they could deceive the Holy Spirit, no doubt they would have answered, no : for they must have known that such an attempt would be in vain. They dared to make the attempt because they had their minds on the apostles as men, and not as inspired men. The test thus unintentionally applied resulted in a triumphant vindication of the Spirit's power as an indwelling guide, and the circumstances were such that no man could dare to repeat the experiment.

VER. 11. The failure of the plot proved as propitious to the cause of Christ as its success would have been disastrous. (11) And great fear came upon the whole church, and upon all that heard these things. This fear was excited not merely by the sudden and awful fate of the guilty pair ; but also by the evidence which the incident furnished of the heart-searching power which dwelt in the apostles. The disciples now had a better conception of the nature of apostolic inspiration, and the unbelieving masses were awed into respect and reverence.

We must not drop this incident without observing its bearing in another direction. This piece of corruption was connected with the Lord's treasury ; and apart from the feature which was emphasized by Peter, it has a bearing on our modern church life. The lie told by Ananias consisted in representing his gift as being more liberal in proportion to his ability than it really was. Every time a member of the church at the present day makes exaggerated statements of the amount he is giving, or understates the amount of his wealth, in order to make out a degree of liberality beyond what is real, he is guilty of the sin of Ananias and Sapphira; and if all such were to drop dead in their tracks, there would be a thinning of the ranks in some places. All who are tempted to act thus should be faithfully notified that the same God who punished Ananias and Sapphira on the spot will not fail to punish, in his own time and place, all who imitate them.

3. PROSPERITY OF THE CHURCH INCREASED, 12–16.

In this paragraph the author states more fully the effects of the exposure and punishment of Ananias and Sapphira. They were seen in the greater number of cures wrought by the apostles, the greater reverence felt for them by the people, and the greater number of additions to the church. (12) And by the hands of the apostles were many signs and wonders wrought among the people; and they were all with one accord in Solomon's porch. (13) But of the rest durst no man join himself to them: howbeit the people magnified them, (14) and believers were the more added to the Lord, multitudes both of men and women; (15) insomuch that they even carried out the sick into the streets, and laid them on beds and couches, that, as Peter came by, at least his shadow might overshadow some of them. (16) And there also came together the multitude from the cities round about Jerusalem, bringing sick folks, and them that were vexed with unclean spirits: and they were healed every one. The latter part of this passage shows that the greater number of miracles now wrought was in consequence, not of any increased power of the apostles, but of increased zeal for healing among the people; and they brought a greater number of sick to be healed because their faith in the healing power was

greater than before. Many of these who were healed
and of those who brought them were doubtless baptized,
and thus churches began to be formed in these "cities
round about." Solomon's portico continued to be the
meeting place of the disciples; but now both saints and
sinners kept at a more respectful distance from the persons of the apostles than before; for each felt his own
unworthiness, and dreaded the possibility of being smitten for some sin, as Ananias and his wife had been. All
these considerations had their natural effect on sinners,
in bringing them in greatly increased numbers to repentance and baptism. The special mention of women
here for the first time is a probable indication that
among the converts there was now a greater relative
number of these than before.

Usually, in our modern experience, a great sin exposed in the church, such as that of Ananias and Sapphira, brings the church into disrepute for a time,
diminishes the respect for it entertained in the community, and renders all efforts to add to its numbers futile.
Why was the effect in Jerusalem the reverse of this?
This is a serious question for those who bear rule in the
church. It is quite evident that the difference depends
on the very different way in which such scandalous conduct is now treated. If the Jerusalem church had
tolerated Ananias and Sapphira, by retaining them in
their fellowship after their exposure, doubtless the
"ways of Zion would have mourned," and sinners
would not have been turned to the Lord. But the sudden punishment visited upon them by the Lord, and the
abhorrence of their deed manifested by burying them
without ceremony in the clothing in which they died,
and while their bodies were scarcely cold, made the

whole community feel that here was a people among whom sin could not be tolerated. It was a safe place for a man who needed holy companionship to help him in the effort to live a holy life—a place in which he might expect every false step to be promptly corrected, and through which he might confidently hope to make his pilgrimage to a better world. People who wish to make a compromise with sin, and who join a church merely because they are afraid to live without some appearance of religion, will always avoid such a church; but those who are in earnest about the desire to save their souls and to do good, seek just such a church as their spiritual home. When shall the rigid discipline which God established in the beginning be seen on earth once more? Let the shepherds of the flock give an answer, as they remember that they must give account to God concerning the souls committed to their care.

4. THE APOSTLES ARE IMPRISONED AND RELEASED, 17–21.

Vv. 17, 18. The excitement which now prevailed throughout Jerusalem and the adjacent cities, finding expression in enthusiastic praise of the apostles, and in the turning of many to the Lord, was too much for the equanimity of the dignitaries who had forbidden any more preaching or teaching in the name of Jesus, and it moved them to action again. (17) But the high priest rose up, and all they that were with him (which is the sect of the Sadducees), and they were filled with jealousy, (18) and laid hands on the apostles, and put them in public ward. Here we have the same Sadducees who had arrested and threatened Peter and John. Made furious with jealousy toward men whose influence they had vainly tried to destroy, and who were now almost worshiped by the people, they seized not only the two whom they had formerly arrested, but all of their companions, being determined to execute on a large scale the threats which they had uttered. The night in prison was a gloomy one to the apostles, and still gloomier to the thousands of their less courageous brethren and sisters outside.

Vv. 19–21. To the apostles the arrest and imprisonment could not have been a surprise, for they knew that the Sanhedrin was governed by determined men who would be likely to put their threats into execution; but that which followed the night of imprisonment must have been a great surprise both to them and to all Jerusalem. (19) But an angel of the Lord by night opened the prison doors, and brought them out, and said, (20) Go ye, and stand and speak in the temple to the people all the words of this life. (21) And when they had heard this, they entered into the temple about daybreak, and taught. The hearers whom they found in the temple "about daybreak" were doubtless few, and they were probably some of the brethren who could not sleep for anxiety, and who went there to pray. As these early worshipers entered the temple and found the apostles there, their first impulse was to run and spread the news; so the apostles had not long to wait ere they were surrounded by a listening throng. I imagine that the sermons which were interrupted the previous day were renewed as if the interruption had been but momentary.

5. THE APOSTLES ARE BROUGHT INTO COURT, 21–27.

Vv. 21–24. To the high priest and his coadjutors, the night had doubtless been one of troubled thought; for they knew that in the morning they would have to confront once more the men who had defied them, and who, in their course of defiance, had won to their side a vast multitude of the best people in the city and surrounding country. What to do with them was a puzzling question. (21) But the high priest came, and they that were with him, and called the council together, and all the senate of the children of Israel, and sent to the prison to have them brought. (22) But the officers that came found them not in the prison; and they returned, and told, saying, (23) The prison house we found shut in all safety, and the keepers standing at the doors: but when we had opened, we found no man within. (24) Now when the captain of the temple and the chief priests heard these words, they were much perplexed concerning them whereunto this would grow. The disappearance of the prisoners was to them a mystery, yet they could not fail to refer it to the working of the miraculous power with which they knew the apostles to be endowed. To us the mystery is that, with such facts confronting them, they thought only of "whereunto this would grow," instead of thinking, What will God do with us if we continue to fight against these manifestations of his power? The wonder is that they did not immediately disperse, and try to conceal the fact that they had come together at all. They were, in reality, staggered by the announcement, and they knew not for a time what to do or say.

Vv. 25-27. It was soon known abroad in the city
that the Sanhedrin had assembled, and the purpose of
the meeting was well understood. By this time also
some of the people who stood with the priests had
learned what was going on in the temple. (25) And
there came one and told them, Behold, the men whom ye
put in the prison are in the temple standing and teaching the people. (26) Then went the captain with the
officers, and brought them, but without violence; for
they feared the people, lest they should be stoned. (27)
And when they had brought them, they set them before
the council. When the news came that the apostles were
in the temple, the captain and his band, having once before been sent for them, needed no further orders; he
went at once for his escaped prisoners. He doubtless
saw in the faces of the people that his task was a dangerous one, and he may have seen a few stones in the hands
of the more excitable part of the crowd; for to the
people, who now understood how the apostles had been
released, their re-arrest appeared to be a daring outrage.
The captain does not handle the men as he would escaped prisoners under ordinary circumstances; but he
escorts them most deferentially into the presence of the
court. It was doubtless the outside multitude from
whom he feared the stoning, and not the disciples; but
it is not improbable that some of the new converts, who
had imbibed only in part the spirit of the gospel, would
have taken part in the fray had it once begun.

6. The Accusation and the Defense, 27-32.

Vv. 27, 28. We now have a lively and graphic
description of the trial of the apostles. Caiaphas is not
so indefinite about the grounds of accusation as in the

case of Peter and John : the injunction with which they had been dismissed gives him a starting point for the present proceedings. (27) **And the high priest asked them, saying, (28) We straitly charged you not to teach in this name : and behold, ye have filled Jerusalem with your teaching, and intend to bring this man's blood upon us.** These words contain two specific charges against the apostles—disobedience to the Sanhedrin, and an attempt to bring upon them the blood of Jesus. The last was the tender point with the accusers, and the mention of it here brings to light a secret feeling which had been animating them from the beginning. If the resurrection of Jesus could have been established without implicating those who had condemned him in the crime of shedding innocent blood, it is highly probable that this series of attempts to suppress the preaching would not have been made. But this could not be ; and these unfortunate men now found themselves involved by their previous crime in the necessity of accepting the brand of murderers at the hands of an indignant people, or suppressing and crushing out the belief in the resurrection. Instead of receding from the course of hypocrisy and crime upon which they had entered in condemning Jesus, they chose the bad alternative of plunging into it still deeper.

Vv. 29–32. The candor and fearlessness of Peter's reply to the demand of the chief priest are worthy of the man and the occasion. (29) **But Peter and the apostles answered and said, (30) We must obey God rather than men. The God of our fathers raised up Jesus, whom ye slew, hanging him on a tree.**[1] (31)

---

[1] On the word " tree," used here for the word cross, see remarks under chap. xiii. 29.

Him did God exalt with his right hand to be a Prince and a Saviour, to give repentance to Israel and remission of sins. (32) And we are witnesses of these things; and so is the Holy Spirit, whom God hath given to them that obey him. To the first charge, that of disobeying the Sanhedrin, they plead guilty. Peter and John had departed from their first trial with the words, " Whether it be right in the sight of God to obey you rather than God, judge ye;" and now they say in reference to their disobedience, "We ought to obey God rather than men." The second charge is met by reiterating that for which they were accused—by boldly hurling into the teeth of their judges the awful fact that it was innocent blood which they had shed, and that this was proved by the resurrection of Jesus and his exaltation in heaven. And lest they should still doubt the fact of the resurrection and exaltation, Peter repeats what he had so often said before, that he and his fellow apostles were witnesses of the former, while he refers to the Holy Spirit as the witness of the latter. This testimony, coming from men who had just been delivered miraculously from a guarded prison, the guards not knowing they had passed out, and who had previously filled Jerusalem with wonderful works wrought by the power of the Holy Spirit, could not be gainsaid, or honestly doubted.

In the statement that Jesus had been exalted a Prince and Saviour to " give " repentance and remission of sins, it is implied that repentance as well as remission of sins is a gift. But to give repentance can not mean to bestow it without an exercise of our own will; for it is itself, as we have seen before, an act of our will.[1] It is an act of the will to which we are led by sorrow for sin. God

---

[1] See the remarks on repentance under chap. iii. 19.

gives it then, not directly, but indirectly, by giving the motives which lead to it. There were adequate motives to sorrow for sin before Jesus was presented as a Saviour ; but it must be admitted that his death, resurrection, and exaltation in our behalf, is the one great motive now, compared with which all others are insignificant. By furnishing this greatest of all motives for repentance, God had given repentance to Israel.

7. THEY ARE SAVED FROM DEATH BY GAMALIEL, 33–42.

Vv. 33, 34. The manner in which Peter, as the mouthpiece of the apostles, repeated in the presence of the Sanhedrin the offense for which they had been arrested, exasperated the leading Sadducees beyond measure, and came near turning the court into a mob : (33) But they, when they heard this, were cut to the heart, and were minded to slay them. (34) But there stood up one in the council, a Pharisee named Gamaliel, a doctor of the law, had in honor of all the people, and commanded to put the men forth a little while. The Pharisees, as we have seen before, were less excited over the progress of the gospel than the Sadducees; and now that the latter were about to precipitate a crisis which would have involved the whole Sanhedrin in a horrible crime, at least one Pharisee was cool enough and prudent enough to interpose wiser counsel. The removal of the prisoners, like that of Peter and John before, was to prevent them from hearing any admissions which might be made in the course of the intended discussion. The statement that Gamaliel "commanded" the men to be put forth, implies that this was the privilege of any member of the court.

Vv. 35–39. Gamaliel seems to have retained his position on the floor until the officers had withdrawn the prisoners and closed the doors, while the Sadducees, with no little impatience, were awaiting his remarks. (35) And he said to them, Ye men of Israel, take heed to yourselves as touching these men, what ye are about to do. (36) For before these days rose up Theudas, giving himself out to be somebody; to whom a number of men, about four hundred, joined themselves: who was slain; and all, as many as obeyed him, were dispersed, and came to nought. (37) After this man rose up Judas of Galilee in the days of the enrollment, and drew away some of the people after him: he also perished; and all, as many as obeyed him, were scattered abroad. (38) And now I say unto you, Refrain from these men, and let them alone: for if this counsel or this work be of men, it will be overthrown: (39) but if it is of God, ye will not be able to overthrow them; lest haply ye be found even to be fighting against God.

It has been charged by unfriendly critics that the author of Acts has here put into the mouth of Gamaliel a speech which, in the nature of the case, he could not have uttered. It is held that while Theudas is here placed before Judas, he really lived at a later period, a mistake of which Gamaliel could not have been guilty; and furthermore, that Theudas flourished twelve years after the time at which Gamaliel is said to have made this speech. The charge is based on the fact that Josephus mentions a Theudas who did flourish at a later period, in the reign of Claudius Cæsar, and whose career was similar to that of the Theudas here mentioned.[1] The truth of the charge depends on the

---

[1] Ant. xx. v. 1.

identity of the Theudas of Josephus and the Theudas of Luke. Neither writer goes into such details as to furnish safe ground for the assumption of identity, while Josephus himself makes room for the supposition that there may have been more than one Theudas, by mentioning a large number of insurrections occurring at the right period to suit the remark of Gamaliel, without naming their leaders. He says of the period just preceding the deposition of Archelaus: " Now at that time there were ten thousand other disorders in Judea, which were like tumults, because a great number put themselves in a warlike posture, either out of hopes of gain to themselves, or out of enmity to the Jews." He also says in another place: " And now Judea was full of robberies ; and as the several companies of the seditious lighted upon any one to lead them, he was created a king immediately, in order to do mischief to the public."[1] Now, that one of these leaders may have been named Theudas, is not at all improbable, and when we have the word of a veracious writer that he was, it is most unjust, in the absence of all conflicting evidence, to charge him with falsehood.[2]

---

[1] *Ibid.* xvii. x. 4, 8.

[2] The question discussed above has been in dispute ever since the second century, when the objection was first urged by Celsus (Origen *vs.* Celsus, B. I. c. 6). All unbelievers and all semi-rationalistic writers who think that our Gospels and Acts were not written by their reputed authors, taking ground against Luke ; while those who give full credit to the Scriptures have held substantially the view stated and defended above. The reader will find in Alford's Commentary, and Meyer's, the two sides of the controversy well stated, and also the names of the most noted writers on both sides. In confirmation of what I have said above, I may add, that while the Theudas of Gamaliel was followed by about " four hundred " men, who were, after he was

Upon the fate of these two impostors Gamaliel bases his advice in reference to the apostles. The merits of his advice must be differently estimated according to the point of view from which we contemplate it. If it were proposed as a general rule of procedure in reference to religious movements, we should condemn it as time-serving. Instead of waiting to see if such a movement is to prove successful, every lover of truth will promptly investigate its claims, if it has any worthy of attention, and decide without reference to public opinion or probable success. But Gamaliel was arguing a different question from this, the question whether this movement should be suppressed by violence ; and from this point of view his advice was certainly good. Assuming, as he did, that the movement was an improper one, the question was, Shall we attempt to crush it out with violence ? or shall we suspend proceedings against it until it begins to grow weak of itself, as it certainly will if it be not of

---

slain, " dispersed ;" the Theudas of Josephus "persuaded a *great part of the people* to take their effects with them and follow him to the Jordan ;" and when the troops of Cuspius Fadus attacked them, they "*slew* many of them, and *took many of them alive*" (Ant. xx. v. 1). The differences are not easily explained, except by supposing that the Theudas of Gamaliel and the Theudas of Josephus are different persons. The probability that two such leaders, living at considerable intervals apart, may have borne the same name, is happily illustrated by similar occurrences in our own century. We quote from Prof. Stokes : "There was an Irish movement in 1848 which numbered among its prominent leaders a William Smith O'Brien, and there is now (1891) an Irish movement of the same character, and it also numbers a William O'Brien among its most prominent leaders. A Parnell leads a movement for the repeal of union in 1890. Ninety years earlier a Parnell resigned high office sooner than consent to the consummation of the same legislative union of Great Britain and Ireland " (*Expositor's Bible, Acts, p.* 237.)

God? Such was the drift of the first part of his remarks; but at the close he betrays a doubt whether the
movement should be opposed at all; for he very clearly intimates that it may be of God, and that in fighting against
it they might be found fighting against God. It is
strange that a man who was capable, under such circumstances, of the calm thought and sound reasoning which
characterize this speech, had not already committed himself to a cause so well supported by incontrovertible
evidence.[1]

Vv. 40–42. The advice of Gamaliel had the effect of
restraining the council from shedding blood; but the
priests and elders were too much exasperated to follow
fully his advice. (40) And to him they agreed; and when
they had called the apostles to them, they beat them, and
charged them not to speak in the name of Jesus, and let
them go. (41) They therefore departed from the presence of the council, rejoicing that they were counted

---

[1] Christian Baur makes use of this consideration to throw
doubt on the reality of the preceding miracles. He says: "If
all these miracles were really performed as is here narrated, and
in so authentic a manner that the Sanhedrin itself could not
ignore them, nor bring anything against them; if the man lame
from his birth was healed by the word of the apostle, and if the
apostles themselves, without any human intervention, were freed
from prison by an angel from heaven—how could Gamaliel, if he
was a man such as is here described, unbiased and thoughtful,
resting his judgment on experience, express himself so problem-
atically as he does here, and leave it to the future to decide
whether this cause were or were not divine?" (*Paul*, vol. i. 35).
If this question had been propounded to Gamaliel himself, it
would doubtless have thrown him into confusion; for he was in
that particular state of mind in which men are often guilty of the
greatest inconsistency. They are unwilling to admit conclusions
which evidence is forcing upon them, and yet they are too honest
to altogether deny the force of the evidence.

worthy to suffer dishoner for the name. (42) And every day, in the temple and at home, they ceased not to teach and preach Jesus as the Christ. The law of Moses limited the scourge to forty stripes, and left it discretionary with the judges for what offenses it should be inflicted.[1] It seems from Paul's experience to have been customary to stop at thirty-nine,[2] perhaps to prevent going beyond the limit of the law by a miscount. It is probable that the apostles received thirty-nine apiece on the naked back. The statement that when they were released they went away " rejoicing that they were counted worthy to suffer dishonor for the name," would be incredible, were it not written in such a book as this, and written of such men as these. Even as the case stands it is a more surprising fact than any of the miracles which they are said to have wrought; especially when we consider that this was their first experience of scourging. After Paul had endured a long continued fight of afflictions like this, it is not so wonderful to hear him say, " I take pleasure in weaknesses, in injuries, in necessities, in persecutions, in distresses for Christ's sake: for when I am weak then I am strong."[3] But that the older apostles had a similar experience the first time they were scourged, is one of the grandest exhibitions of faith to be found in apostolic history. Perhaps the secret of their ability to rejoice is to be found in the consideration that Christ showed confidence in their steadfastness by allowing them to be tested in this way, and they were glad of the opportunity to prove that his confidence was not misplaced.

The preaching was now, as before, in the temple; for there was no thought of excluding the apostles and

---

[1] Deut. xxv. 1-3.   [2] II. Cor. xi. 24.   [3] II. Cor. xii. 10.

their brethren from the open court to which all Jews
had right of access; and it was also daily. They held,
in modern Protestant phraseology, a continuous protracted meeting. But they did not limit their labors, as
so many modern preachers are content to do, to public
preaching: they also taught and preached " at home"
(42)—an expression which points to the homes of their
hearers, rather than to their own home; for in their own
home, if they still lodged in the same house, they could
receive but few persons, whereas in the homes of the
people they could reach everybody who was in need of
instruction or conviction. Thus we have the inspired
apostles as an example for that most directly effective of
all preaching, the face to face work, without much of
which no preacher of the gospel can be thoroughly successful in evangelizing a community.

We have now reached the close of the first persecution, and it is plainly to be seen that it resulted in a
complete triumph for the apostles. When the people
saw them go away from the whipping-post, rejoicing that
they were counted worthy to suffer thus for the name of
their Master, they were amazed; for the like of this had
never before been seen on earth. And when they saw
that the preaching continued without intermission in defiance of all threats and all punishment, the hearts of all
the nobler men and women, of all who could admire
moral heroism, were irresistibly drawn toward the Christ
whose love thus ennobled his followers.

SEC. V.—FURTHER PROGRESS OF THE CHURCH, AND THIRD PERSECUTION.

(VI. 1—VIII. 4.)

1. SEVEN MEN APPOINTED TO SERVE TABLES, 1–7.

VER. 1. Having completed his account of the second persecution, our author continues the plan of this part of his work by turning our attention once more to the progress of the church, and then to a third persecution which followed. The perfect unity which had hitherto bound together the multitude of the disciples was now in jeopardy, though it would be too much to say, with some writers, that it was broken; and we are introduced to both the cause of peril and the steps by which it was averted. (1) Now in these days, when the number of the disciples was multiplying, there arose a murmuring of the Grecian Jews against the Hebrews, because their widows were neglected in the daily ministration. By daily ministration is meant the daily distribution from the fund contributed by benevolent members, which was made " to every one as he had need." That it was made daily, and that the widows were the principal recipients, confirms our former conclusion that there was no general equalization of property, but only a provision for the needy. The Grecian Jews, more properly Hellenists, were Jews of foreign birth and Greek education, so called because they adopted the manners of the Hellenes, or Greeks. The great multiplication of the disciples having rendered it impracticable for the twelve, with so much other work on hand, to look after the wants of all with equal care, very naturally the widows of these comparative strangers in the city were the first to be unintentionally overlooked.

Vv. 2–4. The unity of heart and soul which still prevailed in the church manifested itself by the promptness with which a satisfactory arrangement was made to quiet the murmur as soon as it was heard. Doubtless the need for such an arrangement was foreseen by the head of the church and by the Holy Spirit dwelling in the apostles; but this foresight was not given to the apostles, nor were they moved to make the arrangement until the need for it was manifest to them and to the whole church. Thus the Spirit guided them into additional truth as additional truth was needed. Hitherto the twelve were the only officers in the church; but now they are led to the appointment of others. (2) And the twelve called the multitude of the disciples unto them, and said, It is not fit that we should forsake the word of God, and serve tables. (3) Look ye out therefore, brethren, from among you seven men of good report, full of the Spirit and of wisdom, whom we may appoint over this business. (4) But we will continue steadfastly in prayer, and in the ministry of the word. The alternative with the twelve was to forsake (not wholly, but in some measure) the preaching and teaching of the word, in order to serve the tables satisfactorily, or to turn the latter business over to others, and give themselves wholly to the former. The right course was too obvious to admit of hesitation or delay.

It seemed good to the apostles and to the Holy Spirit that the whole "multitude of the disciples" should take part in the selection of these officers, the apostles doing no more in the matter than to prescribe their qualifications. No ingenuity of argument can evade the conclusion that this gives the authority of apostolic precedent for the popular election of church officers. In what way the choice was made by the multitude, whether by balloting, or by a *viva voce* vote, and whether with or without nominations, we are not informed; and consequently, in reference to these points, every congregation is left to its own judgment.

The three qualifications prescribed should not escape our notice. They indicate what kind of men are alone fitted to be office-bearers in the church of God. They were to be men, first, of "good report;" and this has reference, no doubt, to their reputation both within the church, and within the circle of fair-minded persons outside the church. Second, they were to be "full of the Spirit." As we have had no account thus far of any but the apostles having received miraculous powers from the Spirit, the historian can not be fairly understood as referring, by this expression, to such powers. He means men who were full of the Spirit as respects the fruits of a holy life. That some of these wrought miracles afterward, is no proof that they could do so now. Third, they were to be men "full of wisdom;" by which is meant that they should possess that practical good sense which enables men to manage complicated business affairs with satisfaction.

Vv. 5, 6. The wisdom of the proposal was obvious to all, and none hesitated about prompt compliance with it. (5) And the saying pleased the whole multitude: and they chose Stephen, a man full of faith and of the Holy Spirit, and Philip, and Prochorus, and Nicanor, and Timon, and Parmenas, and Nicholas a proselyte of Antioch: whom they set before the apostles: (6) and when they had prayed, they laid their hands on them. It is a remarkable manifestation of generosity in the church at large that all these are Greek names, indicating that the men were selected from the very party whence the murmuring had proceeded. It was as if the Hebrews had said, We have no selfish ends to accomplish, and no jealousy toward you whose widows have been neglected; we therefore give the whole business into your hands, and fearlessly trust our widows to your care. So generous a trust could not be betrayed except by the basest of men: it was a continuation of the perfect unity which had existed before, and which the murmuring had not been allowed to interrupt.

The title of the office here created is not given, and from this circumstance some scholars have failed to identify it with that of deacon, mentioned in the first chapter of Philippians and the third chapter of First Timothy. But while the name of the office is absent, terms are used which show plainly that the office is the same. If the question had been one about ruling, and the seven had been chosen and appointed to rule, there could certainly be no hesitation about styling them rulers. The case before us is a perfect parallel. The question was about the "daily διακονίαν,"[1] and the seven were chosen

---

[1] The word διάκονος is rendered in our English version by the three words, minister, servant, and deacon. No reader unacquainted with the original could imagine that three English words now currently used in senses so different, could represent the same word in the original; and consequently this rendering leads to confusion. One of the three should be employed uniformly so as to give the English reader the same opportunity to see its usage that the Greek reader enjoys. The term deacon would not answer this purpose, because it is limited in its meaning as an English word to the office so designated, and it would be misleading in every passage in which the original occurs except two; for out of the many occurrences of διάκονος it is rendered

to διαχονεῖν; why, then, hesitate to call them διάχονοι?
Indeed, the verb διαχονεῖν, here used to express the chief
duty of the office, is the very one which in the third
chapter of First Timothy is twice rendered in our version "serve as deacons."[1] Undoubtedly, then, it is the
deacon's office which was here first created, and supplied
with incumbents. The chief duty for which they were
appointed was "to serve tables;" and as reference is had
to the "daily ministration," and the complaints of neglected widows, the tables of the poor are specially those
to be served. But while serving these tables, it was a
natural consequence of having such business in charge

---

deacon only in Phil. i. 1 and I. Tim. iii. 8, 10. Deacon, indeed,
is the Greek word anglicized, and we have to resort to a Greek
lexicon for its meaning. The word minister would also be ob-
jectionable as a uniform rendering, for it is appropriated in
modern usage to the public speakers of the church, whereas the
original word has no such limitation. Should we adopt it, we
would have such renderings as these: "His mother said to the
ministers, Whatsoever he saith unto you, do it" (Jno. ii. 5; see
also 9); "If any man serve me (ἐμοὶ διακονῇ), let him follow me;
and where I am, there shall my minister (διάκονος) be" (Jno. xii.
26); "Phœbe our sister, who is a *minister* of the church at Cenchrea" (Rom. xvi. 1). But the word *servant* would properly express the idea everywhere. This is the precise meaning of the
word, and the Latin word *minister*, by which it is most commonly
rendered in our version, means the same. With servant as the
uniform rendering, the English reader could determine by the
context, as the Greek scholar now does, whether in a given passage the servant was one in the official or in the unofficial sense
of the term. The two classes of officers, now called elders and
deacons, would in this way be known as rulers and servants,
their true relationship.

[1] It is gratifying to know that this argument, made in the first
edition of my Commentary, is made also by Bishop Lightfoot in
his Commentary on Philippians, published several years later
(Lightfoot's Phil. p. 186).

that they also served the Lord's table; and it was an equally natural transition, that forasmuch as the poor fund was in their hands, all the other financial interests of the church were also committed to them. Because these officers were charged with the business affairs of the church, it by no means follows that they were shut off from usefulness in any other way for which they had capacity and opportunity. God exacts the employment of every talent which he has committed to us, and he has appointed no work to be done which is too holy for the humblest disciple. We therefore find one of the seven soon after standing in the front rank of the defenders of the faith in the very city where the apostles themselves were laboring; while another was the first to plant a church among the Samaritans. Those who deny to deacons in the present day the same privilege, impose restrictions in conflict with this manifestation of God's will. Only two of the seven are mentioned afterward in Acts, but this does not prove that the others were either inactive or unfaithful. The service of all as deacons proved temporary; not, as some suppose, because it was so intended; but because the church which they served was soon scattered to the winds, and their ministration was no longer needed. When the church was afterward restored, it may be that some of them returned to the city and resumed the duties of their office.

The first name in the list, that of Stephen, is followed by the words, "a man full of faith and of the Holy Spirit," and these words are not repeated after the other names; but we are not to understand from this that they were not true of the other persons; for as the apostles had prescribed this characteristic as a qualification for the office, we are to understand the words, though not repeated, as applying to all alike.

That Nicholas was a " proselyte of Antioch," which means that he was a convert from heathenism to Judaism, and had previously lived in Antioch, shows very plainly that the disciples entertained no doubt about the reception into the church, and even about the election to office, of Gentiles, provided they had been circumcised. This should be borne in mind when we come to consider the discussions which afterward arose about the relation of the Gentiles to the church, and to salvation in Christ.

VER. 7. The appointment of the seven to administer the business affairs of the church, left the apostles, as was intended, with nothing to do but to preach and teach and pray ; and thus the work of the whole church was more effective than before. (7) And the word of God increased ; and the number of the disciples multiplied in Jerusalem exceedingly ; and a great company of the priests were obedient to the faith. This great multiplication of the disciples in Jerusalem, after such an increase as we have noticed before, puts it beyond our power to estimate, with any approach to accuracy, the number at this time. The tide of success had now reached its flood, and this was signalized not so much by the great number of converts, as by the fact that among these was a " great company of the priests." The peculiar relation which the priesthood sustains to any religion must always render the priests the chief conservators of old forms, and the most persistent opponents of revolutionary changes. When they begin to give way, the system which they have upheld is ready to fall. No fact previously recorded by Luke shows so strikingly the effect of the gospel on the popular mind in Jerusalem.

The remark made concerning these priests, that they "were obedient to the faith," shows that there is something in the faith to be obeyed. This obedience is rendered not by believing; for that is to exercise the faith, not to obey it : but faith in Jesus as the Christ, the Son of God, demands of us a course of life in accordance with that which we believe; and to follow this course is to obey the faith by yielding to its demands. This obedience begins with baptism; and consequently, to say that the priests "were obedient to the faith" is equivalent to saying that they were baptized. Paul, with the same thought in mind, declares that the grace and apostleship conferred on him were for the "obedience of faith among all the nations."[1]

There is another expression in this verse worthy of notice, because of its singular contrast with phraseology often heard in modern times in connection with such events. It is the saying, in connection with the great multiplication of the disciples, and the obedience of so many priests, that "the word of God increased." At the present day such incidents are often introduced by remarks of this kind : "There was a precious season of grace;" "The Lord was present in his saving power;" "There was a gracious outpouring of the Holy Spirit," etc. So great a departure from Scripture phraseology, indicates a departure from Scriptural ideas. With the conception that the conversion of sinners is an abstract work of the Holy Spirit, men may express themselves thus; but Luke, who had no such conception, saw in the increase an increase of the word of God; by which he means an increase not in the amount of the word, but in its effects. The more favor-

---

[1] Rom. i. 5.

able condition of the church when the recent murmuring ceased, and the introduction of a more perfect organization, made the preaching more effective, and greater success was the consequence.

2. STEPHEN ARRESTED AND FALSELY ACCUSED, 8–15.

VER. 8. The great prosperity of the church resulted, as it had done twice before, in arousing the unbelievers to action in the way of persecution. In this instance Stephen was selected as the victim. (8) And Stephen, full of grace and power, wrought great wonders and signs among the people. This is the first exhibition of miraculous power by any but an apostle. Whether Stephen received the power to work wonders and signs before or after his appointment as deacon, we have no means of determining; neither does the writer tell us in what way it was imparted to him. He reserves information on the subject of imparting spiritual gifts to a point in the history further on (viii. 14–17).

Vv. 9, 10. The circumstances which led to this prominence on the part of Philip are stated next. (9) But there arose certain of them that were of the synagogue called the synagogue of the Freedmen,[1] and of the Cyrenians, and of the Alexandrians, and of them of Cilicia and Asia, disputing with Stephen. (10) And they were not able to withstand the wisdom and the Spirit by which he spoke. All the parties here mentioned were Hellenistic Jews, who, from a natural inclination to flock together in the Holy City, had a syna-

---

[1] The word *libertines* in our version is here misleading to the uneducated reader; and as it is the Latin word for freedmen, there can be no good reason for not translating it, and therefore I depart from the R. V. here in rendering it freedmen.

gogue of their own.[1] Stephen, being also a Hellenist, had doubtless been a member of this synagogue before he became a Christian, and by his new connection he had not forfeited his membership. Most naturally, when he began the public advocacy of the new faith, he did so in the synagogue of which he was already a member, and undertook the conviction and conversion of his former associates. This brought on the conflict.

The Freedmen, who constituted a large element of the membership in this synagogue, were Jews who had been slaves, and had by one means or another obtained their freedom. The others were from the several cities and countries named, at least the Cilicians being the countrymen of him who was afterward the apostle Paul. The Jewish learning of the day belonged to the Pharisees, rather than the Sadducees; the faithful among the foreign Jews were chiefly Pharisees, and they were generally men of some wealth and much intelligence. Consequently we now find a new leader on the part of the church and a different party of the unbelievers brought into conflict. It was not now, as in the two former conflicts, a mere struggle between force and endurance; but it was an intellectual struggle—a war of arguments on the great question of the Messiahship. Never, perhaps, even in the life of Jesus, had there been so protracted, and so warmly contested a debate between competent disputants on the great question of the day. It was the first time the disciples had measured arms with their opponents in open discussion. The young converts had hitherto en-

---

[1] I can see no ground in the wording of the text for the conclusion adopted by some writers, that *three* synagogues are here designated (Alford *in loco*), by others *two*, by others *five* (Meyer *in loco*). It is a matter, however, of no special importance.

joyed no opportunity of comparing the evidences by
which they had been convinced with those which learning and ingenuity might frame against them; but now
they heard both sides, with the odds in numbers, learning and social position all on the side of their opponents. It was a critical moment in their experience, and
it needs no vivid imagination to realize the solicitude
with which they listened to Stephen and his foes. Any
fears they may have entertained at first were soon dissipated, as it became evident that Stephen's antagonists
" were not able to resist the wisdom and the Spirit by
which he spoke."

Vv. 11-14. When men whose chief concern it is to
vindicate themselves rather than the truth are defeated
in debate, they very commonly resort to vituperation or
violence. Both were tried against Stephen. The Pharisees, who had the management of the case, entered upon
the same line of policy which they had pursued successfully in the prosecution of Jesus. (11) Then they sub-
orned men, who said, We have heard him speak blasphemous words against Moses and against God. (12)
And they stirred up the people, and the elders, and the
scribes, and came upon him, and seized him, and brought
him into the council, and set up false witnesses, who said,
(13) This man ceaseth not to speak blasphemous words
against this holy place and the law: (14) for we have
heard him say, that this Jesus of Nazareth shall destroy
this place, and shall change the customs which Moses delivered unto us.

This is the first time that the people are represented
as being stirred up against the disciples. Hitherto the
fear of the people had restrained the violence of the
persecutors. This change is accounted for by the fact

that the Sadducees, who had conducted the previous persecutions, had comparatively little influence with the masses, and the further fact, that they had contented themselves with arraying against the apostles the mere authority of the Sanhedrin; but now the Pharisees, who had much more popular influence, are in the lead, and they poison the minds of the people by seizing upon certain utterances of Stephen which needed to be only slightly distorted in order to form the ground of very serious charges. They are cunning enough, too, to make these charges, not against the whole body of the disciples, or against the apostles, who now enjoyed the confidence of the masses; but against a single person who had just risen up from obscurity.

The general charge was that he had committed blasphemy—a crime punishable with death under the law; blasphemy against Moses, in saying that Jesus would change the customs which Moses had delivered; and blasphemy against God, in saying that he would destroy God's holy temple. It is quite probable that Stephen had, in the course of the debate, quoted the prediction of Jesus that the temple would be destroyed, but had not said that Jesus would destroy it; and as his enemies could see that the destruction of the temple would necessarily bring to an end the temple services, they put their own inference into his lips, in charging him with saying that Jesus would change the customs delivered by Moses. The specifications were so nearly true as to form a plausible ground for the accusation,[1] while the falsity

---

[5] The position taken by Baur in his chapter headed "Stephen the Predecessor of Paul," that Stephen looked upon the temple worship "as a thing already antiquated and in ruins," while "the apostles always remained immovably true to their old ad-

of the witnesses lay in the additions they made to Stephen's words, and in construing what he said as blasphemy.

Let us observe here, that the Pharisees avoided the blunder committed by the Sadducees, of bringing men into court for trial with no definite charges framed against them. Charges were formally presented, witnesses were deliberately heard in support of them, and Stephen was called upon for his defense.

VER. 15. When the case had been fully stated, and the testimony of all the witnesses was in, there was a momentary pause, and all eyes were fixed upon Stephen, who stood before his accusers. (15) **And all that sat in the council fastening their eyes on him, saw his face as it had been the face of an angel.** There is no need to suppose anything supernatural in his appearance. He was standing just where his Master had stood when condemned to die; he was arraigned on a similar charge; he had the same judges; and he knew perfectly well that the court had come together not to try him, but to condemn him. He knew that the supreme hour of his life had come; and the emotions which stirred his soul as he thought of the past, of death, of heaven, of the cause which he had pleaded, and of the foul murder about to be perpetrated, necessarily lit up his countenance with a glow almost supernatural. If his features, as is highly probable, were naturally fine and expressive, the

herance to the temple," is without justification in the text, even if we regard the accusations brought against Stephen as strictly true; for there is no evidence that he differed from the apostles in believing the prediction of Jesus concerning the destruction of the temple, or that he held the temple worship as " already antiquated and in ruins." (*Life and Works of Paul*, vol. i. c. 2).

crowning ornament of a noble form, it is not surprising that in such a moment his face should be compared to that of an angel.

3. Stephen's Discourse, vii. 1–53.

I.

THE INTRODUCTION, 1-8.

Vv. 1–8. With his face glowing like that of an angel, at a word from the high priest Stephen proceeds to deliver one of the most remarkable discourses on record. (1) And the high priest said, Are these things so ? (2) And he said, Brethren and fathers, hearken. The God of glory appeared unto our father Abraham, when he was in Mesopotamia, before he dwelt in Haran,[1]

---

[1] It is charged by rationalists generally, that Stephen makes several historical mistakes in this speech, of which the first is his representation here that God gave this command to Abraham " before he dwelt in Haran," whereas it is said in Genesis xii. 1–4, that he gave it to him in Haran. But his language implies that he knew what occurred in Haran, but wished to state an additional and antecedent fact. Knowing that God did appear to Abraham in Haran, and also knowing what some of his hearers overlooked, that he had also appeared before that time, he here speaks of the previous appearance, this being the one that started Abraham in the direction of Canaan. Those who say that he was mistaken should account for the fact stated in Gen. xi. 31, that Terah took his family, " and they went forth with them from Ur of the Chaldees, to go into the land of Canaan." What could have started this whole family of Shemites on a journey of more than a thousand miles into a country occupied by Hamites, unless it were some such command as that which finally took Abraham from Haran into that same country ? Stephen says it was such a command ; and even if he based the statement on a logical inference, with no other source of knowledge, no one can deny that the inference is a just one. If it be objected that the command, if given before, would not have been repeated in words so nearly identical, we may answer, that the command given to

(3) and said unto him, Get thee out of thy land, and from thy kindred, and come into the land which I will show thee. (4) Then he came out of the land of the Chaldeans, and dwelt in Haran : and from thence, when his father was dead,[1] God removed him into this land,

---

Jonah to go into Nineveh was expressed in almost the same terms when first given as when repeated after his experience in the bowels of the fish (Jonah i. 2; iii. 2). Furthermore, there is an important omission in Stephen's quotation of the words as compared with those in Gen. xii. He omits the words, "and from thy father's house," which agrees with the fact that on leaving Ur of Chaldea he did not leave his father's house, as he did when he left Haran.

[1] Here is the second mistake charged upon Stephen. It is claimed that Abraham was born when his father was seventy years old (Gen. xi. 26); that he left Haran when he was himself seventy-five years old, which would make his father 70+75=145 ; and as Terah lived to two hundred and five (Gen. xi. 32), he must have lived 205—145=60 years after Abraham left Haran, instead of dying, as Stephen says, before Abraham's departure. But this whole calculation depends on the correctness of the figures from which it starts. The statement of the text, Gen. xi. 26, is that "Terah lived seventy years, and begat Abraham, Nahor and Haran." Unless we assume that these three were triplets, we can not assert that Terah was just seventy when Abraham was born. But that they were not triplets, and that Nahor and Abraham were much younger than Haran, is evident from the fact that Nahor's wife was Haran's daughter, and that Haran's son Lot was not many years younger than Abraham, as appears from the later history of the two. It is obvious, then, that this statement about the births of the three is not intended to show the time of the birth of Abraham or Nahor, but only that of Haran. It is similar to the statement in Gen. v. 32, that "Noah lived five hundred years: and Noah begat Shem, Ham and Japheth;" whereas, by comparison of the ages of Noah and Shem at the time of the flood, we find that Noah was five hundred and two years old when Shem was born (Gen. iii. 13, *cf.* xi. 10). In other words, the author of Genesis, in his aim at extreme brevity, in both these instances gives the age of a father at the birth of one

wherein ye now dwell : (5) and he gave him no inheritance in it, no, not so much as to set his foot on : and he promised that he would give it to him in possession, and to his seed after him, when as yet he had no child. (6) And God spake on this wise, that his seed should sojourn in a strange land, and that they should bring them into bondage, and entreat them evil, four hundred years. (7) And the nation to which they shall be in bondage will I judge, said God : and after that they shall come forth and dwell in this place. (8) And he gave him the convenant of circumcision : and so Abraham begat Isaac, and circumcised him the eighth day ; and

---

(and apparently, in both cases the oldest) of his sons, and while doing so mentions the births of the other two, without wishing to make the impression that they were all brought forth at one birth. Indeed, he avoids that impressien by other statements in the context which preclude it. Stephen then may be relied on when he says that God removed Abraham from Haran into Canaan after the death of Terah ; and if so, then the age of Terah when Abraham was born was 205—75=130 years. Alford objects to this conclusion in the following terms: "Terah, in the course of nature, begets his son Abram at one hundred and thirty ; yet this very Abram regards it as incredible that he himself should beget a son at ninety-nine (Gen. xvii. 1, 17); and on the birth of Isaac out of the course of nature, most important Scripture arguments and consequences are founded, *cf.* Rom. iv. 17–21 ; Heb. xi. 11, 12 " (*Commentary in loco.*) The learned author forgets that " in the course of nature" this same Abram, long after he was ninety-nine, and apparently after the death of Sarah, when he was one hundred and thirty-seven, took a younger wife and begat six other sons, the sons of Keturah (Gen. xxiii. 1; xxiv. 1–4). The incredulity of Abram, then, so far as it respected himself (for it is evident that it had reference chiefly to Sarah), depended on something else than his mere age. It may have depended largely on the fact that he had now been living thirteen years with a young concubine, Hagar, since the birth of Ishmael, and she had not borne him another son (xvii. 24, 25).

Isaac, Jacob; and Jacob, the twelve patriarchs. Here is a calm, dignified, and very graphic sketch of the story in Genesis, from the first call of Abraham until the birth and circumcision of the twelve sons of Jacob. It was a recital which always interested a Jewish audience, just as an effective recital of the migration of our Pilgrim Fathers always interests an American audience. But what had it to do with the charges brought against Stephen? and why should it be found on the lips of a man about to be condemned to die? These questions it was impossible at the moment for his hearers to answer, though they must have occurred to every mind. It is equally impossible for us to answer them, unless we anticipate the sequel, which we should not do.

II.

THE CASE OF JOSEPH, 9–16.

Vv. 9–16. The speaker next recounts the circumstances growing out of the sale of Joseph, which led to the migration of Jacob into Egypt, and to his death, with that of his sons, in that foreign land. The account is equally graphic with the preceding, and as skillfully abridged. (9) And the patriarchs, moved with envy against Joseph, sold him into Egypt: (10) and God was with him, and delivered him out of all his afflictions, and gave him favor and wisdom before Pharaoh king of Egypt; and he made him governor over Egypt and all his house. (11) Now there came a famine over all Egypt and Canaan, and great affliction; and our fathers had no sustenance. (12) But when Jacob heard that there was corn in Egypt, he sent forth our fathers for the first time. (13) And at the second time Joseph was made known to his brethren; and Joseph's race became manifest unto Pharaoh. (14) And Joseph sent and called to him his father, and all his kindred, three score and fifteen souls.[1] (15) And Jacob went down into Egypt ; and he died, himself, and our fathers; (16) and they were carried over into Shechem, and laid in the tomb that Abraham bought for a price in silver of the sons of Hamor in Shechem.[2] In this division of the discourse,

---

[1] Here Stephen is said to make his third mistake, in putting the number of Jacob's family at seventy-five, whereas the text of Gen. xlvi. 27 makes the number seventy, including two who had died in Canaan. Many conjectures have been advanced to account for this difference, while the only one that should have been thought of has been often overlooked. Stephen, being a Hellenist, read the Scriptures in the Greek translation, as did all of his adversaries in the foreign synagogue, and as did the great majority of the Jewish people, to whom the original Hebrew was already a dead language. His Greek Bible, the Septuagint version, gives precisely the number of names which he here quotes. It reads: "All the souls of the house of Jacob who went with Jacob into Egypt, were seventy-five souls;" and it makes the additional five, by giving, at verse 20, the names of two sons of Manasseh, two of Ephraim, and one grandson of the latter. Stephen then gave the figures as he and his hearers read them in their Bible, and perhaps neither he nor they had ever observed the discrepancy between the version and the original.

[2] In this sentence are two more of the mistakes charged on Stephen, and they are much more like real mistakes than any of the preceding. He appears to say that Jacob was carried over to Shechem and buried, whereas he was buried at Hebron in the cave of Macpelah ; and he does plainly say that Abraham bought a tomb of the sons of Hamor in Shechem, whereas it was the tomb at Hebron which he bought, while it was Jacob who bought a piece of land at Shechem. It is difficult to imagine how Stephen could have made these two mistakes ; for the burial of Jacob is made so prominent in Genesis, and was attended by so remarkable a funeral procession, including not only all the men of his own posterity, but the elders of Egypt, and a great company of Egyptian horsemen, that the account of it must have been very familiar to every Israel'te, and very dear to his heart. So, too,

the ill treatment of Joseph by his brethren is brought
into vivid contrast with his final rescue of the whole
family from starvation; and the way the story is told

---

the purchase of the cave at Macpelah by Abraham, attended as it
was by great sorrow for the loss of his beloved wife at an advanced age, and by the beautiful courtesies which adorned both
his own conduct and that of his Hittite neighbors in making the
transfer, was too prominent and interesting an event for a Jew
of any intelligence in the Scripture, such as Stephen certainly
was, to commit so great a blunder in regard to it. It is far more
likely that some early copyist, knowing of Abraham's purchase,
and not remembering that Jacob also made one at Shechem, here
inadvertently substituted the name Abraham where the name
Jacob was originally written. We are constrained therefore, by
the natural probabilities of the case, to conclude with many eminent critics that the name Abraham is a clerical error, and not a
mistake made by Stephen. The statement made concerning the
burial of Jacob admits another explanation. As the two clauses
stand in our version, "he died, himself, and our fathers; and
they were carried over into Shecham," there can be no doubt
that "himself" and "fathers" are common subjects of the one
verb "died," and that the pronoun "they" before "were carried" refers to both alike. But it is not so in the original. The
construction is different. The verb rendered died is in the singular number, ἐτελεύτησεν, and it agrees only with αὐτός, himself.
The plural substantive "fathers" is not the subject of that verb,
but of the plural ἐτελεύτησαν understood. The construction having
been changed with the introduction of the plural subject, it follows that the plural verb μετετέθησαν, "were carried," belongs to
fathers, and not to Jacob. The two clauses, properly punctu-
ated, and with the ellipsis supplied, read thus: "and he died;
and our fathers died, and were carried over into Shechem." With
this rendering and punctuation, which are certainly admissible,
the contradiction totally disappears; and if the passage had been
thus rendered at first into English, a contradiction would not have
been thought of. The question whether the "fathers," other than
Joseph, were carried over to Shechem for burial, can not be determined by anything said in the Old Testament; for of their
burial place nothing whatever is said. Stephen must have obtained
his information on this point, as he did his knowledge of the edu-

was well calculated to interest Stephen's hearers ; but the use which he intended to make of the facts recited was a mystery to them, and no one present could have been more conscious of this than Stephen himself, who purposely kept his ultimate aim out of sight.

III.

THE CASE OF MOSES IN EGYPT, 17-37.

Vv. 17-29. From this glance at the history of Joseph the speaker advances to that of Moses ; and with a master hand he sketches so much of it as to show that God raised him up in a remarkable way to a position of great learning and power, and that Moses undertook the deliverance of his people, but failed because they turned against him. (17) But as the time of the promise drew nigh, which God vouchsafed to Abraham, the people grew and multiplied in Egypt, (18) till there arose another king over Egypt, who knew not Joseph. (19) The same dealt subtilly with our race, and evil entreated our fathers, that they should cast out their babes, to the end that they should not live. (20) At which season Moses was born, and was exceeding fair ; and he was

---

cation of Moses, from some extra biblical source. As the mummy of Joseph was buried in the piece of land bought from the sons of Hamor (Josh. xxiv. 32), it is not improbable that the same was true of his brothers. Jerome, who lived in Palestine in the fourth century, says : " The twelve patriarchs were buried not [in Arbes (Hebron), but in Shechem ;" which shows that in his day the fact stated by Stephen was the current belief of the Jews. (See the citation in Speaker's Commentary). That a tomb was purchased together with the piece of land bought at Shechem, Stephen must also have learned from some source other than the Old Testament; but it is not at all improbable. Indeed, the possession of a sepulcher may have been one of the motives for the purchase of the land.

nourished three months in his father's house: (21) and when he was cast out, Pharaoh's daughter took him up, and nourished him for her own son. (22) And Moses was instructed in all the wisdom of the Egyptians; and he was mighty in words and works. (23) But when he was well nigh forty years old, it came into his heart to visit his brethren the children of Israel. (24) And seeing one of them suffer wrong, he defended him, and avenged him that was oppressed, smiting the Egyptian: (25) and he supposed that his brethren understood how that God by his hand was giving them deliverance; but they understood not. (26) And the day following he appeared unto them as they strove, and would have set them at one again, saying, Sirs, ye are brethren; why do ye wrong one to another? (27) But he that did his neighbor wrong thrust him away, saying, Who made thee a ruler and a judge over us? (28) Wouldst thou kill me, as thou killedst the Egyptian yesterday? (29) And Moses fled at this saying, and became a sojourner in the land of Midian, where he begat two sons. Although it was afterward discovered that this effort of Moses was premature, the Israelites of later generations must have regretted that their fathers rejected in so ungenerous a manner the offer to deliver them made by Moses at such a sacrifice to himself; for no doubt Stephen here rightly interprets his slaying of the Egyptian as a signal for his countrymen to rise and strike for liberty under his leadership. It was sad to think of their want of appreciation of such heroism.

Vv. 30–37. But Stephen has use for the next section in the career of Moses, in which, after being rejected by his countrymen, God made him their deliverer: and this he proceeds to sketch in the same graphic style. (30)

And when forty years were fulfilled, an angel appeared
to him in the wilderness of Mount Sinai, in a flame of
fire in a bush. (31) And when Moses saw it, he won-
dered at the sight: and as he drew near to behold, there
came a voice of the Lord, (32) I am the God of thy
fathers, the God of Abraham, and of Isaac, and of Jacob.
And Moses trembled, and durst not behold. (33) And
the Lord said, Loose the shoes from thy feet: for the
place whereon thou standest is holy ground. (34) I have
surely seen the affliction of my people which is in Egypt,
and have heard their groaning, and I have come down to
deliver them: and now come, I will send thee to Egypt.
(35) This Moses whom they refused, saying, Who made
thee a ruler and a judge ? him hath God sent to be both
a ruler and a deliverer with the hand of the angel who
appeared to him in the bush. (36) This man led them
forth, having wrought wonders and signs in Egypt, and
in the Red Sea, and in the wilderness forty years. (37)
This is that Moses, who said unto the children of Israel,
A prophet shall God raise up unto you from among your
brethren, like unto me.[1] In this passage the speaker not
only presents the contrast between the rejection of Moses
by his brethren, and God's appointment of him to the
very office which they refused him, but he also introduces the prediction uttered by Moses concerning the
Messiah—a prediction in which Moses evidently anticipated the coming of a prophet greater than himself.

IV.

THE CASE OF MOSES IN THE WILDERNESS, 38–41.

Vv. 38–41. Ungrateful as had been the conduct of
the Hebrews toward Moses when he first attempted to

---

[1] Deut. xviii. 15–19.

deliver them, it bore no comparison to their mistreatment of him after he had led them out into the wilderness; and to this Stephen next invites the attention of
his hearers: (38) This is he that was in the church[1] in
the wilderness with the angel[2] who spoke to him in
Mount Sinai, and with our fathers: who received living
oracles[3] to give unto us: (39) to whom our fathers
would not be obedient, but thrust him from them, and
turned back in their hearts into Egypt, (40) saying unto
Aaron, Make us gods which shall go before us: for as
for this Moses, who led us forth out of the land of Egypt,
we know not what is become of him. (41) And they
made a calf in those days, and brought a sacrifice unto

---

[1] The word here rendered church, ἐκκλησία, is the one usually
so rendered in N. T., but never in O. T. As the body of the
Israelites represented by it is always in O. T. styled the congregation, or the assembly, so it should have been here in the
text as our revisers have given it in the margin. This is
required by uniformity, and it would have prevented some
persons from confounding the assembly in the wilderness with
the New Testament church.

[2] By "the angel who spoke to him in Mount Sinai," Stephen
means the same angel mentioned in verse 30, where he says, "An
angel appeared to him in the wilderness of Mount Sinai, in a
flame of fire in a bush." In the next verse (31) this angel is
called The Lord, as in Exodus he is called both Jehovah and
God (Ex. iii. 2, 4). This shows that visible and audible manifestations of God were made through the persons of angels.

[3] The term oracles was used by the Greeks for communications supposed to have been received from their gods. In contrast with these, which came from no living being, and which
were nothing but empty words, the communications received by
Moses are called by Stephen *living* oracles, because they came
from the living God, and because they had within themselves
power to direct aright the lives of men. Both Paul and Peter
unite with Stephen in applying the title "living" to the word of
God (Heb. iv. 12; I. Pet. i. 23). See further under 53.

the idol, and rejoiced in the works of their hands. The greater flagrance of this sin appears from the fact that it was committed immediately after those splendid manifestations of God's presence with Moses which the people had witnessed in Egypt, at the Red Sea, in the march to Mount Sinai, and in the giving of the law from the summit of that mountain. They rejected Moses after he had accomplished the main part of their deliverance, and yet God made him the instrument for completing the deliverance which he had begun.

V.

GOD'S FINAL REJECTION OF ISRAEL, 42, 43.

Vv. 42, 43. The next division of the speech is apparently more abbreviated in Luke's report than the preceding divisions, and perhaps Stephen himself went less into details here than before. In a single sentence he passes over all the apostasies of Israel, from the time of the calf worship at the foot of Mount Sinai, till the final announcement of the Babylonian captivity by the mouth of the prophet Amos, whom he quotes: (42) But God turned, and gave them up to serve the host of heaven; as it is written in the book of the prophets,

> Did ye offer unto me slain beasts and sacrifices
> Forty years in the wilderness, O house of Israel?

(43) And ye took up the tabernacle of Moloch,
> And the star of the God Rephan,
> The figures which ye made to worship them:
> And I will carry you away beyond Babylon.[1]

---

[1] Stephen here quotes the Septuagint version of Amos v. 25–27, which varies slightly from the Hebrew. A discussion of the variations belongs rather to a commentary on Amos than to one on Acts. Stephen's purpose in the quotation is to show his

With this brief glance at the course of Israel in rejecting their divinely appointed leaders and deliverers during a period of many centuries, the first general division of the speech, as we shall see, is concluded. Before making the application of it, he passes to a topic which was included in his accusation; for we should be careful to observe that nothing which he has said thus far has any connection at all with the charges under which he was arraigned. His hearers could but wonder what use he intended to make of the facts which he had recited, and he was not yet ready to satisfy their curiosity.

---

hearers that one of their own prophets had long since convicted the generation in the wilderness of abandoning the service of Jehovah for that of various idols besides the calf which Aaron made; in consequence of which God then gave them up to worship "the host of heaven," and, as a remoter consequence, was in the days of the prophet about to send them into captivity in a foreign land. The question, "Did ye offer me slain beasts and sacrifices in the wilderness forty years?" is answered by the statement, "Ye took up the tabernacle of Moloch, and the star of the god Rephan;" thus showing, that although, as plainly appears in the Pentateuch, some sacrifices were offered in the wilderness, they were vitiated so as to amount to no worship at all because of the idolatry which was intermingled with them. In the expression "beyond Babylon," Stephen departs from the text of both the Hebrew and the Septuagint, which read "beyond Damascus." He doubtless did this on purpose, because the change more fully expressed the real mind of God in the prediction. God saw fit, in speaking through the prophet, to speak only of sending the people beyond Damascus, which was a short distance, when he really intended, as subsequent events disclosed, to send them much farther. Stephen puts in the word which expresses the full purpose of God. His hearers were acquainted with the facts, and could easily perceive his purpose.

VI.

THE TABERNACLE AND THE TEMPLE, 44–50.

Vv. 44–50. Instead of either admitting or formally denying the charge of blasphemy against the temple, the speaker proceeds to show very briefly the true religious value of that building. This he does by first alluding to the movable and perishable nature of the tabernacle, which was superseded by the temple, and then showing from the prophets that a temple made with hands can not be the real dwelling place of God. (44) Our fathers had the tabernacle of testimony in the wilderness, even as he appointed who spoke unto Moses, that he should make it according to the figure that he had seen. (45) Which also our fathers, in their turn, brought in with Joshua when they entered on the possession of the nations, which God thrust out before the face of our fathers, unto the days of David;[1] (46) who found favor in the sight of God, and asked to find a habitation for the God of Jacob. (47) But Solomon built him a house. (48) Howbeit the Most High dwelleth not in houses made with hands; as saith the prophet,

(49)   The heaven is my throne,
        And the earth the footstool of my feet:
        What manner of house will ye build me? saith the
        Lord:

---

[1] The commentators are nearly equally divided on the question whether the clause, " unto the days of David," is to be connected with the thrusting out of the Canaanites, or the bringing in of the tabernacle; Alford, Meyer and Hackett holding the latter view, and Lechler, Gloag and Jacobson, the former. It is not important to decide the question, for both views are in harmony with the facts of the history, and also with Stephen's train of thought. Our translators appear to have held the latter view,

Or what is the place of my rest ?
(50) Did not my hands make all these things ? [1]

Involved in these remarks is the argument, that inasmuch as the tabernacle was once God's house, but was supplanted by the temple ; and inasmuch as the temple, grand and ancient as it was, was infinitely too small to contain the living God, and was declared by one of their own prophets not to be God's real dwelling place, it could be no blasphemy to say that it was yet to be set aside and destroyed.

VII.

THE APPLICATION, 51–53.

Vv. 51–53. Stephen is now prepared to spring upon his accusers the concealed application of the facts which he had arrayed in the first division of his discourse. The historical introduction had paved the way for the following analogies. As Joseph, the divinely selected saviour of his brethren, had been sold into slavery by these brethren ; as Moses, divinely selected to deliver Israel from bondage, was at first rejected by them to become a fugitive in Midian, but was sent back by the God of their fathers to actually deliver them ; as Moses, after leading them out of Egypt, was again and again rejected by them ; and as all the prophets had met with similar mistreatment ; so now, the final prophet of whom Moses and all the later prophets had spoken, sent to deliver them from a far worse bondage, had been rejected and slain by the sons of those persecuting fathers. The force of all these analogies is concentrated in the few

---

for the comma which they have placed after " fathers " is out of place if the former is the connection of thought.
[1] Isa. xlvi. 1, 2.

words which follow : (51) **Ye stiffnecked and uncircum-**
cised[1] **in heart and ears, ye do always resist the Holy**
Spirit :[2] **as your fathers did, so do ye.** (52) **Which of**
the prophets did not your fathers persecute ? and they
killed them who showed before the coming of the
Righteous One; of whom ye have now become betrayers
and murderers; (53) **ye who received the law as it was**
ordained by angels, and kept it not.[3] The pent-up fires
which had burned in the breast of Stephen from the beginning of these cruel proceedings, and which had given
an angelic glow to his features before he began to speak,
but had been carefully smothered during the progress
of his argument, found vent, to the amazement of his
hearers, in these scorching and blazing words.

[1] On account of the feeling with which Jews came to look upon
all uncircumcised persons, the term uncircumcised was used by
them as a term of reproach and contempt; Moses emphasizes his
want of eloquence by speaking of his "uncircumcised lips" (Ex.
vi. 12, 30); and speaks of Israel in apostasy as having "uncir-
cised hearts" (Lev. xxvi. 41). David denounces Goliath as "this
uncircumcised Philistine" (I. Sam. xvii. 26); while Jeremiah
says of the people, "Their ear is uncircumcised, they can not
hearken " (Jer. vi. 10); and Ezekiel speaks of Elam as "uncircumcised in heart, and uncircumcised in flesh" (chap. xliv. 7, 9).
Adopting this Scriptural usage, Stephen denounces his judges
in the terms hurled at heathen nations and apostate Israel by
Moses and the prophets. No words could have been severer in
their estimation, and none could have been more just.

[2] Their fathers had resisted the Holy Spirit, as Stephen shows
in the next verse, by persecuting the prophets; and they had
done the same, as he shows in verse 53, by persecuting Jesus.
Thus we see that men resist the Holy Spirit when they reject the
words spoken by the Holy Spirit through inspired men.

[3] The Greek words here rendered " as it was ordained by angels,"
εἰς διαταγὰς ἀγγέλων, are very obscure in meaning, and therefore
difficult of translation. Many and conflicting attempts have been
made by the commentators, but Alford is surely correct when he

4. Stephen is Stoned, and the Church is Dispersed, VII. 54—VIII. 4.

Vv. 54–60. The exasperation of the Sanhedrin was as sudden as was the explosion of feeling with which the discourse came to an end; and it was the more intense because the denunciation hurled in their teeth was not a mere burst of passion, but the deliberate announcement of a righteous judgment, sustained by his array of analogies from Scripture, the bearing of which now flashed suddenly upon their minds. They had not been able to resist in debate the wisdom and spirit with which Stephen spoke, and now their efforts to convict him of crime had recoiled with terrific force upon their own heads. Their only recourse was the one usual with unprincipled partisans when totally discomfited, and to this they rushed with fearful rapidity. (54) **Now when they heard these things they were cut to the heart,**[1] **and they gnashed on him with their teeth.** (55) **But he,**

---

says: "The key to the right understanding of them seems to be the similar expression in Gal. iii. 19." He might have added, Heb. ii. 2. In the former place it is said that "the law was ordained through angels by the hand of a mediator;" and in the latter it is referred to as "the word spoken through angels." These passages show that according to apostolic interpretation God gave the law to Moses, not by speaking in his own proper person, but by speaking through angels whom he sent to Moses, and who doubtless appeared to him visibly. This, then, is the conception which Stephen embodies in the words before us; and although the rendering of the Revised Version which we follow does not bring out this thought very clearly, it is perhaps the best rendering which the original admits.

[1] Literally, *sawn asunder in their hearts.* They felt as if their hearts had been cut through with the rough teeth of a saw, so sharp and rasping were the words of Stephen. The literal gnashing of their teeth toward him was a natural consequence.

being full of the Holy Spirit, looked up steadfastly into heaven, and saw the glory of God, and Jesus standing on the right hand of God, (56) and said, Behold, I see the heavens opened, and the Son of man standing on the right hand of God. (57) But they cried out with a loud voice, and stopped their ears, and rushed upon him with one accord; (58) and they cast him out of the city, and stoned him: and the witnesses laid down their garments[1] at the feet of a young man named Saul. (59) And they stoned Stephen, calling upon the name of the Lord, and saying, Lord Jesus, receive my spirit. (60) And he kneeled down, and cried with a loud voice, Lord, lay not this sin to their charge. And when he had said this, he fell asleep. (viii. 1) And Saul was consenting to his death. This was a strange way for a court to break up; the whole body of seventy grave rabbis, whose official duty it was to watch for the faithful execution of the law, leaving their seats and rushing in a wild mob, amid hideous outcries, to the sudden execution of a prisoner uncondemned and untried.[2] But the maddest pranks ever played on earth are witnessed when wicked men set themselves in uncompromising opposition to God and his people.

---

[1] The witnesses had to begin the stoning (Deut. xvii. 7), and they threw off their outer garments to give their arms free movement.

[2] The objection urged by unfriendly critics, that the Sanhedrin had no right to execute a criminal without the consent of the Roman governor, and that therefore this account of Stephen's death is incredible (Baur, Life of Paul, i. 53, 54), is precluded by the narrative itself, which shows that this was an essentially unlawful procedure. It were as sensible to deny the credibility of any other account of mob violence, on the ground that it was not lawful. Mobs, because they are mobs, violate law, yet they often observe some of the forms of law, as did this mob in requiring the witnesses to begin the stoning.

The vision witnessed by Stephen need not be understood as a real opening of the sky, so that things beyond
could be seen by the human eye, but only as a symbol-
ical representation, such as those granted to John in the
isle of Patmos. It was vouchsafed both for his own
encouragement in the hour of death, and for the good
of friends and foes alike in subsequent days. The words
of Stephen, "Son of man standing on the right hand of
God," were an echo in the ears of the chief priests
of those uttered by Jesus when he stood before them on
trial. There was at least one in the audience upon whom,
we have reason to believe, the impression made by this
whole procedure was deep and lasting. The young man
Saul never forgot it, but long afterward, when bending
under the weight of years, he made sad mention of the
scene.[1] From him, as an eye-witness, Luke undoubtedly
obtained the information concerning it on which he relied, and also his report of Stephen's discourse. This is
a sufficient answer to all who have raised doubts about
the practicability of his obtaining a correct report of
the speech.[2]

Vv. 1–4. The enemies of the church had now tried
in vain all ordinary methods of opposing the truth.
Under the leadership of the Sadducees they tried first
threatening, then imprisonment, and then stripes. They
were about to follow these with the death of the twelve,
when the milder counsels of the yet unexasperated
Pharisees prevailed, and resort was had to discussion.
But the cause, which had prospered under the imprisonment and scourging of its chief advocates, bounded forward with a fresh impetus when brought before the

---

[1] Acts xxii. 19, 20; I. Tim. i. 12–17.

[2] See Baur, *Paul*, i. 52, 55; Zeller, *Acts of Apostles*, i. 241.

people in open debate, and the Pharisees were moved to follow the Sadducees in using violence. It was their purpose to proceed in their bloody work with the forms of law ; but in a moment of frenzy they lost all restraint, and dispatched their chosen victim with the violence of a mob. Once embarked in this mad career, nothing less than the extermination of the church could satisfy them.

(1) And there arose on that day[1] a great persecution against the church which was in Jerusalem; and they were all[2] scattered abroad throughout the regions of Judea and Samaria,[3] except the apostles. (2) And devout men buried Stephen, and made great lamentation over him. (3) But Saul laid waste the church, entering into every house, and dragging forth[4] both men and women, committed them to prison. (4) They therefore that were scattered abroad went about preaching the word.[5]

The grief of the good in a community at the loss of a good man is always great ; but it is most intense when

---

[1] The statement of the text is not that the whole of the persecution described below occurred on "that day," but it then "arose." Doubtless many days transpired before the whole church was dispersed.

[2] To assume with some (Baur, Zeller, et. al.), that only the Hellenistic portion of the church was scattered abroad, is to contradict without reason the universal terms of the text.

[3] That Samaria was one of the regions to which these Jews fled, shows that already there was a feeling among the Samaritans toward the disciples quite different from that toward the Jews in general.

[4] The term haling, here employed by our translators, is so thoroughly obsolete, that it should no longer disfigure the text, and I have accordingly discarded it, as was desired by the American section of the Revision Committee.

[5] The preaching here referred to was doubtless both public and private preaching, the latter being participated in by women as well as men.

the death is brought about by injustice and violence. It is not surprising, therefore, that the burial of Stephen was attended by " great lamentation " on the part of the " devout men " who discharged this mournful service. Possibly some of them were not members of the church. But while his death filled the hearts of the disciples with unutterable grief, it possessed a very great value to them from another point of view. They had embarked with all their interests, temporal and eternal, in the cause of one who, though he had proved himself mighty to deliver while present with them, had gone beyond the reach of vision, and no longer held personal converse with his former companions. Thus far, amid many tears, some stripes, and much affliction, they had found satisfaction in his service; but before Stephen's death it was not known by experience how their new faith would sustain them in a dying hour. Now one of their number had tried the dread reality. He had died praying for his murderers, and committing his spirit to the Son of man, whom he saw in a heavenly vision. No man at the present day can tell how great was the strength and consolation which came to all when the death of the first who died was so triumphant. It was a fitting and most providential preparation for the fiery ordeal through which the whole body of the believers was immediately compelled to pass. They could now go forward in their tear-dimmed course without fear or care for that within the grave or beyond it. With much bitterness of heart they left their native city and their individual homes to seek refuge among strangers; but to many of them the bitterness of temporal loss was no doubt slight compared with that of seeing the cause which they loved better than life apparently brought to

ruin. Still, though they had lost all for preaching
the word, they went everywhere preaching it. And
what must have been the feelings of the twelve when
they found themselves alone in a great city, the congregation of many thousands which they had collected all
scattered and gone, and they themselves silenced for
want of hearers? Their own lives must have been in
imminent peril; but, supposing that the time to which
Jesus had limited their stay in Jerusalem had not yet expired, and being undoubtedly solicitous for the future of
their many brethren and sisters who were languishing
there in prison, they courageously stood their ground, regardless of consequences. That they were allowed to
stay, and were unmolested, may be accounted for in part
by the supposition that they would be powerless after
the destruction of the church, and in part by the remembrance of their miracles, especially their miraculous
escape from prison. Moreover, they could no longer
preach in public for want of an audience, and thus they
appeared to be frightened into silence, and were consequently considered harmless.

COMMENTARY ON ACTS.

PART SECOND.

SPREAD OF THE GOSPEL IN JUDEA AND ADJACENT COUNTRIES.

(*VIII. 5—XII. 25.*)

SEC. I.—THE LABORS OF PHILIP.

(VIII. 5-40.)

1. HE FOUNDS A CHURCH IN THE CITY OF SAMARIA, 5-13.

VER. 5. Among the many who now went about preaching the word, the writer first follows Philip, and describes some of his labors. (5) **And Philip went down to the city of Samaria, and proclaimed unto them the Christ.** This Philip was not the apostle by that name, seeing that the apostles are said in verse 1 to have remained in Jerusalem; but he was one of the seven mentioned in vi. 5. His office of deacon had terminated by the dispersion of the church which he had served, and now he becomes an evangelist, the title by which he is called in xxi. 8. He evidently became an evangelist, not by being formally set apart to this work, but by beginning to evangelize under the force of circumstances. Among the older commentators there was much dispute as to whether the city into which he went was *a* city *of*

Samaria, or *the* city of Samaria; but the definite article is now admitted to be a part of the Greek text, and this settles the question.[1] It was the old capital of the twelve tribes, and it had recently been enlarged and embellished by Herod the Great.[2] Luke describes Philip's work in Samaria first, because this was the first success-ful work outside of Judea, and because, in the directions given by Jesus (i. 8), Samaria stands next to Judea.

Vv. 6–12. When Philip entered the city of Samaria the public mind was in a condition apparently unfavor-able to the reception of the gospel. The practice of magical arts was quite common among the Jews and the Samaritans of that age, and the masses of the people of all nations were very superstitious in reference to them. At this particular time the people of Samaria were com-pletely under the influence of a famous magician, and this obstacle had to be overcome before Philip could hope for success. The story of the conflict and the triumph is briefly told. (6) **And the multitude gave heed with one accord to the things that were spoken by Philip, when they heard, and saw the signs which he did. (7) For from many of those who had unclean spirits, they came out, crying with a loud voice: and many that were palsied, and that were lame, were healed. (8) And there was much joy in that city. (9) But there was a certain man, Simon by name, who be-**

---

[1] It was settled by the reading (τὴν πόλιν τῆς Σαμαρείας) in the Sinaitic MS., which, reinforcing the previously known evidence of the Alexandrian and the Vatican MSS., overbalanced all evidence for the omission of τὴν before πόλιν

[2] Herod changed its name to Sebaste, the Greek for Augusta, in honor of Augustus Cæsar; and it still retains this name in the Arabic form, *Sebustiyeh*. For a description of its present ruins, see the author's Lands of the Bible, 294.

foretime in the city used sorcery, and amazed the people
of Samaria,[1] giving out that himself was some great
one : (10) to whom they all gave heed, from the least to
the greatest, saying, This man is that power of God
which is called Great.   (11) And they gave heed to him,
because that of long time he had amazed them with his
sorceries.   (12) But when they believed Philip preaching good tidings concerning the kingdom of God and the
name of Jesus Christ, they were baptized, both men and
women.

This is another case of conversion, with a very brief
account of the means and influences by which it was
brought about.   Philip's preaching, like that of the
apostles on the day of Pentecost, and that of Jesus before
them, was accompanied by miracles.   The first effect on
the people was great joy, accompanied by the most
interested attention to the things which were spoken by
Philip (6–8).   Next, they shook off the spell which Simon had wrought upon them, and believed Philip's
preaching (9–12).   When they believed they were baptized, both men and women (12), and here the brief
story ends.   It is as simple and direct as the commission
under which Philip preached: "He that believeth and is
baptized shall be saved."

This case of conversion was well chosen by Luke,
because the subjects of it, up to the moment in which
Philip began to speak to them, were under the spell of
a magician, and the miracles wrought by Philip were

---

[1] Here the name Samaria designates not the city, but the country of the Samaritans.   The expression in Greek is τὸ ἔθνος τῆς
Σαμαρείας.   Josephus describes its limits (*Wars*, iii. 3, 4); and
they corresponded very closely to those of the tribes of Ephraim
and western Manasseh.

brought into direct comparison with the wonders wrought by Simon. The fact that the people without hesitation gave up their faith in Simon as the great power of God, and implicitly believed in what Philip did and taught, can be accounted for only on the ground that there was such a difference between the tricks of sorcery and the miracles, that the people, even though completely deluded by the former, could plainly see, when once the two were placed side by side, that the latter were divine, and the former human. The tricks of sorcery were, and they are still, as inexplicable to the beholder as miracles; but the former are mere tricks, serving no purpose except to excite idle curiosity, and therefore they are unworthy of God as their author; while the miracles consisted in acts of healing which were altogether beneficent and worthy of the exercise of divine power. Furthermore, the latter served the purpose of accrediting a message of mercy to a lost race, and thus they subserved a purpose far superior in beneficence to their immediate good effects on the afflicted. On account of this distinction, the miracles, instead of being superior exhibitions of magic art, as skeptics have alleged, are found in mortal conflict with magic wherever the two came together. See further evidence of this in xiii. 6–12, and xix. 11–20.

VER. 13. The most signal triumph achieved on this occasion, was that over Simon himself. Luke gives it the prominence of a separate statement in these words: (13) And Simon also himself believed; and being baptized, he continued with Philip; and beholding signs and great miracles wrought, he was amazed. His amazement is proof that he saw, as the people did, the distinction between miracles and his own tricks of jugglery. He could understand the nature of the latter, even such

as he knew not how to work, because of his own experience with such things; but the former were to him, as to
all men, incomprehensible. It was undoubtedly this
which caused him to believe; and to avoid the confusion into which many have fallen in regard to his
faith, it should be observed that the words, " Simon also
himself believed," are written not from Philip's point of
view, but from Luke's. Philip might have been deceived by a pretended faith; but Luke, writing long
after the transaction, and with all the knowledge of
Simon's later career that we have, says that he believed,
and this should preclude all doubt as to the reality of
his faith. The statements made below (18–24) are to
be interpreted in the light of this fact. His baptism
committed him not only to this faith, but to the abandonment of sorcery, as of all other sins.

2. Mission of Peter and John to Samaria, 14–17.

Vv. 14–17. Luke next introduces an incident which,
on account of its singularity in New Testament history,
and the speculations to which it has given rise, demands
very careful consideration: (14) **Now when the apostles
who were at Jerusalem heard that Samaria had received
the word of God, they sent unto them Peter and John:
(15) who, when they were come down, prayed for them,
that they might receive the Holy Spirit: (16) for as yet
he was fallen upon none of them; only they had been
baptized into the name of the Lord Jesus. (17) Then
they laid their hands on them, and they received the
Holy Spirit.**

In order to a correct understanding of this procedure,
we must notice four facts which are conspicuous: first,
that the Samaritans, having believed the gospel and been

baptized, were, according to the commission (Mark xvi. 16), and according to Peter's answer on Pentecost (Acts ii. 38), pardoned and in possession of the "gift of the Holy Spirit." After they had been in possession of this gift long enough for the news to reach Jerusalem, the body of the apostles united in sending to them Peter and John.[1] Third, previous to the arrival of Peter and John the Holy Spirit had fallen with its miraculous powers on none of the Samaritans. Fourth, upon the imposition of hands by the two apostles, preceded by prayer, the Holy Spirit with its miraculous powers fell upon them.

From these facts we may draw several conclusions. (1) Whatever other purposes may have prompted the mission of the two apostles, such as confirming the faith of the disciples, or assisting Philip in his labors, it is quite certain that the chief purpose was the impartation of the Holy Spirit. What they did on their arrival was certainly that for which they went: but the chief thing which they did was to confer the Holy Spirit; therefore this was the chief purpose of their visit. If, however, Philip could have conferred this gift, the mission would have been useless so far as its chief purpose is concerned. This affords strong evidence that the miraculous gift of the Holy Spirit was bestowed through no human hands but those of the apostles; and this conclusion is confirmed by the consideration that in the only other instance of the kind recorded in Acts, that of the twelve in Ephesus (xix. 1–7), the gift was bestowed by the hands of an apostle. The case of Saul is not an exception (see the remarks on ix. 17); neither is that of Timothy; for

---

[1] That Peter and John were "sent" by the other apostles, conflicts with the Roman Catholic doctrine of the primacy of Peter, by showing that he was subject to his brethren.

although the latter is said to have received a gift through the laying on of the hands of the eldership (I. Tim. iv. 14), yet he received the same or some other gift by the putting on of Paul's hands (II. Tim. i. 6). From Paul he doubtless received the miraculous gift, and from the elders the gift of position as an evangelist.

(2) The fact that these disciples enjoyed pardon and membership in the church before receiving the miraculous gift, proves that this gift has no connection with the enjoyment of either of these blessings; yet the mystic power of an ultra spiritualism has involved some great minds in confusion as to this important matter. Witness the following from Neander in reference to the condition of the Samaritans previous to the visit of Peter and John: "They had not yet attained the consciousness of a vital communion with the Christ whom Philip preached, nor yet to the consciousness of a personal divine life. The indwelling of the Spirit was as yet something foreign to them, known only by the wonderful operations which they saw taking place around them."[1] This assertion is in direct conflict with the commission, and with the apostolic promise that they who would repent and be baptized should receive the gift of the Holy Spirit. It also conflicts with Paul's teaching, that the indwelling of the Spirit is characteristic of all who are Christ's (Rom. viii. 9–11); for certainly those who had been properly "baptized into the name of Christ," as the Samaritans had been (16), were his.

(3) The statement, "as yet he had fallen upon none of them: only they had been baptized into the name of the Lord Jesus," shows that there was no such connection between baptism and the miraculous gift of the

---

[1] Planting and Training of the Church, *in loco.*

Spirit, as that the latter might be inferred from the former. This gift, then, was not common to the disciples, but it was enjoyed only by those to whom it was specially imparted.

Seeing that this extraordinary gift of the Spirit was not necessary to the conversion and pardon of these persons, nor to the indwelling of the Spirit, it is proper to inquire for what purpose it was bestowed. We have already remarked under chapter i. 8, that the design of bestowing it on the apostles was to endow them with power to establish the kingdom, and to furnish miraculous attestation of their mission. In general, miracles were designed to indicate divine sanction of the precedure with which they were connected; but when the miracle assumed a mental form, it was intended also to impart to the person a supernatural mental power. The young church in Samaria had hitherto been guided by the teaching of Philip, and more recently by that of Peter and John; but these men must, in executing their high commission, soon depart to other fields of labor; and if, in doing so, they had left the church in the condition in which Peter and John found it, it would have been without means of increasing its knowledge of the new institution, and with none but the uncertain memories of the members of retaining with accuracy what it had already learned. To supply this defect, primarily, and secondarily to leave with the church the means of convincing unbelievers, the gift of inspiration was bestowed.[1] It was bestowed we may presume, not on all,

---

[1] The suggestion made by Alford, that another purpose of imparting the Spirit to the Samaritans was to remove the alienation between them and the Jewish brethren, by showing the latter that God gave to the Samaritans the same gifts as to themselves,

both men and women, but on a sufficient number of chosen individuals. The design of such gifts, and the way in which they were exercised in the congregation, are fully set forth by Paul in I. Cor. xii.–xiv. These gifts served a temporary purpose, until the facts, doctrine, commandments and promises of the new covenant were committed to writing by inspired men, when the prophecies, tongues, and miraculous knowledge of individual teachers gave place to the written word.

3. A Wicked Proposal by Simon, 18–24.

Vv. 18, 19. In the preceding remarks on the incident before us, it has been assumed that the gift of the Spirit imparted was miraculous. This assumption is justified by the fact that it was a matter of observation to the bystanders, as is evident from the next statement of the text : (18) **Now when Simon saw that through the laying on of the apostles' hands the Holy Spirit was given, he offered them money, (19) saying, Give me also this power, that on whomsoever I lay my hands he may receive the Holy Spirit.** This proposal shows, as does the previous statement of verse 17, that the Spirit did not come upon these persons directly from heaven, as upon the apostles on the day of Pentecost ; but that it was imparted through the imposition of hands, and came from the person of the apostles in whom the Spirit dwelt. This is one mark of distinction between the

points to a probable effect of the gift ; but after the Lord had personally directed the apostles to preach in Samaria (chap. i. 8), it is by no means certain that any prejudice on the subject remained in the minds of the disciples, especially as the Samaritans were a circumcised people.

baptism in the Spirit and the gift of the Spirit. See
further under chap. xi. 16.

In order to account for the infamous proposal of
Simon, we must remember his former mode of life, and
consider the mental habits which it generated. As a
sorcerer, it had been his business to increase his stock in
trade by purchasing from other sorcerers the secret of
tricks which he could not himself perform, and watching for opportunities to make such purchases. When
he saw the apostles impart to men the power to work
real miracles, he at once perceived that here was a
chance for profit far beyond that which he had aban-
doned. His overruling avarice, mingled with a passion
for popular applause, a passion which his former habits
had also cultivated, prompted him to make the offer; and
the blinding effect of these passions prevented him from
seeing the wickedness of either offering money for this
power, or of intending to sell it to others.

Vv. 20-23. Nothing could be more abhorrent to an
apostle than such a proposal. It aroused the impulsive
spirit of Peter, and his response is marked by his characteristic vehemence. (20) But Peter said to him, Thy
silver perish with thee, because thou hast thought to obtain the gift of God with money. (21) Thou hast neither
part nor lot in this matter : for thy heart is not right before God. (22) Repent therefore of this thy wickedness,
and pray the Lord, if perhaps the thought of thy heart
shall be forgiven thee. (23) For I see that thou art in
the gall of bitterness and in the bond of iniquity. This
description of Simon's spiritual condition is explicit and
emphatic. The "gall of bitterness" is a forcible expression for the wretchedness of his condition ; and "the
bond of iniquity," for the dominion under which in-

iquity held him. His heart was not right before God, and he was on the way to perdition. The declaration, " Thou hast no part nor lot in this matter," is not to be limited to the matter of imparting the Spirit, as appears from the reason given : " for thy heart is not right before God." If his heart had been right before God, he would still have had no part or lot in imparting the Holy Spirit. The reference is to the whole subject in hand,[1] in which a baptized person would have a part if his heart was right.

Simon's destitute and miserable condition has been construed by many as proof that he had been a hypocrite from the beginning. Whether this inference is justifiable, depends upon the question whether conversion involves so complete a renovation that old mental habits are entirely eradicated, never to exert their power again. If this is true, then Simon was certainly not a genuine convert. But if, as both Scripture and experience teach, the turning of a sinner to God leaves his passions still within him in a latent state, ready to spring into activity under temptation, it must be admitted that Simon may have been a truly penitent believer when he was baptized ; and inasmuch as Luke says, with all the facts before him, that he did believe (13), we must not deny this inspired testimony. The unfortunate man had become a child of God, but he was yet a babe ; and all the weaker from the degradation to which his moral nature had been reduced before his conversion. He was therefore an easy prey to temptation, coming to him in

---

[1] The Greek words are ἐν τῷ λόγῳ τούτῳ, literally rendered, *in this word*, as in the margin of R. V. ; but such is the latitude which usage attached to the word λόγος, that the rendering, *in this matter*, correctly expresses the meaning in this instance.

its old form, and in an unexpected way. He fell, as many a man still falls, when an old slumbering passion is suddenly aroused. Peter therefore does not say to him as to an alarmed man of the world, Repent and be baptized; but, as to a sinning disciple, "Repent and pray God, if perhaps the thought of thy heart shall be forgiven thee." The "perhaps" very clearly indicates a doubt whether forgiveness would be attainable. The doubt was based on the uncertainty in Peter's mind, whether the repentance of such a man under such circumstances could be sufficiently thorough to secure forgiveness.[1]

Ver. 24. The doubt indicated by the "perhaps" of Peter was confirmed in a measure by Simon's response: (24) And Simon answered, and said, Pray ye for me to the Lord, that none of the things which ye have spoken come upon me. This response shows plainly that Peter's scathing speech terrified Simon, but there it stops. He was told to pray for himself, and for the forgiveness of his sin; but instead of doing this, he calls on the two apostles to pray for him, and he limits his request to the thought of merely escaping the things which they had spoken. Here the record leaves him, and although he disappears in a more hopeful condition, he leaves no assurance of final repentance and salvation. Many traditions are related of his subsequent career by Justin Martyr, Cyril of Jerusalem, Irenæus, Tertullian, and the author of the Clementine Recognitions, all writers of the second century; but most of them are certainly

---

[1] Peter could have had no allusion to the unpardonable sin, as several commentators have supposed (Plumptre, Alford, *et. al.*) ; for he knew very well what that sin is (Mark iii. 28–30) ; and he knew that Simon had not committed it.

legendary, and none of them are at all reliable. It is
not wise to fill the memory with idle tales in regard to
Biblical characters.

4. OTHER LABORS OF PETER AND JOHN, AND THEIR RETURN, 25.

VER. 25. The next statement of our author illustrates another phase of the labors on which the apostles
had now entered. (25) **They therefore, when they had
testified and spoken the word of the Lord, returned to
Jerusalem, and preached the gospel to many villages of
the Samaritans.** The first clause of this sentence refers
to their further testifying and speaking in the city of
Samaria; and the last to their work on the way to
Jerusalem. The route of travel from Samaria to Jerusalem led them through Shechem, so often mentioned in
the Old Testament, and through Sychar, near Jacob's
well, where Jesus had conversed with the woman of
Samaria (Jno. iv. 39–43). If that woman was still
alive, and if she had not already gone over to Samaria
to hear Philip preach, she had now an opportunity to
learn what Jesus meant by his puzzling remarks about
"living water" (Jno. iv. 10–15). The apostles probably adopted a circuitous route to Jerusalem, so that they
might touch other villages than those on the main
thoroughfare; and in each they doubtless remained long
enough to reap some of the fruits of their labor.

5. PHILIP IS SENT TO AN ETHIOPIAN EUNUCH, 26–31.

VER. 26. When the congregation in Samaria had
been supplied with spiritual gifts, and sufficiently instructed to justify leaving it to its own resources for
edification, Philip was called to another field of labor,

and we are introduced to a case of conversion in which
a single individual is the subject, and the details are
given with unusual fullness. It is a case in which God
is seen to lay plans, as it were, to bring about the result,
and we are able to trace distinctly the method of his
procedure.

The first step taken in the case was the mission of an
angel from heaven ; but when the angel made his appearance on earth, it was not, as in case of many imaginary angelic visits for such a purpose, in the presence of
the man to be converted, but in the presence of the
preacher. (26) **But an angel of the Lord spake unto
Philip, saying, Arise, and go toward the south unto the
way that goeth down from Jerusalem unto Gaza : the
same is desert.** This is all that the angel has to say.
His part of the work, which was simply to start the
evangelist in the direction of the person to be converted,
is accomplished ; so he retires from the scene.

The words, " the same is desert " (whether spoken by
the angel, or appended by Luke, is immaterial), were intended to note the singularity of a preacher being sent
away from a populous district to an uninhabited region.
The term desert is not here to be understood as meaning
a barren waste ; for no such waste has ever existed
between Jerusalem and Gaza ; but as meaning that part
of the way which leads through a comparatively unpopu-
lated district.[1] Much error and confusion concerning
this way, or road, is found in the older commentaries,
which were written before the recent thorough explorations of the country ; but these, and especially the actual

---

[1] That the Greek word, ἔρημος, has this meaning, may be seen
by reference to the following passages: Matt. xiv. 15, 19 ; Mark
vi. 35, 39 ; Jno. vi. 10.

surveys made by the Palestine Exploration Fund of Great Britain, have cleared up the subject by showing that there was a Roman paved road leading from Jerusalem direct to Gaza, some traces of which are still visible, though the route, in the roughest part, is now impassable for vehicles. This road is laid down on the great map of Palestine made from the surveys, and can be easily traced by any one in possession of the map. The whole distance from city to city is about fifty miles, and the direction from Jerusalem is nearly due southwest. Some five or six miles from the latter city the road begins to descend from the central ridge, which it follows that far, through a rough and narrow ravine called *Wady el Mesarr,* into *Wady es Sunt,* known in the Old Testament as the valley of Elah. After traversing this valley a few miles nearly due south, the road turns to the west, and rises through another *wady* to the level of the great Philistine plain, which it follows the rest of the way to Gaza. The passage along the mountain ravine must be the part called desert, for all the rest of the way the road passes through the midst of villages, pastures, and cultivated fields; that is, it did so when the country was well populated. If Philip's path intersected the road in this desert, he traveled due south from the city of Samaria, and passed to the west of Jerusalem, all in compliance with the direction of the angel.

Vv. 27, 28. Philip promptly obeyed the voice of the angel, and by a journey of nearly fifty miles he came into the designated road in the rear of a chariot. The occupant was the man in whose behalf he had come, but as yet he knew nothing of him. (27) **And he arose and went: and behold, a man of Ethiopia, a eunuch of great**

authority under Candace, queen of the Ethiopians, who
was over all of her treasure, who had come to Jerusalem
to worship; (28) and he was returning and sitting in
his chariot, and was reading the prophet Isaiah. All
that is said here about the man was learned by Philip
afterward, and was doubtless communicated by him to
Luke. His being a eunuch debarred him from the
privilege of mingling in the Jewish congregation, or entering the Jewish court of the temple;[1] but it did not
debar him from the court of the Gentiles, in which men
of all nations, clean or unclean, were at liberty to worship. That he had been in Jerusalem to worship, and
that he was now engaged in the study of the Jewish
Scriptures, make it almost certain that he was either a
Jew or a proselyte, more probably the former; and
when we add to these considerations the circumstance
that Luke introduces farther on the baptism of uncircumcised persons as if it were a startling innovation, we
are constrained to think that it was Luke's intention
that we shall regard this eunuch as a circumcised man.
It was not uncommon for Jews born and reared in
foreign lands to attain to eminent positions, such as this
man enjoyed, and especially in the department of finance,
for which they have always possessed natural fitness.

A remarkable prescience is observable in the timing
of the angel's mission and the movements of Philip to
the beginning and progress of the eunuch's journey.
Philip must have started from Samaria at least as early

---

[1] While emasculated persons were shut out from the assembly of Israel as Gentiles were—the former for the purpose of
preventing Jews from allowing themselves or their sons to be
thus mutilated (Deut. xxiii. 1)—yet both, if obedient to the law of
God, were encouraged to worship God, and to send in sacrifices
with the assurance that they would be accepted (Isa. lvi. 1-8).

as the day previous to that in which the eunuch left
Jerusalem; yet the Lord who sent the angel knew so
well when the eunuch would start, how long it would
take him to reach the point at which Philip came in behind him, and how long it would take Philip to reach
the same point, that the angel's mission was so timed as
to make all the movements fit one another: thus the
providence of God united with the miraculous mission
of the angel to bring about the intended conversion of
the eunuch, and to send the gospel in him to a distant
nation.

VER. 29. When Philip entered the road to which he
was directed, his mission was accomplished so far as he
could know from the message of the angel; for this was
all that the angel had told him to do. Here he would
doubtless have paused for further orders had not another
divine admonition moved him on. Just at this moment
the Holy Spirit began to take part in the proceedings;
and, like the angel, he began, not with the sinner, but
with the preacher. (29) **And the Spirit said unto Philip,
Go near, and join thyself to this chariot.** The purpose
of this communication was evidently the same as that of
the angel, to bring the preacher and the subject for conversion face to face. But for it Philip might have
allowed the chariot, which was already some distance
ahead of him, to pass out of sight.

VER. 30. In order to do as the Spirit directed, Philip
had to move energetically. (30) **And Philip ran to him,
and heard him reading Isaiah the prophet, and said,
Understandest thou what thou readest?** The man was
reading aloud—a good way to keep the mind fixed on
what we read. Considering the relative positions of the
parties, Philip's question, Dost thou understand what

thou readest? strikes us as a rather abrupt if not an impertinent method of introducing himself to the grandee. It was, however, an appropriate question, and wisely propounded. Philip as yet knew not his man; he knew not whether to approach him as a fellow disciple, or as an unbeliever. He knew that if he was an unbeliever he could not tell the meaning of the well known prediction which he was reading, one of the plainest predictions in all the prophets concerning the sufferings of Christ. The Jews, not being willing to apply it to the Christ, because they expected him to be a great earthly king, knew not what to do with it. On the other hand, he knew that if the man was a believer the passage would be unmistakably clear to him. The purpose of the question, then, was to draw out the religious position of his man, so as to determine how to proceed with him further.

6. Philip Preaches to the Eunuch, Baptizes Him, and then Preaches in Philistia, 31–40.

Vv. 31–35. The eunuch's answer to Philip's question was prompt and satisfactory: (31) **And he said, How can I except some one shall guide me? And he besought Philip to come up and sit with him.** (32) **Now the place of the Scripture which he was reading was this,**

> **He was led as a sheep to the slaughter;**
> **And as a lamb before his shearer is dumb,**
> **So he openeth not his mouth:**

(33) **In his humiliation his judgment was taken away:**
> **His generation who shall declare?**
> **For his life is taken from the earth.** [1]

---

[1] This quotation is taken from Isaiah liii. 7, 8; but it follows the Septuagint, which was the Bible of all foreign born Jews, and which the eunuch must have been reading. The clause, " In

(34) And the eunuch answered Philip, and said, I pray thee, of whom speaketh the prophet this ? of himself, or of some other ? (35) And Philip opened his mouth, and beginning from this Scripture, preached unto him Jesus.

Philip now understands his man, and he better understands what had just taken place with himself. The man is a devout worshiper of God, who, though the treasurer of a distant kingdom, does not fail to come to Jerusalem, as the law requires, to worship. He has been there now; and, on his way home he is scarcely out of sight of the holy city when he takes in hand, as he rides along, the book of Isaiah. He is a thoughtful reader, carefully inquiring, as he reads, the meaning of every passage. He is an unbeliever in Christ, or he would not doubt to whom the passage he is reading refers. It so happens that he is reading and studying

---

his humiliation his judgment was taken away," is best explained by the fact that in the trial of Jesus he was deprived of right judgment by an unfair trial and condemnation. So Plumptre, Gloag, Hackett and Alford understand it. Meyer and others hold that the judgment that was taken away was his right to judge ; but this right Jesus treated as one yet to be exercised in the future world (Jno. v. 22–38; xii. 47, 48), and therefore he was not robbed of it in his humiliation The clause, " His generation who shall declare ?" must be interpreted in the light of the clause, " for his life is taken from the earth." The fact that his life was taken, raised the question, Who shall declare his generation. The meaning depends on that of the expression, " his generation." This expression usually means a man's posterity, and the question implies a negative answer. The meaning seems to be, no one shall set forth his posterity, because he had no posterity when his life was cut off. The meaning suggested by Meyer, " Who shall declare the multitude of his spiritual offspring?" is read into the passage from subsequent developments, and could not well have been in the prophet's views; and it is not suggested by his words.

the very passage of all others in Isaiah which, when understood, will be most likely to bring him to Christ: and could Philip have failed to say to himself, " God sent the angel to me, to bring me here at the exact moment in which he foresaw that this man would be reading this very passage, and raising in his own mind a question concerning it which I can answer by the name Jesus ?" There was no time to pause and wonder over this outcropping of God's knowledge and wisdom ; but doubtless Philip's soul was fired by it as he proceeded from that Scripture to preach Jesus as its fulfillment. And if his puzzled hearer had offered David's prayer, " Open thou mine eyes, that I may behold wondrous things out of thy law," he realized an answer when he saw, beaming from the page which was so dark before, the glory of a suffering Saviour. The Scriptures were opened to him by the ministration of angels and of the Holy Spirit, but all became effective to him through the words of the preacher.

Vv. 36–40. The account of this conversion terminates, like those on Pentecost and those in Samaria, with the baptism of the person. (36) And as they went on the way, they came unto a certain water; and the eunuch saith, Behold, here is water; what doth hinder me to be baptized ? (38) And he commanded the chariot to stand still: and they both went down into the water, both Philip and the eunuch; and he baptized him. (39) And when they came up out of the water, the Spirit of the Lord caught away Philip; and the eunuch saw him no more, for he went on his way rejoicing. (40) But Philip was found at Azotus: and passing through he preached the gospel to all the cities, till he came to Cæsarea.

The first natural water to which they came, unless it were a spring on the wayside, was the brook which flows through the valley of Elah, the brook which David crossed in going forth to meet Goliath.[1] It is a mountain stream, which goes dry in the summer, but flows with a strong current through the winter and the spring.[2] Such streams always wear out pools here and there very suitable for baptizing. If the chariot had already crossed this stream when the eunuch requested baptism, there was another in the Philistine plain, now called *Wady el Hasy*, which Robinson, the first to institute any intelligent inquiries on this subject, fixed upon as the place of baptism.[3] It is a perennial stream, and suitable for baptizing at any season of the year. It is not at all improbable, however, that the real place of this baptism was one of the many artificial pools with which the country abounded at that time, and the ruins of which are found in every section.[4] The rainless season of seven months, which is experienced there every year, made it necessary, when the country was filled with people and flocks and herds, to make extraordinary provision of water for stock, and for irrigating the summer crops; and no country was ever so well supplied in this way as Judea.

The question, "What doth hinder me to be baptized?" was suggested immediately by the appearance of the water; but it could not have occurred to the eunuch had he not been previously instructed concerning the ordinance. He had learned not only that there was such

---

[1] I. Sam. xvii. 40.

[2] See an account of it in the author's Lands of the Bible, 259.

[3] *Biblical Researches,* ii. 514, note xxxii.

[4] See *Lands of the Bible,* 48.

an ordinance, but that it was the duty and the privilege of men to observe it when properly prepared for it. He also desired to be baptized, and his only question was whether he was a suitable candidate. As he had known nothing of Jesus as the Christ up to the moment of Philip's preaching to him, he had certainly learned nothing definite concerning the baptism which Jesus had ordained; and we are consequently forced to the conclusion that what he now knew he had learned from Philip's preaching.[1] From this we learn that in preaching to him Jesus, Philip had instructed him concerning baptism; that when men preach Jesus as they should, baptism is a part of the sermon. It was a part of Peter's sermon on Pentecost, and of Philip's preaching to the Samaritans; and we shall see, as we proceed with this commentary, that it had a place in every completed apostolic sermon addressed to sinners. The evangelists of the present day who omit it preach a mutilated gospel, and they do so to please men by catering to a sectarian prejudice which they should rather seek to uproot and destroy.

As soon as he had propounded the question, he commanded the chariot to stand still, showing that Philip's answer, which is not recorded, presented no hindrance. To some persons in a later age it appeared that Philip is here represented as making no answer, and that he acted too hastily; hence the interpolation into some

---

[1] The conceit that he had learned it from the words, "So shall he sprinkle many nations," near the close of the previous chapter of Isaiah, has been advanced by some controversialists; but it has not been approved by any of the critical commentators, and it is proved to be groundless by the fact that the Septuagint, which the eunuch was reading, has in that passage, instead of the Greek for sprinkle, the word, θαυματάζω, which means *to astonish*.

copies of Acts of the words : " And Philip said, If thou
believest with all thy heart, thou mayest. And he
answered and said, I believe that Jesus Christ is the Son
of God." [1] The interpolator obtained the idea which he
inserted from such passages as Romans x. 8, 9 ; I. Tim.
vi. 13; and Matt. xvi. 16, which show that such a confession was taken by the apostles ; and it is not improbable that this apostolic custom was still prevalent when
the interpolation was made.[2]

It is impossible to frame a sentence in English or in
Greek which could more unmistakably declare the fact
that previous to the baptism of the eunuch both he and
Philip went down into the water, and that after the
baptism they came up out of it. It is painful to observe
the disingenuousness with which some commentators, like
many unlearned controversialists, have taxed their ingenuity to obscure this fact,[3] in the interest of a perverted

---

[1] In regard to scarcely any reading are the textual critics more
unanimously agreed, or on better manuscript evidence, than the
rejection of this verse as an interpolation. See the evidence in
Tregelles, or Westcott and Hort, or in Tischendorf's Eighth
Edition.

[2] It was found in at least one MS. in the latter half of the
second century; for it is quoted by Irenæus, who was in active
life from the year 170 to 210. His words are : ὡς αὐτὸς ὁ εὐνοῦχος
πεισθείς καὶ παραντίκα ἀζιῶν βαπτισθῆναι, ἔλεγε, Πιστεύω τὸν υἱὸν εἶναι
Ἰησοῦν Χριστόν; when the eunuch himself was persuaded, and
thought proper to be baptized immediately, and said, I believe
that Jesus Christ is the Son of God. Cyprian quotes the passage
as follows: " Behold water ; what is it that hinders me to be baptized?" Then Philip said, " If thou believest from the whole
heart, thou mayest." Ecce aqua, quid est quod me impedit bap-
tizari ? Tunc dixit Philippus, si credis ex toto cardo tuo licit
(Cyprian's Works, 318).

[3] As a recent and striking example, we quote the following remarks from the Expositor's Bible, by Prof. G. T. Stokes, on this

form of the ordinance of baptism. It is clearly seen
that neither Philip nor the eunuch would have gone into
the water if the purpose had been to merely sprinkle or
pour a small quantity of water upon the latter. The
same reasons precisely which now keep preachers who
practice sprinkling out of the water would have kept
Philip and the eunuch out of it. On the other hand,
the same necessity which now compels those who practice
immersion to go into the water for the purpose compelled Philip and the eunuch to do so ; and from this
conclusion the candid mind can find no escape. If we
knew nothing at all of the meaning of the word baptize,
whether in English or Greek, except the single fact that
some say it means to sprinkle, and others that it means
to immerse, this passage alone would settle the question
forever with all whose minds are free to follow implicitly
the obvious meaning of the Scriptures. The account of
the eunuch's conversion administers rebuke at several
points to many teachers of our age, and it should call
them back with trembling to the teaching and practice
of the inspired evangelists.

The removal of Philip after the baptism may have
been miraculous, so far as the meaning of the expression
"caught away" is concerned ; and this meaning agrees
best with the expression, "found at Azotus ;" or it may
have been by a sudden command, such as that which

passage : "The Ethiopian eunuch baptized by St. Philip in the
wilderness could not have been immersed. He came to a stream
trickling along, scarcely sufficient to lave his feet, or perhaps
rather to a well in the desert; the water was deep down, and
reached only, as in the case of Jacob's well, by a rope or chain.
Even if the water could have been reached, common sense, not to
speak of any higher motive, would have forbidden the pollution
of an element so needful for human life " (page 143).

caused him to run and overtake the eunuch's chariot (29, 30); and this agrees better with the reason given why the eunuch saw him no more, "for he went on his way rejoicing." This reason implies that if he had not gone on his way, he might have followed Philip on *his* way. The evident purpose of the writer is to show that it was the Spirit who caused his departure from the presence of the eunuch, and to leave the exact method of his removal in obscurity, as a matter of no importance to his readers. The circumstance worthy of note is that Philip was not allowed to remain longer in company with his new convert, as he would naturally desire to do in order to his further instruction. It was God's will that the man should go on his way to his native land, and work out his own salvation (together, perhaps, with that of many other persons) by building upon the elementary instruction which he had now received. With many men this would doubtless be unsafe ; but God knew his man; and it was because he knew him that he had taken the deliberate steps which we have traced to bring him to himself in Christ.

Notwithstanding this sudden separation from his teacher, and the necessity of going on his way with so little knowledge of his newly found Saviour, the eunuch "went on his way rejoicing." His rejoicing sprang from the experience of that which Paul afterward set forth to an audience of Jews : " Through this man is proclaimed unto you remission of sins : and in him every one that believeth is justified from all things, from which ye could not be justified in the law of Moses" (xiii. 38, 39). It is impossible that Philip failed to tell him, as did Peter his converts, the connection of remission of sins with repentance and baptism ; and now that he had complied with the conditions of pardon, he rejoices in the experience of it.

Our conception of this case of conversion will lack completeness if we fail to look at it from another point of view which the account enables us to take. Should a friend have met the eunuch after he parted from Philip, and inquired as to the cause of the joy so manifest in his countenance, the recital would have presented the facts of the conversion from his point of view, rather than from that of the historian. He would not have begun the story, as our author does, with the visit of the angel to Philip; for of this he knew nothing; he would not have mentioned the command of the Holy Spirit, "Go join thyself to this chariot;" for of this he was equally ignorant; but his story would have been about this: I had been to Jerusalem to worship. I had started for home; and as I rode in my chariot I opened the book of Isaiah and commenced reading. I came upon the passage so much puzzling to our scribes, in which the prophet speaks of the humiliation and death of some one for the good of the world; and I was laboring hard to determine in my own mind of whom the prophet wrote those words, when suddenly there appeared running by the side of my chariot a footman, who inquired, "Understandest thou what thou readest?" His manner indicated that he understood it, and it seemed providential that he came to me at the very moment when I needed his help. I invited him to take a seat with me; I pointed to the passage, and stated to him my difficulty. In a short time he made it perfectly plain to me that the passage referred to the long looked for Messiah; and that this great personage, instead of reigning here on earth, as our scribes have taught us, was to die a sacrifice for our sins ; to rise from the dead, ascend to heaven whence he came, and to establish his kingdom over both men and angels. He convinced me of the truth of all this, and showed me that through that man's blood, by faith in him and repentance and baptism in his name, we are to receive the remission of sins which the law could not give us. While he was still speaking to me these good tidings of great joy, we came to a certain water, and I requested the baptism in which he had instructed me. He baptized me ; he then turned away as abruptly as he had come to me ; but I have come on my way rejoicing in the forgiveness of sins, and in the assured hope of everlasting life. Such was the experience of this man up to the moment that the curtain of history drops and hides him from our view. Happily, as we lose sight of him the sounds that come back to us are notes of joy, and we may hope to meet him at the point where all our journeys end, and to rejoice with him forever. His ready faith and prompt obedience give evidence of such a character that we may believe he will bring many sheaves with him in the great harvest.[1]

The Azotus at which Philip was found is the Ashdod of the Old Testament, one of the five cities of the Philistines. It stood a few miles from the seashore, nearly at a right angle to the line of the eunuch's travel, and probably fifteen miles distant. From that place to Cæsarea, the terminal point of the labors of Philip here mentioned, is about sixty miles ; and the region in which

---

[1] Very naturally, the Christians of Ethiopia (now Abyssinia) afterward ascribed to the eunuch the introduction of Christianity into their country; and they have some traditions in regard to his subsequent career, but none of them is sufficiently authenticated to deserve our attention.

he labored was the old land of Philistia as far north as
Joppa, and the plain of Sharon thence thirty miles north
to Cæsarea.   At Azotus this plain is about sixteen miles
wide, and about ten at Cæsarea; and all the way it is
exceedingly productive.   At that time it was thickly set
with villages and small cities, many of which, in a state
of decay, remain to the present time.   It was a field for
evangelization sufficient to occupy many years of Philip's life.   We shall see traces of the probable effects of
his work as we proceed.

SEC. II. — THE CONVERSION AND EARLY LABORS OF SAUL.

(IX. 1–31.)

1. HIS JOURNEY TO DAMASCUS, 1–9.

Vv. 1, 2. From the conversion of a nobleman,
whose home was in a distant land, our author now turns
to that of the most noted enemy of the church at the
time.   He has already introduced Saul to his readers, in
the account of Stephen's martyrdom; for this most
laborious and self-sacrificing of all the apostles first appears on the page of history standing by when Stephen
was stoned, with the clothing of the witnesses against
him lying at his feet.   His own statements concerning
himself enable us to trace his history to a still earlier
period.   The early education and ancestral remembrances
of a man have much to do with forming his character
and shaping his career.   Those of Saul were well calculated to thrust him into the very course of action in

which he first figures in Luke's narrative. He was born in the famous Greek city of Tarsus, on the banks of the river Cydnus in Cilicia.[1] This city was then a seat of Greek learning, almost rivaling Athens and Alexandria;[2] and on account of its situation on a navigable river, and near to the mountain passes leading into the interior of Asia Minor to the north, and of Syria to the east,[3] it was the center of an extensive commerce. Here he acquired in childhood a knowledge of the Greek language, and of the manners and customs of the Greeks, which served him a good purpose in after life. At the same time he was carefully guarded by other influences against the evil effects of the heathen society around him. He was of pure Jewish extraction, "a Hebrew of the Hebrews, of the tribe of Benjamin, and descended from pious ancestors."[4] This insured his careful instruction in Jewish history, and in the law of Moses. His parents

---

[1] Acts xxii. 3.

[2] "So great is the zeal of the inhabitants for philosophy and all other encyclic training, that they have surpassed even Athens and Alexandria, and every other place one could mention in which philosophical and philological schools have arisen" (Strabo, xiv. 4).

[3] The plain in which Tarsus is situated is bounded on the north and northwest by a lofty range of mountains, covered with snow the greater part of the year. The region beyond is reached by a pass through this range called the Gates of Cilicia, because it was the only means of access to Cilicia from the west. Another range bounds Cilicia on the east, and through it there are two other well known passes, called the Amanid and the Syrian Gates, which give access to Syria. Tarsus is now an insignificant town of about ten thousand inhabitants; but a railway has been recently constructed from the sea coast through and beyond Adanah, and this may lead to a partial renewal of its ancient importance.

[4] Phil. iii. 4, 5; II. Tim. i. 3.

were Pharisees,[1] and his understanding of the Scriptures was therefore modified by the peculiar interpretations and traditions of that sect.

Besides this religious instruction, he was taught the trade of a tent-maker.[2] The goat's hair which was used for the manufacture of rude garments and tent cloth, was produced in great quantities in the mountains of Cilicia, and the manufactured article acquired the name κιλίκιον (Latin, *Cilicium*), from the name of the province. The fact that he afterward received an expensive intellectual education proves that his father put him to this humble trade, not through necessity, but in compliance with the Jewish conception, that some form of manual labor was an important part of the education of every boy.[3] The trade was of great service to him in some of the darker days of his subsequent life.[4]

It was only his childhood that was thus devoted to parental instruction and to the acquirement of the Greek language and a trade; for he was "brought up" at the feet of Gamaliel in Jerusalem.[5] Under the instruction of this learned Pharisee, whose prudence and calmness we have had occasion to notice in connection with the trial of the twelve apostles (v. 33–39), his knowledge of the law was enlarged, his zeal for it inflamed, and his Pharisaic prejudices intensified. His progress in this Bible school is thus described by himself: "I advanced

---

[1] Acts xxiii. 6.　　[2] Acts xviii. 3.

[3] In the Talmud Gamaliel is quoted as saying, "Learning of any kind, unaccompanied by a trade, ends in nothing, and leads to sin;" Rabbi Meir, as saying, "Let a man always teach his sons pure and easy trades;" and Rabbi Judah, as saying, "Not to teach one's son a trade is like teaching him robbery" (Farrar's Life of Paul, p. 14, n. 1).

[4] Acts xviii. 3; xx. 34; I. Thess. ii. 9.　　[5] Acts xxii. 3.

in the Jews' religion beyond many of mine own age among my countrymen, being more exceedingly zealous for the traditions of my fathers."[1] This preëminence in scholarship and zeal was accompanied by the strictest religious deportment, so that after the lapse of many years he could appeal to those who knew him in his youth, though now his enemies, to testify that according to the strictest sect of their religion he had lived a Pharisee; and he could even declare that as touching the law he was blameless.[2] Such was his character and reputation previous to his appearance on the pages of Acts.

It is not probable that Saul was in Jerusalem at the time of the crucifixion of Jesus, or for several years previous. If he had been, it is unaccountable that in all his speeches and epistles he makes no allusion to a personal knowledge of events in the life of Jesus. At the time of Stephen's death he must have been at least thirty years of age,[3] and he had probably been out of school for ten or more years. The supposition that he had returned to Tarsus previous to the beginning of John's ministry, and had reappeared in Jerusalem after the ascension of Jesus, is most agreeable to all the known facts in the case. When the conflict arose between Stephen and the Jews of the foreign synagogue, Saul was almost certainly one of the Cilicians who encountered him (vi. 9); and his superior learning in the law naturally placed him in the front rank of the disputants. He was apparently a member of the Sanhedrin,[4] and he

---

[1] Gal. i. 14.   [2] Acts xxvi. 4, 5; Phil. iii. 6.

[3] He is called "a young man" at the time, but his leadership implies an age as well advanced as would be consistent with styling him a young man, and points to about thirty.

[4] If we are to understand his remark (chap. xxvi. 10), "When they were condemned to death, I gave my vote against them,"

certainly took the part of a leader of that body when
they turned into a mob and stoned Stephen; for "the
witnesses laid down their garments at the feet of a
young man named Saul;" and the formal statement is
made that "Saul was consenting unto his death."[1]
After the death of Stephen he still maintained the position of a leader in the persecution, until the church was
dispersed. In the course of this persecution others besides Stephen were put to death, while many were
scourged in the synagogues to make them blaspheme the
name of Jesus.[2]

When the church in Jerusalem had been scattered
abroad, Saul doubtless thought that he had effectually
destroyed the hated sect: but the news soon began to
come back from various quarters, that the scattered disciples were establishing congregations in every direction.
One less persistent than Saul might now have despaired
of success in suppressing a faith which had thus far been
promoted by every attack made upon it, and which had
seemed to gather renewed life from apparent destruction;
but he had a will that rose to higher resolve as obstacles
multiplied before it, and thus he is represented in the
text which must now come before us. (1) **But Saul, yet**

literally, he was certainly a member of some tribunal which decided the fate of the disciples in this persecution; and no other is
known except the Sanhedrin. Against the supposition that he
was a member of this body, nothing is alleged except a tradition
among later Jewish writers, that no one could be a member who
was not of mature age, or who was not a married man (Gloag,
Lechler, Hackett on xxvi. 10). As for the latter qualification,
Farrar gives very plausible if not conclusive reasons for believing that Saul was married in early life, and had become a
widower (Life of Paul, chap. iv). Both objections, however, are
without the support of well established facts.

[1] Chap. vii. 58; viii. 1.   [2] Chap. xxvi. 11.

breathing threatening and slaughter against the disciples
of the Lord, went unto the high priest, (2) and asked of
him letters to Damascus unto the synagogues, that if he
found any that were of the Way, whether men or women,
he might bring them bound to Jerusalem.   The plurality
of synagogues in Damascus here indicated shows that
the city contained a very considerable Jewish population; and with this agrees the statement of Josephus,
that not less than ten thousand Jews were slain in a
tumult there in the reign of Nero.[1]   When the news
reached Jerusalem that the faith of Jesus was being
propagated in this large Jewish community, the exasperation of Saul and his fellow persecutors knew no bounds;
and as Damascus was the nearest foreign city of great
importance, it was at once selected as the first point for
the pursuit of the scattered disciples.   Under ordinary
circumstances such letters as Saul carried would not have
empowered him to arrest men in a foreign city, and to
bring them away in bonds; but he had reason to believe,
from considerations which must now be only a matter of
conjecture, that the authorities in Damascus would permit him thus to act; and that he was correct is apparent
from the readiness with which the governor of the city
afterward lent the aid of his guards for the purpose of
arresting Saul himself.[2]

Vv. 3, 4. It is impossible for a man to be in a frame
of mind less favorable to conversion to Christ, than was
Saul when he started on this mad expedition. How
striking the contrast between him, breathing out threatening and slaughter against the disciples of Christ, as he
started for a foreign city to arrest and imprison them,
and the eunuch, reading thoughtfully the prophet

---

[1] Wars, ii. 25.   [2] II. Cor. xi. 32.

Isaiah as he started on a peaceful journey to his distant
home. Yet the gospel of Christ shows its wonderful
power of adaptation by turning both into the way of salvation. The distance from Jerusalem to Damascus is
about one hundred and forty miles. The most usual
route of travel was northward along the dividing ridge
of the mountain range through Bethel and Shechem to
Jezreel; thence westward to Bethshan on the bluff leading down into the Jordan valley; thence up that valley
to a stone bridge across the Jordan which is standing in
good condition to this day;[1] and thence along the elevated plateau east of the Jordan valley to Damascus.
During the last day's journey the road passes along the
eastern base of Mount Hermon, whose snow-capped
summit bounds the horizon on the left. The storm of
passion with which Saul started on this journey would
naturally have subsided in some degree during the four or
five days of travel, leaving him in a mood better suited to
the interview which Christ had made ready for him. (3)
And as he journeyed, it came to pass that he came nigh
unto Damascus: and suddenly there shone round about
him a light out of heaven: (4) and he fell upon the earth,
and heard a voice saying to him, Saul, Saul, why persecutest thou me? Luke omits several important details
of the scene which he now describes, because they are
supplied to his readers in two speeches which he quotes
from Paul farther on.[2] It is proper that we also leave
them out of sight while we attempt to realize the scene
as Luke aims to set it before us. We are not here told
how Saul knew that the light which suddenly shone

---

[1] See a description of this bridge in the author's Lands of the
Bible, 354.

[2] Chap. xxii. 6-10; xxvi. 12–18.

around him was a " light out of heaven :" it is sufficient
to know that it was of such a character as to leave no
doubt on this point. It was of such a nature that when
it shone upon him "he fell upon the earth ;" and he was
too brave a man to be thus unnerved without an adequate
cause. That it was a miracle, he must have instantly
perceived ; and when the voice came, saying, " Saul,
Saul, why persecutest thou me ?" the word persecute conveyed too plain a reference to his course toward the disciples to be misunderstood. It was also unmistakably
manifest that the voice, as the light, came out of heaven ;
but who the speaker was, whether Stephen, or some
other disciple whom he had slain, or some other mysterious personage, he could not know from these words,
so he immediately inquires who it is.

Vv. 5, 6. (5) And he said, Who art thou, Lord ? And
he said, I am Jesus whom thou persecutest : (6) but
rise, and enter into the city, and it shall be told thee
what thou shalt do. It is impossible for us, who have
been familiar with the glory of the risen Christ from
infancy, to fully realize the thoughts and feelings which
flashed like lightning into the soul of Saul, on hearing
these words. Up to this moment he had held Jesus to
be an impostor cursed of God and man, and his followers blasphemers worthy of death ; but now this hated
being is suddenly revealed to him in a blaze of divine
glory. The evidence of eyes and ears can not be doubted.
There he stands,[1] with the light of heaven and the glory
of God around him, and he says, " I am Jesus." Stephen
then was right, and I have shed innocent blood. " O

---

[1] That Saul saw Jesus, though not stated here, is expressly
stated by Ananias (17), by Barnabas (27), and by Saul himself
(I. Cor. xv. 8).

wretched man that I am, who shall deliver me from the body of this death?" The die is cast. The proud spirit yields, and the current of that mighty soul is turned back in its channel, to flow forever deeply and strongly in the opposite direction.

VER. 7. At this point Luke reveals the fact that Saul was not alone, and he mentions briefly the deportment of the men who were with him. (7) **And the men who journeyed with him stood speechless, hearing the voice, but beholding no man.** This is not the statement of a writer who is conscious of inventing a story, and taking care to bolster it up with fictitious evidence: otherwise he would not have admitted that the only persons who could have been joint witnesses with Saul of the presence of Jesus did not see him. The fact that they did not, if he really appeared, can be accounted for on one of only two suppositions; either that Jesus purposely kept himself concealed from them while appearing to Saul; or that they failed, for some cause unmentioned in the text, to turn their eyes in that direction. The real cause will appear farther on.[1] In the meantime these companions, though not able to say who spoke to Saul, were competent witnesses to the facts that the light appeared, that a voice was heard from the midst of it, and to the blindness of Saul which followed as an immediate result.

Vv. 8, 9. But for the last words spoken by Jesus, " Rise, and enter into the city, and it shall be told thee what thou shalt do," Saul would not have known what step next to take; but having received this command, he obeyed it as best he could. (8) **And Saul arose from the earth; and when his eyes were opened, he saw noth-**

---

[1] See under chap. xxii. 9; xxvi. 14.

ing : and they led him by the hand, and brought him
into Damascus. (9) And he was three days without
sight, and did neither eat nor drink. The words, " when
his eyes were opened," do not imply that they had been
closed from the instant that the light first appeared ; for
then he could not have seen Jesus. Moreover, had he
closed them then, the light would not have blinded him.
The narrative plainly implies that he gazed into the
light as long as he could endure the glare; and that he
closed his eyes when he could bear the pain no longer.
When he arose, which may have been after some moments spent in an effort to steady his nerves, he instinctively opened his eyes, and found himself blind. The
words, " they led him by the hand and brought him into
Damascus," imply that he and they were on foot, a very
common mode of journeying in those days, and not on
horses or camels, as imagination has so often painted
them. His abstinence from both food and drink can be
accounted for only by his extreme misery while brooding
over his awful crimes and waiting to be told what to do.
The three days are doubtless to be understood, according
to the Jewish count, as including the remnant of the day
in which he arrived, the following day, and so much of
the third day as had passed when he obtained relief.

2. SAUL IS BAPTIZED, 10–19.

Vv. 10–12. The Lord purposely left Saul three days
in the throes of agony which his new convictions had
brought upon him, before telling him, according to
promise, what he should do. This delay fixed the attention of all the unbelieving Jews who surrounded him,
and tried in vain to comfort him, upon the cause of his
distress and of his blindness ; and thus, as we shall see

below, a good purpose was subserved.[1] The manner in which relief was at last sent to him is now described. (10) **Now there was a certain disciple at Damascus, named Ananias; and the Lord said unto him in a vision, Ananias. And he said, Behold, I am here, Lord. (11) And the Lord said unto him, Arise, and go to the street which is called Straight, and inquire in the house of Judas for one named Saul, a man of Tarsus, for behold, he prayeth; (12) and he hath seen a man named Ananias coming in, and laying his hands on him, that he might receive his sight.** In this communication the Lord speaks to Ananias as if Saul were totally unknown to him, and he reveals the fact, which we might have conjectured, that in the midst of his remorse Saul was engaged in earnest prayer. The vision here mentioned had been granted to Saul for the obvious purpose of giving him hope that his eyesight would be restored; and it was made to conform to that which actually occurred, in order that when it occurred Saul might see in the correspondence the hand of God. The street called Straight is still unmistakably identified in Damascus by its contrast with all the other streets of the city; for while all the others are very crooked, making curves or abrupt angles at intervals of from fifty to one hundred yards, this runs nearly a mile with only five slight angles. The mention of this street by name, together with the name of Judas, in whose house Saul was staying, affords no mean evidence of the authenticity of this narrative.

Vv. 13–16. This communication from the Lord imposed on Ananias a very unwelcome task. (13) **But Ananias answered, Lord, I have heard from many of this man, how much evil he did to thy saints at Jerusalem:**

---

[1] See under 19–22.

(14) and here he hath authority from the chief priests to bind all that call upon thy name. (15) But the Lord said to him, Go thy way : for he is a chosen vessel unto me, to bear my name before the Gentiles and kings, and the children of Israel : (16) for I will show him how many things he must suffer for my name's sake. Here the term saints is applied to the disciples by Ananias in a way to indicate that it had already acquired this use, although this is the first occurrence of it in the New Testament. It designates them as men of holy living. The equivalent expression, them that " call on thy name," is also used for the same persons. The name referred to is that of the Lord Jesus; for it is he who holds the conversation with Ananias. The latter speaks of Saul's persecuting career in Jerusalem as a matter of hearsay with himself, from which we infer that he was not one of those who had fled from Jerusalem after the death of Stephen, but rather one who had been baptized there during the peaceful period previous to that persecution. How he had heard that Saul came to Damascus to bind all who there called on the name of Jesus, when none seemed to know this but the companions of Saul, is not easily determined, unless we suppose that the apostles who had remained in Jerusalem had sent runners ahead of Saul's company, to warn the Damascus disciples of the impending danger. This is highly probable.

Ananias found, as all others have who have ventured to argue against a command of the Lord, that he listens to no such argument. The answer, "Go thy way," settled this; but the Lord vouchsafed to inform him that he had placed an estimate on Saul far different from that which any one would have supposed. In the figure of a " chosen vessel " to bear the name of Jesus before Gen-

tiles and kings and Israelites, he compares Saul to a
carefully selected casket, in which a jewel rich enough
for a present to a king is to be deposited, that jewel being
his own precious name. Jewelers always keep costly
gems in caskets of corresponding value; and so, when
Jesus is about to send his name to kings and the great
ones of earth, he chooses this persecuting Saul as the
fittest vessel in which to enclose it. The selection was
a most surprising one to Ananias; but subsequent events
proved its wisdom. Long afterward Saul himself employed the same figure of speech, having doubtless
caught it from the lips of Ananias; but he changes it
materially, saying, " We have this treasure in earthen
vessels, that the exceeding greatness of the power may
be of God, and not of us." [1] While to Christ he was a
choice vessel, in his own eyes he was but a vessel of
pottery. Ananias was perhaps not much less surprised
when the Lord added, as showing a consequence of Saul's
being so choice a vessel, " I will show him how many
things he must suffer for my name's sake." This remark
fixes attention on the fact, observable in all of God's
dealings with the choice spirits of this earth, that when
he calls men to positions of high honor and distinguished
usefulness, he calls them to a life of suffering. This
proved afterward to be preëminently the case with Saul.

Vv. 17–19. By these words of the Lord the natural
fear of the persecutor, which made Ananias object to going to him, was removed. (17) And Ananias departed,
and entered into the house; and laying his hands on
him, he said, Brother Saul, the Lord, even Jesus, who
appeared unto thee in the way which thou camest, hath
sent me, that thou mayest receive thy sight, and be

_____

[1] II. Cor. iv. 6, 7.

filled with the Holy Spirit. (18) And straightway there
fell from his eyes as it were scales, and he received his
sight; and he arose and was baptized; (19) and he received food and was strengthened. It does not appear,
from the narrative how Ananias had learned that Jesus
had appeared to Saul on the way. It is most likely that
he had learned it from what was told by those who conversed with Saul in the house of Judas, the report of it
having spread rapidly among the Jews of the city. He
addressed him with the endearing title, "brother," not because he was a brother Israelite, but because he was now
a fellow believer, and in the way of obedience. That
which fell from his eyes, compared to scales, was undoubtedly a deposit caused by the acute inflammation consequent upon the glare of the light from heaven. Observe, too, that it was not something that merely appeared
to Saul as if it fell from his eyes, as some interpreters
would have it,[1] but something which did so fall, as Luke
expressly declares. In the statement, "and he arose
and was baptized," there is an omission of the command
to that effect, which must have been uttered; and this
is further proof that Luke has purposely abbreviated the
narrative. The omission is supplied in Paul's account
quoted at xxii. 14–16. The place of the baptism is likewise omitted; but the river Abana runs through the
midst of the city, and affords abundant facilities for
baptism in itself, besides supplying many artificial pools
in the courts of the larger buildings.[2]

The statement of Ananias, that he had been sent that
Saul might "be filled with the Holy Spirit," is commonly
interpreted as implying that the Holy Spirit was to be

---

[1] Lechler, Hackett, and others.
[2] See Plumptre *in loco*, and Lands of the Bible, 551, 552, 558.

imparted by imposition of hands.[1] But we have seen already that when the Samaritan converts of Philip were to receive the miraculous gift of the Spirit, two apostles were sent to them for the purpose of imparting it, from which we inferred that Philip had not this power. This makes us slow to believe that the power was given to Ananias; yet we would be shut up to this conclusion if there were no alternative. There is, however, an alternative which makes this conclusion not only unnecessary, but highly improbable. We have learned, from Peter's first discourse, that all who repented and were baptized received the Holy Spirit; and it follows that Saul received the Spirit when Ananias baptized him. This made his reception of the Holy Spirit dependent on the coming of Ananias, and it sufficiently accounts for the words of the latter, without resorting to the improbable supposition that he was empowered to do that which none but apostles could ordinarily do. Let it also be observed at this point that Ananias was almost certainly an unofficial disciple (verse 10), and that we here have an example of a baptism by unofficial hands. It shows that, whatever may be true as a matter of ordinary propriety, the validity of the ordinance by no means depends upon its administration by an officer of the church, or a preacher.

The fact that immediately after his baptism Saul "took food and was strengthened," implies that the remorse which had led to his extreme fast had then passed away; and this agrees with the promise of remission of sins in baptism. See more on this point under xxii. 16.

If now, before we leave this case of conversion, we pause to distinguish the human and the divine in the

---

[1] Plumptre, Gloag, Lechler.

agencies by which it was effected, and their connections one with the other, we shall better understand how Saul was brought to Christ. The foremost characteristic of this case is the fact that the Lord Jesus was himself the preacher. It was his word proclaimed out of the light from heaven, and proved to be divine by that miraculous light in which he appeared, that made Saul a believer, and brought him to repentance. Faith came, as in all other cases, from hearing the word. But while the Lord was the preacher, and while his word caused the sinner to believe and repent, there was still something for the sinner to do before finding peace, and for information concerning this the Lord sends him to Damascus instead of giving it himself. While waiting for this information, although he suffers the keenest pangs of penitence, and pours out his soul in prayer, his sins are still unforgiven, showing that justification is not immediately consequent upon faith and repentance. In this unhappy condition he remains for three days, because no one has come to tell him what to do. This is another peculiarity of his case, no other convert of whom we read having experienced a similar delay. The delay was the Lord's doing; for no one who could tell him what to do dared to go near him, and the Lord had not yet sent Ananias. As Saul knew not for whom to send, and as neither Ananias nor any other disciple would come if left to himself, a divine interposition was necessary, as in the case of Philip's mission to the eunuch; and so, instead of sending an angel, as in that case, the Lord himself spoke to Ananias. Thus a human messenger is made to tell the sinner what to do, even after the Lord himself has appeared to him, and the human messenger helps him to do what he is told to do by baptizing him. When

he is baptized his grief and fasting are at an end, his sins
are forgiven, and here the story of his conversion comes
to an end.

3. Saul Preaches in Damascus, 19–25.

Vv. 19–22. No sooner had Saul obeyed the gospel
and received pardon than he began to devote all his
energies to building up what he had sought to tear down.
(19) And he was certain days with the disciples which
were at Damascus. (20) And straightway in the synagogues he proclaimed Jesus, that he is the Son of God.
(21) And all that heard him were amazed, and said, Is
not this he that in Jerusalem made havoc of them who
called on this name ? and he hath come hither for this
intent, that he might bring them bound before the chief
priests. (22) But Saul increased the more in strength,
and confounded the Jews who dwelt in Damascus, proving
that this is the Christ. The " certain days " (ἡμέρας
τινάς) of verse 19 are most naturally understood as
including the time of the preaching next mentioned ;
and the " straightway " (εὐθέως) of verse 20, as starting
not from the close of the certain days, but from Saul's
baptism. Undoubtedly the very day he was baptized all
the disciples in the city gathered about him and took
him at once into their fellowship ; and on the very next
Sabbath, whether it was one day or six days later, he
began his preaching in the synagogue, this being his first
opportunity. It may be that some of the synagogues
were opened on other days of the week after he had begun
to preach, thus giving him more frequent opportunities
than the regular meetings allowed. The first effect of
this preaching was amazement to hear the man who had
" made havoc" of the church in Jerusalem, and had

come to Damascus for a similar purpose, preaching the
faith which he had sought to destroy. The next effect
is that they were "confounded" by Saul's proofs that
Jesus is the Christ. In the words, "Saul increased the
more in strength," the comparison is with the strength
mentioned in 19 v., " he took food and was strengthened;"
and the reference is to the restoration of his physical
strength after the exhausting fast and agony of the three
days previous. Such an experience would greatly en-
feeble a very stout man, and he might be many days re-
covering from its effects.

This preaching by Saul was a protracted effort to
convert to the faith the Jews who dwelt in Damascus;
and although we have no evidence that any were convinced, they were at least "confounded." This was the
result of Saul's fresh and independent testimony to the
resurrection and glorification of Jesus. He had not,
like the original apostles, seen the Lord after his resurrection and previous to his ascension, but he had seen
him descend from heaven in his glorified body, and his
testimony was fully equal to that which had been borne
by Peter. If any man in Damascus doubted his truthfulness, his traveling companions could testify with him
to the reality of the light from heaven, and the voice
which proceeded out of the midst of the light, while his
own blindness, better known to the unbelievers than to
the believers, could not have resulted from conceiving
or telling a lie. If in any mind the thought arose that
he had been deceived by some optical or mental illusion,
it was dissipated by the consideration that the blindness
could not have resulted from such a cause. Thus the
blindness served to cut off all escape from the conclusion
that his report of the vision was true; and if the vision

was a reality, there was no room to doubt that Jesus had
risen from the dead and ascended to heaven. The
blindness had been protracted, involving the delay of
his baptism mentioned above (p. 179), for the very purpose of fixing it in the minds of the people, and especially in the minds of the unbelieving Jews, that it might
finally serve this important purpose. Such is the force
of his testimony as it appeared to those who heard him
in Damascus. To ourselves it stands thus : If the vision
which he claimed to have witnessed was a reality, then
Jesus is the Christ, and his religion is divine. His
blindness, which there can be no reason to doubt, precludes the supposition that he was deceived. Was he
then a deceiver? His whole subsequent career, as related both by Luke and himself, declares that he was
not : for all the motives derived from both time and
eternity which can move men to deception were arrayed
against the course which he afterward pursued. His
reputation among men, his hopes of wealth and power,
his love of friendship, and his personal safety, all demanded that he should maintain his former religious
position. In making the change he knowingly sacrificed
all of these, and, if he was practicing deception, he exposed himself to the punishment which he believed the
wicked would receive in eternity. It is possible to believe that a man might, through miscalculation as to immediate results, begin to practice a deception involving
such consequences, but it is incredible that he should
continue to do so after his mistake was discovered, and
that he should persist in it through a long life. It is
incredible, therefore, that Saul was a deceiver ;[1] and as

---

[1] It is evidence such as this which constrains the author of
' Supernatural Religion," one of the most radical infidel works

he was neither deceived himself, nor a deceiver of others, his vision must have been a reality, and Jesus who appeared to him is what he proved him to be, the Son of God.[1]

Vv. 23–25. Saul now sees enacted in Damascus a scene like some in which he had played a part in Jerusalem, but with his own part reversed. He experiences some of the ill treatment which he had heaped upon others. (23) And when many days were fulfilled, the Jews took counsel together to kill him: (24) but their plot became known to Saul. And they watched the gates also day and night that they might kill him: (25) but his disciples took him by night, and let him down through the wall, lowering him in a basket. From this account it appears that when he heard of their plot he hid himself; but his enemies, thinking that he would try to escape through one of the gates of the city, and that thus they would be sure of finding him, kept constant watch for him. This watching also became known to his friends, which shows that they too were on the watch, and they provided for him another mode of escape. Along the eastern wall of Damascus some of the houses are built against the wall, with upper stories of wood resting on the top of the

published in England within the present generation, to say: "As to the apostle Paul himself, let it be said in the strongest and most emphatic manner possible, that we do not suggest the most distant suspicion of the sincerity of any historical statement he makes" (vol. iii. 496).

[1] Lord Lyttleton's small work on the conversion of Paul, in which he proved the divine origin of the Christian faith from this incident alone, has never been answered. The theories by which Renan, Baur and Strauss have attempted to account for Paul's belief that he saw Jesus, without admitting the fact, are considered in my Evidences of Christianity, Part III., chap. xi.

wall; and there are also a few such on the southern wall.[1] Out of a window in any of these a man might now be let down in the way described in the text;[2] and the same was doubtless true in ancient times. In case of a siege, when the wall must be surmounted by soldiers, these wooden superstructures could be torn away in a few hours.

This attempt to kill Saul is the third effect of his preaching on the unbelieving Jews. The first was amazement that he should preach Jesus at all (21); the second, confusion when they heard his testimony for Jesus (22); and third, their plot to kill him. This last effect was seen "when many days were fulfilled," an indefinite expression which might mean a few weeks, a few months, or a few years. We learn from Saul's own statement in Galatians (i. 17, 18), that his escape occurred three years after his conversion, and that within this period he had made an excursion into Arabia.[3] How

---

[1] Lands of the Bible, 559.   [2] Cf. II. Cor. xi. 32.

[3] Two contradictions are here alleged between Luke's account and that of Paul's: first, that Luke's "many days" can not include Paul "three years;" and second, that whereas Luke says that Saul preached in Damascus "immediately," Paul says he went "immediately into Arabia." As to the first, we may as well say, that when Joshua remarks to the Israelites, "Ye dwelt in the wilderness a long season" (Josh. xxiv. 7), while Moses says they were there forty years, there is here a contradiction, because a long *season* is not equal to forty years. Or, taking the opposite expression, as well say of Job's remark, "Man is of few days and full of trouble," that according to this men in Job's days lived only a *few days*, contradicting the statement that Job himself lived one hundred and forty years after his affliction (Job xiv. 1; xlii. 16). The case of Shimei is still more in point. When spared by Solomon on condition that he should not depart from Jerusalem, he "dwelt in Jerusalem many days;" yet he went out of the city "at the end of three years" (I. Kings ii. 36-40). As

far he had gone into Arabia, or how long he had remained there, he does not intimate; but he says that
after that excursion he returned to Damascus, and it is
easy to see that the attempt to kill him occurred
after this return.   He also says that " the governor under
Aretas the king guarded the city of the Damascenes, in
order to take me " (II. Cor. ii. 32); which shows that
Damascus was then under the dominion of Aretas, who

---

for the second allegation, it is not true that Paul's language contradicts that of Luke. If we read it with the question in mind,
Does he say that he went immediately into Arabia? I think we
shall answer that he does not. He says : " But when it was the
good pleasure of God, who separated me, even from my mother's
womb, and called me through his grace, to reveal his Son in me,
that I might preach him among the Gentiles; immediately I conferred not with flesh and blood : neither went I up to Jerusalem
to them who were apostles before me: but I went into Arabia;
and again I returned into Damascus " (Gal. i. 15–17). Here are
four statements: first, that he did not confer with flesh and blood;
second, that he did not go up to Jerusalem to the older apostles;
third, that he went into Arabia; and fourth, that he returned into
Damascus. Which of these does " immediately " qualify? Certainly not the last; for he did not immediately return to Damascus. And if not the last, why the third? These two are the
things which he did; and they are set over by the conjunction
" but " against the two things which he did not do. But does
" immediately " really qualify either of these directly? Did he
mean to say, I immediately did not confer? I immediately did
not go? Or is there not something understood which immediately qualifies more directly? He is speaking of being called to
preach; and what can he mean, but that he immediately commenced preaching without conferring with flesh and blood, without going up to Jerusalem to confer with the apostles. That,
still further, in prosecution of this preaching, which he immediately began, he went into Arabia, and returned again to Damascus, all of this, before he went up to Jerusalem to see Peter? If
this is the train of thought in the passage, and it seems to yield
no other, then instead of contradicting Luke's assertion that he
preached immediately in Damascus, it confirms it.

was king of Arabia, and that the Jews had his coöperation in the attempt to arrest Saul in the gates.   Furthermore, as Damascus was at that time under the king of
Arabia,[1] the country south of and adjacent to it must
also have been overrun by his forces, and for the time
in which he held it it would be styled a part of Arabia.
Saul's excursion, then, may have been into this region
for the purpose of preaching in its cities and villages;[2]

[1] Because there is no other historical account of this temporary
possession of Damascus by Aretas, Paul's statement of it has
been called in question; but he was thoroughly well informed
concerning the political relation of the city at the time he was
preaching in it; and as his statement is that of an eye witness,
and a thoroughly reliable man, no better authority for the fact
can be desired.

[2] I here quote from my Evidences of Christianity, Part III.,
chap. viii. : " The conjecture that Paul's excursion into Arabia
was not for the purpose of preaching, but for the purpose of
meditating on his new relations to Christ, and preparing himself
mentally for the work now before him, although it is adopted by
such men as Alford, Lightfoot and Farrar, appears to me to be
so utterly at variance with the restless activity and burning zeal
of the apostle, as to be altogether incredible.   The addition to
this conjecture, that he went as far as Mount Sinai, more than
four hundred miles from Damascus, whither Elijah had retired
before him, instead of confirming the original hypothesis, seems
rather to weaken it; for Paul knew very well that when Elijah
went thither he was rebuked by the Lord, who said, ' What doest
thou here, Elijah?' and that he was ordered back to his work.
In the absence of all evidence for this conjecture, we should be
governed in judging of the purpose of the excursion by what we
know of Paul's habits during the remainder of his life; and by
this standard we should judge that he was one of the last men on
earth to waste any precious moments, not to speak of a year or
two, in meditation in the desert, while the cause which he had
espoused was now struggling for its very existence.   See the
views of Alford and Lightfoot in their commentaries on Galatians, and those of Farrar in his Life of Paul, chap. xi.

and it may have been his activity in this work which aroused the Jewish opposition to its highest pitch, and at the same time enabled them to enlist the Arabian governor in their plot.

4. SAUL RETURNS TO JERUSALEM, AND IS SENT TO TARSUS, 26–30.

Vv. 26, 27. The mortification of Saul at being compelled to thus escape from the scene of his first labors in the gospel was long remembered to be mentioned many years after when he would speak of the things which concerned his weakness.[1] He had not yet seen any of those who were apostles before him, since he left them in Jerusalem to go on his murderous mission to Damascus. He now turns his steps in that direction, determined to go up and see Peter.[2] Early in the night's journey he passed the spot were Jesus had met him. We shall not attempt to depict his emotions when the walls of Jerusalem and the battlements of the temple came once more into view. As he approached the city, he saw the place of the crucifixion, and he may have passed near the spot where Stephen was stoned, and where he himself had stood "consenting to his death." He was about to meet again, on the streets and in the synagogues, his old allies whom he had deserted, and some of the disciples whom he had persecuted. The tumult of his emotions we leave to the imagination of the reader, and their portrayal to the pages of more voluminous writers,[3] while we follow Luke's account of his reception among the disciples. (26) **And when he was come to Jerusalem, he assayed to**

---

[1] II. Cor. xi. 30–33.   [2] Gal. i. 18.

[3] See especially *Life and Epistles*, by Conybeare and Howson; and Farrar's Life of Paul.

join himself to the disciples: and they were all afraid of him, not believing that he was a disciple. (27) But Barnabas took him and brought him to the apostles, and declared unto them how he had seen the Lord in the way, and that he had spoken to him, and how at Damascus he had preached boldly in the name of Jesus.   From this it appears that at first "all the disciples were afraid of him, not believing that he was a disciple;" and that his attempt to "join himself" to them was repulsed.   However painful this may have been to him, it was probably not a surprise ; for how could he expect them to believe him a genuine disciple, after experiencing what they had at his hands?   It is scarcely possible that they had not heard some report of his conversion; but as they must have supposed him capable of any device by which to gain an advantage over them, it was impossible for them, except on the strongest evidence, to believe that his conversion was genuine.   Barnabas was the first to become fully convinced.   Moved by the generous impulses characteristic of him, he may have sought an interview with Saul, or the latter, having some knowledge of Barnabas, may have approached him as the one most likely to grant him a candid hearing.   In either case, it would not be difficult for Barnabas to credit the unvarnished story, told, as it must have been, with an earnestness and pathos which no impostor could assume.   When Barnabas was once convinced, it was easy for him to convince the apostles, and for them to convince the brethren.   All this was probably the work of a single day.   Peter received him into the house where he was then residing, and entertained him fifteen days.[1]   He now had ample time and a good opportunity to learn

[1] Gal. i. 18.

from Peter's lips the whole story of the life of Jesus, concerning which his previous knowledge must have been very limited. "Of the other apostles," he says in the same connection, "I saw none, save James the Lord's brother." From this we learn that this James, though not one of the twelve, was in some sense regarded as an apostle; and Luke undoubtedly includes him, and perhaps others of similar rank among the brethren, in the "apostles" to whom Barnabas brought Saul.[1]

Vv. 28–30. The brethren may have received Saul with some misgiving, but the course which he pursued must have won their confidence very soon. (28) **And he was with them going in and out at Jerusalem, (29) preaching boldly in the name of the Lord: and he spoke and disputed against the Grecian Jews; but they went about to kill him. (30) And when the brethren knew it, they brought him down to Caesarea, and sent him forth to Tarsus.** During his absence from Jerusalem the persecution which he had led had so far subsided that these foreign Jews were once more willing to debate the questions at issue; and in the intervals of his conversations with Peter, Saul met them in discussion; but ere two weeks had passed they found their new opponent equally invincible with Stephen; and in the madness of

---

[1] The assertion made by Zeller (i. 299), following Baur and other German infidels, that Luke contradicts Paul in saying that Barnabas brought the latter to "the apostles," is based on the double assumption that by the term apostles he means all of the apostles, or the majority of them; and that the term applies to none but the twelve. But Lightfoot, in his commentary on Galatians, has shown clearly that the term was applied to various others, as Paul and Luke both apply it to James the Lord's brother; and this fact refutes the charge. See for this use of the term, chap. xiv. 4, 14; Rom. xvi. 7; II. Cor. viii. 23; chap. xi. 13; Phil. ii. 25; Rev. ii. 2.

defeat they resolved that Stephen's fate should be his.
In this emergency the brethren found opportunity to
make amends for the suspicion with which they had at
first regarded him, by taking him away to a place of
safety. We learn from his own lips, farther on, that the
concern of the brethren for his personal safety was not
the controlling reason for his departure; and that he had
a very strong desire to stand his ground in Jerusalem,
notwithstanding the purpose of the Jews to kill him.[1]
After reaching Cæsarea, a short voyage on the Mediterranean and up the Cydnus brought him to Tarsus, the
home of his childhood, and perhaps of his earlier man-
hood. He returns to the friends of his early days, a
fugitive from two great cities, and a deserter from that
strictest of sects in which he had been educated; but he
comes to bring them glad tidings of great joy. He disappears at this point from the pages of Luke, but he
does not go into inactivity. His own pen at a later date
fills this blank in the history, by informing us that he
went into the regions of Syria and Cilicia, where he
preached the faith which he once destroyed.[2] We shall
yet meet with brethren in both these countries, who
were doubtless brought to Christ by this preaching.[3]
We shall find reason to believe, also, that during this interval he encountered a portion of the sufferings which
he enumerates in the eleventh chapter of Second Corinthians, and that before the close of it he experienced his
well known vision of paradise.[4] While he is passing

---

[1] Acts xxii. 18-21. [2] Gal. i. 21-24. [3] Acts xv. 40, 41.

[4] The epistle in which he mentions this vision was written in
the year 57; and as the vision had been witnessed fourteen years
previous, its date was the year 43, which, as appears from the
chronology (*Int.* ix.) was the year in which Paul closed his labors
in Syria and Cilicia, and went with Barnabas to Antioch.

through these experiences, our historian introduces to us some important and instructive scenes in the labors of the apostle Peter.

SEC. III.—PETER PREACHES IN JUDEA, AND IS SENT TO THE UNCIRCUMCISED.

(IX. 31—XI. 18.)

1. The Church Enjoys Peace and Prosperity, 31.

Ver. 31. Our author makes the transition from the labors of Saul to those of Peter, by stating the condition of affairs which invited Peter to leave Jerusalem and go abroad. (31) **So the church throughout all Judea and Galilee and Samaria had peace, being edified ; and, walking in the fear of the Lord and in the comfort of the Holy Spirit, was multiplied.** This time of peace had probably begun before Saul's return to Jerusalem, and had been interrupted by the persecution waged against him. Now that he was gone, it was restored. It might have been imagined by some that, as the church had sprung into existence amid strife and persecution, it would languish when opposition was withdrawn ; but its present prosperity proved that it was not the obstinacy of human passion, but the legitimate working of unchangeable truth, which had brought it into existence. According to Gamaliel's philosophy (v. 34–39), its claim to a divine origin was now vindicated. The church was edified, in the sense of being built up in Christian character ; and multiplied, in the sense of very rapid increase of numbers. It should be noticed that the term church, or congregation, is here applied so as to include all the disciples in these three districts, the region of our Saviour's personal labors. It is a secondary use of the word, the whole body being contemplated as if congregated together.[1]

2. Peter, Evangelizing, Comes to Lydda, 32–35.

Vv. 32–35. When the Lord ordered Saul away from Jerusalem he said he would send him "far hence to the Gentiles;" but thus far no uncircumcised Gentiles had been admitted into the church. Luke is now about to show how Peter opened the gates of the kingdom for their admission; and he approaches the subject by recounting the labors which led Peter to the spot where the messengers who called him to this task found him. (32) And it came to pass, as Peter went through all parts, he came down also to the saints who dwelt at Lydda. (33) And there he found a certain man named Æneas, who had kept his bed eight years; for he was palsied. (34) And Peter said unto him, Æneas, Jesus Christ heals thee: arise and make thy bed. And straightway he arose. (35) And all that dwelt at Lydda and in Sharon saw him, and they turned to the Lord. From this it appears that there were saints at Lydda before Peter's arrival. They may have been baptized in Jeru-

---

[1] The original (ἐκκλησία) is the common Greek word for an assembly of the people. It is used in this sense in chap. xix. 32, 39, 41, where it applies to an assembly of the people of Ephesus, whether orderly or disorderly. It is unfortunate that it is not everywhere translated congregation, as in the Geneva version, so that the uninformed English reader would see its exact meaning. Its figurative use when applied to more than a single congregation, as in the present instance, would then be apparent to every reader as well as to the learned.

salem during the early days of the church there; or they may have been brought in by Philip while he was evangelizing from Azotus to Cæsarea (viii. 40). It was doubtless their presence in the town which led Peter, as he was going " throughout all parts," to come thither. The " all parts " referred to were the parts of Judea, Galilee and Samaria, mentioned in the preceding verse; and the remark shows that before reaching Lydda Peter had visited congregations in all of these districts. The almost unprecedented effect of this one miracle, causing the mass of the population of Lydda and of the surrounding plain of Sharon to turn to the Lord, is attributable to two causes: first, the fact that the man cured was, like the cripple cured at the Beautiful gate in Jerusalem (iii. 10; iv. 22), a widely known victim of an incurable disease; and second, the fact that the people, like ripe fruit on a tree, which needs only a little shaking to bring it down, were already most favorably inclined to the truth.

3. Peter is Called to Joppa, 36–43.

Vv. 36–38. From the midst of these happy and exhilarating triumphs of the gospel, Peter was called to a house of mourning in the city of Joppa. (36) Now there was at Joppa a certain disciple named Tabitha, which by interpretation[1] is called Dorcas: this woman was full of good works and almsdeeds which she did. (37) And it came to pass in those days, that she fell sick

---

[1] For the words, " by interpretation," which so frequently occur in the English New Testament, we should have *by translation;* for it is in every instance a matter of translation, and not of interpretation. Here the name Tabitha, translated into Greek, means Dorcas, and translated into English it means Gazelle.

and died : and when they had washed her, they laid her
in an upper chamber. (38) And as Lydda was nigh unto
Joppa, the disciples, hearing that Peter was there, sent
two men to him, intreating him, Delay not to come on
unto us. (Joppa) has always been the principal seaport
of Judea,[1] except during the comparatively short period
in which the artificial harbor constructed by Herod at
Cæsarea was in use.[2] It lies in a northwesterly direction
from Jerusalem, from which it is distant (thirty-eight
miles) by the macadamized road which now connects the
two cities.   Lydda is some two or three miles north of
this road, and about twelve miles out from Joppa.   The
old road to Jerusalem, which was used before the turn-
pike was constructed, passed through Lydda, and entered
Jerusalem from the north, while the present road enters
it from the west.   A walk of three hours brought the
two men with their sad message to Peter.   We are left
by the historian entirely to conjecture as to the purpose
for which Peter's presence in Joppa was desired, whether
to minister comfort to the distressed little band of believers, in the way which is the only one left to modern
preachers under such circumstances, or with the hope
that he would raise the sleeping saint from the dead.   It
is more probable that the former was their thought ; for
it was not the custom of the apostles to bring back to
life their deceased brethren and sisters merely because

---

[1] It is the port at which the rafts of cedar from Lebanon for Solomon's temple were landed (II. Chron. ii. 16) ; and also those for the
second temple (Ezra iii. 7) ; and it is the one from which Jonah
set sail, that he migh flee to Tarshish (Jonah i. 3).   It now has a
population of between fifteen and twenty thousand, and is connected by regular lines of steamers, visiting it weekly, with all
the ports of the Mediterranean Sea.

[2] See an account of it under chap. x. 1.

they had been useful in their lives; otherwise Stephen and others who had been cruelly slain in the midst of their usefulness would have been resuscitated. The message to Peter, as we read it, was simply this: "Delay not to come on unto us." Doubtless the whole story of Dorcas was told to him; for the hearts of the messengers were full of it, and Peter had his own thoughts about it as the three went on their way to Joppa.

Vv. 39-43. Death in that warm climate, where no facilities exist for preserving dead bodies, is followed by a speedy burial, usually before the close of the same day; and if Peter was to be there in time to witness the burial of Tabitha, there was no time for delay. (39) And Peter arose and went with them. And when he was come, they brought him into the upper chamber: and all the widows stood by him weeping, and showing the coats and garments[1] which Dorcas made while she was with them. (40) But Peter put them all forth, and kneeled down, and prayed; and turning to the body, he said, Tabitha, arise. And she opened her eyes; and when she saw Peter, she sat up. (41) And he gave her his hand, and raised her up; and calling the saints and widows, he presented her alive. (42) And it became known throughout all Joppa: and many believed on the Lord. (43) And it came to pass, that he abode many days in Joppa, with one Simon a tanner. Nothing could be more graphic than this brief narration, or more touching then the incident itself. Amid the march of imposing events which are moving before us, it drops in like

---

[1] The two words rendered coats and garments (χιτῶνας and ἱμάτια) mean *tunics* and *mantles*—the former the inner garment then worn, which fitted close to the body, and the latter the outer garment, which was loose and flowing.

the passage

a wild flower in a stately forest. (It) opens a vista through the larger events of the history, lets light in upon the social sorrows of the early saints, and discloses a scene with the like of which our own experiences have made us familiar. Here is the same tender care for the lifeless body, the same distress felt by all, the same desire for the presence of him who has been our religious counselor; the same company of weeping women, and of men standing by in mournful silence; the same recounting with sobbing voices of the good deeds done by the departed; and, beyond all this to which we are accustomed, a group of poor widows holding up before Peter as he comes in the tunics and mantles which Dorcas had made for them and their children while she was yet with them. What a memorial! How much richer and more to be desired than monuments of marble and bronze covered with flattering inscriptions! Blessed are the dead who die in the Lord; and blessed are the living in whose softened hearts is treasured at such an hour the remembrance of such a life as Dorcas had lived. As Peter stood there for a moment in tearful silence, did he not seem to himself to be standing once more at the tomb of Lazarus, by the side of his Master, and surrounded by the Jews who wept with Mary and Martha? But he remembers that his compassionate Lord is now in heaven. With deep solemnity he motions the mourners all aside. He is left alone with the dead. He kneels down, and prays. (The prayer of faith he knows is heard.) With a voice of authority, and yet of tenderness, a voice which can be heard by the dead, he says to the cold body, " Tabitha, arise." Her eyes open, and she sees Peter. Does she recognize him, or is he a stranger to her? We know not. She sits up, and looks him in the face. Not another word passes between them; but he gently gives her his hand, and helps her to her feet. He calls in the saints and widows, and there in her white shroud she stands before them alive. Here the narration closes, as well it might; for not even Luke's graphic pen could describe the scene which followed. And if the restoration of one saint to the little band which she has left is indescribable, what shall we say or think of that hour when all the sainted dead shall rise in glory and greet one another on the shores of life? (Is not this event in Joppa intended to give us a slight foretaste of the joys of the resurrection morning?) No wonder that this " became known throughout all Joppa," and that " many believed on the Lord." Joppa was now a field white for the harvest, and Peter found inviting work for many days. He came to weep with those who wept; he remained to rejoice with those who rejoiced.

4. Cornelius, a Gentile, Directed to Send for Peter, x. 1–8.

Vv. 1, 2. The scene of the narrative changes from Joppa to Cæsarea,[1] about thirty miles north on the Medi-

---

[1] This city was founded by Herod the Great for the purpose of providing on the coast of Judea, which has no natural harbor, an artificial one in which ships could anchor at any time of the year. Its completion as a walled city, together with the completion of the artificial harbor, was celebrated in the year 13 B. C; and all the procurators of Judea after Pilate made it their seat of government. After passing through many vicissitudes during the centuries of war and desolation to which all Judea was subjected, it was finally destroyed in the year 1226. Since then its harbor has silted up, the breakwater having long since crumbled beneath the ceaseless wash of the waves, and it is now too shallow

terranean shore, and we are introduced to another case of conversion, that of a Gentile and a soldier. (1) **Now there was a certain man in Cæsarea, Cornelius by name, a centurion of the band called the Italian band, a devout man, and one that feared God with all his house, who gave much alms to the people, and prayed to God always.** At first glance it might appear strange that a man whose character is thus described should need conversion. There are many men in the present day, in whose favor not so much can be said, who flatter themselves that their prospects for final salvation are good. They are honest in their dealings, honorable in their intercourse with men, good husbands and fathers, generous to their neighbors, and benevolent to the poor; what have they to fear at the hands of a just and merciful God? But Cornelius was all this, and beyond this he was a devout and prayerful man; yet it was necessary for even him to hear words whereby he might be saved (xi. 14). Our self-righteous men of the world must then be deceiving themselves. They forget that while they are discharging in a creditable manner their obligations to their fellow men, they are neglecting the much higher obligation to render direct service to God by observing the ordinances of his appointment. The most inexcusable of all sins is a refusal to render to God, our Maker and Redeemer, the homage which is his due. Moreover, in acting thus we do great harm by our example to our fellow-men, and most of all to those who love us most.

That Cornelius was an Italian, born and reared in a heathen land, is made almost certain by his Latin name,

---

for any sea-going vessels. Its ruins are among the most extensive and interesting in Palestine. For a decription of them the reader is referred to the author's Lands of the Bible, p. 275 *ff.*

combined with the fact that he was an officer in an Italian cohort. How then could he have acquired the character which is here ascribed to him? No possible heathen education could have imparted it to him. It could be acquired only by contact with the Jewish people. (From the very people, then, whom he was helping to keep in subjection to the Roman yoke he had learned the only true religion.) With the exception of being uncircumcised, he stood before God as did any pious Jew of that age, or of this, who had not accepted Christ. Christ had now come in between all men and God, so that there was no access to the forgiveness of sins except through him, and we are to see how Cornelius was brought to Christ, and through him to God.

Vv. 3–6. The first step taken in bringing this good man to Christ is described in these words: (3) He saw in a vision openly, as it were about the ninth hour of the day, an angel of God coming in unto him, and saying to him, Cornelius. (4) And he, fastening his eyes upon him, and being affrighted, said, What is it, Lord? And he said unto him, Thy prayers and thine alms are gone up for a memorial before God. (5) And now send men to Joppa, and fetch one Simon whose surname is Peter: (6) he lodgeth with one Simon a tanner, whose house is by the seaside.

The vision here described did not appear in a dream or a trance; but to a man wide awake, and, as we learn farther on (30), engaged in prayer. That he observed one of the Jewish hours of prayer (iii. 1), the hour of evening incense, is additional proof that he owed his religious character to Jewish instruction. The fear which the visible presence of the angel excited was instinctive; for there is no reason why men should fear angels or spirits; yet all men, even the most godly, have been frightened when they have seen, or thought they have seen, supernatural beings.

From a modern point of view the words of the angel render it still more surprising (*cf.* remarks under 1, 2) that such a man should be made a special subject for conversion. If, in addition to all that is said of his exalted religious character, his prayers were heard, and his alms had gone up for a memorial before God, what did he yet lack of salvation from sin? Let a man with such an experience as his appear before any church at the present day, and say: "I have been for many years a devout man, worshiping God as well as I knew how, giving much alms to the poor, praying continually, and teaching my household the fear of God. Yesterday afternoon at three o'clock I was praying according to my custom, when suddenly an angel stood before me, and said, 'Thy prayers and thine alms are come up for a memorial before God.'" Who would hesitate to pronounce him a thoroughly converted man? He certainly was a convert from heathenism to Judaism, yet the angel, as we learn from Peter's subsequent recital of the facts (xi. 14), after telling him to send for Peter, said, "He shall speak unto thee words whereby thou shalt be saved, thou and all thy house." Though the angel had spoken to him, and though God had heard his prayers, he must yet hear words from a man's lips before he will be saved. We must watch the narrative as it continues, to see what words were spoken, and what they contained that was so necessary.

Let us not fail to observe that here is the prayer of a man not yet wholly converted to Christ, and that the prayer is answered. But how different is the answer from that which persons in a similar spiritual condition are taught to expect in our own time. The angel does not bring him word that his sins are forgiven; nor does he leave him rejoicing in the forgiveness of sins because he is assured that his prayers are heard. Instead of this, he is told to send for a man who will tell him what he must do to be saved. If similar prayers were answered now, who can doubt that the same God would answer them in the same way, by telling the inquirer to send for a preacher, or for some other disciple, who would rightly instruct him?

It is interesting and instructive to observe that we here have another instance of the intervention of an angel in securing the conversion of a man. In comparing the angel's work with that of the one who appeared in the case of the eunuch (viii. 26), we observe that though the latter appeared to the preacher, and the former to the person to be converted, both appeared for essentially the same purpose; that is, to bring the preacher and the subject for conversion face to face. Thus we learn that supernatural interventions never superseded the indispensable work of the human agent. Even when the Lord himself, as in the case of Saul's conversion, appeared to the sinner, the human agency was still indispensable, and the Lord himself directed Ananias to go to the still unforgiven Saul. (These facts can not be too urgently pressed upon the attention of an age like ours, in which they are totally ignored by the majority of religious teachers. In all three of these instances the supernatural intervention became necessary, because without it the parties would not have come together at all.) Philip would not otherwise have known that there was an Ethiopian on the road to Gaza; Ananias would

not have dared to approach Saul; and Cornelius would
not have known that it was his privilege to send for
Peter.

Vv. 7, 8. Although it was now (late in the afternoon,)
Cornelius did not hesitate to start three messengers at
once on the journey. (7) **And when the angel that spake
unto him was departed, he called two of his household
servants and a devout soldier of them that waited on him
continually; (8) and having rehearsed all things unto
them, he sent them to Joppa.** Here it appears that the
religious zeal by which he had brought his household to
the fear of God (2) had reached out also to some of the
soldiers under his command. The soldier, in his Roman
uniform, was sent along as a protection to the two servants; for then, as now, the attendance of even a single
soldier, representing the supreme power of the empire,
was a protection to travelers.

5. PETER IS DIRECTED TO GO TO CORNELIUS, 9–23.

Vv. 9–16. The scene now changes again, and we
pass (from) Cæsarea back to Joppa, where we left Peter
in the house of the tanner. Our author anticipates the
arrival of the messengers of Cornelius, by showing how
the Lord prepared Peter for a favorable reception of
their message. (9) **Now on the morrow, as they were on
their journey, and drew nigh unto the city, Peter went
up upon the housetop to pray, about the sixth hour: (10)
and he became hungry, and desired to eat: but while
they made ready, he fell into a trance; (11) and he beheld the heaven opened, and a certain vessel descending,
as it were a great sheet, let down by the four corners
upon the earth: (12) wherein were all manner of four-**

footed beasts and creeping things of the earth and fowls
of the heaven. (13) And there came a voice to him,
Rise, Peter, kill and eat. (14) But Peter said, Not so,
Lord; for I have never eaten anything that was common
and unclean. (15) And a voice came unto him again
the second time, What God hath cleansed, make not thou
common. (16) And this was done thrice : and straightway the vessel was received up into heaven. Although
Peter was in a trance, he was still completely at himself
in thought and feeling; hence the outgush of his characteristic impetuosity, when he answered the command
from heaven, "Not so, Lord." His thoughts went no
farther in justification of his boldness than the fact that
he had never in his life eaten anything unclean, as were
some of the things he was commanded to eat; but in
thus abstaining he knew that he was obeying a law which
God had himself given to his fathers, and he could not
at the instant take in the thought that God was now
abolishing one of his own laws. When the sheet and
the voice came to him the second and the third time, he
was silent; for then he saw that God meant what he
said, and no man was ever more prompt to obey when a
command was understood. This vision came when Peter
was engaged in prayer, because then he was in the most
favorable mood for acquiescence in an unwelcome command; and when he was hungry, because the command
had reference to the legal distinctions concerning animal
food. He was on the housetop, because, in a small
house, with perhaps only two or three rooms, he could
find privacy better on the roof than below. A battle-
ment may have hidden him from the view of persons on
neighboring houses, if any were on their housetops in
the heat of the day.

Vv. 17–20. The occurrence of this vision, and the movements of the messengers sent by Cornelius, like the journey of Philip and the movement of the eunuch's chariot (chap. viii. 26, 27), were well timed by the angels who had them in charge. (17) **Now while Peter was much perplexed in himself what the vision he had seen might mean, behold, the men who had been sent by Cornelius, having made inquiry for Simon's house, stood before the gate, (18) and called, and asked whether Simon, who was surnamed Peter, were lodging there. (19) And while Peter thought on the vision, the Spirit said to him, Behold, three men seek thee. (20) But rise, get thee down, and go with them, nothing doubting: for I have sent them.** Peter could not fail to see that by means of this vision God had abolished the legal distinction between clean and unclean animals; hence we infer that his perplexity and his protracted thought on the meaning of the vision had reference to something else. That which was abolished was a prominent part of God's law; and he may have been perplexed as to why it should be abolished. He may also have raised the question whether the rest of the law was also to be abolished; if so, this would perplex him still more. But he was not left very long in doubt; for in the skillful adjustment of the vision to the movements of the messengers of Cornelius, the latter had now arrived, and found the right house, and the Holy Spirit in Peter reveals to him that three men are below seeking for him, and bids him go with them. It is not necessary to think that Simon's house was outside the city, because, as many of the commentators have supposed,[1] his business

---

[1] This supposition is based exclusively on the statement of rabbis of a later age; but there is nothing in the law of Moses

was considered unclean; for, whatever may be true as to that, his tannery may have been outside the walls while his residence was inside.

Vv. 21, 22. As Peter goes down stairs to meet the men whose arrival was so strangely made known to him, he is still perplexed as to the meaning of the vision; but he soon begins to see a meaning in it which he had not suspected. (21) And Peter went down to the men, and said, Behold, I am he whom ye seek: what is the cause wherefore ye are come? (22) And they said, Cornelius a centurion, a righteous man, and one that feareth God, and well reported of by all the nation of the Jews, was warned of God by a holy angel to send for thee into his house, and to hear words from thee. Connecting this message, sent by the order of a "holy angel," with the vision, and with the command of the Spirit to go with the men, nothing doubting, Peter now in an instant sees that he is called by divine authority, through the angel, through the vision, through the Spirit, to do what he had always before thought sinful, to go into the house of a Gentile, and to speak to him the word of the Lord. Nothing less than an unmistakable divine call could have induced him to do this; but now he has no alternative unless he would withstand God. He now sees what he afterward expressed so happily, that he was to call no man common or unclean (25).

6. The Meeting of Peter and Cornelius, 23–33.

Vv. 23, 24. The messengers themselves were most probably Gentiles, and the soldier certainly was; and under ordinary circumstances Gentiles could scarcely

to justify it, and it is not at all certain that the business was regarded as unclean by the Pharisees of the apostolic age.

have found entertainment in the house of Simon the tanner. But his mind and that of Peter were sufficiently moved in the right direction by what had already occurred, to remove all hesitation about receiving them to the hospitalities of the house. (23) So he called them in and lodged them. And on the morrow he arose and went forth with them, and certain of the brethren from Joppa accompanied him. (24) And on the morrow they entered into Cæsarea. And Cornelius was waiting for them, having called together his kinsmen and his near friends. Peter did not start for Cæsarea as promptly as Cornelius had started his messengers to Joppa. He may have waited to the next day in order that the brethren who were to go with him, six in number (chap. xi. 12), might get ready; or because the place at which they had to spend the night on the way was at such a distance as to make it best to start in the morning. Cornelius knew the time that the journey would require, and so, with military promptness, he had a select audience ready and waiting. Notice, this audience was not composed of a miscellaneous crowd, but of kinsmen and near friends of Cornelius, who were doubtless invited to be present because of their known interest in the object for which they came together.

Vv. 25-29. It was not without emotion that Peter first approached the door of a Gentile's house, and it must have been with the deepest emotion that Cornelius first met the man for whom he had sent in obedience to the command of an angel. An overpowering sense of humility marked the deportment of the soldier, while the apostle bore himself with an easy dignity, which nothing but a noble nature and a high calling could have imparted to a fisherman. (25) And when it came to pass that Peter entered, Cornelius met him, and fell down at his feet, and worshiped him. (26) But Peter raised him up, saying, Stand up; I myself also am a man. (27) And as he talked with him, he went in, and findeth many come together: (28) and he said unto them, Ye yourselves know how that it is an unlawful thing for a man that is a Jew to join himself or come unto one of another nation; and yet unto me hath God showed that I should not call any man common or unclean: (29) wherefore I came without gainsaying when I was sent for. I ask therefore with what intent ye sent for me. Cornelius worshiped Peter only in the sense of paying him that homage which, according to oriental custom, was due to one of greatly superior rank. The term is frequently used in this sense, and his knowlege of the true God forbids the supposition that he intended to pay divine honors to a man. He was moved to this homage in consideration of the high esteem in which Peter seemed to be held by the " holy angel." But Peter, not knowing his man as yet, could not know that only this kind of homage was intended,[1] and hence his remark " I myself also am a man." Peter's explanation of his departure from Jewish custom in entering the house of a Gentile shows that he now clearly understood the vision as including men in its scope; and his remark, based upon this understanding, was satisfactory to his hearers without the recital of the vision itself. The messengers had told him for what purpose he was sent for, but he thought it proper to have a statement of this purpose from the parties themselves, before proceeding further.

---

[1] See Matt. ii. 2, 8; viii. 2; ix. 18; xiv. 33; xv. 25; xviii. 26; xx. 20.

Vv. 30–33. Peter's inquiry was addressed to the company at large, but Cornelius was the proper person to answer it, and he did so in a most direct and satisfactory manner. (30) **And Cornelius said, Four days ago, until this hour, I was keeping the ninth hour of prayer in my house; and behold, a man stood before me in bright apparel, (31) and saith, Cornelius, thy prayer is heard, and thine alms are had in remembrance in the sight of God. (32) Send therefore to Joppa, and call unto thee Simon, who is surnamed Peter; he lodgeth in the house of Simon a tanner, by the seaside. (33) Forthwith therefore I sent to thee, and thou hast well done that thou art come. Now therefore we are all present here in the sight of God, to hear all things that have been commanded thee of the Lord.** His first remark in this answer shows that according to the mode of counting then prevalent, it had been four days since the appearance of the angel, although, according to our own method, as we can see by counting back, it was precisely three days. He here styles the being who had spoken to him "a man in bright apparel," but he evidently recognized him by the communication which he brought, if not by the peculiar brightness of his apparel, as an angel, as he is styled by Luke (3), and by the messengers (22). The last statement in the answer shows that the whole company had assembled in the conscious presence of God, for the express purpose of hearing, and of hearing as they should hear it, the message from God with which Peter was charged. When such an audience is assembled to hear such a preacher, the results most to be desired are sure to follow.

7. Peter's Sermon to the Uncircumcised, 34–43.

Vv. 34, 35. The occasion furnished Peter a most happy introduction to the remarks which he had to submit, and like a trained rhetorician, which he was not, he proceeded to make use of it. **(34) And Peter opened his mouth, and said, Of a truth I perceive that God is no respecter of persons; (35) but in every nation he that feareth him, and worketh righteousness, is acceptable to him.** The expansive thought here expressed was sufficient, in Peter's mind, to burst asunder the exclusive bonds of the Mosaic covenant; and it should be sufficient now to dispel from the minds of men the equally exclusive theory of an arbitrary predestination of certain men and angels to their eternal destiny. It is a positive and inspired declaration that God respects not persons, but character. To fear him and work righteousness, and not any other distinction between persons, is the ground of acceptability with him.

Vv. 36–39. As we have observed above, the experience which Cornelius had now related to Peter is such as would secure him instant recognition as a Christian among modern Protestants; but Peter was so far from thus regarding it, that he proceeds to preach to him the words whereby he might be saved; and first, as on Pentecost, he briefly describes the personal career of Jesus. **(36) The word which he sent unto the children of Israel, preaching good tidings of peace by Jesus Christ (he is Lord of all), that saying ye yourselves know, (37) which was published throughout all Judea, beginning from Galilee after the baptism which John preached; (38) even Jesus of Nazareth, how that God anointed him with the Holy Spirit and with power: who went about**

doing good, and healing all that were oppressed by the devil; for God was with him. (39) And we are witnesses of all that he did both in the country of the Jews, and in Jerusalem; whom they slew, hanging him on a tree. From the words, "ye know," with which this recital is introduced, we learn that the personal career of Jesus was already known to Cornelius and his friends; and that they were acquainted with the "good tidings of peace" which Jesus had preached to the children of Israel. Peter rehearses the story for the apparent purpose of confirming their belief in it by the assertion that he and his companions were witnesses of it all. That of which the auditors were as yet ignorant was their own interest in the message of peace, which had been looked upon as intended for Israel alone.

Vv. 40, 41. The crowning fact of the gospel comes next in the narrative, as it did in the sermon on Pentecost. (40) Him God raised up the third day, and gave him to be manifest, not to all the people, (41) but unto witnesses that were chosen before of God, even to us who did eat and drink with him after he arose from the dead. Here, by way of commending the evidence of the resurrection, Peter states to his hearers a fact which has been so differently construed by unbelievers as to be made a ground of objection; that is, that the witnesses were chosen beforehand. He says that they were chosen by God; but he doubtless has reference to their choice by the Lord Jesus. Whether Peter or the unbelievers are right in this, depends entirely on the grounds of the choice. If they were chosen because of their willingness to testify without regard to facts, or because of the ease with which they might be deceived, it might be rightly regarded as a suspicious circumstance. But the reverse is true in both particulars. Such was the situation of the witnesses that there was imminent danger to both property and person in giving their testimony, and therefore every motive to dishonesty prompted them to keep silence. They were also the least likely of all men to be deceived, because of their long and intimate familiarity with him who was to be identified. On the other hand, if he had appeared to all the people, a large majority of them would have been unable to testify with entire certainty to his identity. Peter, then, was right; for the fact that such witnesses were chosen beforehand proves that no deception was intended; but that, on the contrary, the aim was to provide the most reliable witnesses then living.[1] To Cornelius the testimony of Peter to what had been done was ample, from the fact of his having been warned of God by a holy angel to send for Peter; and the company had already declared themselves ready to hear all things that had been commanded him by the Lord (33).

---

[1] "If their point had been to have their story believed, whether true or false, or if they had been disposed to present their testimony, either as personal witnesses or as historians, in such a manner as to render it as specious and unobjectionable as they could—in a word, if they had thought of anything but the truth of the case as they understood and believed it—they would, in the account of Christ's several appearances, at least have omitted this restriction. At this distance of time, the account as we have it is perhaps more credible than it would have been in the other way, because this manifestation of the historian's candor is of more advantage to their testimony than the difference in the circumstances of the account would have been to the nature of the evidence. But this is an effect which the evangelists could not foresee, and is one which by no means would have followed at the time when they wrote" (Paley, *Evidences of Christianity*).

Vv. 42, 43. Having now sketched the career of Jesus, and stated the evidence of his resurrection, Peter proceeds in regular order to the next historical fact, the giving of the apostolic commission. (42) And he charged us to preach to the people, and to testify that this is he who is ordained of God to be the judge of quick and dead. (43) To him bear all the prophets witness, that through his name every one that believeth on him shall receive remission of sins.

The command to preach to the people was expressed in the commission (Mark xvi. 15), and that they were to "testify that this is he who is ordained of God to be the judge of quick and dead" was implied in the preface to the commission, "All authority hath been given unto me in heaven and on earth" (Matt. xxviii. 18). Before this, however, in the lifetime of Jesus, he had declared to the Jews that all judgment was given to him, and that the Father would judge no man (Jno. v. 21, 22). In the promise of remission of sins (43) we must not overlook the force of the words, "through his name." The promise is to every one who believeth on Jesus, but it "is through his name" that the promise is to be made effective. These very persons were a little later commanded to be baptized "in the name of Jesus Christ" (48); and all are baptized "into the name of the Father, and of the Son, and of the Holy Spirit" (Matt. xxviii. 19). This perfectly harmonizes with Peter's command in his first sermon, "Repent and be baptized every one of you in the name of Jesus Christ for the remission of sins;" and the passage by no means supports the doctrine of justification by faith only. Peter's reference to the prophets as the witnesses for this promise is a surprise, especially as it occurs immediately after his reference to the apostolic commission in which was the most explicit statement of it. His probable purpose was not to indicate a primary reliance on the prophets, but to show that instead of being a new promise coming from Jesus alone, it was an old one taught generally in the Old Testament.

8. The Uncircumcised Receive the Holy Spirit and are Baptized, 44–48.

Vv. 44–46. Peter's sermon was interrupted and broken off by an incident that stands alone in apostolic history, and was a great surprise to Peter and his Jewish companions. (44) While Peter yet spake the words, the Holy Spirit fell on all them who heard the word. (45) And they of the circumcision who believed were amazed, as many as came with Peter, because that on the Gentiles also was poured out the gift of the Holy Spirit. (46) For they heard them speak with tongues, and magnify God. The ground of amazement to the Jewish brethren was not the mere fact that these Gentiles received the Holy Spirit; for if Peter had finished his discourse, promising them the Holy Spirit on the terms which he had laid down on Pentecost, and had then baptized them, these brethren would have taken it as a matter of course that they received the Spirit. And if, after this, he had laid hands on them and imparted the miraculous gift of the Spirit, as in the case of the Samaritans, they would not have been so greatly surprised. The considerations which caused the amazement were, first, that the Holy Spirit was "poured out" upon them directly from God, as it had never been before on any but the apostles; and second, that this unusual gift was bestowed on Gentiles. This second circumstance

will be explained in discussing the design of this miracle
under verses 47, 48, below. The fact that this gift of
the Spirit was manifested by the miracle of speaking in
tongues[1] distinguishes it from that gift of the Spirit
promised to all who repent and are baptized (ii. 38);
and the fact that it came directly from heaven, without
the imposition of apostolic hands, distinguishes it from
such gifts as that bestowed on the Samaritans, and that
afterward bestowed on prominent members of many
churches.[2] We have no event with which to classify it

---

[1] It is a matter of surprise to find so judicious a commentator
as Plumptre expressing himself on this miracle as follows: " As
there is no mention here of the utterance of praise being in any
other language than those with which the speakers were familiar,
there is no ground for assuming that this feature of the Pente-
costal gift was reproduced, and the jubilant ecstatic praise which
was the essence of that gift must be thought of as corresponding to
the phenomena described in I. Cor. xiv. 7–9." It is less surprising to find Meyer expressing in substance the same opinion.
They both overlook the fact to which Alford calls attention, that
Peter, in describing the incident afterward, says: " God gave unto
them *the like gift as he did also unto us*" (chap. xi. 17), thus
identifying it with the gift of tongues bestowed on Pentecost. As
Luke has once described speaking in other tongues on Pentecost,
and showed that men of these other tongues understood the speakers, it was but natural that in his second reference to the same
phenomenon he should use a briefer form of expression; and if,
by "speaking in tongues," he does not mean other tongues than
were natural to the speakers, his words are without meaning."
The supposition that either this phenomenon or that mentioned
in the fourteenth chapter of First Corinthians was mere "jubilant ecstatic praise," not uttered in any human tongue, is to suppose that these inspired persons spoke nonsense; and it is far
more likely that the nonsense is with those who adopt this
supposition. See Alford's notes on the latter passage, and on
Acts ii. 4.

[2] See xix. 1–7; I. Cor. i. 4–6; xiv; Gal. iii. 1–6; I. Thess. v.
19, 20.

except the gift bestowed on the apostles on Pentecost; and thus it is actually classified by Peter farther on (xi. 15, 16). He says: " As I began to speak, the Holy Spirit fell on them, even as on us at the (beginning) And I remembered the word of the Lord, how that he said, John indeed baptized in water, but ye shall be baptized in the Holy Spirit." In these words he identifies it as a baptism in the Holy Spirit ; and these two are the only events that are thus designated in the New Testament. The one was the divine expression of the admission of the first Jews into the new Messianic kingdom, and the other, that of the first Gentiles.

The baptism of Cornelius and his friends in the Holy Spirit previous to their baptism in water has been urged as evidence that remission of sins takes place before baptism. It could furnish such evidence if remission of sins was simultaneous with the miraculous gift of the Spirit ; but such is not the case. In every other instance of a miraculous gift, remission of sins preceded it. This is true of the apostles on Pentecost, for they had long before been accepted disciples of Christ ; it is true of the Samaritans, for they had been baptized by Philip before the apostles sent Peter and John to them to impart the miraculous gift ; it is true of the twelve disciples in Ephesus, to whom Paul imparted this gift after he had baptized them (xix. 1–7) ; and it is true of all in the Corinthian church who had received similar gifts (I. Cor. i. 4–7 ; xii. 1–7). In none of these instances was it connected with remission of sins ; therefore such a connection can not be assumed in the present instance. If it be thought incongruous that this miraculous power should be manifested in persons whose sins are not forgiven, let it be remembered that it was (a miracle) wrought upon these persons for a purpose external to themselves (see below under 47, 48); and that, although they were unpardoned, they were godly persons according to Jewish faith. There is no greater incongruity, if the thought of incongruity could be tolerated at all, in their receiving a (momentary) miraculous gift of the Spirit, than in the previous mission of an angel to Cornelius to assure him that his prayers were heard and that his alms were had in remembrance by God.

This incident in the conversion of Cornelius can not in any way be held as a precedent for subsequent ages; for it was (certainly a miracle) and no miracles are now wrought. We may as well expect sinners now to see an angel, as Cornelius did, before their sins are forgiven, as to receive the Spirit as he did.

Vv. 47, 48. The true explanation of this unusual circumstance, though given most fully in Peter's speech recorded in the next chapter (xi. 15–18), is clearly implied in the following words: (47) Then answered Peter, Can any man forbid the water, that these should not be baptized, who have received the Holy Spirit as well as we? (47) And he commanded them to be baptized in the name of Jesus Christ. Then prayed they him to tarry certain days. There are two ways of ascertaining the purpose of an incident: the purpose may be stated; or we may learn what it is by the use which is made of it. Here there is no statement of the purpose of the gift of the Spirit; but Peter, who knew the purpose, plainly indicates what it was by the use which he makes of it. He uses it to remove from the minds of his Jewish companions any doubt which they might still entertain as to the propriety of baptizing Gentiles. This, then, is the purpose for which the miracle was wrought. Furthermore, we find Peter using it afterward in Jerusalem, to remove the same doubts from the minds of the Jewish brethren there (see last citation). Unquestionably, then, this was its purpose; and herein we find the reason why no such event as this ever occurred afterward, or is now to be expected; for when it was once demonstrated that uncircumcised Gentiles might be baptized, the question was settled forever, and needed not to be settled again.[1]

Before he was interrupted, Peter had proceeded with his discourse so far as to reach the subject of faith and the remission of sins; and baptism would have been the next word on his lips if he had continued according to the model of his sermon on Pentecost. The interruption, however, did not break the thread of his discourse; it only enabled him to advance with still greater confidence to the very conclusion which he had intended; for he first demands of the brethren whether any one could forbid baptism, and then commands the Gentiles to be baptized in the name of the Lord. Let us now recall the fact that Cornelius had been directed to send for Peter to hear words whereby he and all his house should be saved (xi. 14). Peter has come, and spoken these words. He has told the company of Christ, in whom they now believe. He has told them to be baptized, and it has been done. What the pious, prayerful, and almsgiving Cornelius had lacked of being a Christian

---

[1] On this point Dean Plumptre expresses himself in the following satisfactory manner: "The exceptional gift was bestowed in this instance to remove the scruples which 'those of the uncircumcision' might otherwise have felt as to admitting Gentiles, as such, to baptism; and having served that purpose, as a crucial instance, was never afterwards, so far as we know, repeated under like conditions" (*Com. in loco*).

has now been supplied, and nothing has been required of him but to believe in Christ and be baptized. This closes the account of another conversion, and it coincides in essential details with all that have gone before it in this narrative.

We should be glad to know more of Cornelius, so as to judge whether, even in times of peace, the profession of arms was considered by the apostles compatible with the service of the Prince of Peace. He is the only soldier of whose conversion we have an account in the New Testament, and of his subsequent career we know nothing. Not many years afterward the army in which he held a commission visited a most cruel and unjust war upon the Jews, and whether he continued in the service through that period we can never know in this life. Let it be noted, however, that this is an instance of a soldier becoming a Christian, not of a Christian be-becoming a soldier. It furnishes a precedent for the former, but not for the latter.

9. Peter's Defense for these Proceedings, xi. 1–18.

Vv. 1–3. The novel and startling scene which had transpired in Cæsarea was soon reported abroad. (1) Now the apostles and the brethren that were in Judea heard that the Gentiles also had received the word of God. (2) And when Peter was come to Jerusalem, they that were of the circumcision contended with him, saying, (3) Thou wentest in to men uncircumcised, and didst eat with them. While the persons who made this complaint against Peter are called "they of the circumcision," and are not said to include any of the apostles, it is clearly implied that the apostles, who in the first verse are said to have heard of Peter's proceedings, had not expressed any approval of it. They doubtless thought and felt as the brethren did who made the complaint. They are now to be enlightened on the subject, as Peter had been, and the method in which it was accomplished is very instructive.

Vv. 4–17. (5) But Peter began, and expounded the matter unto them in order, saying, I was in the city of Joppa praying: and in a trance I saw a vision, a certain vessel descending, as it were a great sheet let down from heaven by four corners; and it came even unto me: (6) upon which when I had fastened my eyes, I considered, and saw the four-footed beasts of the earth, and wild beasts, and creeping things and fowls of the heaven. (7) And I heard also a voice saying unto me, Rise, Peter; kill and eat. (8) But I said, Not so, Lord: for nothing common or unclean hath ever entered into my mouth. (9) But a voice answered a second time out of heaven, What God hath cleansed, make not thou common. (10) And this was done thrice; and all were drawn up again into heaven. (11) And behold, forthwith three men stood before the house in which we were, having been sent from Cæsarea unto me. (12) And the Spirit bade me go with them, making no distinction. And these six brethren also accompanied me; and we entered into the man's house: (13) and he told us how he had seen the angel standing in his house, and saying, Send to Joppa, and fetch Simon, whose surname is Peter: (14) who shall speak unto thee words, whereby thou shalt be saved, thou and all thy house. (15) And as I began to speak, the Holy Spirit fell on them, even as on us at the beginning. (16) And I remembered the word of the Lord, how that he said, John indeed baptized in water; but ye shall be baptized in the Holy Spirit. (17) If then God gave unto them the like gift as he did also unto us, when we believed on the Lord Jesus Christ, who was I, that I could withstand God? In this speech Peter confines himself to a careful recital of those incidents mentioned in the preceding chapter which came under his own observation, and to the conclusion which he deduces from them. His argument is, that after seeing the vision, hearing the voice, and receiving the order of the Spirit to go with the men sent for him, he properly went into the man's house; and that when he saw that the Gentiles whom he had begun to address were baptized in the Holy Spirit, he could not withstand God. By this last remark, taken in its historical connection, he certainly meant that he would have been withstanding God had he refused to baptize the persons, or had he made a difference in other respects between them and Jews. He does not mention the act of baptizing them, neither had it been mentioned by the complainants. The latter had mentioned only the offense of going into the house of Gentiles, and eating with them, leaving out the much graver fault of baptizing them, because, if the former were wrong, much worse was the latter. This was a case in which the less included the greater. In his answer, Peter in express terms justified going into the house, and, by a necessary implication, the act of baptizing them.

Ver. 18. The facts rehearsed by Peter had the same effect on the minds of the objectors that they had on that of Peter. (18) And when they heard these things, they held their peace, and glorified God, saying, Then to the Gentiles also hath God granted repentance unto life. Instead of being bigots, as they are sometimes said to have been, these Jewish brethren, who had been hitherto untaught on the relation of uncircumcised persons to the Church of God, accepted the truth as soon as they heard it : and they accepted it not murmuringly, as men who were forced to its acceptance, but joyfully, as men who were glad to be relieved from a conviction which had caused them anxiety. They not only "held their peace," but they "glorified God" for what they had learned.

In this section of the history we have a striking example of one of the ways in which the apostles were led into all the truth, according to the Lord's promise (Jno. xvi. 13). Peter did not know by virtue of his inspiration that the uncircumcised were to be admitted to baptism ; neither did the other apostles, after Peter had baptized some uncircumcised persons, know by virtue of their inspiration that he had done right. As a matter of course, the Holy Spirit could have illuminated all of their minds internally on this as on any other topic; but it chose, instead of this, to adopt a different method. By visions addressed to his eye, a voice addressed to his ear, messages sent to him through the command of an angel, reinforced by just one command from the Holy Spirit, Peter was guided into this new truth ; and by a verbal account of the same to his brethren, the latter were brought to the same light. The latter indeed were convinced by the same facts which convinced Peter ; the only difference being that the facts reached Peter through direct observation, while they reached the others through the words in which Peter recounted them. In precisely this way the power of all Scripture facts reaches the minds and hearts of men at the present day, and thus the Holy Spirit operates on us through the

word. This method had an obvious advantage in the
instance before us in that, the other brethren, both inspired and uninspired, were not dependent on Peter's
statement of an inward revelation to himself on this
important subject, a method which might have left some
in doubt; but they could see as clearly as Peter did, the
force of the evidence which convinced him. The consequence was that amid all the controversies which afterward disturbed some sections of the church in connection
with circumcision, no doubt was ever afterward intimated of the propriety of baptizing uncircumcised
Gentiles.

SEC. IV.—A CHURCH FOUNDED IN ANTIOCH, AND ANOTHER PERSECUTION IN JERUSALEM.

(XI. 19—XII. 25.)

1. BEGINNING OF THE WORK IN ANTIOCH, 19–21.

Vv. 19–21. Our author, in pursuance of the plan of
this part of his work, now turns back once more to the
dispersion of the Jerusalem church, and surveys rapidly
another section of the wide field before him. (19) They
therefore that were scattered abroad upon the tribulation
that arose about Stephen, traveled as far as Phœnicia,
and Cyprus, and Antioch, speaking the word to none
save only to Jews. (20) But there were some of them,
men of Cyprus and Cyrene, who, when they were come
to Antioch, spake unto the Greeks also, preaching the
Lord Jesus. (21) And the hand of the Lord was with
them: and a great number that believed turned unto the

Lord. From these verses we learn that while Philip was preaching in Samaria, Saul in Damascus and Arabia, and Peter, a little later, in all parts of Judea, Samaria and Galilee, other brethren were evangelizing among the Jews as far north as Phœnicia, the island of Cyprus, and the famous city of Antioch, the last being their farthest point in that direction. In preaching to " none save only to Jews" these brethren were but following the example of the apostles, until Peter opened the door to the Gentiles, as described in the last section. The statement that some of these, when they came to Antioch, preached also to the Greeks, limits this latter preaching, as respects the places named, to Antioch. It was not till they reached Antioch that they began to preach to Greeks. It appears also that these men came to Antioch at a latter period than did those who spoke only to Jews. It is clearly implied that something had taken place in the interval to cause this change; and as the last preceding series of events mentioned by Luke is connected with the baptism of Gentiles by Peter, he seems to have desired his readers to infer that this latter event preceded the preaching to Greeks in Antioch. This probability is reduced almost to certainty when we look to the chronology of these events. It is well ascertained that the death of Herod, mentioned in the twelfth chapter, occurred in the year 44 A. D.; and we learn from our present chapter that Barnabas and Saul labored together in Antioch one whole year previous to that event (26). Barnabas brought Saul to Antioch, then, in the year 43 ; and the statements of verses 22–25 below imply that the former had not been many months in Antioch before he went for Saul ; consequently, Barnabas must have been sent from Jerusalem not earlier than the latter part of the year 42. But he was sent as soon as the brethren in Jerusalem learned of the successful preaching in Antioch; and consequently we must conclude that the latter part of this preaching, that to the Greeks, had not taken place earlier than the early part of 42, or the last of 41; and as the baptism of Cornelius occurred in 40 or 41, this event preceded the preaching to Greeks in Antioch.[1] Thus the conclusion which is naturally suggested by the order of Luke's narrative is that which the closest investigation establishes, that uncircumcised Gentiles were not baptized until after Peter opened the door to them in Cæsarea. But while Peter's work opened the way, this work in Antioch was the first vigorous invasion of the Gentile world by the advanced forces of the Lord's army.

The preaching in Phœnicia here mentioned, suggests the origin of the churches which are afterward found there;[2] and the fact that the preachers who first spoke to Greeks in Antioch were from Cyprus and Cyrene suggests the probability that they had first done some preaching in their own homes, before going upon these foreign missions. This they had an abundance of time to do, in the five or six years which had passed since the death of Stephen. It is possible, as many have suggested, that Simon of Cyrene, who bore the cross of Jesus part of the way to Golgotha, was one of these Cyrenian preachers. In the words, "a great number that believed turned unto the Lord," we have a recognition of the fact that turning to the Lord is a different act from believing, and subsequent to it. As in iii. 19, where turning to the Lord follows repentance, the

---

[1] See the Chronology of Acts, p. xxviii. [2] Chap. xv. 3; xxi. 3, 4; xxvii. 3.

specific reference is to baptism, which is the turning act. An equivalent expression, used elsewhere, would be, a great number " believed and were baptized."[1]

2. BARNABAS IS SENT TO ANTIOCH, 22–24.

Vv. 22–24. Jerusalem was still the center and base of operations, being the headquarters of the apostles. The latter kept watch over all the movements of the other preachers, and sent help or counsel according to circumstances. Even when no apostles were present in the mother church, they doubtless made provision for such oversight by other competent persons. (22) **And the report concerning them came to the ears of the church which was in Jerusalem: and they sent forth Barnabas as far as Antioch: (23) who, when he was come, and had seen the grace of God, was glad; and he exhorted them all, that with purpose of heart they should cleave unto the Lord: (24) for he was a good man, and full of the Holy Spirit and of faith: and much people was added unto the Lord.** It is not often that Luke pronounces an encomium on persons of whom he speaks, as he does here on Barnabas; but it was proper that the selection of the latter for this important mission should be justified by mention of the noble qualities which led to the choice. The purpose of his mission can be learned only by the work which he did in Antioch; and from this we learn that it was somewhat different from that of the mission of Peter and John to Samaria. It was not to impart miraculous spiritual gifts, which Barnabas had not the power to impart; but to do that for which Barnabas was famous, and from his superiority in which he had derived his present name—to exhort the brethren

---

[1] Chap. xviii. 8.

BAR-WARS

to cleave unto the Lord. The brethren in Jerusalem well knew the need of such exhortation to young disciples, and they sent for the purpose their best exhorter. Observe, too, that while he was exhorting the brethren, many who were not brethren became such. After men are convinced that Jesus is the Christ, they are very frequently brought to repentance and obedience by hearing exhortations addressed to the disciples.

3. Barnabas Brings Saul to Antioch, 25, 26.

Vv. 25, 26. Barnabas seems to have been engaged but a short time in these labors, when he felt the need of help more efficient than that of his predecessors, if they were still present, and for reasons not stated in the text his thoughts turned toward Saul, the former persecutor, whom he had befriended in Jerusalem. All that he knew of Saul's work since the brethren in Jerusalem had sent him away to Tarsus was the report which had come to Jerusalem: "He that once persecuted us now preacheth the faith of which he once made havoc" (Gal. i. 23); unless he had heard more since coming to Antioch, which is quite probable. At any rate, of all the men who were accessible to him, Saul was his choice for the work which was now opening in this great city,[1]

---

[1] I can not introduce the city of Antioch to the reader unacquainted with its history so well as by quoting the following graphic description of it by Farrar: "The queen of the East, the third metropolis of the world, this vast city of perhaps five hundred thousand souls must not be judged by the diminished, shrunken and earthquake-shattered Antakieh of to-day. It was no mere oriental town, with flat roofs and dingy, narrow streets, but a Greek capital, enriched and enlarged by Roman magnificence. It is situated at the point of junction between the chains of Lebanon and Taurus. Its natural position on the northern slope of Mount

and so we read: (25) **And he went forth to Tarsus to
seek for Saul.** (26) **And when he had found him, he
brought him unto Antioch. And it came to pass that
even for a whole year they were gathered together with
the church, and taught much people ; and that the disciples were called Christians first in Antioch.** The united
labors of two such men for a whole year, in a community
to which the gospel had already been favorably introduced, could not fail of great results ; and the ultimate
results were far beyond any hope which they could then
have entertained ; for they were now erecting as it were
the second capital of the Christian world, whence were

Silpius, with a navigable river, the broad, historic Orontes, flowing
at its feet, was at once commanding and beautiful. The windings
of the river enriched the whole wooded plain, and as the city was
but sixteen miles from the shore, the sea breezes gave health and
coolness. These natural advantages had been largely increased
by the lavish genius of ancient art. Built by the Seleucidæ as
the royal residence of their dynasty, its wide circuit of many
miles was surrounded by walls of astonishing height and thick-
ness, which had been carried across ravines and over mountain
summits with such daring magnificence of conception as to give
the city the aspect of being defended by its own encircling mountains, as though these gigantic bulwarks were but its natural
walls. The palace of the kings of Syria was on an island formed
by an artificial channel of the river. Through the entire length
of the city, from the Golden or Daphne gate on the west, ran for
nearly five miles a grand corso, adorned with trees, colonnades
and statues. Originally constructed by Seleucus Nicator, it had
been continued by Herod the Great, who, at once to gratify his
passion for architecture and to reward the people for their good
will towards the Jews, had paved it for two miles and a half with
blocks of white marble. Broad bridges spanned the river and its
various affluents ; baths, basilicas, villas, theaters clustered on
the level plain, and overshadowed by picturesque and rugged
eminences, gave the city a splendor worthy of its fame as only
inferior in grandeur to Alexandria and Rome."

sent forth not long afterward the most fruitful missions of the apostolic age.

The new name which here and now originated proved the most potent name that has ever been applied to a body of men. The question, who originated it, whether Barnabas and Saul, or the disciples of Antioch, or the unbelievers of Antioch, has occasioned more discussion than its importance justifies. To an untrained reader of the Greek it might appear that the passage should be rendered, " they were gathered together with the church, and taught much people, and called the disciples Christians first at Antioch," thus representing Barnabas and Saul as the authors of the name ; but this rendering is condemned, and that of our text is justified by the almost unanimous judgment of scholars. To call the followers of Christ Christians is so obviously proper and natural that it might have occurred to almost any one acquainted with the Greek language ; and this renders it difficult to decide whether it was given by unbelievers, or by the disciples themselves. In favor of the former supposition is the fact that bodies of men very commonly receive the names by which they are permanently known from others ; but the supposition adopted by many, that this name was given by the enemies of the faith in derision, is groundless, as is very clear from the consideration that there is nothing in it belittling or contemptuous. It is just such a name as a number of grave and dignified friends of the cause, had they been sitting in council on the subject, may have adopted. For its divine approval, we need no other assurance than that found in its acceptance by the apostles. True, in the only later occurrences of it in the New Testament, it appears as the name by which the disciples were called, rather than that by which they called themselves ;[1] but it is only natural that in the epistles, which are all addressed to Christians, other and more intimate titles should be usually employed.[2]

4. BARNABAS AND SAUL ARE SENT TO JUDEA, 27–30.

Vv. 27–30. As the husbandman annually exchanges the labor of tillage for that of gathering in his harvest, so Barnabas and Saul, after a year's toil in preaching and teaching, laid aside that work for awhile, in order to bear some of the fruits of the benevolence which they had cultivated to the suffering in another country. (37) Now in those days there came down prophets from Jerusalem unto Antioch. (28) And there stood up one of them named Agabus, and signified by the Spirit that there should be a great famine over all the world : which came to pass in the days of Claudius. (29) And the disciples, every man according to his ability, determined to send relief unto the brethren who dwelt in Judea : (30) which also they did, sending it to the elders by the hand of Barnabas and Saul. This is the first mention of the gift of prophecy among the disciples, but Agabus and his companions seem to have been already well known as prophets, which shows that their gift had been previously exercised. The conduct of the brethren at Antioch shows also that the predictions uttered by these prophets were implicitly believed ; for they did not wait till the predicted famine had actually set in, but they made pro-

---

[1] See chap. xxvi. 28, where it is found in the lips of king Agrippa II. ; and I. Peter iv. 16, were Peter uses it as the name under which the disciples were persecuted.

[2] For a discussion of the significance and value of names for the followers of Christ, see Excursus, Vol. II.

vision for it in advance. This prompt action on their part, which seems to have been spontaneous, and not to have sprung from exhortations by Barnabas and Saul, is the more to their credit, from the consideration that the famine was to extend over their own country, and the world generally, as well as over Judea. Had they been characterized by the selfishness of our own age, they would have said, Let us see first how severe the famine is going to be with ourselves and our immediate neighbors; and then, if we have anything to spare, we will send it to our more distant brethren. They indulged in no such selfish parleying; but, knowing that in the crowded population of Judea, where there was more poverty at best than in the region around Antioch, which was made rich by foreign trade, a famine would be more distressing than here, they determined at once to take the risk for themselves, and to make sure at all hazard of relieving their poorer brethren. It is clear that they understood the wonderful benevolence of the Jerusalem church, not as a fanatical outburst of communism, but as an example to be imitated under like circumstances by all Christians. Barnabas and Saul could well afford to suspend for a few weeks their work of preaching and teaching for the purpose of promoting a benevolent enterprise such as the world had seldom or never witnessed before. There is no preaching so eloquent as that which sounds out from whole-hearted benevolence.

The manner in which the elders of the churches in Judea are here mentioned, without a previous notice of their having been appointed, shows the elliptical character of Luke's narrative, and it results from the circumstance that he wrote after the churches had been fully organized, and all of the officials and their duties had become well known. The elders, being the rulers of the congregations, were the proper persons to receive the gifts, and to see to the proper distribution of them among the needy.

5. James is Beheaded and Peter is Imprisoned, xii. 1–11.

Vv. 1, 2. The historian does not follow Barnabas and Saul in their tour of the churches of Judea, but, leaving them in this work, he turns into Jerusalem, and introduces a thrilling episode concerning affairs then transpiring in that city. (1) Now about that time Herod the king put forth his hand to afflict certain of the church. (2) And he killed James the brother of John with the sword. The persecutions which we have hitherto noticed were conducted by religious partisans in Jerusalem, without assistance from the civil rulers; but here is one in which the reigning prince is the leader, while the old enemies of the truth are working behind the curtain, if at all. This Herod was a namesake of Agrippa, the noted minister of Augustus Cæsar whose life by Tacitus is one of the noblest of Latin classics, and he was commonly called Agrippa. He was a grandson of the Herod *the Great* by whom the infants of Bethlehem were slaughtered, and a nephew of Herod the Tetrarch by whom John the Baptist was beheaded. He grew up in Rome, where he wasted what fortune he had inherited in princely extravagance; but while doing so he contracted an intimacy with Caius Cæsar, afterward the notorious Emperor Caligula. When the latter ascended the throne after the death of Tiberius, he elevated his friend Agrippa to a small kingdom composed of part of his grandfather's dominions, which was subsequently enlarged by Claudius

until it included all of the territory ruled by the first
Herod. He was now in the zenith of his power, and
was living in the utmost magnificence.[1] There is not a
hint as to the exciting cause of this murder; and there
are so many causes which may have instigated it that
conjecture in regard to it is vain. A more profitable
subject for reflection is the very singular fact that God
could so soon spare from the world and the church one
of the apostles, when he had only twelve; for this death
occurred only about ten years after the death of Jesus.
Surely James had accomplished but a very small part of
the work which had been assigned to him and his fellow
apostles in the great commission, when God permitted
his life to be suddenly and cruelly cut off. How striking
an illustration of the oft-repeated saying, that God's
ways are not as our ways. And how distinctly must
James have remembered, when his head was placed on
the block, what Jesus had predicted of himself and his
brother John on a memorable occasion when their ambition got the better of them.[2] By this time he understood better than then what it is to sit on the right hand
of Jesus in his kingdom.

The death of James, the first apostle who suffered
martyrdom, must have been a source of indescribable
grief to the church in Jerusalem; and to an uninspired
historian it would have furnished matter for many pages
of eloquent writing: what shall we think, then, of Luke
as a writer, who disposes of it in a sentence of seven
words in Greek, represented by eleven in English?
Surely there is an indication here of some supernatural

---

[1] For a full and most interesting account of his career, see
Josephus' Antiquities, Books xviii., xix.

[2] Matt. xx. 20-28.

restraint upon the impulses of the writer, and it is accounted for only by his inspiration.

Vv. 3–5. A man engaged in a wicked enterprise is often made timid by conscience when left to himself; but when applauded by the multitude he is emboldened to press forward in his mad career. Agrippa may have hesitated when he had shed the blood of an apostle—a crime which none of the previous persecutors in Jerusalem had dared to perpetrate; but when the people applauded he hesitated no longer. (3) And when he saw that it pleased the Jews, he proceeded to seize Peter also. And those were the days of unleavened bread. (4) And when he had taken him, he put him in prison, and delivered him to four quaternions of soldiers to guard him; intending after the passover to bring him forth to the people. (5) Peter therefore was kept in the prison, but prayer was made earnestly of the church unto God for him. Evidently the king was seeking the destruction of the Jerusalem church, as the Pharisees, under the leadership of Saul, had done before; but, in contrast with their method, he sought to accomplish his purpose by beheading the leaders, rather than by persecuting the members. He doubtless congratulated himself on the wisdom of the new method, when he had succeeded in slaying one apostle, and in locking up, ready for execution, the chief man of them all. He must have heard of a previous imprisonment of the twelve, and of their escape from the prison in the night without the knowledge of the guards (v. 17–23); so he determined to improve upon the method of confinement then adopted, as well as upon the general method of the persecution. Not content with confining Peter in a prison whose outer gate was of iron (10), he added a guard of sixteen soldiers, some of whom he placed in front of that gate (6), and some at two distinct points between the gate and the cell in which Peter was confined (10). Finally, to make surety doubly sure, he had him bound with two chains to two soldiers, between whom he slept (6). When all these precautions had been taken, he doubtless said to the chief priests, I will show you how to keep a prisoner. Let him get out of my hands, if he can.

In the earnest prayer which the church was now making for Peter, the brethren were but following the example of the apostles themselves at the time of their first persecution (iv. 23–30). We have reason to believe that they were not praying for his release; for they well knew that without miraculous interposition this was impossible; and as God had not thus rescued James, they had no reason to believe that he would thus rescue Peter. Moreover, when he was released, as we see below (13–15), they were so far from expecting it or hoping for it, that they could not at first believe it, as they would have been ready to do had they been praying for it. It was most natural under the circumstances that their petition to God should take a different direction; for, remembering how Peter had once faltered in the presence of imminent danger, and fully expecting that he would now be required to face the block, they had good cause to pray that his faith and courage might not fail him in the final crisis, but that, like Stephen and like James, as we may suppose, he might glorify the Lord by a triumphant death.

Vv. 6–11. Time wore away in painful suspense until the last night of the Passover week, and this night was to the brethren the most painful one of all; but though Peter was undoubtedly expecting to die the next morning, he seems to have slept as soundly as the soldiers to whom he was chained.) (6) **And when Herod was about to bring him forth, the same night Peter was sleeping between two soldiers, bound with two chains : and guards before the door kept the prison. (7) And behold, an angel of the Lord stood by him, and a light shined in the prison cell : and he smote Peter on the side, and awoke him, saying, Arise up quickly. And his chains fell off from his hands. (8) And the angel said unto him, Gird thyself, and bind on thy sandals. And he did so. And he said unto him, Cast thy garment about thee, and follow me. (9) And he went out, and followed ; and he knew not that it was true which was done by the angel, but thought he saw a vision. (10) And when they were passed the first and second ward, they came unto the iron gate that leadeth into the city ; which opened to them of its own accord, and they went out, and passed on through one street ; and straightway the angel departed from him. (11) And when Peter was come to himself, he said, Now I know of a truth, that the Lord hath sent forth his angel, and delivered me out of the hand of Herod, and from all the expectation of the people of the Jews.** It is no wonder that Peter thought he was dreaming while this deliverance was being accomplished, or that it required the sight of the moon [1] and stars above him, and of the houses around him, to convince him that he was actually out of prison. No miracle more complicated or more unexpected had ever been wrought.

---

[1] As the paschal lamb was eaten at the time of full moon, being the night between the fourteenth and fifteenth day of the lunar month, and as this deliverance was on the seventh night afterward, the moon was just a week past the full ; and as this was the dry season, it was almost certainly visible.

6. Peter Leaves the City, and the Guards are Slain, 12-19.

Vv. 12–16. After coming to himself Peter was not long in deciding what to do. Either because the house of Mary was the nearest among the homes of the disciples, or because of the well known character of its inmates, or both, he went immediately thither. (12) And when he had considered the thing, he came to the house of Mary the mother of John whose surname was Mark ; where many were gathered together and were praying. (13) And he knocked at the door of the gate,[1] and a maid[2] came to answer named Rhoda. (14) And when she knew Peter's voice, she opened not the door for joy, but ran in and told that Peter stood before the gate. (15) And they said unto her, Thou art mad. But she confidently affirmed that it was even so. And they said, It is his angel. (16) But Peter continued knocking: and when they had opened, they saw him, and were amazed. Mary was not only the mother of Mark, doubtless the Mark of the second Gospel, but also an aunt of Barnabas (Col. iv. 10). She was apparently a widow in good circumstances financially, and her commodious house was a place of resort for the brethren

---

[1] "The door of the gate," though an unmeaning expression with us, is strictly accurate as here used ; for the entrance to large houses in Palestine is through large folding gateways, wide enough for loaded animals to pass in, while, for the admission of persons when the large gate is closed, there is a small door through one of the folds of the gate, just large enough to admit one person at a time.

[2] The Greek word, παιδίσκη, here rendered "maid," commonly means a young female slave. Whether slave or hired servant, Rhoda seems to have been in full sympathy with the inmates of the house in regard to Peter.

of the church. The many who were gathered together there that night were by no means all the church, as some writers suppose; for the church was at this time far too numerous to be collected in a single private residence. This was probably one of many houses in which brethren were gathered together praying on what all supposed to be the last night of Peter's life. Few nights more solemn had ever been experienced by the brethren of that oft persecuted church. The unwillingness of those in Mary's house to believe the words of Rhoda, and their amazement when they saw Peter with their own eyes, were but natural under the circumstances; and doubtless the same incredulity was manifested by other groups of brethren in the city, as the news gradually came to them during the rest of the night, and early the next morning. The thought, before they saw him, that it must be his angel, is based on the supposition that every man has an angel, which is a true Scriptural idea;[1] and that this angel might sometimes assume the voice and personal appearance of his ward, which is doubtless a superstition.

VER. 17. The deliverance of Peter by the angel was a clear indication that it was God's will that he should flee from his enemies, and his plans to this end were promptly formed. His visit to the house of Mary was for the purpose of relieving the anxiety of his brethren; but the greatest secrecy was necessary in order to prevent his plans from being frustrated, so his stay at Mary's house was but momentary. (17) But he, beckoning unto them with his hand to hold their peace, declared unto them how the Lord had brought him forth out of the prison. And he said, Tell these things unto James and

_____

[1] Matt. xviii. 10; Heb. i. 14.

to the brethren. And he departed, and went to another place. Silence was necessary in order to prevent arousing some of the neighbors, who might learn what was going on and report to the authorities. James, and the brethren generally, were to be told of the release, in order that their anxiety for Peter both now and on the morrow might be allayed. The manner in which James is mentioned shows that he, since the death of the elder James, and in the absence of Peter, was the chief man of the church. The probability is that this was not James the sons of Alphæus, one of the twelve, but James the Lord's brother.[1] The "other place" into which Peter now went was doubtless some other place than Jerusalem; for in the latter it would be very difficult for him to safely hide himself. He purposely avoided telling the brethren where he was going, so that they could truthfully say, if questioned, that they did not know; and it is by no means certain that Luke had learned where it was when he wrote this narrative. When Peter appeared in Jerusalem again there was doubtless great curiosity among friends and foes alike to know where he had been concealed; but prudence even then may have suggested that he should keep the secret to himself.

Vv. 18, 19. Naturally the morning light brought great confusion to the soldiers; first to the two between

---

[1] He is the James who was associated with Peter in Jerusalem at the time of Paul's first visit to the city after his conversion (Gal. i. 19): and also with Peter and John, as the context in Galatians would indicate, in the conference about circumcision (chap. ii. 9); and at this time, intermediate between the two, it is a fair presumption that we have the same James. Of the apostle James, Acts furnishes us no information after the first dispersion of the Jerusalem church.

whom he had been chained, and afterward to them all. Herod, too, was surprised and chagrined. He learned that he had no more skill in keeping apostles imprisoned than had the chief priests before him. (18) Now as soon as it was day, there was no small stir among the soldiers, what was become of Peter. (19) And when Herod had sought for him, and found him not, he examined the guards, and commanded that they should be put to death. And he went down from Judea to Cæsarea, and tarried there. According to the strict letter of Roman military law, the execution of the soldiers was a necessity. When those standing in front of the gate were examined, we can see that the only answer they could give was, We kept our post all night, we remained wide awake, and no one passed in or out of that gate. When the man who kept the key of the iron gate was called, he truthfully said that it had not been out of his hand, nor had it been placed in the lock. The two guards between the outer door and Peter's cell were positive that no one had passed by them during the night; and the two to whom Peter had been chained could only say, When we went to sleep he was here with the chains all secure, and when we awoke he was gone; and that is all we know. Of course none of these statements could be true unless a stupendous miracle had been wrought; and there was absolutely no alternative but to admit the miracle, or to hold that all of the soldiers had conspired together to voluntarily release the prisoner. The last horn of the dilemma could not be accepted by any sane man, seeing that the soldiers knew perfectly well that their lives would pay the forfeit of such a release. It seems then impossible to believe that Herod doubted the reality of the miracle, or the truthfulness of the soldiers; but he was determined not to admit the miracle, and he deliberately chose in preference to murder sixteen innocent men. There was not a man in Jerusalem who could doubt the true state of the case when the facts became known. No wonder that the bloody wretch soon left the scene of so foul a crime, and made Cæsarea his place of residence.

7. The Death of Herod, and the Return of Barnabas and Saul, 20–25.

Vv. 20–23. Our author continues the history of this murderous prince to its close. (20) Now he was highly displeased with them of Tyre and Sidon : and they came with one accord to him, and, having made Blastus the king's chamberlain their friend, they asked for peace, because their country was fed from the king's country. (21) And upon a set day Herod arrayed himself in royal apparel, and sat on his throne, and made an oration to them. (22) And the people shouted, saying, the voice of a God, and not of a man. (23) And immediately an angel of the Lord smote him, because he gave not God the glory : and he was eaten of worms, and gave up the spirit. The dependence of Tyre and Sidon on Herod's country for food was not absolute ; for their own territory produced some grain, and Egypt was not very far away ; but the territory of Phœnicia was only a narrow mountain range along the seashore, altogether insufficient for the support of these two large cities, and it was much cheaper to bring the additional supply from the country adjoining theirs than from Egypt ; so, as a matter of public policy, peace with the former was much to be desired. It seems that those who came to Cæsarea to secure this peace were not a small body of ambassadors, but quite a multitude of the citizens. It was probably by bribery that they made Blastus the chamberlain (treasurer) their friend, and it may be that through him some of the money reached the king. Josephus, who gives a more detailed account of Herod's death, says that the occasion of this oration, here called " a set day," was a festival which Herod was celebrating in honor of Claudius Cæsar; and that the royal apparel in which Herod was arrayed was a robe woven entirely out of silver, which glistened in the morning sun. He also says that Herod was seized with violent pains in the bowels, and that he lingered in great torture for five days. His account, though containing some details besides these given by Luke, and omitting some which Luke gives, contains nothing inconsistent with what is here said.[1] Thus was the righteous judgment of God, which is usually reserved for the future state, displayed in this world, as a warning to wicked men, and an encouragement to those who do well.

VER. 24. It was inevitable that this providential death of Herod, so soon after the murders which he had committed in Jerusalem, should seriously affect the public mind. We are not surprised, therefore, when Luke adds: (24) But the word of God grew and multiplied. It grew in the reverence with which the people regarded it, and it multiplied in the increase of its converts to the truth. Another formidable and boldly executed plot to destroy the faith in Christ only advanced it among the people, as all the others had done.

VER. 25. The account which we have just gone over, of the death of James, the imprisonment of Peter, and the miserable death of Herod, is thrown in between the arrival of Barnabas and Saul on their mission to the

---

[1] Antiquities, xix. 8.

poor saints, and their return to Antioch; and the author seems to mean by this arrangement that these events occurred in this interval. Whether Barnabas and Saul went into Jerusalem to attend the passover which was being observed while Peter was in prison, is not stated; and it is most probable that, on account of the danger imminent, they kept away. But after Herod left the city this danger was diminished, so before their return to Antioch they entered the city, though it is not probable that they found there either Peter or any of the other apostles. (25) **And Barnabas and Saul returned from Jerusalem, when they had fulfilled their ministration, taking with them John whose surname was Mark.** Here we are first introduced to the son of the Mary to whose house Peter went when released from prison by the angel. He was doubtless at home on that memorable night; he was Peter's son in the Gospel;[1] and he must have been very deeply impressed by the events of that passover. The Gospel which he afterward wrote furnishes none of his personal history, but we shall meet with him again more than once in this narrative. On returning to Antioch, Barnabas and Saul had very startling news to tell, in addition to their report concerning the mission on which they had been sent.

Here the second part of Acts comes to a close, and with it Luke's account of the general spread of the gospel. From this point his narrative is confined to certain prominent events in the career of the apostle Paul, and it assumes the character of a biography.

I. Peter v. 13.

EXCURSUS A.

CONNECTION OF BAPTISM WITH REMISSION OF SINS.

The thought of any connection at all between baptism and remission of sins is repulsive to many Protestants of the present age. This state of feeling is largely due, I am constrained to believe, to a misconception of the nature of remission of sins. The latter is confounded with a change of heart, and is supposed to be a renewing of the soul effected by the direct agency of the Holy Spirit. It is regarded as an inward experience, a matter of consciousness; and men are taught to look within themselves for the evidence of it, and to find that evidence in the state of joy which immediately succeeds it. To one who has this conception of remission of sins, and of the agency by which it is brought about, it must necessarily appear absurd to suppose that it is in any way dependent on baptism, unless, with the Romanists, we attach to baptism some kind of magical power to effect a change in the soul.

But this conception of remission of sins is a mistaken one. It is not found in the New Testament. On the contrary, remission of sins is clearly distinguished from that change within which we commonly style a change of heart. This latter change takes place in repentance; for in the course of repentance the love of sin is removed, sorrow for it intervenes, the love of righteousness springs up, and there is a deep resolve to sin no more. But repentance is constantly distinguished in the Scriptures from remission of sins, and the latter is constantly assumed to be consequent upon the former, not included in it. This is seen in the frequent occurrence of the expression, "repentance and remission of sins." It is also seen in such expressions as these: "The baptism of repentance unto remission of sins" (Mark i. 4; Luke iii. 3); "Repent and be baptized every one of you in the name of Jesus Christ unto the remission of your sins" (Acts ii. 38). Here is not only a very marked distinction between the two, but remission of sins is most clearly set forth as subsequent to repentance."

This mistaken conception is still further corrected, and the true idea brought out, by observing the meaning of the word rendered remission (ἄφεσις). As defined in the lexicons, it means, primarily, "release, as from bondage, imprisonment, etc. Secondarily, when connected with sins, it means, forgiveness, pardon of sins (properly, the letting them go, as if they had not been committed), remission of their penalty."[1] It is used in its primary sense in the quotation from the Septuagint, Luke iv. 18, 19, where it occurs twice in the sense of deliverance or liberation of captives. It is used in its secondary sense everywhere else in the New Testament, and in one place (Mark iii. 29, "hath never forgiveness") the term forgiveness is its only admissible rendering in English. But forgiveness, pardon, is not an act which takes place within the soul of the person who is guilty; it takes place within the mind of the person who forgives, and it can not be known to the person forgiven except by some medium of communication. This is obviously true

---

[1] Grimm. *Greek Lexicon N. T.*; also Trench, *Greek Synonyms*, *sub verbo*

when one man forgives another; and when it is God who forgives, it is an act of the divine mind in reference to the sinner, and not a change within the sinner himself. Furthermore, it is an act which, from its very nature, can not take place until there has already occurred within the sinner such a change of heart and purpose as can make it proper in God, even on the ground of atonement in Christ, to extend pardon. In other words, the whole inward change which the sinner is required to undergo, must take place before sin can be forgiven. This being true, the apparent absurdity of connecting remission of sins in some way with baptism is removed, and it is left an open question, whether, in addition to faith and repentance, God also requires baptism before forgiveness. To the minds of the majority of present-day Protestants, the mere announcement of this question brings up the objection that justification is by faith only, and that the possibility of baptism being a prerequisite is by this fact excluded. But while justification, which involves remission of sins, is undoubtedly dependent on faith as a condition, it is nowhere said or implied that it is dependent on faith alone; that is, on faith apart from the outward manifestations of faith. If justification is withheld until faith manifests itself in some outward action, the sinner is still justified by faith, but it is by faith in action as distinguished from faith as a mere state of mind. Abraham is the typical example of justification by faith; yet what we have just said is true of him, as his case is expounded by the apostle James. He says: " Was not Abraham our father justified by works, in that he offered up his son Isaac upon the altar? Thou seest that faith wrought with his works, and by works was faith made perfect; and the Scripture was fulfilled which saith, And Abraham believed God, and it was reckoned unto him for righteousness" (ii. 21-23). Here the apostle, instead of seeing an inconsistency between justification by faith and justification by faith manifested in an act of faith, holds the latter in the case of Abraham to be the fulfillment of the former. In other words, the Scripture statement that Abraham believed God, and it was reckoned unto him for righteousness, was realized when Abraham by faith offered up his son on the altar. In precisely the same way, and in perfect harmony with justification by faith, a man may be justified by faith when, as an act of faith, he is baptized. The question is still open, then, whether this is the fact in the case.

It is still further objected that some statements respecting faith, not included in those connecting it with justification, exclude the possibility of forgiveness being connected with baptism. For example: "God so loved the world, that he gave his only begotten Son, that whosoever believeth on him should not perish, but have eternal life" (Jno. iii. 16); and, "He that believeth on the Son hath eternal life" (*ib.* 34). Here it is plainly affirmed that the believer is in possession of eternal life; but it is still an open question whether this is affirmed of the obedient believer, or of the believer who has not yet manifested his faith by action; whether, to use James' phraseology, it is faith made perfect by works of faith, or faith yet silent in the soul. This question is to be determined, not by such general statements as these, but by specific statements as to the conditions on which forgiveness of sins is offered.

The persistent objector has yet another set of texts which, to him, preclude the connection of which we speak, texts in which justification is affirmed of faith without works of law. For example: "We reckon therefore that a man is justified by faith apart from the works of the law;" or, leaving out the articles, "apart from works of law" (Rom. iii. 28). But by works of law in this place Paul means such acts of obedience to law as would justify a man on the ground of innocence, and make him independent of the grace manifested in pardon. Now, acts of faith, such as the offering of Isaac on the altar, do not belong to this category. On the contrary, this act of Abraham, viewed in the light of law, would have been a crime. The same is true of the act of Rahab in receiving the spies and protecting them, which James specifies as the act by which she was justified (Jas. ii. 25). This act, viewed in the light of law, was treason, while that of Abraham was murder. Now baptism is certainly an act of faith, deriving its propriety from a positive command; and not a work of law in the sense attached to that expression by Paul; consequently, it may be required of a believer to be baptized before he is forgiven, and yet justification may be apart from "works of law."

All connection between baptism and remission of sins is supposed to be precluded on still another ground, the fact that salvation is a matter of grace and not of works: "For by grace have ye been saved through faith; and that not of yourselves: it is the gift of God: not of works, that no man should glory" (Eph. ii. 8, 9). But here again, as in the epistle to the Romans, the works excluded from the ground of salvation are works of perfect obedience, by which, if any man had wrought them, he would be saved on the ground of merit. This would exclude grace. But remission of sins is in its very nature a grace bestowed, and not a debt paid; and whether it is bestowed on certain conditions or on no condition, it remains a matter of grace. Only in case the works done are of such a nature that the person doing them deserves salvation, can grace be excluded; and in that case there would be no remission, because there would be no sins to be remitted. So, then, if God has seen fit to require the believer to be baptized before he forgives him, forgiveness is none the less a matter of grace than if he made no such requirement. When a state executive pardons a criminal, no one ever thinks of saying it is not an act of grace because the criminal is required, as a condition, to sign a pledge never to repeat his crime; and if it were a case of theft, and the governor should require a restoration of the stolen property as a condition of pardon, no one would think of denying that the pardon was an act of grace.

Seeing now that a connection between baptism and remission of sins is not precluded by any of the doctrinal statements of the Scriptures, which have so commonly been supposed to have this force, we are at liberty to examine without prejudice those passages of Scripture which seem to declare such a connection, and to ascertain, if possible, what that connection is. First, then, we examine some passages which plainly teach that remission of sins follows baptism in order of time.

Foremost among these is Peter's well-known answer, in his Pentecost sermon, to the question, "Brethren, what shall we do?" It is foremost, because this is the first time that Peter, making use of the keys which had been committed to him (Matt. xvi. 19), opened the gates of the kingdom to believers by declaring what they should do to find admittance. He said, "Repent ye, and be baptized every one of you in the name of Jesus Christ unto the remission of your sins; and ye shall receive the gift of the Holy Spirit." Here, as we have pointed out in the commentary under this passage, whether the preposition be rendered *unto, for,* or *in order to,* remission of sins is unmistakingly placed after repentance and baptism. No words can make this more certain. The same connection precisely is stated in almost identical terms by both Mark and Luke with reference to the baptism of John. They both say that John preached " the baptism of repentance unto the remission of sins" (Mark i. 4; Luke iii. 3). Here John's baptism is called the "baptism of repentance," because repentance was the only prerequisite demanded of a believing Jew. If the baptism instituted by Christ were distinguished from it by a corresponding epithet, the latter would be styled the baptism of faith; not because faith is the only prerequisite, but it is the one most prominent in the preaching of the apostles. That this baptism of repentance was " unto remission of sins," unmistakably points to remission as subsequent to it in order of time. In all these passages, however, if " unto " is used strictly, the baptism is contemplated as bringing the baptized person *to* remission, and no lapse of time is supposed between the baptism and that to which it brings the person. When, therefore, we speak of remission following baptism, we mean that it follows immediately. The command of Ananias to Saul teaches the same thing. The words, " Arise, and be baptized, and wash away thy sins " (Acts xxii. 16), clearly imply that his sins were washed away (a metaphor for remission of sins) as the immediate result of baptism. These are all of the passages in which sins are mentioned in immediate connection with baptism, and they unite in showing that remission of the former is an immediate consequent of the latter.

In another class of passages the same truth is set forth by implication. Paul makes the statement, and re-iterates it, that we are baptized into Christ: "Or are ye ignorant that all we who were baptized into Christ Jesus were baptized into his death?" (Rom. vi. 3); "For as many of you as were baptized into Christ did put him on" (Gal. iii. 27). Now when a man is in Christ his sins are certainly forgiven, and before he is in Christ they are certainly not forgiven. They are for-given in passing into Christ, and a part of the process by which one passes into Christ is the act of baptism; and it follows that, as he is not in Christ until he is baptized, until he is baptized he is not forgiven. The words of our Lord in the apostolic commission justify the same inference: "Go ye therefore and make disciples of all nations, baptizing them into the name of the Father, and of the Son, and of the Holy Spirit" (Matt. xxviii. 19). The man who has not yet entered into the relation expressed by the words "into the name of the Father and of the Son, and of the Holy Spirit," is yet in an unforgiven state, whatever may be his belief and his emotions; and this relation is established as soon as all of his sins are forgiven; but he enters into this rela-tion in the act of baptism, he is baptized into it, and it follows that his sins are forgiven in connection with his baptism.

Still another class of passages present *facts* which imply the same relation between baptism and remission. It is of the nature of forgiveness to impart joy to the person forgiven, and it is a matter of universal experience that the consciousness of unforgiven sins is a burden to the soul. If, then, in tracing the experiences of men whose conversion to Christ is described in the New Testament, we should find that they rejoiced before they were baptized, this would be evidence that remission of sins precedes baptism. On the other hand, if we find this rejoicing uniformly following baptism, we must accept the opposite conclusion. Now there is not one instance of the former on record; on the contrary, in every instance of the mention of this rejoicing, it comes after baptism. For example, it was after he was baptized that the eunuch went on his way "rejoicing;" while before baptism he was in a state of anxiety and preplexity (Acts viii. 34–40). Before Saul was baptized, and up to the moment that Ananias told him to arise and be baptised and wash away his sins, he was in great agony of soul, and had neither eaten nor drunk for three days; but as soon as he was baptized, his soul was at ease, "for he took food and was strengthened" (ix. 9–18). In like manner the Philippian jailer was in distress and perplexity before his baptism, but after he was baptized he brought Paul and Silas into his house and set food before them, "and rejoiced greatly, with all his house, having believed in God" (xvi. 30–34).

A fourth class of passages teach the same doctrine by the manner in which they connect baptism with salvation. Salvation in Christ consists essentially in the forgiveness of sins; for only when the soul is redeemed from sins by the power of Christ working within, and the guilt of sin taken away by pardon, can a man be in a state of salvation. If, then, when salvation and baptism are spoken of together, it is in a way to indicate that there is no connection between them, this might force us to re-examine the passages already noticed, to see if we had by any possibility misread them. Or if in such passages we should find that salvation is spoken of as if it precedes baptism, this might demand a similar re-examination. But neither of these conditions is found to exist; the reverse is uniformly the order which we find. In the commission we read, "He that believeth and is baptized shall be saved" (Mark xvi. 16). Here salvation is placed after baptism, and it is certainly the salvation which consists in forgiveness of sins; for the final salvation depends on much more than believing and being baptized. In the epistle to Titus we read, "When the kindness of God our Saviour, and his love toward man, appeared, not by works done in righteousness, which we did ourselves, but according to his mercy he saved us, through the washing of regeneration, and the renewing of the Holy Spirit, which he poured out upon us richly, through Jesus Christ our Saviour; that, being justified by his grace, we might be made heirs according to the hope of eternal life" (iii. 4–7). Here, by the washing (literally, laver) of regeneration, the apostle means baptism, which is so called because it is a species of washing connected with the process of regeneration; and it is affirmed that by this and the renewing of the Holy Spirit (the inward work of the Spirit which precedes baptism) we are saved. At the same time, lest any might think of merit of any kind as the ground of this salvation, he says that this salvation is not accorded because of anything which we had previously done in the way of righteousness, but only because of God's mercy. Furthermore, he identifies the salvation thus spoken of with justification, by the added clause, "that, being justified by his grace, we might be made heirs according to the hope of eternal life." Again we read in the first epistle of Peter that "eight souls were saved through water; which also after a true likeness doth now save you, even baptism, not the putting away of the filth of the flesh, but the interrogation of a good conscience toward God, through the resurrection of Jesus Christ" (I. Pet. iii. 31). Here the negation of putting away the filth of the flesh is aimed against a Jewish misconception, and to us its meaning is obvious. The clause rendered, " but the interrogation of a good conscience," is confessedly obscure; but whatever its meaning, it leaves unaffected the fact previously stated, that water does now, in a true likeness to that of the flood, save us in baptism ; and if baptism saves in any sense whatever, it must precede salvation, and bring the sinner to it.

Finally, the connection in question is implied in our Lord's remark to Nicodemus as to the conditions of entering into the kingdom of God: " Except a man be born of water and the Spirit, he can not enter into the kingdom of God." All ancient Christian scholars, and all the abler expositors of modern times, agree in declaring with one voice, that by the term water Jesus here refers to baptism. Dr. Wall, in his history of Infant Baptism, says: " There is not one Christian writer of any antiquity, in any language, but who understands the new birth of water as referring to baptism ; and if it be not so understood, it is difficult to give any account how a person is born of water, more than born of wood " (vol. i. 110). Alford testifies: " All the better and deeper expositors have recognized the coexistence of the two, water and the Spirit" (Com. *in loco*); and to the same effect it is said by Dr. Westcott: " All interpretations which treat the term water here as 'simply 'figurative and descriptive of the cleansing power of the Spirit, are essentially defective, as they are also opposed to all ancient tradition" (Com. on John *in loco*). In another part of his notes on the passage, Alford goes still farther in the direction of these assertions, and also gives the meaning of the verse, in these words: "There can be no doubt, on any honest interpretation of the words, that to be born of water refers to the token or outward sign of baptism—to be born of the Spirit, to the thing signified, or inward grace of the Holy Spirit. All attempts to get rid of these two plain facts have sprung from doctrinal prejudices, by which the views cf expositors have been warped." We may set aside, therefore, as exceptional and sectarian, all interpretations which take out of this passage its obvious allusion to baptism, and we are justified in saying that according to the united judgment of unbiased scholars of all churches, Jesus here meant that except a man experience the inward work of the Holy Spirit, and be baptized, he can not enter into the kingdom of God. Now before a man is in the kingdom of God, his sins are unforgiven; and when his sins are forgiven he is no longer an alien, but a citizen of that kingdom. By whatever process, then, he enters into that kingdom, by that or in that he obtains the remission of sins; but that process is the birth of water and the Spirit, of neither alone, but of both; and therefore he obtains forgiveness not before, but when he is baptized. It is but an echo of these words of our Lord, when Paul says He saved us "through the washing of regeneration and the renewing of the Holy Spirit" (Titus iii. 5).

These evidences establish, as clearly as any fact can

be established, an immediate connection between baptism and remission of sins, and they show with equal clearness that the divine act of forgiving sins takes place when the sinner, in whose heart the Holy Spirit has wrought faith and repentance, is baptized into Christ.

Here we might draw this discussion to a close but for the fact that by many this is supposed to be a heretical doctrine, unsupported by the scholarship of either past or present ages. To disabuse the reader of this impression, we proceed to show how these evidences have been regarded by men of learning. In the first place, the voice of antiquity is united upon it, as on the meaning of "born of water and the Spirit." Sufficient proof of this, without quoting individual authors, is found in the fact that the article on the subject in the Nicene Creed, adopted in the beginning of the fourth century without a dissenting voice, declares : "We believe in one baptism for the remission of sins." It is a well known fact also, that the Greek Church, the Armenian, and the Roman Catholic, still teach and have ever taught this doctrine, with the additional and unscriptural idea that baptism, independently of faith and repentance, takes away original sin in the case of infants. Infant baptism indeed owes its origin to this mistaken conception. The process is traced by Neander in the following well known passage : "But when, now, on the one hand, the doctrine of corruption and guilt, cleaving to human nature in consequence of the first transgression, was reduced to a more precise and systematic form, and on the other, from the want of duly distinguishing between what is outward and what is inward in baptism (the baptism by water and the baptism by the Spirit), the error became more firmly established that without external baptism no one could be delivered from that inherent guilt, could be saved from the everlasting punishment that threatened him, or raised to eternal life; and when the notion of magical influence, a charm connected with the sacrament, continually gained ground, the theory was finally evolved of the unconditional necessity of infant baptism. About the middle of the third century, this theory was generally admitted in the North African Church." Among the evidences which he gives of the truth of this representation, is an extract from Cyprian (Epistle 59), in which the writer contends for the baptism of infants immediately after their birth, and closes with these words: "But if even the chief of sinners, who have been exceedingly guilty before God, receive the forgiveness of sins on coming to faith, and no one is precluded from baptism and from grace, how much less should the child be kept back, which, as it is but just born, can not have sinned, but has only brought with it, by its descent from Adam, the infection of the old death; and which may the more easily obtain the remission of sins, because the sins which are forgiven it are not its own, but those of another" (Church History, i. 313, 314).

The unfortunate circumstance that this doctrine of baptism for remission of sins, universally taught in the ancient church, was thus corrupted by the church of the dark ages, was undoubtedly the cause of a reaction against it among the leaders of the Protestant Reformation; yet Luther and Calvin, while repudiating the doctrine as taught by Rome, and failing to adopt it in its original form, did both stumble upon it in their exposition of various passages of Scripture in which it is plainly taught. Thus Luther, commenting on the words (Gal. iii. 27), "All ye that are baptized into Christ, have put on Christ," makes these remarks: "This old man must be put off with all his works, that of the children of Adam we may be made the children of God. This is not done by changing of a garment, or by any laws or works, but by a new birth, and by the renewing of the inward man; which is done in baptism, as saith Paul: 'All ye that are baptized, have put on Christ.' Wherefore, to be appareled with Christ according to the gospel is not to be appareled with the law or with works, but with an incomparable gift; that is to say, with remission of sins, righteousness, peace, consolation, joy of spirit, salvation, life, and Christ himself. This is diligently to be noted, because of the fond and fantastical spirits, who go about to deface the majesty of baptism, and speak wickedly of it. Paul, contrarywise, commendeth and setteth it forth with honorable titles, calling it 'the washing of the new birth, the renewing of the Holy Spirit' (Titus iii.). And here also he saith, that all they which are baptized have put on Christ. As if he said, Ye are carried out of the law into a new birth, which is wrought in baptism. Therefore ye are not now any longer under the law, but ye are clothed with a new garment; to-wit, with the righteousness of Christ. Wherefore baptism is a thing of great force and efficacy" (Luther's Com. on Galatians). In these extracts Luther confirms the views expressed above, not only on the passage which he has immediately in hand, but also on our Lord's remark about the new birth, and Paul's in regard to the washing of regeneration. And all this comes from him who is the prime author of the modern doctrine of justification by faith alone.

John Calvin expresses himself to the same effect, and brings into view a still larger number of the passages which I have cited above. He says: "From baptism our faith derives three advantages, which require to be distinctly considered. The first is, that as proposed to us by the Lord, as a symbol and token of our purification; or, to express my meaning more fully, it resembles a legal instrument properly attested, by which he assures us that all our sins are canceled, effaced, and obliterated, so that they will never appear in his sight, or come into his remembrance, or be imputed to us. For he commands all who believe to be baptized for the remission of their sins. Therefore those who have imagined that baptism is nothing more than a mark or sign by which we profess our religion before men, as soldiers wear the insignia of their sovereign as a mark of their profession, have not considered that which is the principal thing in baptism; which is, that we ought to receive it with this promise: 'He that believeth and is baptized, shall be saved' (Mark xvi. 16). In this sense we are to understand what is said by Paul, that Christ sanctifieth and cleanseth the church 'with the washing of water by the word' (Eph. v. 26); and in another place that 'according to his mercy he saves us, by the washing of regeneration, and renewing of the Holy Spirit' (Titus iii. 5); and by Peter, that 'baptism doth now save us' (I. Peter iii. 21)."[1] From this extract the reader can see at a glance that all the passages cited in it are understood by Calvin to have the very meaning which I have attached to them; and the fact that these

---

[1] Calvin's Institutes, B. iv. 15, § § 1, 2. Similar views are expressed in § § 3, 4: though in § 15 he inconsistently represents the sins of Cornelius as being forgiven before he was baptized.

interpretations are given by a theologian who did not consistently apply them in his system, gives them the greater weight because it shows that they are not the result of doctrinal prepossession, but of the simplicity and clearness with which they are expressed in the passages themselves.

It is well known, also, that another great reformer of more recent times, John Wesley, fell upon this doctrine in the course of his exegetical studies, although it constituted no part of his system. He says: "Baptism administered to real penitents, is both a means and a seal of pardon. Nor did God ordinarily, in the primitive church, bestow pardon on any, unless through this means" (*Notes on N. T.*, p. 350).

Not to multiply evidences of this kind to any unnecessary extent, we pass by the utterances of many other eminent scholars of orthodox churches, and add a few from writers of our own age, eminent for their learning and their exegetical skill.

H. B. Hackett, one of the most eminent scholars and commentators in the Baptist Church of America, in commenting on Acts ii. 38, says: "*In order to the forgiveness of sins,* we connect naturally with both the preceding verbs. The clause states the motive or object which should induce them to repent and be baptized. It enforces the entire exhortation, no one part of it to the exclusion of the other." On Acts xxii. 16, he says: "*And wash away thy sins.* This clause states a result of the baptism in language derived from the nature of that ordinance. It answers to ' for the remission of sins ' in ii. 38—that is, submit to the rite in order to be forgiven." Clearer or more explicit testimony to the doctrine upheld in this excursus could not be uttered.

Dr. Jacobson, Bishop of Chester, and author of the notes on Acts in The Speaker's Commentary, under Acts xxii. 16 quotes with approval the words of Waterland: "Baptism was at length his [Paul's] grand absolution, his patent of pardon, his instrument of justification granted him from above; neither was he justified till he received that divine seal, inasmuch as his sins were upon him till that very hour."

Dr. J. A. Alexander, of Princeton, writes: "The whole phrase, to (or toward) remission of sins, describes this as the end to which the multitude had reference, and which, therefore, must be contemplated in the answer." Again: "The beneficial end to which all this led was the remission of sins" (*Com.* Acts ii. 38).

Lechler, author of Commentary on Acts in Lange's Bible Work, says under ii. 38: "The apostle promises to those who repent and receive baptism, (1) the remission of sins, and (2) the gift of the Holy Spirit." Under xxii. 16, he says: "We have here a noble testimony to the value which was assigned to holy baptism by the pure apostolic church. It was not a mere external ceremony, but a means of grace for washing away sins, and was the first actual entrance into the church of Jesus."

Dr. Gloag (Presbyterian), says in his Commentary, under xxii. 16: "Baptism in the adult, except in the peculiar case of our Lord, was accompanied by a confession of sin, and was a sign of its remission; hence called baptism in order to forgiveness of sins" (Acts ii. 38).

Plumptre, after quoting the words of Ananias to Paul, says: "They show that for the apostle baptism was no formal or ceremonial act, but was joined with repentance, and, faith being presupposed, brought with it the assurance of a real forgiveness. In St. Paul's language as to the ' washing' (or bath) of regeneration (Tit. iii. 5), we may trace his continued adherence to the idea which he had thus been taught on his first admission to the Church of Christ " (*Com. on Acts*, xxii. 16).

Finally we quote the testimony of two eminent philologists. Meyer says under Acts ii. 38 : " $\grave{\epsilon}\iota\varsigma$ denotes the object of the baptism, which is the admission of the guilt contracted in the state before $\mu\epsilon\tau\alpha\nuo\tilde{\iota}\alpha$." Grimm, in his great lexicon of the Greek N. T., defines $\grave{\epsilon}\iota\varsigma$ $\check{\alpha}\varphi\epsilon\sigma\iota\nu$ $\check{\alpha}\mu\alpha\rho\tau\iota\omega\nu$, Acts ii. 38, " to obtain the forgiveness of sins " ($\beta\alpha\pi\tau\iota\xi\omega$ II. b. aa.).

These citations are abundant to show that we have not misinterpreted the passages in question; and they show clearly that we are right in rejecting the rendering of the R. V., " *unto* remission of sins," and retaining that of the A. V., " *for* remission of sins." Peter's purpose in the expression was not to indicate the mere fact that baptism brings one to remission, but to state the blessing in order to the attainment of which his hearers were to be baptized. In other words, he states a motive for the act. In many other passages the R. V. is liable to the same criticism in its rendering of the preposition $\epsilon\check{\iota}\varsigma$. We might add many more testimonies if it were necessary. They show that the connection between baptism and remission of sins for which we contend is one of the most universally recognized doctrines of the New Testament. We have occupied so much space with its presentation, from a desire to restore this most solemn ordinance of our Lord to the place which it occupied in the primitive church, and to bring into practice the views of its meaning so clearly expressed by the scholars of all schools and ages. It has been common, in these latter days, to decry the doctrine, connected as it must be with the right action of baptism, because of consequences ascribed to it with reference to the salvation of myriads of pious persons in past ages who have not been really baptized; but such consequences, whether real or imaginary, can not alter the truth of Scriptures, while the consideration of them tends to bias our judgment and to hide the truth from us. It is the part of wisdom to unhesitatingly accept the truth as we discover it, knowing that we are to be judged in the great day according to the measure of light which we have, or may have; and that if our fathers were saved in neglect of any duty of which they were ignorant, we may not hope to be saved in neglect of any duty which is plainly pointed out to us. The right action of baptism is very rapidly gaining recognition among the serious minds of our time; let us endeavor to restore also its right design, and thus we may put to silence those " fond and fantastic spirits," as Luther styles them, " who go about to deface the majesty of baptism, and speak wickedly of it."

NEW COMMENTARY

ON

ACTS OF APOSTLES

BY

J. W. McGARVEY, A. M.

VOLUME 2

THE STANDARD PUBLISHING FOUNDATION
CINCINNATI, OHIO

COMMENTARY ON ACTS.

PART THIRD.

PAUL'S TOURS AMONG THE GENTILES.

(*XIII.—XXI.*)

SEC. I.—THE FIRST TOUR.

(XIII.—XIV).

1. BARNABAS AND SAUL SET APART TO THE WORK, XIII. 1–3.

VER. 1.   The opening sentence of this part of Acts
stands closely connected with the preceding part, taking
its start from the return of Barnabas and Saul to Antioch;
and yet, because of the new subject here introduced, its
style is the same as if it were the beginning of an independent narrative.[1] (1) **Now there were at Antioch, in
the church that was there, prophets and teachers, Barnabas, and Symeon that was called Niger, and Lucius
of Cyrene, and Manaen foster-brother of Herod the tetrarch, and Saul.**

The distinction between prophets and teachers is not
clearly drawn in the New Testament, except to the ex-

---

[1] The new and quite different subject matter now introduced,
sufficiently accounts for the author's style here, without aid from
any of the suppositions mentioned by Meyer, including one of
his own.

tent that the former were men who spoke by inspiration, while the latter sometimes did and sometimes did not. The previous statement of Luke, that "there came down prophets from Jerusalem to Antioch" (xi. 27), of whom Agabus was one, may have included the prophets who are here mentioned.

The order in which the five names are written is probably that of the relative reputation of the men. Barnabas, having been sent from Jerusalem, and having been an eminent man there, was naturally looked upon as the most important person, while Saul was at this time the least noted of the five. Symeon, as his name proves, was a full-blooded Jew; and though his surname Niger (black) can scarcely justify the conclusion that he was an African Jew,[1] it could scarcely have been given to him without some allusion to his complexion. Symeons were so numerous among the Jews that it was necessary to distinguish them in some way, and it is highly probable that this one, from having an unusually dark complexion, was called black Symeon.[2] As some of the second group of preachers who had come to Antioch were men of Cyrene (xi. 20), it is natural to suppose that Lucius of Cyrene was one of these, and that he was therefore one of the founders of the church. Manaen is the Greek form of the Hebrew name Menahem. Having been the foster-brother of Herod the tetrarch, his mother having nursed the two when they were infants, he had in all likelihood kept up through life an acquaintance

---

[1] "From his appellation Niger, he may have been an African proselyte." (Alford, *in loco*).

[2] It is quite common in America, when two or three men with the same name live in the same vicinity, to distinguish them by their shades of complexion, or the color of their hair: *e. g.*, Red Tom, Black Tom, etc.

with that prince; and it is not improbable that Luke learned through him something of Herod's thoughts and words concerning John the Baptist and Jesus, which he had recorded in his previous narrative (Luke ix. 7–9).

Vv. 2, 3. Symeon, Lucius and Manaen had been the chief teachers of the church during the absence of Barnabas and Saul on their mission to Jerusalem, and now this work is to be left to them again. (2) And as they ministered to the Lord, and fasted, the Holy Spirit said, Separate me Barnabas and Saul for the work whereunto I have called them. (3) Then when they had fasted and prayed and laid their hands upon them, they sent them away. The ministering to the Lord here mentioned has no special reference to the public worship, but rather to their service in supplying the wants of their brethren; for such is the meaning of the original word when used in reference to Christian[1] service. It was their habitual, daily work. For what cause they were fasting just at this time we have no intimation; but from the instruction of the Master on the subject (Matt. ix. 15), we may safely infer that it was in consequence of some affliction which had befallen them.

The command of the Holy Spirit, to separate Barnabas and Saul, must have been addressed to the other three brethren, and it was doubtless communicated through one of them to the others. The clause, "the work whereunto I have called them," implies that they had both been called to this work before this time. Paul

---

[1] Such is the usage of the verb, λειτουργέω, to minister; and of the nouns, λειτουργία, and λειτουργὸς, ministry, and minister, as is seen in Rom. xv. 16, 27; II. Cor. ix. 12; Phil. ii. 17, 30. The fact that the word liturgy is derived from it is suggestive of the great departure from Scriptural ideas and usage indicated by ancient and modern liturgies.

was called to it in the commission given to him by the Lord at the time of his conversion, as we learn from his own lips farther on (xxvi. 16–18); but when Barnabas was called we have no means of determining. Saul had been preaching to Gentiles as well as to Jews, as we may safely conclude, ever since he had heard of the baptism of Cornelius by Peter; but he had never yet made the former his chief work. It should be observed, that the thought of separating the two to this work did not originate with the brethren; but it was expressly communicated to them by the Holy Spirit.

The purpose of the fasting, prayer and laying on of hands is clearly indicated in the context: for what they did was doubtless what they were told to do; but what they were told to do was to "separate" the two to the work indicated; and, therefore, fasting, praying and laying on of hands was the method of separating them. This is the ceremony deemed suitable for such a separation by those under the guidance of the Holy Spirit, and it follows that on all similar occasions, such as separating a brother to the ministry of the word, or separating one who is already an experienced preacher, as were both Barnabas and Saul, to some new and different field of labor, it is proper for those concerned in the movement to lay hands on him with fasting and prayer. The modern conception, that hands may be imposed only by those holding an office superior to that which is to be filled, is the invention of an unscriptural hierarchy, having no support in the New Testament. In the instance before us, hands were imposed on Barnabas by three men who were his inferiors in the estimation of the church; and on Paul, the called apostle of Jesus Christ, by men who were not apostles, and, so far as our information extends,

not even elders of the congregation in which they were
teachers and prophets. This incident clearly demonstrates another fact in regard to this ceremony, that it
possesses none of the magical power to impart spiritual
graces which has been superstitiously ascribed to it; for
surely Barnabas and Saul were not destitute of any grace
which could be imparted to them by Symeon, Lucius
and Manaen. The truth is, that this ceremony, now no
longer called ordination[1] in the English Scriptures, was
nothing more than a method of solemnly commending a
man to God for the ministration to which he was being
set apart. The subject will come before us again in
regard to Timothy under xvi. 1–3.

Only the teachers and prophets are mentioned in
connection with this proceeding, but we are not to suppose that they acted in private. Doubtless the ceremony
of laying on hands was in the presence of the congregation; and after the command of the Spirit was received,
there was doubtless time given for the apostles to prepare
for the journey, and for the congregation to be notified.
These considerations make it probable that the fasting
connected with the imposition of hands was not the one
in which the teachers and prophets were already engaged,
but one specially appointed for the occasion.

2. THEIR LABORS IN CYPRUS, 4–12.

Vv. 4, 5. The journeys now entered upon by Saul are
among the most momentous ever undertaken, whether
by one man or many. They are worthy therefore of the
space allotted to them by our author, and of the most

---

[1] The revisers have wisely disconnected this English word
from the accounts of appointments to office, and confined it to
decrees and appointments of God.

careful study by every one interested in human progress.
(4) So they, being sent forth by the Holy Spirit, went
down to Seleucia ; and from thence they sailed to Cyprus.
(5) And when they were at Salamis they proclaimed the
word of God in the synagogues of the Jews : and they
had also John as their attendant. (Seleucia was the seaport of Antioch, sixteen miles distant, where all large
vessels lay at anchor; for although the Orontes, on the
banks of which Antioch was situated, was navigable for
small vessels, it was too shallow for those of the deepest
draught. Embarking here on some trading vessel, they
sailed to the port of Salamis,[1] which is at the eastern end
of the island of Cyprus.

In choosing this island as the first point in the wide
world to which they directed their course, they were
moved in part, no doubt, by the fact that it was the birthplace of Barnabas, where his personal acquaintance would
be of advantage to them; but also in part by the consideration that there were many Jewish synagogues there,
furnishing starting points for the work, and that the
gospel had been proclaimed there already with some
success (xi. 19, 20).

The John mentioned as the attendant of Barnabas
and Saul is the " John surnamed Mark" of xii. 25. He
had not been set apart to the work, as had his older
companions, but he had undertaken voluntarily to go
with them as an attendant. His work was to assist them
in every way in which a young man can serve his elders.

Luke is entirely silent in regard to the success of the
preaching in Salamis, leaving us to suppose that it was

---

[1] Salamis was afterward destroyed by war and earthquakes,
and its site is now marked by ruins about four miles north of the
modern town Famagosta.

not great, and that the stay of the apostles there was probably void of stirring incidents.

Vv. 6, 7. It was not till the preachers reached the other extremity of the island, about one hundred miles distant to the west, that the writer pauses to relate any of the incidents of their labors in Cyprus. (6) And when they had gone through the whole island unto Paphos, they found a certain sorcerer, a false prophet, a Jew whose name was Bar-Jesus; (7) who was with the pro-consul,[1] Sergius Paulus, a man of understanding. The same called unto him Barnabas and Saul, and sought to hear the word of God. Paphos was not the original city of that name, the birthplace, according to the Greek mythology, of the goddess Venus, but a small city of later origin which inherited the name after its predecessor had gone to ruin. It is now an insignificant village called Baffa, or Bafo. At the time of our text, although situated at the western extremity of the island, it was the seat of the Roman government.

---

[1] For a long time modern skeptics contended that Luke here made the mistake of styling Sergius Paulus a proconsul, when he should have called him proprætor, the latter, and not the former, being the Roman title borne by the chief ruler of the island. In vain believers insisted that, though the latter was the usual title, there may have been exceptions, and that Luke was therefore to be credited. "To set the matter finally at rest," says Farrar, "coins and inscription of this very epoch have been found at Curium and Citium, in which the title of proconsul is given to Cominius Proclus, Julius Corduo, and L. Annus Bassus, who must have been immediate predecessors or successors of Sergius Paulus." (Life of Paul, *Excursus*, xvi.) Still later, M. de Cesnolo found at Soli, in the same island, a coin with the inscription "Paulus the Proconsul." (Cuprus, p. 125). Thus the defense of Luke, based at first on the presumption that he is a reliable historian, is made complete by the demonstration of that which had been presumed in his favor.

Lest the reader should think that Luke makes an overestimate of Sergius Paulus in styling him "a man of understanding," seeing that he had with him a false prophet, we may remark that statesmen and generals in that age were in the habit of consulting oracles and auguries about all important matters, and of keeping about them some one who was credited with interpreting the signs of approaching good and evil. As there certainly had been true prophets among the Jews, Paulus showed good sense in trusting to a so-called prophet of that nation, rather than to any other; and when the two Jews came to Paphos, claiming to bring fresh revelations from the God of Israel, the same good sense prompted him to send for them. Such a mind as his could not fail to hear with profit what Barnabas and Saul had to say.

VER. 8. Bar-Jesus saw at once that the success of Barnabas and Saul in convincing the proconsul would be an end of his influence with him, and of the profits which his pretences were yielding; so he put forth his utmost efforts to defeat them. (8) But Elymas the sorcerer (for so is his name by interpretation)[1] withstood them, seeking to turn aside the proconsul from the faith. It would be vain to conjecture the mode of argumentation or vilification which he employed. Whatever it was, it proved to Paul that he was a villain of the deepest dye, fighting against what he knew to be right, and perverting that which he knew to be true. Perhaps Barnabas, as the chief man of the company, had been the speaker up to this moment; but Saul saw that something

---

[1] More properly, " by translation." Luke translates the name Elymas, by some supposed to be an Arabic, and by others an Aramaic word (Grimm's Lexicon), into Greek, by the word here rendered sorcerer. His other name, Bar-Jesus, is Hebrew, and means son of Jesus.

more decisive than words was demanded, and a most extraordinary scene followed.

Vv. 9–12. (9) But Saul, who is also called Paul, filled with the Holy Spirit, fastened his eyes upon him, (10) and said, O full of all guile and all villainy, thou son of the devil, thou enemy of all righteousness, wilt thou not cease to pervert the right ways of the Lord? (11) And now, behold, the hand of the Lord is upon thee, and thou shalt be blind, not seeing the sun for a season. And immediately there fell on him a mist and a darkness; and he went about seeking some to lead him by the hand. (12) Then the proconsul, when he saw what was done, believed, being astonished at the teaching of the Lord. This is the only miracle wrought by an apostle to the injury of any one's person. It was a case much like that of Moses in Egypt, who found it necessary to bring some irresistible afflictions on the magicians, in order to destroy Pharaoh's confidence in them. Saul saw that the readiest way to convince the proconsul that Bar-Jesus was a base impostor was to denounce him in his true character, and then prove the sentence pronounced upon him true and just by blinding him. As he groped about, calling on one and another of the frightened bystanders to lead him by the hand, the falsity and iniquity of his pretensions stood practically confessed, and the divine mission of the apostles was demonstrated. It had the desired effect on the proconsul, and perhaps Barnabas and Mark were as much surprised, though not so much frightened, as the rest of the company. Whether the proconsul followed his belief with the proper obedience, Luke fails to inform us, and the omission rather implies that he did not. The hindrances in the way of a heathen of high rank becoming a Christian in life were almost insurmountable, and if Paulus had accomplished the mighty task, it is unaccountable that at least a word to that effect is not spoken. How long the "season" during which Bar-Jesus was to remain blind proved to be, is left to conjecture. It was certainly long enough for him to have become a believer if his corrupt nature was capable of any good.

With the clause, "Saul, who is also called Paul," this apostle ceases to be called Saul, and begins to be called Paul. Hitherto he has occupied a subordinate position, and his name has come last in the list of himself and his companions; but hereafter he is to occupy the forefront of almost every scene in which he figures. Heretofore it has been "Barnabas and Saul;" hereafter it is to be "Paul and Barnabas." It is impossible not to connect this change with the name of Paulus, who was convinced by the vigorous and unexpected action of Paul. Many eminent scholars think that he had previously borne both names, the one Hebrew and the other an adopted Roman name; and that the change consisted in using the latter henceforward exclusively. This would be satisfactory, if we had any evidence, of which we have not the slightest, that he had ever borne the name Paul previous to this time; for the mere fact that many Jews had Greek or Roman surnames can not be held as evidence that Paul had. The obvious explanation is, that just as his companion Barnabas has been so called by his brethren, his original name being Joseph, because he was a good exhorter (iv. 36); so he, on account of convincing the first proconsul who ever paid respectful attention to the faith in Christ, and especially on account of the exceptionally bold and startling way in which he did it, his brethren, not himself, changed his name to Paulus. The change was the more easily made, and the more naturally suggested, from the circumstance that there was already a difference of only one letter between the two names. As a matter of course, after everybody else had put upon him this new name, he was compelled, willing or unwilling, to use it himself, as he does in all his epistles.

3. The Journey from Paphos to Antioch, 13–15.

Ver. 13. Cutting short the account of events in Paphos in a way that disappoints our curiosity, the historian hurries us with the two apostles on the further prosecution of their tour. (13) **Now Paul and his company set sail from Paphos, and came to Perga in Pamphylia: and John departed from them and returned to Jerusalem.** So completely has Paul now become the central figure in Luke's narrative, that Barnabas and John Mark are called simply "his company." Why they chose this portion of Asia Minor as their next field of labor, is not stated; but it was probably because Paul had already evangelized Cilicia, and wished now to introduce the gospel to the districts adjacent to Cilicia on the west, with a view to the systematic evangelization of the whole peninsula. We shall see a further indication of such a plan in xvi. 1–8. His long residence in Cilicia made him more or less familiar with the state of society in the region which he now penetrates, and he enters it with intelligent foresight.

Luke is equally silent in regard to the reason which governed John Mark in turning back from Perga, and going home. He does not even hint at this point that his reason was unsatisfactory to either of John's companions; though he shows plainly farther on (xv. 37–39) that it was extremely so to Paul. It is very plausibly conjectured by Mr. Howson that he was moved by fear of robbers in the mountains which they would have to cross in passing into the interior. He says: " No population through the midst of which Paul ever traveled abounded more in those 'perils of robbers' of which he himself speaks, than the wild and lawless clans of the Pisidian highlands." [1] The preachers were not burdened with money to attract robbers, but John knew that robbers sometimes kill men and then search for their money.

Vv. 14, 15. Luke does not recount the dangers and hardships of the journey across the mountains, but follows the two travelers in silence from Perga to Antioch. (14) But they, passing through from Perga, came to Antioch of Pisidia; and they went into the synagogue on the sabbath day, and sat down. (15) And after the reading of the law and the prophets the ruler of the synagogue sent unto them, saying, Brethren, if ye have any word of exhortation for the people, say on. This is a graphic, though altogether informal account of the order of service in a Jewish synagogue. First, a section of the law is read; then a section of the prophets; then came exhortations based on what had been read. Paul and Barnabas had taken their seats modestly in the audience among the people; for so Jesus had taught his disciples (Matt. xxiii. 5–12); and the reason why the ruler gave them permission to speak was doubtless because they had previously sought it. They had come into this community for the purpose of speaking to the people; they had fully intended, as was their custom, to begin in the synagogue; and they did as any preacher at the present day would do under similar circumstances

---

[1] *Life and Epistles of Paul*, i. 162, 163.

—they took pains, before the service began, to introduce themselves to the rulers, and ask the privilege of addressing the audience ere it should be dismissed.

This Antioch was one of many cities founded or enlarged by Seleucus Nicator, and named Antioch in honor of his father Antiochus, who was made king of Syria after the death of Alexander the Great. On account of the good roads which radiated from it in every direction, and its comparative proximity to the sea, being about one hundred and twenty miles from Perga, it was the center of a considerable trade, and this had attracted a considerable Jewish population.

4. Paul's Sermon in Antioch, 16–41.

I. The Introduction, 16–22.

Vv. 16-22. To the invitation of the synagogue rulers Paul responded by immediately arising and addressing the audience. There had no doubt been a previous agreement between him and Barnabas that he should thus take the lead. He introduced his discourse by a brief sketch of the history of Israel from the exodus to the time of David: (16) And Paul stood up, and beckoning with his hand, said, Men of Israel, and ye that fear God, hearken. (17) The God of this people Israel chose our fathers, and exalted the people when they dwelt in the land of Egypt, and with a high arm led them forth out of it. (18) And for about the time of forty years suffered he their manners in the wilderness. (19) And when he had destroyed seven nations in the land of Canaan, he gave them their land for an inheritance, for about four hundred and fifty years: (20) And after these things he gave them judges until Samuel the prophet. (21) **And afterward they asked for a king: and God gave unto them Saul the son of Kish, a man of the tribe of Benjamin, for the space of forty years.** (22) **And when he had removed him, he raised up David to be their king; to whom he also bore witness, and said, I have found David the son of Jesse, a man after my heart, who shall do all my will.**

The gesture made by Paul as he began, described as "beckoning with his hand," was habitual with him;[1] and though quite an unusual gesture, it was well calculated to arrest the attention of an audience. It indicated that he knew what he was about to say, and felt confident of its importance.

His brief sketch of the history of Israel served the two chief purposes of an introduction—it led the minds of the hearers forward to the main theme of the discourse, and it did so in a manner well calculated to interest and please them. The Jews had a glorious history, of which they were justly proud; and any happily expressed allusions to its more glorious incidents always awakened their most lively emotions. These incidents furnished the inspiration of their songs, the themes of their orators, and their comfort in persecution. He had the readiest access to their sympathy who showed the highest appreciation of these great events. Paul, knowing this, passed readily into the hearts of his hearers through this open door.

In the statement of verse 19, that "when he had destroyed seven nations in the land of Canaan, he gave them their land for an inheritance for about four hundred and fifty years," the period given can not be understood as beginning before the destruction of those nations, neither can it be limited to the period of Joshua's con-

---

[1] See xxi. 40; xxvi. 1.

quest, which is usually estimated at twenty-five years. It must then refer to the whole period in which God was gradually giving them full possession of the land. It was well known that after the death of Joshua many strongholds were still in the possession of the Canaanites, and of course they held the territory immediately adjacent to these fortified cities. The Philistines, too, the most indomitable of all these tribes, held their own territory almost without dispute till after the death of Saul, who perished in a battle in which they defeated the hosts of Israel. It was not until late in' the reign of David that this obstinate power was at last completely broken down, never again to make war upon Israel (II. Sam. viii. 1; I. Chron. xviii. 1). Now, if the period of four hundred and eighty years, given in I. Kings vi. 1, as the time from the exodus to the founding of Solomon's temple in the fourth year of his reign, be understood as counting, not from the start out of Egypt, but from the arrival in Canaan ; and the time of destroying the nations of Canaan by Joshua be estimated at twenty-five years, we have just four hundred and fifty-one years from the latter date to the end of David's reign ; and thus the period in which God was giving the land to Israel by the gradual extermination of the remnants of heathen left by Joshua, was "about four hundred and fifty years," as Paul says. It lacked as much of it as the space between the final conquest of the Philistines and the end of David's reign, concerning which no figures are given in the Old Testament. Stephen, like Paul, counted the subjugation of the Canaanites as in progress until the time of David, for he refers to them as the "nations which God thrust out before the face of our fathers unto the days of David" (vii. 45).

The next statement (20), "and after these things he gave them judges until Samuel the prophet," can not mean that he gave them judges after the four hundred and fifty years, seeing that this period includes both the time of the judges, and the reigns of Saul and David. The words are not, after this time, but "after these things (μετὰ ταῦτα) ;" and they may therefore be construed as referring to the *events* preceding the figures given. The last of the events is the destruction of the seven nations, that is, the breaking down of their national power by Joshua; and it is true that after these things he gave them judges, for it is at this very point, according to the book of Judges, that these rulers began to have sway.

The length of Saul's reign is not given in the Old Testament, so Paul must have learned that it was forty years from some extra-biblical source which was current in his day.

The words, "I have found David the son of Jesse, a man after my heart, who shall do all my will," express a thought gathered from Psa. lxxxi. 20, "I have found my servant David ;" and I. Sam. xiii. 14, "The Lord hath sought him a man after his own heart, and the Lord hath appointed him to be prince over his people." These words are not spoken concerning the whole life of David, in which there were some things not at all after God's own heart; but they had reference to David's character when chosen to be the successor of Saul ; he was to do all God's will in those particulars in which Saul had failed.

The commentators have nearly all noticed the similarity between this introduction, and a portion of that of Stephen, of whom Paul was a hearer (vii. 36–45). The similarity consists only in the fact that both speakers

make use of the deliverance from Egyptian bondage;
for the details which they mention are almost totally different, and they make the reference for totally different
purposes—Paul's purpose being to favorably introduce
his main theme, while Stephen was gathering up a bundle of misdeeds in the history of the fathers, with which
to lash the consciences of sons who were wickedly imi-
tating their fathers in resistance to the Holy Spirit.

II. JESUS PREACHED AS A SAVIOUR, 23-29.

(a) *THE PROPOSITION, 23, 24.*

Vv. 23, 24. Having reached the name of David in
his introductory sketch, Paul passes immediately from
this name to his main theme, the appearance and work
of David's promised Son: (23) **Of this man's seed hath
God according to promise brought unto Israel a Saviour
Jesus; (24) when John had before his coming preached
the baptism of repentance to all the people of Israel.** In
this brief sentence Paul skillfully introduces Jesus as the
promised Son of David who was to deliver Israel (Ps.
lxxxix. 19–37), and also states the time of his public
appearance, in accordance with the Gospel narratives,
as immediately after the close of John's ministry. Thus
he fixes attention not upon the time of his birth, but
upon the time that God "brought him to Israel as a
Saviour."

(b) *JOHN'S TESTIMONY, 25.*

VER. 25. Having pointed to the close of John's ministry as the time at which Jesus had been brought to
Israel as a Saviour, the speaker next introduces the
direct testimony on this point which was borne by
John. (25) And as John was fulfilling his course, he said,

What suppose ye that I am? I am not he.   But behold,
there cometh one after me, the shoes of whose feet I am
not worthy to loose.   This quotation from John is not
given in the words of either of our Gospels; yet it may
nevertheless be a literal quotation from his lips: for
doubtless John very frequently, and in varying forms of
speech, corrected the idea which began to prevail among
the people, that he was the Christ.   The purport of the
quotation as used by Paul is that John bore formal
testimony that one was coming after him so much more
exalted than himself that he was not worthy to perform
for him the menial service of untying his sandals; and
who could this be but the Christ, the Son of David? No
other conclusion could appear possible to his hearers;
and thus the words of John furnished proof of the two
affirmations contained in the proposition which Paul had
announced; first, that the Saviour had appeared; and
second, that he appeared after John had preached repentance to all the people of Israel.   It is highly probable
that this very preaching of John was familiar to Paul's
hearers, as a consequence of the visits which some of
them had made to the festivals in Jerusalem, where
they would hear all about it ; and consequently Paul had
no occasion to dwell upon it.

(c) *PROPHECIES FULFILLED IN THE DEATH OF JESUS, 26–29.*

VER. 26. At this point in his discourse, moved, perhaps, by some favorable expression in the countenances
of his hearers, or possibly by some apparent want of
attention, the speaker interrupts the course of his argument momentarily, and vehemently urges upon his
hearers their personal interest in the matters of which he
is speaking. **(26)** Brethren, children of the stock of

Abraham, and those among you that fear God, to us is
the word of this salvation sent forth. But his impetuosity was not so great as to make him forget the convincing and persuasive proofs which he had yet to
present, so he advances quickly to a fuller statement of
his argument.

Vv. 27–29. After asserting that the messiahship of
Jesus was authenticated by the testimony of John, it was
incumbent on the speaker to explain the singular fact
that the Jews in Jerusalem had put him to death as an
impostor. Had he proceeded to state this fact without
qualification, it would have appeared to his hearers as
proof that Jesus could not be the Christ; consequently,
he states it in such a way as not only to guard against
this objection, but to furnish additional evidence. (27)
For they that dwell in Jerusalem, and their rulers, because they know him not, nor the voices of the prophets
which are read every Sabbath, fulfilled them by condemning him. (28) And though they found no cause of
death in him, yet asked they of Pilate that he should be
slain. (29) And when they had fulfilled all that was
written of him, they took him down from the tree, and
laid him in a tomb. This statement of the case made it
appear that the Jerusalem Jews had condemned and
slain him because they did not know him; that their
failure to know him was a result of their ignorance
of what the prophets had said concerning the Christ;
and that both in his condemnation, and in the details of his crucifixion, they fulfilled what had been
written by the prophets concerning him. Doubtless
Paul here quoted some of these prophecies, in order that
his hearers might see the correctness of his statements;
but Luke, for brevity's sake, omits them. Thus the

crucifixion of Jesus, which, as a naked fact, would be regarded by any Jew in the world as *prima facie* evidence that he was not the Messiah, was turned into an unanswerable argument in his favor, and at the same time the misconception of the messiahship itself which was held by the Jews was corrected.

In this condensed account of the death and burial of Jesus, the mention of their taking him down from the tree, without a previous mention of their hanging him on the tree, implies either that Paul's hearers were familiar with the fact of the crucifixion, or that Luke, in abbreviating, has omitted much of what Paul said. The latter is the more probable explanation; for throughout the speech Paul speaks as if his hearers were ignorant of the facts about Jesus. He makes no distinction between those who condemned him and those who took him down and buried him, for the very obvious reason that he is telling what "they that dwell in Jerusalem, and their rulers," did, and these expressions include Joseph and Nicodemus, who buried him. He calls the cross a tree, as Peter does (v. 30; x. 39; I. Pet. ii. 24), for the reason, most likely, that the main shaft of it was the rough undressed trunk of a small tree.[1] Sawed timbers were not then in use, and the soldiers were not likely to hew a piece for the sake of appearances.

(d) THE RESURRECTION OF JESUS, 30–37.

Vv. 30–33. The speaker next presents the crowning fact in the gospel evidence, and he fails not to connect

---

[1] The word employed is not the usual one for tree (δένδρον). but ξύλον, which strictly means wood, though it is employed by Paul and Peter, and by John in Revelation, in the sense of tree. See, besides the citations made above, Gal. iii. 13; Rev. ii. 7; xxii. 2; 14.

it with Old Testament predictions, so as to make his
Jewish hearers more willing to receive it. (30) **But God
raised him from the dead: (31) and he was seen for
many days of them that came up with him from Galilee
to Jerusalem, who are now his witnesses unto the people.
(32) And we bring you good tidings of the promise made
unto the fathers, (33) how that God hath fulfilled the
same unto our children, in that he raised up Jesus; as
also it is written in the second psalm, Thou art my Son,
this day have I begotten thee.** That the ancient promise to the fathers, " In thee and in thy seed shall all the
families of the earth be blessed," had been fulfilled, was
in the nature of the case good tidings to these Jews; but
that it was fulfilled in raising Jesus from the dead, was a
new thought to them; and that in this were fulfilled the
words of the second psalm, " Thou art my Son; this day
have I begotten thee," was equally new and startling.
Both propositions needed proof. It is scarcely possible
that Paul stated the testimony of the witnesses of the resurrection as briefly as it is here given; for it is the capital fact of the whole sermon, and it needed the most
ample verification to his hearers. He doubtless gave the
testimony of the original witnesses in full; but he seems
to have omitted his own. As he was addressing total
strangers, this was a matter of prudence. They would
be more ready to believe what he said of the testimony
of others, than of his own, because in stating the former
he would appear more disinterested.

The words, " Thou art my Son, this day have I begotten thee," would naturally be referred at first glance
to the birth of the person addressed; but they are here
applied to the resurrection of Jesus. In other instances
of their occurrence in the New Testament they are ap-

plied in the same way. In Hebrews **v.** 5, it is said : " So
Christ glorified not himself to be made a priest, but he
that spake unto him, Thou art my Son, this day have
I begotten thee." Now as he was not a priest until
after he had died as a victim, and was prepared to enter
heaven with his own blood, it is clear that these words
refer to his being begotten from the dead. In Hebrews
i. 5, the question, " To which of the angels said he at
any time, Thou art my Son, this day have I begotten
thee ?" is adduced as evidence that he was superior to
angels, and it can not therefore refer to the birth by
which he was " made a little lower than the angels "
(Heb. ii. 7). The context in the psalm, too, supports
this application ; for the words are addressed, not to an
unconscious infant, that day born into the world ; but to
an intelligent being :

> " I will tell of the decree :
>   The Lord said unto me, Thou art my Son ;
>   This day have I begotten thee."

The whole of the second psalm, from which the quotation is made, is evidently Messianic ; for none of it is
applicable to any other person than the Christ.

Vv. 34–37. Paul now adds to the testimony of the
witnesses of the resurrection a still more formal proof
that this was the purpose of God concerning the Christ.
(34) And as concerning that he raised him up from the
dead, now no more to return to corruption, he hath
spoken on this wise, I will give you the holy and sure
blessings of David. (35) Because he saith also in another
psalm, Thou shalt not give thy Holy One to see corruption. (36) For David, after he had in his own generation
served the counsel of God, fell on sleep, and was laid unto
his fathers, and saw corruption : (37) but he whom God

raised up saw no corruption. The quotation, " I will give you the holy and sure blessings of David," is taken from Is. lv. 3, and the context shows that it has reference to him of whom it had been promised that God would raise him up to sit on David's throne. Paul uses the past tense in regard to the fulfillment of this promise, because his hearers believed in the prophecies, and would readily grant that every one of them must be fulfilled in its season. If he proved, as he had done, that Jesus had been raised from the dead, they would readily grant that in this the prediction was fulfilled.

The reader will at once recognize the next prediction quoted (35) as the one made use of by Peter in the first division of his sermon on Pentecost, and the argument based upon it in the next two verses as the same used by Peter on that occasion. There is perhaps no passage in the whole of the Old Testament which contains a more explicit prediction of the resurrection of the Christ than this; and for this reason it became a favorite proof-text with the early preachers. To accuse Paul of copying in any unbecoming manner from Peter, or Luke of falsely putting into Paul's mouth an argument which the latter would not have deigned to borrow, as some have done, is absurd; for if two men are to argue the truth of any proposition, how is it possible for them to do so successfully except by both employing the evidences which support it? And these evidences, whatever the nature of the proposition, or of the subject matter, must from the nature of things be always largely the same.

(e) REMISSION OF SINS PROCLAIMED THROUGH JESUS, 38, 39.

Vv. 38, 39. Having now established by conclusive evidences the messiahship of Jesus, Paul proceeds to offer the audience the benefit of his mediation : (38) **Be it known to you therefore, brethren, that through this man is proclaimed unto you the remission of sins : (39) and by him every one that believeth is justified from all things, from which ye could not be justified by the law of Moses.** Here Paul joins with John the Baptist, Jesus himself, and Peter in setting forth remission of sins as the one distinguishing blessing to be enjoyed in Christ. The revised version, like that of King James, is wrong here in the rendering, "by him," and "by the law." The original means "in him" ($\dot{\epsilon}\nu$ $\tau o\acute{\nu}\tau\omega$) and "in the law " ($\dot{\epsilon}\nu$ $\tau\tilde{\omega}$ $\nu\acute{o}\mu\omega$).[1] The thought is, that the believer who is "in Christ," a characteristic expression with Paul, is justified in the sense of enjoying remission of sins (38), which blessing those in cr under the law could not enjoy. He here teaches concerning the law what he abundantly taught later in his epistles, that in it there was no remission of sins, and that the promise of forgiveness which was made to those who offered the sacrifices of the law was dependent for its fulfillment on the subsequent shedding of the blood of Christ.[2] The benefits of the Jewish law were extended only to those who were born in or properly initiated into the body of people to whom the law was given ; and just so, the remission of sins is here proclaimed to the believer who shall be " in Christ ; " and as we learn by another characteristic expression of Paul, the believer is " baptized into Christ," baptized into his body."[3] Thus the connection of the remission of sins with baptism, which was plainly stated

---

[1] " Literally, *in him*, as the sphere in which forgiveness was found, rather than as the instrument through which it came." (Plumptre). Meyer, Alford and Lechler give the same rendering.
[2] Heb. x. 1–4 ; ix. 15.   [3] Rom. vi. 3 ; Gal. iii. 27 ; I. Cor. xii. 13.

in Peter's first discourse (ii. 38), is implied in this, the first reported discourse by Paul. The reason that he did not, like Peter, urge his hearers to repent and be baptized, that they might be in Christ and enjoy the remission of their sins, was because, as we shall see below, he saw that they were not prepared for such an exhortation.

III. A WARNING, 40, 41.

Vv. 40–41. The announcement which closed the preceding division of the speech was most unwelcome to Paul's hearers; for it was an express disparagement of the law of Moses, and such remarks always grated harshly upon Jewish ears. Peter had said by implication the same thing, when he said to the sanhedrim, "neither is there any other name under heaven, that is given among men, wherein we must be saved" (iv. 12). That which was implied in Peter's speech was boldly expressed in Paul's. He doubtless discovered after this utterance an unfavorable expression in the faces of his Jewish hearers; for otherwise so watchful a speaker would not have closed his address with the words which follow: (40) Beware therefore, lest that come upon you which is spoken in the prophets;

(41) Behold, ye despisers, and wonder, and perish;

  For I work in your days,

   A work which ye shall in no wise believe, if one declare it unto you.

The quotation was intended to warn them against rejecting the good tidings which he preached to them, and to show them that if they did, they would identify themselves with the class to which these fearful words of the prophet had reference. The words, "though one should declare it unto you," imply that the declaration of it would contain such evidence as would make the rejection of it inexcusable. The words are quoted from Habakkuk i. 5 (Septuagint version), and the context there shows that the reference is to an impending destruction at the hands of the Chaldeans. Paul applies them to the destruction impending over all who reject the gospel; for in this the words have another fulfillment.

5. Immediate Effect of the Sermon, 42, 43.

Vv. 42, 43. Though no one in the audience was prepared to obey the gospel; and no one, perhaps, fully believed what had been spoken, the majority were favorably impressed, as appears from the way in which they spoke and acted. (42) And as they were going out they besought that these words might be spoken to them the next Sabbath. (43) Now when the synagogue broke up, many of the Jews and the devout proselytes followed Paul and Barnabas; who, speaking to them, urged them to continue in the grace of God. The request mentioned in the former of these two verses was made as the people pressed around the apostles after leaving their seats; while the breaking up of the synagogue mentioned in the latter means the departure of the people from the place. The dismission by the elders preceded both. The "proselytes," here first mentioned, were that portion of the audience twice addressed in the course of the sermon as "ye that fear God" (16, 26). The picture which Luke draws of these devout Gentiles and many of the Jews following Paul and Barnabas in a crowd to their lodging, and keeping up an earnest conversation, shows at once the simple habits of the people, and the deep interest which they felt in the new and thrilling theme of the discourse. They were already "in the grace of God," an expression which means only that God regarded them with favor, as he does all earnest seekers after truth; and should they continue in it, as the apostles exhorted them, they would soon attain to the remission of sins which he had offered in Christ.

6. Results on the Next Sabbath, 44-48.

Ver. 44. The profound impression made by Paul's sermon in the synagogue, and by the conversation of both the preachers with those who followed them to their lodging, very naturally spread like a contagion throughout the city during the succeeding week; and we are not to suppose that the preachers were in the meantime idle. Paul's characteristic zeal, which afterward caused some sober men to style him a babbler (xvii. 18), would not permit him to remain silent for a whole week, when the tide of public opinion was running so strongly in his favor. The first result was seen in the next assemblage at the synagogue. (44) **And the next Sabbath almost the whole city was gathered together to hear the word of God.** The previous audience had assembled merely to hear the usual readings and exhortations of the synagogue; but this one assembled for the purpose of hearing the word which was to be preached by Paul. The synagogues were not built with a view to such crowds, and therefore it is highly probable that the speaker stood in the door, as has been done so often in our western country, and spoke to a large crowd without, as well as to those within the building. The building was not cumbered, like our modern chapels, with benches; but the people sat on mats laid on the floor, and could

easily turn their faces toward the door, while those outside sat in the same way on the ground.

VER. 45. So large an assemblage of the people to
hear a doctrine which had appeared disparaging to the
law of Moses, and which had on this account already
offended some of the Jews, could but arouse the indignation of the disaffected, and was calculated to disaffect
those who had been favorably impressed on the previous
Sabbath. The leaders among them acted as their countrymen of like spirit in other countries uniformly acted
under such circumstances. (45) But when the Jews saw
the multitude, they were filled with jealousy, and contradicted the things which were spoken by Paul, and
blasphemed. This contradicting and blaspheming did
not of course precede Paul's remarks. We must understand that he delivered a discourse, omitted by the historian, in which the doctrine of the previous Sabbath
was again set forth, and that during the course of its
delivery he was interrupted by outspoken contradictions
and reproaches. Such interruptions are not unknown
at the present day in oriental congregations.

Vv. 46, 47. Thus far the apostle had addressed the
Jews directly, and the Gentiles present only indirectly;
but it now appeared that it was useless to reason further
with the former, or to attempt to conciliate them.
(46) And Paul and Barnabas spoke out boldly, and said, It
was necessary that the word of God should first be spoken
to you. Seeing that ye thrust it from you, and judge yourselves unworthy of eternal life, lo, we turn to the Gentiles. (47) For so hath the Lord commanded us, saying,
      I have set thee for a light of the Gentiles,
      That thou shouldst be for salvation to the uttermost
      part of the earth.

In these utterances both of the apostles took part (46), and they were bold utterances from the consideration that they were certain to provoke the hatred of the Jews, and would probably result in violence. The statement, " it was necessary that the word of God should first be spoken to you," shows that the apostles understood that the preaching was not only to begin at Jerusalem (Luke xxiv. 47), but that it was in every community to be presented to the Jews first. "To the Jew first, and also to the Greek," was the standing rule with Paul (Rom. i. 16 ; ii. 10). The propriety of this we have discussed under i. 8.

VER. 48. The next statement of our historian has been the subject of no little controversy. (48) **And as the Gentiles heard this, they were glad, and glorified the word of God : and as many as were ordained to eternal life believed.** The controversy turns on the meaning of the word translated "were ordained" ($\dot{\eta}\sigma a\nu \ \tau\epsilon\tau a\gamma\mu\acute{\epsilon}\nu o\iota$). Calvinistic writers unite in referring it to the eternal election and foreordination taught in their creeds. If this were the correct interpretation, it would involve some difficulties which they seem not to have observed. If "as many as were foreordained to eternal life" believed on that day, then all the rest were reprobates, doomed to everlasting punishment, and Paul's further preaching to them was useless. Now it is unaccountable that so complete a separation of the two classes took place throughout a large assembly in a single day ; and still more unaccountable that this was revealed to Luke so that he could record it. Our surprise is even yet greater when we remember that, according to the theory, not even the elect themselves can ever know with certainty that they are elect. We should surely not adopt a conclusion so anomalous, unless we are compelled to do so by the obvious force of the words employed. Dr. Hackett, after rendering the passage, "and as many as were appointed to eternal life believed," says: "This is the only translation which the philology of the passage allows." Grimm, in his lexicon, expresses the Calvinistic idea more fully by giving as the meaning, "as many as were appointed (by God) to eternal life, or to whom God had decreed eternal life."

The word thus translated is from the root τάσσω, the primary meaning of which is to *set in order;* or, as Grimm expresses it, *to place in a certain order.* In composition with διά it is so rendered in I. Cor. xi. 34: "The rest will I *set in order* when I come." In only one other of its eight occurrences in the New Testament is it rendered ordained; and in this it may as well have been rendered by its primary meaning: "The powers that are ordained [set in order] by God" (Rom. xiii. 1). It is usually rendered appoint; as, to appoint a place (Matt. xxviii. 16) ; to appoint something to be done (Acts xxii. 10) ; to appoint a day (xxviii. 23). But in making appointments order is brought out of preceding confusion, or want of order, and the primary meaning of the word is not lost sight of in this use of it. The same is true when it is applied to a mental act. When the mind has been in confusion on a subject, not knowing what to think, and finally reaches a definite conclusion or purpose, the thoughts are brought out of confusion into order, and this term properly expresses the change. A striking example is found in xvi. 2, where the brethren in Antioch are said to have heard "no small dissension and questioning," between Paul and Barnabas on one side, and certain men from Judea on the other, in reference to a vital question. While this dissension was in progress, the rank and file of the brethren and sisters must have been in the utmost confusion; but they finally reached a conclusion as to what should be done, and this change is expressed by the word in question; " they determined (ἔταξαν) that Paul and Barnabas and certain others of them should go up to Jerusalem to the apostles and elders about this question." This is the rendering of A. V., and it correctly represents the mental change which occurred. Dr. Hackett affirms that the term " was not used to denote an act of the mind; " but the translation to which this idea forced him is conclusive evidence to the contrary. He renders the clause in question, " they appointed that they should go up," etc.; and in this he is followed by the authors of R. V. This is not good English. It is an ungrammatical use of the word appoint. When a mission is determined on, we appoint the men who shall be sent, but we do not appoint that they shall go. Evidently the state of the case was this: the brethren were at first undetermined what to do; and they finally determined to do what they did. Our English word *disposed* has a similar usage. It means to arrange in a certain order, and it applies primarily to external objects; but when one's mind is arranged in accordance with a certain line of conduct, we say he is disposed to pursue it.

We scarcely need to observe, after the preceding remarks, that the specific meaning of this verb in a given passage is to be determined by the context. In the passage before us the context presents no allusion to something done by God for one part of the audience, and not done for the other; or to some purpose entertained respecting the one, and not the other; but it speaks

of two contrasted states of mind among the people, and
two consequent courses of conduct. Of the Jews present it is said, first, that they were filled with jealousy;
second, that they contradicted the things which were
spoken by Paul, and blasphemed; third, that they judged
themselves unworthy of eternal life. In contrast with
these, the Gentiles, first, were glad; second, they glorified the word of God; third, they were τεταγμένοι for
eternal life. Now which of the specific meanings of the
Greek word shall we here insert? It stands contrasted
with the mental act of the Jews in judging themselves
unworthy of eternal life, and the law of antithesis requires
that we understand it of some mental act of the opposite
nature. The rendering, were *determined*, or were *disposed* for eternal life, is the only one of which the case
admits. The verb is in the passive voice, and a past
tense, and therefore it represents a mental state which
had been brought about before the moment of which the
writer is speaking. In other words, the statement that
" as many as were determined for eternal life believed "
implies that they were brought to this determination before they believed. At some previous time in their history these Gentiles, who had been born and reared in heathenism, had heard of eternal life as taught by the Jews.
Either under the teaching of the Jews, or under the teaching of Paul since his arrival in Antioch, or under both
combined, they had been brought out of a state of mental
confusion on this transcendently important subject, into
a determination to obtain eternal life if possible.[1]

---

[1] " Better, ' as many as were disposed for.' " (Plumptre). " All
who, by the grace of God, desired to range themselves in the
ranks of those who desired eternal life accepted the faith."
(Farrar, *Life of Paul*, 211). " Rather, were set in order for, *i. e.*,
disposed for eternal life." (Jacobson in *Speaker's Com.*) " As many

Let it be noted that the being determined for eternal life, and the believing, stand here as cause and effect, or at least as antecedent and consequent. This is not at all unnatural or uncommon. A man who has learned that eternal life may be obtained, and has made up his mind to obtain it if within his power, is the very man to readily accept the true way of obtaining it when that way is clearly pointed out to him; while the man who is so much absorbed in worldly matters as to be indifferent to eternal life is the very man to allow the testimony concerning the way of obtaining it to pass in at one ear and out at the other. We find it so in all of our congregations at the present day. Two men sit side by side under the sound of the same gospel sermon; one is awake to the importance of the life to come, while the other is absorbed in the life that now is. The latter will turn a deaf ear to the preaching, incurring Paul's reproach of judging himself unworthy of eternal life, while the former will believe the glad message, and fly to the seat of mercy. It is precisely this difference as respects eternal life which Luke here points out; and he points it out because it accounts for the fact that one class in Paul's audience believed, and the other did not. It leaves the responsibility for belief and unbelief, with their eternal consequences, on men, and not on God.

7. FINAL RESULTS IN ANTIOCH, 49–52.

VER. 49. The devout proselytes who believed under Paul's second sermon proved to be the first fruits of a

---

as were disposed to eternal life. The meaning of the word dis. posed must be determined by the context. The Jews had judged themselves unworthy of eternal life: the Gentiles, as many as were disposed to eternal life, believed." (Alford).

large harvest. **(49) And the word of the Lord was spread abroad throughout all the region.** This means that not only in Antioch, but in all Pisidia lying adjacent to it, converts to the truth were made. Paul's labors were apparently confined to the city, but the report of his work, as it spread from place to place, brought interested hearers from every direction, even as we see in our own age.

VER. 50. The jealousy of the Jews, which had been aroused by the presence of the great audience that heard Paul's second sermon, was intensified by these triumphs of the word, and it led, as similar triumphs had done from the beginning in Jerusalem, to the violence which Paul and Barnabas had anticipated (46). **(50) But the Jews urged on the devout women of honorable estate, and the chief men of the city, and stirred up a persecution against Paul and Barnabas, and cast them out of their borders.** These devout women were among the Gentile proselytes who heard Paul; for such is the usage of the word rendered devout; but they were not of those who had been determined for eternal life; and this shows that not all the Gentile attendants of the synagogue became believers under the second sermon. That these women were of honorable estate, that is, of high connections in the political world, and satisfied with the present life, accounts for their being less determined for eternal life than those who believed. They doubtless belonged to the families of the "chief men of the city," and it was through their influence that the latter were stirred up to persecute the apostles by banishing them from the city. Women have always been among the most steadfast friends of Jesus, and yet some women have been ready and effective tools of his enemies. It seems that the Jews acted with practical unanimity in this wicked procedure, and that the favorable impression made on some of them by Paul's first sermon (43) was but transitory.

Vv. 51, 52. Paul and Barnabas were not without indignation when they were thus ignominiously expelled from the city. They were pained to think of the ingratitude which it manifested, and to anticipate the prejudice which the fact would excite against them when they should enter into other cities with this stigma upon them. Luke tells us briefly how they acted, and how the disciples felt after their teachers were driven from them. (51) **But they shook off the dust of their feet against them, and came unto Iconium.** (52) **And the disciples were filled with joy and with the Holy Spirit.** The act of the departing apostles, witnessed no doubt by those for whom it was intended, was not an idle or childish mark of resentment, as it would be in an uninspired teacher; but it was designed as a solemn " testimony against them "—a prophecy of the righteous judgment of God, whom they had rejected in rejecting his chosen messengers (Mark vi. 11 ; Luke x. 16). The statement that the disciples, under these painful circumstances, were " filled with joy and the Holy Spirit," is to us a surprise ; for we should have expected them to be filled with grief and fear. It shows that their assurance concerning the everlasting life for which they had been determined, and their belief that the Spirit of God now dwelt in their mortal bodies, gave them a joy which could now be maintained without the aid of human teachers, and of which no human power could deprive them. They were capable now of standing alone, and of edifying one another.

8. Events in Iconium, xiv. 1–7.

Ver. 1. On leaving Antioch the apostles took a road leading to the southeast, as if they were aiming to reach Cilicia, Paul's native province. They pursued this course over a vast plain grazed by innumerable flocks of sheep for about (ninety[1] miles,) when, after crossing a mountain ridge, they reached Iconium, the largest and most important city in that part of Asia Minor, both then and now. Lofty mountains rise to the west, to the north, and to the south of it, while to the east there opens another vast plain with a beautiful lake in the midst of it. Here the principal routes of travel from the cardinal points of the compass meet and cross one another, making Iconium a center of traffic and travel for an extensive region. The apostles had passed by all smaller places on the way, and kept this city in view, both because it was such a center, and because it contained a synagogue, within and around which they could find a people prepared to hear the gospel. (1) **And it came to pass in Iconium, that they entered together into the synagogue of the Jews, and so spake that a great multitude both of the Jews and the Greeks believed.** The multitude who believed was great, not in proportion to the whole population of the city, but to the number who usually believed in such places, and especially to those in Antioch. The Greeks, who made up part of the number,

---

[1] The geography of the interior of Asia Minor is very imperfectly known by western scholars. This is strikingly illustrated by the conflicting statements of the distance from Antioch to Iconium, found in recent commentaries. It is represented by Farrar, Jacobson, and Plumptre, as 60 miles; by Gloag as 50; and by Hacket as 45. Prof. Ramsey, who must be accepted as authority on the subject because of his very recent explorations in that region, furnishes the figures given above.

were doubtless proselytes in the main. The immediate cause of their belief is distinctly stated by Luke; the apostles "so spake" that they believed. It was the conclusiveness of the evidence, and the earnestness with which it was presented, that carried conviction to the hearers, thus verifying Paul's subsequent doctrine, that "faith comes by hearing, and hearing by the word of Christ" (Rom. x. 17).

Vv. 2, 3. More Jews were won to Christ there than in Antioch, but those who were not won exhibited the spirit universal with their class. (2) But the Jews that were disobedient stirred up the souls of the Gentiles, and made them evil affected against the brethren. (3) Long time therefore they tarried there, speaking boldly in the Lord, who bare witness unto the word of his grace, granting signs and wonders to be done by their hands. The Gentiles whom the disobedient Jews stirred up included others besides Greeks; that is, the native Lycaonians, and perhaps persons of other nationalities residing in the city. It must have been by false and malicious representations that the Jews succeeded in stirring them up. This opposition seems to have increased the boldness of the apostles, and it caused them to continue there "a long time;" but how many days, weeks, or months, we can not say. This is the only note of time given by Luke in the whole account of this tour.

The manner in which the Lord bore witness to the word of his favor, as here stated by Luke, is worthy of notice for the contrast which it presents with much of the phraseology of modern times. The proof with many in these days, that a man's ministry is "owned and accepted" by the Lord, is found in the "abundant outpourings of the Holy Spirit" which attend it; and this means the number of "powerful conversions" which reward it. But the Lord's method, according to Luke, was by "granting signs and wonders to be done" by the hands of the preachers. Not a word is said by him, or by any other inspired writer, of such an attestation as is now constantly brought forward. This difference shows that our modern revivalists confound the attestations of the word by signs and miracles, which was common in the apostolic age, with the exciting scenes which now occur in revivals, many of which were not dreamed of by the early evangelists. This whole subject needs to be restudied in the light thrown upon it by the book of Acts.

Vv. 4–7. The bold and persistent efforts of Paul and Barnabas stirred the city to its depths, but they failed to overcome the obstinacy of the Jews, and the depravity of the Gentiles. (4) But the multitude of the city was divided; and part held with the Jews, and part with the apostles. (5) And when there was made an onset both of the Gentiles and of the Jews with their rulers, to entreat them shamefully, and to stone them, (6) they became aware of it, and fled unto the cities of Lycaonia, Lystra and Derbe, and the region round about: (7) and there they preached the gospel. Here, as in Antioch, the Jews dared not use violence toward the preachers, for fear that they would themselves suffer as disturbers of the peace; so they worked through others until they gained the coöperation of the city rulers. As the onset which was concocted involved stoning as well as other mistreatment, we suppose that the Jews had obtained permission to do that part of the work, for it was their national form of capital punishment. As in all such cases, although the multitude of the city was divided, the party for truth and right were less active than the

party for injustice; and, because they were for the right,
they were not willing to use violence. The escape of
the missionaries must have been narrow; and it was due,
no doubt, to the watchful kindness of some friend, it
may be from among the disobedient, who exposed the plot
in time to prevent its execution. The next journey of
the apostles, like the preceding, was toward the south-
east, across the extensive plain which we have already
mentioned (1), to Lystra, about forty miles from Iconium.

9. LABORS AND RESULTS IN LYSTRA, 8–20.

Vv. 8–12. Lycaonia, the district into which the
apostles fled, was east of Pisidia, and north of the Taurus
mountains. The exact site of Lystra was not known in
modern times until it was recently identified by Prof.
Ramsay. (Historical Geography of Asia Minor).

Finding at Lystra no Jewish synagogue to afford
them an assembly of devout hearers, the missionaries
were constrained to preach in the open air. The narrow
streets universal in the cities of that age were unsuited
to gatherings of the people; but in every city there was
more or less unoccupied space about the gates, both inside and outside, and these were always favorite places
of concourse. It seems from the context below (13)
that Paul was addressing a crowd at the principal gate
when the following incident took place: (8) And at
Lystra there sat a certain man, impotent in his feet, a
cripple from his mother's womb, who never had walked.
(9) The same heard Paul speaking; who, fastening his
eyes upon him, and seeing that he had faith to be made
whole, (10) said with a loud voice, Stand upright on thy
feet. And he leaped up and walked. (11) And when
the multitude saw what Paul had done, they lifted up

their voice, saying in the speech of Lycaonia, The gods
are come down to us in the likeness of men. (12) And
they called Barnabas, Jupiter; and Paul, Mercury, because he was the chief speaker. The "faith to be made
whole," which Paul discovered in the countenance of the
cripple, is no more nor less than belief that Paul could
make him whole. The idea that it was a faith which
would *enable* Paul to make him whole finds no countenance in the Scriptures. (See remarks under iii. 16).
He could not have obtained this faith from anything
miraculous which Paul had yet done; for evidently this
was the first cure effected in Lystra. The source of his
belief then must have been something which Paul had
said. Paul had probably spoken of the miraculous cures
wrought by Jesus, and of the power given by him to his
apostles to work similar cures in proof of their divine
mission. He may even have mentioned the miracles
which he had wrought at Iconium (3), and have commenced looking in the crowd around him for a proper
subject. Seeing the cripple, and fastening his eyes upon
him, he saw that the cripple, with that credulity which
always characterizes persons with chronic diseases, believed, from the solemn statements made, that Paul had
the power which he claimed. Instantly, therefore, with
a loud voice, Paul commanded, "Stand upright on thy
feet." With amazement the crowd fell away from him
as he leaped and walked, and as quickly as the shock of
surprise would allow them to think, with one accord
there flashed into their minds the only conclusion which
their heathen education would allow, that two gods in
the form of men had come down to them. We shall see
another heathen crowd jump to the same conclusion from
a similar event farther on (xxviii. 1–6). As instantane-

ous as the conviction that the preachers were gods, was the opinion as to which gods they were; for who could one of them be but Jupiter, whose temple stood before their gate as the patron god of the city? And as the other was the chief speaker, who could he be but the god of eloquence, and Jupiter's interpreter? Their excitement caused them very naturally to break forth in their native tongue, instead of the Greek in which Paul had addressed them, and which they spoke as an acquired language. Their shouts necessarily silenced Paul for the time being, and perhaps, while he was waiting for silence to be restored so that he could continue his remarks, he failed to notice that a part of the crowd darted away, some to bring two or more fat bulls which were in readiness for a sacrifice to Jupiter, and some to bring garlands of flowers with which to decorate the horns of the victims.

VER. 13. While Paul was still waiting to renew his discourse, the people made a rush toward the temple, and he learned from their outcries what was about to take place. (13) And the priest of Jupiter whose temple was before the city, brought oxen[1] and garlands unto the gates,[2] and would have done sacrifice with the multi-

---

[1] The original is ταύρους, bulls.

[2] The position is taken by Mr. Howson (Life and Epistles of Paul), and he is followed in it by several commentators, that the word here rendered gates, πυλῶνας, never means the gates of a city, but always the gates of a private house; and that we are therefore to understand that Paul and Barnabas had retired to their place of lodging, and that the idolators brought the victims to the gate of the latter to make the sacrifice. But the criticism on the use of the Greek word is proved to be inaccurate by the fact that in the Apocalypse it is used repeatedly for the gates of a city. See xxi. 12, 13, 15, 21, 25; xxii. 14. Furthermore, as there was a temple to Jupiter in front of the city gate (13), the priest could

tudes. The priest was doubtless moving toward the
altar in front of the temple, which may have been but a
few steps from where Paul stood, and the people at once,
by a common impulse, rushed forward to join in the
honors so promptly made ready for their heavenly visitors.

Vv. 14–18. Paul and Barnabas were shocked beyond
measure to see themselves about to be honored as gods.
(14) But when the apostles, Barnabas and Paul, heard of
it, [1] they rent their garments, and sprang forth among
the multitude, crying out (15) and saying, Sirs, why
do ye these things? We also are men of like passions
with you, and bring you good tidings, that ye should
turn from these vain things unto the living God, who made
the heaven and the earth and the sea, and all that in
them is: (16) who in the generations gone by suffered
all the nations to walk in their own ways. (17) And
yet he left not himself without witness, in that he did
good, and gave you from heaven rains and fruitful seasons, filling your hearts with food and gladness. (18)
And with these sayings scarce restrained they the multitudes from doing sacrifice unto them.

It should be observed that Luke here applies the
title apostle to both Barnabas and Paul (14), as we have

not have thought of leaving it, and going into the street to offer
sacrifice. These considerations constrain us to take the view of
the whole transaction which we have given.

[1] Not "heard of it," as if they were at a distance, and did not
see it; or as if they did not understand the Lycaonian dialect,
and therefore knew not that they had been called gods until some
one who could speak Greek told them of it; but simply "heard
it" (ἀκούσαντες). They may have seen the priests and others
bringing the bulls and flowers without the thought of what was
intended until some outcry from the priests, or from the crowd
immediately about the apostles, made it known to them. The

done occasionally in preceding remarks. While Barnabas was not one of the twelve, and therefore not an apostle in the same sense that they were, he still bore the title in common with some others.[1] This was probably due to their having been under the personal instruction of Jesus, or possibly to their having been present when the great commission was given as recorded by Matthew.[2]

The habit of rending one's clothing when suddenly and violently agitated, though as old as the time of Jacob (Gen. xxxvii. 29–34), appears here (14) the last time in the Bible. The self-possession which the Christian faith inculcates and imparts soon made it disappear from the customs of the Christian Jews.

Though Barnabas, on this occasion, received the chief honor from the people, Luke on that account placing his name foremost in the paragraph just quoted, yet Paul was the master spirit in all these exciting scenes. He continued to play the part of Mercury, which the people had assigned him; for the speech to the idolaters is his in thought and diction. Mr. Howson notes the coincidence between the exhortation to the Lystrians, that they should "turn from these vain things to the living God," and his remark to the Thessalonians, that they had "turned from idols to serve the living and true God;" between the remark, that "in generations past God had suffered the Gentiles to go in their own ways," and his statement to the Athenians, the "time of this ignorance God has

narrative furnishes no ground at all for the supposition that neither Paul nor Barnabas understood what the Lycaonians had said.

[1] Rom. xvi. 7; II. Cor. xi. 13; Gal. i. 19; Rev. ii. 2.
[2] For an elaborate discussion of the N. T. use of this title, see the essay on the subject in Lightfoot's commentary on Galatians.

overlooked;" and finally, between the argument to prove that God had not left himself without witness among the heathen, and that in Romans (i. 20), where he says: "The invisible things of him since the creation of the world are clearly seen, being perceived through the things which are made, even his everlasting power and divinity; that they may be without excuse." To which I may add, that the coincidence in thought between this speech and that made in Athens to another company of idolaters (xvii. 22–31) is so striking that the latter might be regarded as the same speech altered to suit another audience. The speech was successful in preventing the sacrifice intended, but it left the idolatrous crowd sorely perplexed as to who their two visitors might be.

VER. 19. Paul continued his labors from day to day, but so dense was the darkness in which these idolaters were enshrouded, that he labored in vain to make them understand the revelation which he brought to them. In the meantime the news of that strange scene, in which men were about to be worshiped as gods, flew like wild fire from city to city, until it reached the ears of Paul's enemies in Iconium and Antioch, when a number of these, urged by hatred, made a swift journey to Lystra. (19) But there came Jews thither from Antioch and Iconium: and having persuaded the multitudes, they stoned Paul, and dragged him out of the city, supposing that he was dead. It is difficult to comprehend the malignity of these Jews. Those who came from Antioch had journeyed one hundred and thirty miles, and those from Iconium forty, to maltreat a man who had not harmed them, but whom they hated without a cause. It is not so difficult to imagine the representations by which they persuaded the Lystrians. They could say, We understand that you have taken these two countrymen of ours for gods in human form. We can tell you who they they are. They are Jews who came to Antioch and acted so base a part as to disgust all of their fellow Jews in the city, and to cause the honorable women and chief men of the city to rise up and drive them away. They then went to Iconium, and made themselves such pests that the city rulers, with the aid of Jews and Gentiles acting together, prepared to stone them, when they fled like thieves and came to Lystra. We are not willing for them to disgrace our name and nation any longer, and with your permission we will put an end to their sorcery; for it is by the power of evil spirits that they work wonders among the people. On hearing such representations from the countrymen of Paul and Barnabas, the Lystrians readily consented to let them have their own way.

Knowing from past experience how certainly Paul would escape their hands if he should learn what was on foot, they waited till he came forth as usual to preach near the gateway, when they made a rush with stones already prepared, and pelted him to death in a moment. He fell inside the city gate. Two or three of the rudest and strongest of the crowd were directed to remove his body; so, seizing him by the hands, or perhaps by the feet, they dragged him to a place outside the city where his body was left, like that of a dead beast, to any fate which might await it. Satisfied with what they had done, and fearing, possibly, that some authority higher than that of the city rulers might call them to account for their bloody work, the murderers in all probability started the same hour on their journey homeward.

They supposed that they would never hear of Paul again as a living disturber of their peace.

Ver. 20.   Up to this moment Luke has given us no intimation that Paul's labors in Lystra had been rewarded with converts.   Now they appear on his page, and in a most pitiable condition.   (20) **But as the disciples stood round about him, he rose up, and entered into the city : and on the morrow he went forth with Barnabas to Derbe.**   How long the disciples waited before they ventured out to where the body lay; how long they stood over him before he showed signs of returning consciousness; and how long after that before he and they ventured back into the city, Luke leaves to the imagination of his reader.   We can readily imagine the bitter tears and cries of that little band, while they gazed upon the wounds and bruises of one whom they had learned to love so tenderly; while they thought of the cruelty with which he had been murdered; and when they glanced at the future awaiting themselves, like lambs, as they were, in the midst of wolves.   We can rejoice with them when Paul opened his eyes; and wonder with them that, after he was stoned to unconsciousness, the last spark of life which may have lingered in his body was not extinguished by the horrid manner in which he was dragged over the rough pavements, and through the dust and filth of the street and of the highway, to the place where they found him.   And how was he able, so soon, to rise up and walk ?   How is it possible that he was able to start on a new journey with Barnabas the next day ?   Does not the last fact especially tell us of gentle hands and loving ministrations all through the night, bathing and dressing his many wounds and bruises, and cheering him with words of deepest sympathy ?

Thank God, we are not left altogether to imagination for the names of those tender and loving friends. Timothy was a native of Lystra, baptized during this very visit of Paul; and many years after this we hear, from the depths of the Roman prison whence Paul was led forth to the executioner's block, these melting words addressed to this most beloved of all his companions in tribulation: "I thank God, whom I serve from my forefathers in a pure conscience, how unceasing is my remembrance of thee in supplications, night and day longing to see thee, remembering thy tears, that I may be filled with joy; having been reminded of the unfeigned faith that is in thee; which dwelt first in thy grandmother Lois and in thy mother Eunice; and, I am persuaded, in thee also" (II. Tim. i. 3–5). Were those remembered tears the tears which Timothy, then a boy of fifteen,[1] shed over Paul's bruised and mangled body? And were the faithful Eunice and the venerable Lois in the group which stood around that body till animation was restored? If it was into their house that Paul was led, and by their hands that he was nursed through the night, the mystery of his speedy recovery is in part at least explained. What a scene was that to be witnessed by a boy of fifteen, who had been trained from infancy to the holiest sentiments of the Jewish Scriptures, who was but newly born into the kingdom of the Redeemer, and whose soul was responsive to everything noble in human character! No wonder that his heart was ever

---

[1] As this event occurred not later than the year 48, and as Timothy was still a youth at the date of Paul's first epistle to him (I. Tim. iv. 12), which was written not earlier than 64, Timothy could not at the time of the stoning have been much older than fifteen.

after bound to Paul's like that of a dutiful son to a loving father. And what a compensation did Paul himself afterward find for all his sufferings in Lystra, in the life-long devotion of him concerning whom he could say, "I have no man likeminded?" The very hour in which the whole world seemed to forsake him and hate him brought to his side the dearest friend he ever knew.

10. Success in Derbe, and Return to Antioch, 21-28.

Vv. 21, 22. Having been compelled to fly from Antioch, from Iconium, and from Lystra, who can tell the feelings of the wounded missionary as he approached the gates of another heathen city, bearing visible marks of the indignity which he had suffered? But He who brings light out of darkness caused a refreshing light to shine on the dark pathway of his faithful servant by granting him here a peaceful and abundant harvest of souls. (21) And when they had preached the gospel to that city, and had made many disciples, they returned to Lystra, and to Iconium, and to Antioch, (22) confirming the souls of the disciples, exhorting them to continue in the faith, and that through many tribulations we must enter into the kingdom of God.

At Derbe, where the apostles seem to have suffered no persecution, they were some miles farther eastward than at Lystra, and were not far from the well known pass called the Gates of Cilicia, which leads through the Taurus mountains down into the plain of Cilicia in the direction of Tarsus. Had Paul allowed the thought of rest for a time among friends and kindred to control his movements, he would now have revisited the home of his childhood; but he thought of the disciples whom he

had left behind him to an unknown fate, and he turned
back at great hazard to revisit them. How he succeeded
in re-entering Lystra, and Iconium, and Antioch, and
remaining in each long enough to instruct and organize
the disciples, without a renewal of the persecutions which
had driven him away from all of these cities, Luke does
not inform us. It is possible that the fury of the mob
had spent itself, and that his presence was tolerated because he made no further effort to gain converts to the
new faith. The meetings were doubtless held in private,
and perhaps in the night. The apostles confirmed the
souls of the disciples by exhorting them to continue in
the faith, and by assuring them that the pathway into
the everlasting kingdom, at least in their day, was
through many such tribulations as they had already endured. They were made to realize that the prize at the
end of the journey was worth all the hardships of the
way, and thus they were made strong to endure. There
were many tearful scenes, as the two brethren, who had
come among these people like visitors from a better
world, were bidding them a final farewell, and leaving
them to make their own way through the temptations
and conflicts which beset them.

VER. 23. They were left as "sheep in the midst of
wolves;" but they were committed to the care of the
great Shepherd of the sheep, and were supplied with
under-shepherds to keep them in the fold. (23) **And
when they had appointed**[1] **for them elders in every**

---

[1] The word here translated appointed (χειροτονέω) means primarily to stretch out the hand; secondarily, to appoint by a show
of the hand; and thirdly, to appoint or elect without regard to
the method. See Grimm's N. T. Greek Lexicon. Whether it
designates here an act of Paul and Barnabas, or one which they
caused the people to do, is not made clear. The force of the

church, and had prayed with fasting, they commended them to the Lord, on whom they had believed.   Here we see fasting and prayer connected with the appointment of elders, as we saw prayer and the imposition of hands in the appointment of the seven servants of the church in Jerusalem (vi. 6), and as we saw the last two with fasting in the separation of Barnabas and Saul to their appointed work (xiii. 3).   The laying on of hands, which was part of the ceremony in those two services, is not mentioned here; but as we have seen that it was a part of the service of appointment to office, we may safely infer that it was not omitted.

It should be observed that a plurality of elders were appointed in " every church ; " and this, so far as we are able to trace the facts, was the universal practice of the apostles.   In appointing these, Paul and Barnabas were. but following the example of the older apostles, by whom this office was instituted in the churches of Judea (xi. 30).   An elaborate discussion of the subject would belong properly to a separate treatise, or to a Commentary on I. Timothy.   If any one is surprised that men were found in these newly founded congregations possessed of the high qualifications for the office laid down by Paul in his epistles to Titus and Timothy, he should remember that although these disciples had been but a comparatively short time in the church, many of them were, in character and knowledge of the Scriptures, the ripest fruits of the Jewish synagogue ; and they needed only the

word favors the former view, while the previous act of the twelve in requiring the multitude to choose the deacons (vi. 1-3), favors the latter.   For a summary of many opinions on the subject, see Meyer's commentary, note L by the American editor after chapter xiv.

additional knowledge which the gospel brought, in order to be models of wisdom and piety for the churches. They were not "novices" (I. Tim. iii. 6) in the sense of being newly turned away from wickedness. Cornelius the centurion might represent the class, as respects Gentile converts, and Nathaniel those brought in from the Jews.

Vv. 24–26. Having done all in their power for the churches which they had planted, the apostles continued their homeward journey by descending from Antioch to Perga, where they had first landed in their voyage from Cyprus. **(24) And they passed through Pisidia, and came to Pamphylia. (25) And when they had spoken the word in Perga they went down to Attalia; and thence they sailed to Antioch, from whence they had been committed to the grace of God for the work which they had fulfilled.** Why they did not "speak the word" in Perga at their first visit, and what success they had now, are alike left out of the account of Luke, whose omissions, like those of all other New Testament writers, are not less remarkable than what he records. It is probable that the preaching done here now was actuated more by the desire to usefully occupy the time of waiting for a vessel bound to Antioch, than by a decided hope of accomplishing visible results; and this view is confirmed by the fact that they at last went by land to Attalia,[1] about sixteen miles distant on the sea coast, where they would be more certain to find a vessel than up the river Cestrus at Perga. Thence they "sailed to Antioch," without going ashore at any intermediate point.

---

[1] Attalia is still a seaport of some importance at which the coasting steamers of the Levant make regular calls.

Vv. 27, 28. It is doubtful whether the church in Antioch had heard from Paul and Barnabas since they first left Perga. John, on his return, may have brought them news of the journey to that point. When, therefore, they appeared unheralded on the streets of the city, after an absence of three or four years, we may well suppose that they were met with hearty greetings and much questioning. They had gone on the first mission ever sent out to the heathen world, and they were as eager to tell their story as the disciples were to hear it. He who returns from a hard fought field bearing good tidings, pants beneath the burden of his untold story. **(27) And when they were come, and had gathered the church together, they rehearsed all things that God had done with them, and how that he had opened a door of faith to the Gentiles. (28) And they tarried no little time with the disciples.** The metaphor of an open door to represent men's access to the privileges of the gospel, or the access of the preacher to the hearts of the people, was first employed by our Lord (Jno. x. 1, 2, 7, 9) ; it was a favorite with Paul (I. Cor. xvi. 9 ; II. Cor. ii. 12 ; Col. iv. 3) ; and it is found in the lips of our Lord after his glorification (Rev. iii. 8, 20). Its employment here to represent the access to faith which had now been opened to the heathen world by the mission of the apostles, is probably, as Plumptre suggests, an echo in Luke's narrative of Paul's own language, in the report under consideration. The " no little time " which the apostles now spent in Antioch counts forward to their journey to Jerusalem mentioned in the next chapter, and if we estimate it by comparison with their previous stay in the same city, it was more than a year (*cf.* xi. 26).

SEC. II. A CONTROVERSY ON CIRCUM-
CISION.

(xv.)

1. THE BEGINNING OF THE CONTROVERSY, 1–5.

VER. 1. At this point our historian makes a sudden transition from the conflicts of the disciples with
Jews and Gentiles, to one of momentous importance
among themselves. One phase of this controversy had
taken its origin from the baptism of uncircumcised Gentiles in the house of Cornelius. The question then was
whether such persons should be baptized; and by the
evidences of the divine will which had been presented to
Peter, and which he presented to the brethren, it was
settled, definitely and finally (xi. 18). This fact, strangely
overlooked by many commentators, it is necessary to
bear distinctly in mind, if we would distinguish the suc-
cessive phases which this controversy assumed. The
question now raised in Antioch was a different one.
Without controverting the propriety of baptizing Gentiles, as Paul and Barnabas had been doing, both abroad
and here in Antioch, the disputants took the position that
after being baptized, and receiving forgiveness of sins,
they must be circumcised as a condition of their final
salvation. The position, and the men who assumed it
are thus introduced: (1) And certain men came down
from Judea and taught the brethren, saying, Except ye
be circumcised after the custom of Moses, ye can not be
saved. The fact that these men came from Judea,
where the gospel was first preached, and where the
original apostles had been the teachers, gave their utterances much authority with the Antioch brethren, so it

is not necessary to suppose that they claimed express authority from the apostles for their teaching, though it is possible that they did. They insisted on circumcision, not because of the covenant with Abraham, which was the original ground of the obligation, but because of the law of Moses; and they did so because, as a part of the law of Moses, circumcision bound those who submitted to it to keep all of the law, while circumcision as a mere Abrahamic rite did not; for the Ishmaelites, the Edomites, the Midianites, and other descendants of Abraham, were confessedly not brought under the law of Moses by their circumcision. The phraseology employed shows, what is brought out expressly farther on (5), that they insisted on circumcision "after the custom of Moses," because they held that all the baptized, whether Jews or Gentiles, must keep the law of Moses in order to final salvation. They could not conceive, as yet, that this divinely given law, which had been in existence so long, and for the preservation of which their fathers had suffered so much, could be disregarded by any who would be heirs of eternal life. When they thought of the apostolic commission, they must have included circumcision and the keeping of the law among the things referred to in the words, "teaching them [the baptized] to observe all things whatsoever I have commanded you" (Matt. xxviii. 20).

VER. 2. Paul, who had long ago received by direct revelation from Christ a correct knowledge of the gospel which he preached (Gal. i. 11, 12), knew perfectly that this teaching was erroneous, and Barnabas had learned the same from him, if not from some other source; so the two united with all their might in opposing the Judean teachers. We have to think of a congregation in our own day, distracted by an earnest controversy between its teachers over a vital question of doctrine, in order to realize the distress and confusion which must have racked the minds of the brethren in Antioch while this controversy was in progress. Paul and Barnabas did not succeed in silencing their opponents, but they so conducted the discussion as to bring about a fortunate decision of a provisional character. (2) And when Paul and Barnabas had no small dissension and questioning with them, the brethren determined[1] that Paul and Barnabas, and certain other of them, should go up to Jerusalem, unto the apostles and elders about this question.

If the brethren at Antioch had properly estimated the authority of an inspired apostle, they would have accepted implicitly Paul's decision without this mission to Jerusalem; but their familiarity with the person of the apostle, like that of the Nazarenes with the person of Jesus, made them slow to realize that he spoke with divine authority; and the fact that he was not one of the original twelve caused them to think his utterances less authoritative than theirs. They learned, as the result of the mission, what they should have realized at first; and it is not probable that they ever doubted Paul's teaching again.

As the proposal to send Paul and the others to Jerusalem about this matter involved the implication that the former was inferior in authority to the apostles and elders there, it is probable that Paul, for the maintenance of his apostolic prerogative, would have refused to go, had not the Lord expressly commanded him to do

---

[1] On the correctness of the rendering, "determined," instead of "appointed," (R. V.), see the discussion under xiii. 48.

so; for he himself says in reference to this journey, "I went up by revelation" (Gal. ii. 2). This revelation requiring him to go was made because it was the divine purpose to settle the question at issue, not for the church in Antioch alone, but for all the world and for all time.

Before we leave this verse, let it be distinctly noted that this procedure was not an appeal from the decision of a church to some higher tribunal; for in fact no decision had been rendered. Neither was it an overture from a congregation to a representative body, asking for instruction; for the body applied to was composed of the elders of another single congregation, together with such apostles as might be found there. In truth only three of the older apostles, as the sequel shows, took part in rendering the decision (Gal. ii. 9). In these two essential particulars the step taken by the Antioch church differs from all modern appeals from lower to higher ecclesiastical courts, and it furnishes no precedent for the latter.

Ver. 3. The journey to Jerusalem was made by land, and the messengers passed through two districts which had been evangelized already to a considerable extent. (3) They therefore being brought on their way by the church, passed through both Phœnicia and Samaria, declaring the conversion of the Gentiles; and they caused great joy unto all the brethren. The Samaritans, although circumcised like the Jews, had far less antipathy to Gentiles than the latter; while the disciples in Phœnicia, though made up largely of Jews, were closely identified with Gentiles; and so both were prepared to rejoice at the triumphs of the gospel in the heathen world.

VER. 4. After a pleasant journey through the midst of rejoicing churches, they reached Jerusalem, where the name of Barnabas was held in sacred remembrance on account of his usefulness in the church's infancy; where Paul was now well known as a courageous and self-sacrificing evangelist; and where the news of the successful tour of both into heathen lands had preceded them. The reception which was accorded them was most natural. (4) **And when they were come to Jerusalem, they were received by the church and the apostles and the elders, and they rehearsed all things that God had done with them.**[1] It was a thrilling story which

---

[1] There has been much discussion as to whether this visit of Paul to Jerusalem is the one mentioned in the second chapter of Galatians, or some other; but recent writers are almost unanimous in deciding that it is the same. Farrar puts the decisive evidence in a nutshell as follows: "In the two narratives the same people go up at the same time, from the same place, for the same object, in consequence of the same interference by the same agitators, and with the same results. Against the absolute certainty of the conclusion that the visits described were one and the same, there is nothing whatever to set but trivial differences of detail, every one of which is accounted for in the text." (*Life and Work of Paul*, 228, *n.* 5). Rationalists admit this, but they use the fact to show that as Paul represents this as his second visit to Jerusalem since his conversion, therefore Luke's account of his visit with Barnabas on the alms-giving trip mentioned in xi. is false. (Baur, *Life of Paul*, i. 114, 115; Zeller on Acts ii. 8). But Paul does not say that the visit of Gal. ii. was his second visit. He merely says, "Then after the space of fourteen years I went up again" (Gal. ii. 1). This was, however, the second visit with which his line of argument in Galatians was concerned; for his purpose is to show that he had not before this enjoyed an opportunity to be instructed by the older apostles, except during the fifteen days of his first visit (Gal. i. 18); and during his brief visit mentioned in the eleventh chapter, Peter, the only apostle in the city, was shut up in prison during the passover week,

they told, and it must have drawn many tears from the
eyes of the sympathizing audience, while it aroused them
to fresh enthusiasm in the cause of human redemption.

VER. 5. Touching and inspiring as was the occasion, some brethren in the church were not willing to
miss the opportunity of suggesting what they regarded
as a serious defect in the instruction which Paul and
Barnabas had given their Gentile converts.   (5) **But
there rose up certain of the sect of the Pharisees who
believed, saying, It is needful to circumcise them, and
to charge them to keep the law of Moses.**[1]   After reading so much in the earlier chapters of Acts respecting
the hostility of the sect of the Pharisees to the church, it
is a surprise to here meet with some of that party inside
the church, and occupying a position of some influence,
though it is not a surprise to find them on the wrong
side of an important question.   They found it no longer
possible to resist the evidence in favor of Jesus, and had
therefore been baptized into his name; but they still
clung tenaciously to some of their former ideas.   Long
after this meeting, when Paul had come to fully understand their motives, even if he did not at the time, he
styles them " false brethren privily brought in, who came

and then fled from the city. Paul and Barnabas seem not to have
gone into the city at all until their mission among the churches
of Judea was accomplished, and then their stay must have been
very brief on account of the danger imminent.   See xi. 29—xii. 25.

[1] Baur (*Life of Paul*, i. 117–119; *Church Hist.* i. 52), followed by
the whole school which he represents, declares, without reason
worthy of the name, that Luke here falsifies the facts, and that
the older apostles themselves, and not certain Pharisees who
believed, were Paul's opponents. Paul's own statements about
the perfect agreement between himself and the other apostles
(Gal. ii. 6–10), show clearly the falsity of this assertion, and the
truthfulness of Luke.

in privily to spy out our liberty which we have in Christ
Jesus, that they might bring us into bondage " (Gal. ii. 4).
From this judicial sentence upon them we ascertain that
when they despaired of destroying the church by persecution from without, they deliberately confessed Christ
and came into the church for the purpose of controlling
it from within. It was their design to keep the church
under the bondage of the law, and thus prevent it from
very seriously modifying the state of things among the
Jews in which the Pharisees were the predominant
party. Partisan zeal, the bane of their former life, was
still their controlling passion. It is highly probable
that among them Paul recognized some of his old
acquaintances, who had once been his helpers in persecution, and had more recently been of the number who
sought to put him to death. He knew them through
and through.

The essential issue between Paul and the Pharisees
had reference to the perpetuation of the law of Moses in
the church of God ; and the same issue has been in
debate under different phases from that day to this.
Paul defeated the attempt to fasten circumcision on the
church, but later Judaizers succeeded in perpetuating it
under the form of infant immersion, and afterward of
infant sprinkling. That which the Pharisees failed to
accomplish openly was thus accomplished under a thin
disguise. The Pharisees failed to consolidate the law
and the gospel ; but their imitators have largely succeeded in teaching men that the church of Christ originated in the family of Abraham, and that the Jewish
tribes and the Christian congregations constitute one
identical church. The Roman apostasy perpetuates the
daily sacrifice and pompous ritual of the temple ; relig-

ious zealots have slaughtered Canaanites in the persons of modern heretics; professed Christians go to war under the old battle-cry of the "sword of the Lord and of Gideon;" the "Latter-day Saints" emulate Solomon in the multiplication of wives; and for all these corruptions authority is found in the laws and customs of ancient Israel. The intelligent reader of the New Testament knows scarcely which of these errors is farthest from the truth; and he feels bound to struggle with untiring energy and ceaseless vigilance to uproot them all from the minds of men.

2. Another Meeting, and a Speech by Peter, 6-11.

Ver. 6. After the Pharisees had stated their position, distinctly affirming that the Gentiles should be circumcised and keep the law, the assembly adjourned without discussing the question. The second meeting is announced in these words: (6) **And the apostles and the elders were gathered together to consider of this matter.** Neither this nor the first meeting was composed exclusively of the apostles and the elders; for we have seen (4) that at the first the messengers were "received by the church," and from verse 22 below we learn that the church was now present. There was, however, between these two public meetings a private meeting of Paul and Barnabas with the three apostles who were then in the city. This we learn from Paul's epistle to the Galatians, in which he both states the fact, and gives his reason for seeking the interview. He says: "Then after the space of fourteen years I went up again to Jerusalem with Barnabas, taking Titus also with me. And I went up by revelation; and I laid before them the gospel which I preach among the Gentiles, but privately before them who were of repute, lest by any means I should be running, or had run, in vain." The force of the reason given is seen in the fact that if he had found the old apostles on the side of the Pharisees, their influence would have overborne his with the brethren, and all of his work, both past and future, would have been overthrown by bringing his converts under the bondage of the law.[1] The result of the interview he states in these words: "But from those who were reputed to be somewhat—whatsoever they were, it maketh no matter to me; God accepteth not man's person—they, I say, who were of repute imparted nothing to me; but contrariwise, when they saw that I had been intrusted with the gospel of the uncircumcision, even as Peter with the gospel of circumcision, (for he that wrought for Peter unto the apostleship of the circumcision wrought for me also unto the Gentiles); and when they perceived the grace that was given unto me, James and Cephas and John, they who were reputed to be pillars, gave to me and Barnabas the right hands of fellowship, that we should go unto the Gentiles, and they unto the circum-

---

[1] I can not withhold my surprise that Farrar has so completely misunderstood Paul's meaning here as to write the following sentence: "When he says to the Galatians that he 'consulted them about the gospel he was preaching, lest he might be or had been running to no purpose,' he shows that at this period he had not arrived at the quite unshaken conviction, which made him subsequently say that, 'whether he or an angel from heaven preached any other gospel, let him be anathema," (*Life of Paul*, 228.) This is totally inconsistent with Paul's repeated declaration in the previous chapter of Galatians, that he had received his knowledge of the gospel by direct revelation, and that therefore he could not have any doubts concerning it. Compare Lightfoot on the passage in his commentary on Galatians.

cision " (Gal. ii. 6–10).   From this account of the interview it appears that as soon as the three older apostles
heard Paul's statement of the case, they heartily approved it, and indicated the fact by extending their
right hands to him and Barnabas.   The words, " imparted nothing to me," are well chosen ; for the question
was whether or not Paul had taught the Gentiles their
whole duty ; if not, something additional would have
been imparted.   With this information as to the perfect
understanding and agreement between the inspired apostles before us, we can plainly see that the second public
meeting of the whole church was called, not for the purpose of bringing about an agreement between the apostles, but for the purpose of enabling the apostles to
bring the whole church into agreement with themselves.
In this light we must study the proceedings, or we shall
totally misconstrue them.

Vv. 7–11.   Men who are in error can never be convinced that they are wrong by denying them freedom of
speech.   Not till they have been allowed to express
themselves to the last word are they capable of listening
dispassionately to the other side.   The apostles, knowing
this, or at least acting on it, permitted the judaizers in
the church to say all that they wished to say before any
reply was made to their position and arguments.   Then,
when they had completely emptied themselves, the apostles, one by one, and in a succession apparently pre-
arranged, gave utterance to facts and judgments which
compelled assent.   (7) **And when there had been much
questioning, Peter rose up, and said unto them,**

**Brethren, ye know how that a good while ago God
made choice among you, that by my mouth the Gentiles
should hear the word of the gospel, and believe. (8) And**

God, who knoweth the heart, bare them witness, giving
them the Holy Spirit, even as he did unto us; (9) and
he made no distinction between them and us, purifying
their hearts by faith. (10) Now therefore why tempt ye
God, that ye should put a yoke upon the necks of the disciples, which neither our fathers nor we were able to
bear? (11) But we believe that we shall be saved through
the grace of the Lord Jesus, in like manner as they.

The Greek word rendered questioning in verse 7
($\zeta\acute{\eta}\tau\eta\sigma\iota\varsigma$) literally means a question; but here it has the
sense of debate or disputation (Grimm's Lexicon); and it
is used here rather than the more usual word for debate
($\sigma\upsilon\zeta\acute{\eta}\tau\eta\sigma\iota\varsigma$), to indicate, I think, that the discussion was
conducted chiefly by asking questions— a very common
way of putting an adversary to a disadvantage. The
debate was probably one-sided, the Pharisees putting all
the questions, and putting them so that each one carried
in it an argument, or implied a conclusion. It is perhaps
because they had adopted this form of argumentation
that Peter put the main point of his answer (10) in the
same form.

Peter's speech contains just three points of argument:
First, that in the well known case of the first Gentile
converts in the house of Cornelius, God, by giving them
the Holy Spirit as he had given it to the apostles, made
no distinction between Jews and Gentiles; from which
the silent inference is that as God had made no distinction men should make none. Second, to put on the
necks of these Gentile converts the yoke of the law,
which no generation of Jews had been able to bear,
would be, in the light of the preceding fact, tempting
God; that is, trying his forbearance by their own presumption. Third, the settled belief, indicated in the

words "we believe," that both Jews and Gentiles were to be saved through grace, the grace of the Lord Jesus Christ, implies necessarily that they were not to be saved by keeping the law. In affirming that the law was a yoke that the Jews had not been able to bear, he meant that they had not been able so to keep it as to be saved by the perfection of their obedience to it. This speech, it would seem, should have been enough to end the whole controversy; but it was wisely planned among the apostles that the evidence on the subject should be multiplied in a way to leave no room for more, and no room for subsequent caviling.

3. Speeches by Barnabas and Paul, 12.

Ver. 12. After Peter sat down, Barnabas spoke next, and then Paul, each setting forth other evidences of God's will on the question at issue. (12) **And all the multitude kept silence; and they hearkened unto Barnabas and Paul rehearsing what signs and wonders God had wrought among the Gentiles by them.** Their line of argument was a continuation of Peter's. As the miracle of giving the Holy Spirit in the case of Cornelius and his friends gave proof of God's approval in that case, so the "signs and wonders" which he wrought by the hands of Barnabas and Paul while they were bringing in the Gentiles and organizing them as congregations without circumcision, and without requiring them to keep the law, gave proof of his approbation in these cases also. The argument of the three speeches was exactly the same, though based upon different facts, and these facts were presented in their chronological order.

4. A Speech by James, 13-21.

Vv. 13-21. ~~As in the case of the death and resurrection of the Messiah, no amount of contemporary evidence could convince the average Jew, unless he could be made to see that such a death and resurrection were spoken of in the predictions concerning the Messiah, so, in reference to the question in hand, they could not be silenced without evidence from the prophets.~~ To James was assigned the task of setting forth the evidence on this point, and also of proposing a decision in harmony with the result of the private conference. (13) **And after they had held their peace, James answered, saying,**

Brethren, hearken unto me: (14) **Symeon hath rehearsed how first God did visit the Gentiles, to take out of them a people for his name.** (15) **And to this agree the words of the prophets; as it is written,** (16) **After these things I will return, and I will build again the tabernacle of David, which is fallen, and I will build again the ruins thereof, and I will set it up;** (17) **that the residue of men may seek after the Lord, and all the Gentiles upon whom my name is called,** (18) **saith the Lord, who maketh these things known from the beginning of the world.** (19) **Wherefore my judgment is, that we trouble not them who from among the Gentiles turn to God;** (20) **but that we write unto them, that they abstain from the pollutions of idols, and from fornication, and from what is strangled, and from blood.** (21) **For Moses from generations of old hath in every city them that preach him, being read in the synagogues every Sabbath.**

The words, "James answered" (13), indicate that this speech was in answer to the positions of the Pharisees. The argument is, that the statements of Peter, of which those made by Barnabas and Paul were a mere supplement, and needed not special mention, were in fulfillment of prophecy concerning the Messiah's reign; and it supplied all that was lacking to convince the brethren. While he quotes only one prophet (Amos ix. 11, 12), he says, "to this agree the words of the prophets," meaning that other prophets besides the one quoted had used words of the same import. The quotation is made from the Septuagint, as appears from its agreeing more closely with that version than with the Hebrew. The prophet had in previous verses predicted the downfall of the Jewish kingdom, which would be the overthrow of the tabernacle or house of David, whose descendants were the reigning kings; and in the verses quoted he predicts the rebuilding of the same, which could occur only by some descendant of David again ascending the throne. But after that downfall, no man of David's race became a king until Jesus was enthroned in heaven. This, then, was the rebuilding of the ruins, and it was to be followed by "the residue of men," that is, the Gentiles, seeking after the Lord, as Gentiles had been doing ever since Peter's visit to the house of Cornelius.

The fact that James introduces the decision which he proposes with the words, "Wherefore my judgment is," has been construed by many as evidence that he was president of the conference, and as such rendered a decision which the others were bound to accept. But there is no evidence whatever that he acted in this capacity, or that his judgment in the case was more authoritative than that of Peter, or of John, who also was present. The four things from which James proposed that the Gentiles should be required to abstain had been

made unlawful, not by the Mosaic law, but by the revelations of the patriarchal age. From the beginning
it had been known to the patriarchs that it was sinful
to have any responsible connection with idols, or to
indulge in fornication; and from the time of the law
given to the race in the family of Noah, eating blood,
and consequently eating things strangled which retained
their blood within them, had been wrong, and it will
continue to be until the end of the world.[1]　So, in
regard to the question at issue, whether the Gentile
disciples must observe the law of Moses, James' proposal that " we trouble them not," was fully carried out
by imposing nothing on them that was peculiar to the
law.

The remark with which James closes his speech, that
Moses was preached in every city by being read in the
synagogues, was intended, I think, to meet an objection
which he knew to be in the minds of some of his hearers,
and it may have been expressed by some of the speakers

---

[1] Farrar and Lightfoot, followed by others, hold that these
provisions were intended to be temporary and local. Both refer
for proof of this to Paul's subsequent discussion of eating things
offered to idols, assuming that he permitted it; and the former
appeals to the fact that the Judaizing party in the church afterward disregarded the decree (*Farrar's Life of Paul*, 243, 244;
Lightfoot on Galatians, 127 [1].) But the fact that it was repudiated
afterward by the Judaizers only, shows that they deserved the
stern rebukes which Paul administers to them in the epistle to
the Galatians (i. 6–9; iv. 17; v. 1; vi. 12, 13); and in Paul's
discussion of the question, while he admits that to eat meat
offered to idols is not sinful when the fact of its being so offered
is not known to the eater; and while he shows that, if for no
other reason, one should abstain on account of the harm which
eating might do to weak brethren; he finally takes the very position of the decree, forbidding it altogether as a communion with
demons. See I. Cor. viii. 8–13; x. 14–22.

whom he was answering—the objection that, if the Gentiles were not required to keep the law of Moses, the law would fall into disrepute, and be forgotten among men. Of this James would assure them there would be no danger, seeing that the synagogue service would prevent such a result.

It naturally seems strange to our generation that the apostles thought it worth while to warn the Gentile disciples against "pollutions of idols, and fornication." But they had been trained for generations back to regard the latter vice as an innocent gratification of a natural desire, and to look upon the former as a solemn religious duty; and it was not easy, when they became believers, to shake off convictions which had been thus imbedded in their moral nature. The same difficulty is encountered to this day by missionaries among the heathen.

5. THE DECISION OF THE APOSTLES AND ELDERS, 22–29.

Vv. 22–29. The speech of James brought the discussion to a close. The combined force of the four speeches made the will of God so clear that the opposition was totally silenced, and the only remaining question was, how best to carry out the proposal submitted by James. (22) Then it seemed good to the apostles and the elders, with the whole church, to choose men out of their company, and send them to Antioch with Paul and Barnabas; namely, Judas, called Barsabbas, and Silas, chief men among the brethren: (23) and they wrote thus by them, The apostles and the elder brethren unto the brethren which are of the Gentiles in Antioch and Syria and Cilicia, greeting: (24) Forasmuch as we have heard that certain who went out from us have troubled

you with words, subverting your souls; to whom we
gave no commandment; (25) it seemed good to us, having
come to one accord, to choose out men and send them unto
you with our beloved Barnabas and Paul, (26) men who
have hazarded their lives for the name of our Lord Jesus
Christ.   (27) We have sent therefore Judas and Silas,
who themselves also shall tell you the same things by
word of mouth.   (28) For it seemed good to the Holy
Spirit, and to us, to lay upon you no greater burden
than these necessary things; (29) that ye abstain from
things sacrificed to idols, and from blood, and from things
strangled, and from fornication ; from which if ye keep
yourselves, it shall be well with you.   Fare ye well.

Athough this document was written in the name of
" the apostles and the elder brethren " (23), the latter
expression being the equivalent of " the elders " of 22,
yet "the whole church " (22) was present, and the expression of verse 25, " having come to one accord,"
refers to the apostles having brought all the members of
the church to the judgment in which they themselves
had previously united.   Observe that it begins by repudiating all responsibility for the teaching of the men
who had started the trouble in Antioch, declaring that
the apostles and elders had given them no commandment at all.   The wisdom of sending Judas and Silas is
seen in the fact that they had not been connected at all
with the work among the Gentiles, and that their personal influence would tend to silence any objections
which might be raised by refractory Jews.   They could
explain, without suspicion of bias, anything in the written document which might appear to any one obscure.

This is the earliest document, so far as we know, that
issued from the pen of any apostle.   It antedated all of

the Gospels, and all of Paul's epistles. It circulated as
a separate document among the churches until it was in-
corporated into Acts, when previously existing copies of
it were naturally allowed to perish. It is called an
epistle (30), and also the "decrees [τὰ δόγματα] which
had been ordained by the apostles and elders that were
at Jerusalem" (xvi. 4). It makes a formal claim of
inspiration by the words, "it seemed good to the Holy
Spirit and to us." No uninspired men could dare to use
such language; and this circumstance differentiates it
from all the decrees and deliverances of all the ecclesiastical courts from that day to this, not excepting those
of the Roman Catholic Church, which makes blasphemous
pretences of infallibility. Be it observed, too, that while
this conference is constantly referred to by Romanists
and other supporters of episcopacy, as the first general
council, it was no general council at all. It was not
composed of representatives from the congregations of a
district, however small, but of the members of a single
church.[1] Furthermore, it decided, on the authority of
the inspired men who directed its decisions, a question
of doctrine affecting the salvation of souls; and this no
set of men except the apostles have ever had the right to
do. In no sense, then, can its action be pleaded as a
precedent for the existence of any ecclesiastical court

---

[1] It is gratifying to observe that Archdeacon Farrar, himself a
high dignitary of the Church of England, with a tender side
toward Romanism, unites with the non-episcopal writers in the
view expressed above. He says: "The so-called Council of Jerusalem in no way resembled the general councils of the church,
either in its history, its constitution, or its object. It was not a
convention of ordained delegates, but a meeting of the entire
church of Jerusalem to receive a deputation from the church at
Antioch." (Life of Paul, 243).

whatever outside of the individual congregation, or for the purpose of settling by authority any question of doctrine.

6. Peace Restored in Antioch, 30–35.

Vv. 30, 31. The return journey of the messengers, and the effect in Antioch of the decision which they brought, is briefly stated. (30) **So they, when they were dismissed, came down to Antioch; and having gathered the multitude together, they deliverd the epistle. (31) And when they had read it they rejoiced for the consolation.** As the Jewish brethren in Antioch had not become partisans in the controversy, and had desired only a peaceable settlement of the question, their rejoicing at the result was a natural consequence. If any of those who had raised the question at first were still in the city, doubtless they were crestfallen, but their mouths were stopped, and it is possible that, like their sympathisers in Jerusalem, they acquiesced in the decision. Thus the triumph of Paul and Barnabas was most signal and complete. It was rendered more so in the eyes of the Antioch brethren from the fact mentioned by Paul (Gal. ii. 1-4), but not by Luke, that Titus, a Gentile, had gone with Paul; that a strenuous effort was made to have him circumcised; and that he had come back uncircumcised, Paul having refused to give place to the Judaisers for a single hour.[1]

Vv. 32–34. Judas and Silas had now accomplished the main purpose for which they were sent to Antioch,

[1] The attempt of some writers, including Farrar (*Life of Paul*, 233-237), to make it appear that Titus was circumcised, and that Paul's language about the incident means, he was not *compelled* to be circumcised, but I circumcised him for the sake of peace, appears to me like a mere conceit. Even Baur repudiates it, saying, "Nothing can be more absurd." (*Life of Paul*; i. 122, *n.* 1).

but they found opportunity to make themselves still
further useful. As they had been "chief men among
the brethren" in Jerusalem, it was a source of delight to
the brethren in Antioch to hear them. (32) **And Judas
and Silas, being themselves also prophets, exhorted the
brethren in many words, and confirmed them. (33) And
after they had spent some time there, they were dismissed in peace from the brethren to those who had sent
them forth.**[1] The fact that they were "themselves also
prophets," gave inspired authority to all their utterances,
and made their exhortations the more edifying to the
brethren.

Ver. 35. The city of Antioch was still a profitable
field for apostolic labor, and the scene of interesting
events. (35) **But Paul and Barnabas tarried in Antioch,
teaching and preaching the word of the Lord, with many
others also.** To justify the united labors of so many
eminent men, the number of disciples to be taught and
the number of others willing to hear the preaching
must have been very great.

It is during this period that the most judicious commentators, and I may say all recent scholars, locate the
visit of Peter to Antioch, and the rebuke administered
to him by Paul, as recorded in the second chapter of
Galatians. It has been erroneously affirmed that in
this affair Peter acted in direct conflict with the epistle
which he and others are represented as having so recently
written to this church. The harshness of this supposition has led some to deny the truthfulness of Luke's
representations about that epistle. It is argued that

---

[1] Verse 34 of the A. V., from the *Textus Receptus*, is rightly
omitted from the corrected Greek text and R. V., for want of MS.
evidence.

Peter would not have been guilty of such inconsistency; and if he had, Paul, instead of rebuking him in the terms which he reproduces in Galatians, would have appealed to the epistle itself as the most direct method of refuting Peter.[1] Both of these considerations involve a misconception of the relation between that epistle and Peter's present conduct. The epistle, or the decree, as we should rather style it, had reference to imposing the law of Moses on the Gentiles, and it said nothing at all about the kind of social intercourse which should be maintained between them and the Jews. Now it was with reference to the latter alone that Peter was at fault in Antioch. "When Cephas came to Antioch," says Paul, "I resisted him to the face, because he stood condemned. For before that certain came from James, he did eat with the Gentiles; but when they came he drew back and separated himself, fearing them that were of the circumcision" (Gal. ii. 11, 12). To quote the decree against him for this would have been irrelevant; therefore Paul says nothing about the decree; but he brings up that which was strictly in point, Peter's eating with Gentiles in the house of Cornelius, which he had defended and justified when censured for it in Jerusalem (xi. 1–3). Paul alludes to this in the remark: "If thou, being a Jew, livest as do the Gentiles [he had done this only in Cæsarea before this time], and not as do the Jews, how compellest thou the Gentiles to live as do the Jews?" "For if I build up again those things which I destroyed, I prove myself a transgressor" (Gal. ii. 14–18). Peter had lived like a Gentile in the house of Cornelius, and had done the same for a time in Antioch; but now, by withdrawing, he was virtually

---

[1] Baur, *Life of Paul*, i. 28 *ff.*, followed by all of his school.

saying to the Gentiles, You must live like the Jews if you have social intercourse with me. The trouble doubtless lay in the fact that Gentiles placed on their table dishes which the Jews had been taught to consider unclean, and they also neglected the legal purifications of their own persons. It would be hazardous to say that James agreed with the men who came from him ; for we are warned against this by the fact that the men from Jerusalem who stirred up the first strife in Antioch had received no commandment at all (xv. 24).

The truthfulness of Luke's whole account of the mission of Paul and Barnabas to Jerusalem has been denied by rationalists, because in his account of it there is an omission of almost every particular which is mentioned in Paul's own account given in Galatians. We have seen, as we passed along, that there is no contradiction between the two ; but it can not be denied that the difference just mentioned exists. It is accounted for, in a most natural way, by the fact that Paul's epistle was written at least five years before Acts, and a much longer time before according to the estimates of the rationalists themselves, and probably the facts mentioned in it were well known to Luke's readers, and needed not to be repeated. All that was needed was to set forth those details which Paul had omitted.

SEC. III. PAUL'S SECOND TOUR.

(XV. 36—XVIII. 22.)

1. CHANGE OF COMPANIONS, AND BEGINNING OF THE TOUR, 36–41.

VER. 36. We have lingered long on the interval spent by Paul and Barnabas in Antioch. We are now to follow the former in his second tour among the Gentiles. **(36) And after some days Paul said unto Barnabas, Let us return now and visit the brethren in every city wherein we proclaimed the word of the Lord, and see how they fare.** We shall find as we proceed that the visit extended far beyond the remotest church which they had previously planted; but Paul's proposal contemplated, as the primary purpose of the tour, the care of the brethren whom they had baptized. This shows that his solicitude for the congregations which he had planted was no less ardent than his zeal for the conversion of sinners.

Vv. 37–39. The best of friends sometimes differ on questions of expediency and of personal preference; and we now learn that on such questions even inspired men were liable to differences. **(37) And Barnabas was minded to take with them John also, who was called Mark. (38) But Paul thought not good to take with them him who withdrew from them from Pamphylia, and went not with them to the work. (39) And there arose a sharp contention, so that they parted asunder one from the other, and Barnabas took Mark with him, and sailed away unto Cyprus:** Paul's judgment was controlled in the matter by his high estimate of the courage and self-sacrifice which ought to characterize a preacher of the gospel, while

Barnabas was undoubtedly warped by his personal relationship to Mark, who was his cousin (Col. iv. 10).
Which of the two acted the more wisely we are not now
able to determine, for want of acquaintance with the
motives which actuated Mark in turning back, and with
the circumstances under which he did so; and even if we
could decide, the decision might be of no practical utility.   Suffice it to say, that Mark was afterward fully
restored to Paul's confidence, and that no permanent
alienation from Barnabas took place, as we learn from
the manner in which Paul afterward expressed himself
in regard to both.[1]   Notwithstanding their disagreement
and separation, they did not allow the good cause to
suffer, nor did they fail to accomplish separately that
which Paul proposed that they should accomplish together; for Barnabas, in revisiting Cyprus, saw a portion
of the brethren to whom he and Paul had preached,
while Paul, by a different route, visited the others.   The
separation of Barnabas from Paul is our separation from
Barnabas; for his name is not again mentioned by Luke.
But as we bid him a final farewell, the sails are spread
which are to bear him over the sea, that he may make
the islands glad with the knowledge of salvation; and
the later incidents of his noble life will be made known
to us when we sit down with him in the everlasting
kingdom.

Vv. 40, 41.   We turn with Luke to follow the steps
of him who was in labors more abundant and in prisons
more frequent that all the apostles, and to form a better
acquaintance with his new companion.   (40) but Paul
chose Silas, and went forth, being commended by the
brethren to the grace of the Lord.   (41) And he went

---

[1] I. Cor. ix. 6; Col. iv. 11; II. Tim. iv. 11.

through Syria, and Cilicia, confirming the churches.
The fact that Silas, who had been one of the "chief men
among the brethren" in Jerusalem (22), and had been
selected by the apostles and elders there to represent
them in settling the controversy at Antioch, consented
now to unite with Paul in his work among the heathen,
is a proof to us of the perfect agreement which existed
between Paul and the authorities of the church in
Jerusalem; and it was a guarantee to the Jewish brethren whom the two might visit in their journey that
there was no antagonism between their teaching and that
of the older apostles. The fact that, in addition to this,
Silas was a prophet (32), completed his fitness as Paul's
fellow laborer.

The statement that "they were commended by the
brethren to the grace of the Lord" implies a meeting of
the church for this purpose; and it is not improbable
that the prayer of commendation was accompanied, as in
the case of Barnabas and Paul in the beginning, by
imposition of hands (*cf.* remarks under xiii. 3).

During the interval between Paul's departure to
Tarsus (ix. 30) and his arrival in Antioch (xi. 25, 26), he
had preached the gospel in Syria and Cilicia (Gal. i.
21); and now he revisits with Silas the churches which
he had planted at that time. His proposal to Barnabas
(36) contemplated only a revisitation of the churches
which they together had planted; but as Barnabas went
with Mark to some of these, Paul was left free to revisit
some which he alone had planted, and thus the work of
revisitation was made the more complete by the separation which took place.

Some of the advocates of the episcopal rite of confirmation affect to find in the words, "confirming the

churches " (41), authority for this rite ; but it requires
only a glance at the four passages in which the original
term occurs (ἐπιστηρίζω) to see that it has reference not
to laying hands on new converts in order to admit them
to full fellowship, but to making firm by proper instruction and exhortation the souls of those already in the
full fellowship of the church.[1]

2. CHURCHES OF THE FIRST TOUR REVISITED,
XVI. 1–5.

Vv. 1, 2. Omitting the details of Paul's labors in
Syria and Cilicia, Luke hurries us forward to his arrival
in Derbe and Lystra, the scenes respectively of the most
painful and the most consoling incidents of his former
tour.   Had he been disposed to indulge in descriptions
of scenery, which he never does, he might have given us
a vivid picture of the Gates of Cilicia, the magnificent
pass through the Taurus mountains which opens a way
from the lowlands of Cilicia to the uplands of Lycaonia.
The grandeur of the view must have deeply impressed
Paul and Silas, as it does all modern travelers ; but Luke
found no room on his living pages for even an allusion
to such things.   He is hurrying to introduce to us a new
and most interesting character, destined to play an important part in the subsequent portion of the narrative.
(1) **And he came also to Derbe and to Lystra : and behold,**

---

[1] This is clearly perceived and admitted by Plumptre, and yet
he makes an attempt, though a feeble one, to connect the term
with the episcopal rite of confirmation : " Confirming is, it need
hardly be said, used in the general sense of strengthening ; but as
the bestowing of spiritual gifts by laying on of hands was a chief
part of the work so done, it at least approximates to the idea of
confirming in the later and more technical sense of the term."
(*Com. in loco*).

a certain disciple was there, named Timothy, the son of a
Jewess who believed; but his father was a Greek. (2)
The same was well reported of by the brethren that
were at Lystra and Iconium. The grandmother as well
as the mother of this disciple was a believer, and both
had preceded him into the kingdom. By these two
godly women he had been instructed from his infancy in
the Holy Scriptures (II. Tim. iii. 14, 15); he had been
baptized during Paul's previous visit to Lystra; he had
witnessed the stoning of Paul; had wept over his pros-
trate form; had seen him, as if raised from the dead,
rise up and return into the city; and had seen him depart on the next day with unconquerable determination
into another field of conflict for Christ.[1] It is not wonderful that now, with several added years of Christian
experience, he was well spoken of by the brethren.
The fact that he was thus attested not only at Derbe and
Lystra, close about his home, but also at the distant city
of Iconium, renders it probable that he was already a
young preacher, and that the imposition of hands by the
elders of the church, which is mentioned later, had
already taken place.[2]

VER. 3. The discerning eye of Paul soon discovered in this youth qualities which would render him a fit
companion and assistant, and he secured him for this
position. (3) Him would Paul have to go forth with
him; and he took and circumcised him because of the
Jews who were in those parts: for they all knew that
his father was a Greek. The "Jews who were in those
parts," like all other Jews, could not look favorably on

---

[1] See remarks under xiv. 19, 20.

[2] See I. Tim. iv. 14, where the original word, $\pi\rho\epsilon\sigma\beta\upsilon\tau\epsilon\rho\iota\upsilon\nu$, is improperly rendered presbytery, instead of eldership.

a man of Jewish blood who was uncircumcised. He appeared to be repudiating his nationality. His father having been a Greek is mentioned as the cause of the neglect of the rite in Timothy's infancy.

To a reader not fully informed as to Paul's position in regard to circumcision, it seems very strange that he circumcised Timothy so soon after refusing to do the same with Titus in Jerusalem.[1] It seems also to conflict with statements of Paul in his epistles, especially with that in Galatians v. 2–4: "If ye receive circumcision Christ will profit you nothing. Yea, I testify again to every man who receiveth circumcision, that he is a debtor to do the whole law. Ye are severed from Christ, ye who would be justified by the law; ye are fallen away from grace." But the very terms of this passage show that he is contemplating one who receives circumcision in order that he may come under the law, and be saved by keeping the law. To cases in which this was not the purport of the act this censure could not apply. If Titus had been circumcised, this would have been precisely the import of it; for it was for the purpose of bringing him under the law as a means of final salvation, that it was demanded by the Pharisees. But the circumcision of Jews like Timothy stood on an altogether different footing. Circumcision, as our Lord had taught, was " not of Moses, but of the fathers " (Jno. vii. 22). The obligation to observe it did not originate in the law, but in the covenant with Abraham; and its connection with the law grew out of the fact that the law was given to a portion of Abraham's circumcised offspring. As then the obligation did not originate with the law, the abrogation of the law could not annul it. For this reason the propriety

---

[1] See the remarks under xv. 30, 31.

of circumcising children of Jewish blood was never called in question by Paul; but he and all the disciples recognized it to the very last (xxi; 20–25). The covenant with Abraham in regard to this rite is an everlasting covenant, and the only penalty of neglecting it is the same to-day that it has ever been, that of being cut off from Abraham's recognized posterity (Gen. xvii. 9–14). As it was a national mark, it had no connection with salvation, or with a man's relation to Christ; hence Paul's declaration, "In Christ Jesus neither circumcision availeth anything, nor uncircumcision; but faith working through love" (Gal. v. 6).

At some time Paul laid hands on Timothy to impart to him a spiritual gift (II. Tim. i. 6); but whether at this time, or after he had tried him in the field for a while, we have no means of knowing. The same is true of the imposition of hands by the eldership mentioned in I. Timothy iv. 14. It is highly probable, though, that inasmuch as Paul himself had been separated to this work by imposition of hands (xiii. 3), the elders followed this precedent in the case of Timothy. At any rate, there can be no reasonable doubt that this ceremony on the part of the eldership was intended to set him apart to the work of preaching; for there is no other purpose that can account for it. The conceit that Paul ordained him on the recommendation of two or three churches, is read into the text by those who think they find it there.

Vv. 4, 5. Resuming now the thread of his narrative where he had broken it to speak of Timothy, Luke tells us of the other work done by the apostles in the cities which they had reached. (4) **And as they went on their way through the cities, they delivered them the de-**

crees for to keep, which had been ordained of the apostles and elders that were at Jerusalem. (5) So the churches were strengthened in the faith, and increased in number daily. This statement shows that the decrees were not intended for Syria and Cilicia alone, but for all the Gentile churches. They were everywhere needed to unite in harmonious fellowship the Jewish and Gentile converts. As Paul had founded these churches, and as Silas had been sent out from Jerusalem by the apostles for the express purpose of coöperating with him in maintaining the teaching of the decrees, the latter came to the ears of both Jews and Gentiles with all their force, and produced the happiest effects. The churches " increased in number daily," in consequence of being " confirmed in the faith."

3. PREACHING IN PHRYGIA AND GALATIA, AND A CALL TO MACEDONIA, 6–10.

Vv. 6–8. A line drawn from Derbe westward to Antioch of Pisidia might be styled, in military phraseology, the base line of Paul's present advance into the interior of Asia Minor, with a view to spreading the gospel over all its districts. In person he went no farther in this direction than Phrygia, which lay to the northwest from Antioch; and Galatia, which lay to the north; but churches planted in these regions, if active and zealous, would soon cause the truth to be sounded out through more distant provinces. Journeys and labors which must have occupied many months are recounted by Luke in the few words which follow: (6) And they went through the region of Phrygia and Galatia, having been forbidden of the Holy Spirit to speak the word in Asia; (7) and when they were come over against Mysia, they assayed to go into Bithynia, and the Spirit of Jesus suffered them not; (8) and passing by Mysia they came down to Troas. We are warned by this brief sentence not to assume from the brevity of Luke's narration at any given point that he is brief because he has nothing interesting or important to tell, for we learn from Paul himself that it was far otherwise with the journeys here so hurriedly passed over. Many congregations sprang into existence under his labors in Galatia (I. Cor. xvi. 1), and their subsequent unhappy condition called forth one of his most valuable epistles. The Galatians were Gauls, whose ancestors, as predatory warriors, had wandered from Gaul (modern France) over into Asia Minor before the Christian era, and had by the time of Paul's visit become a settled agricultural people.[1] It was not Paul's intention at first to preach among them, because doubtless he was looking to what he supposed more fruitful fields; but he was constrained by sickness to tarry until he found among them unexpectedly a field ripe for the sickle. He wrote to them afterward, "Ye know that because of an infirmity of the flesh I preached the gospel unto you the first time." The infirmity, as we ascertain from what he further says about it, was that "thorn in the flesh" which he had prayed the Lord in vain to take from him. It was of such a character that strangers like these would be likely to despise and reject him on account of it; but they received him so differently that he wrote to them afterward these grateful words: "That which was a temptation to you in my flesh ye despised not, nor rejected; but ye received me

---

[1] An elaborate account of the Galatians is given by Bishop Lightfoot in an essay on their history and character appended to his commentary on the epistle written to them.

as an angel of God, even as Christ Jesus." And he adds, " I bear you witness, that if possible, ye would have plucked out your own eyes and given them to me" (Gal. iv. 14, 15). His distress of mind and weakness of body may have imparted a mellow tone to his preaching which at once awakened the quick sympathies of the excitable people, and encouraged him to continue his labors far beyond his first intention. Out of the most unpropitious circumstances under which he had ever introduced the gospel to a new community, with the single exception of his going from Lystra to Derbe, there sprang up the sweetest fruits of all his labors ; for there are no other churches of whose devotion to him he speaks in similar terms. Such experiences as this illustrated to him the Lord's meaning, when he said to him in answer to his prayer about this thorn in the flesh, " My grace is sufficient for thee, for my power is made perfect in weakness ; " and it was experience like this which enabled him at length to say, " Most gladly therefore will I rather glory in my weaknesses, that the strength of Christ may rest upon me. Wherefore I take pleasure in weaknesses, in injuries, in necessities, in persecutions, in distresses for Christ's sake : for when I am weak, then am I strong" (II. Cor. xii. 9, 10).

Another new and strange experience befell Paul in this interval. Not only had he been led by sickness to preach in Galatia contrary to his intention, but when he formed the purpose of carrying the gospel next into the province of Asia, the Holy Spirit would not permit him to do so. The name Asia at that time was chiefly used for the Roman province of which Ephesus was the principal city ; and doubtless Ephesus, in which he afterward preached two years and three months, was his objective point. This is the first time of which we read that his own judgment as to his next field of labor was overruled by the Holy Spirit. But this was not all ; for when he was forbidden to go into Asia, which was southwest of him, he next proposed to go into Bithynia, a rich and important province to northward, and he was likewise forbidden to go thither. Having finished up the work behind him, and being thus forbidden to turn either to the left or the right, he had no alternative but to go right forward ; and this took him through Mysia in a northwesterly direction. He went through this district without stopping (for such is the meaning of the expression, " passing by Mysia "), because he saw no opening for work on the way, and he came down to Troas, which was on the seashore, and here he ran upon the barrier of the sea. It is not possible that he and his companions failed to be very much puzzled by these mysterious directings of the Holy Spirit. The questions must have pressed upon them with increasing interest at every step, Why are we turned back from these inviting fields ? and whither is the Lord directing us ?

Vv. 9, 10. During the first night of their stay in Troas the mystery was solved, at least in part. (9) And a vision appeared to Paul in the night ; there was a man of Macedonia standing, beseeching him, and saying, Come over into Macedonia, and help us. (10) And when he had seen the vision, straightway we sought to go forth into Macedonia, concluding that God had called us for to preach the gospel to them. They now understand a part of God's purpose ; they afterward understood it more fully. At this point our author first indicates his own presence by the use of the pronouns " we " and " us." The words, " concluding that God had called us to preach the gospel to them," imply that the author was one of those who had been turned aside from the places in which they had intended to preach (6, 7), and that therefore he had joined the company in the interior of Asia Minor. The traveling companions are now Paul, Silas, Timothy and Luke.

4. ARRIVAL IN MACEDONIA, AND BAPTISM OF CERTAIN WOMEN, 11–15.

Vv. 11, 12. It was not every day that a ship could be found in the harbor of Troas, and still less frequently one bound for the unimportant seaport of Neapolis, and ready to set sail. When, therefore, the apostolic company found one to suit their purpose, and just ready to weigh anchor, they must have realized that God was at last favoring their journey. (11) Setting sail therefore from Troas, we made a straight course to Samothrace, and the day following to Neapolis; (12) and from thence to Philippi, which is a city of Macedonia, the first of the district, a Roman colony: and we were in this city tarrying certain days. The remark, "we made a straight course to Samothrace," implies a favorable wind; for only with such a wind can a sailing vessel make a straight course. We have evidence, too, that this favorable wind was blowing a stiff breeze, which bore the ship along rapidly; for on a subsequent journey (xx. 6) five days were occupied in the same voyage. Here was another indication of a favoring providence which the voyagers, after their strange experience just past, could not fail to observe.

Samothrace is an island in the Archipelago, and Neapolis (Newtown, now called Kavalla) was a seaport for Philippi. The latter city is about ten miles from Neapolis in a northwesterly direction. The road passes over a high ridge which runs east and west, and thence descends into an extensive plain in which Philippi stands on an elevation. As the travelers approached the city, they crossed the river Gangites, on opposite banks of which the armies under Brutus and Cassius on one side, and Octavianus and Antony on the other, were formed in order of battle before that final struggle which decided the fate of the Roman Republic. The missionaries walked through the field of battle as they drew near the city. They found it a Roman city with a Greek population all around it; for such is the force of the remark that it was a colony. Augustus Cæsar, in commemoration of the great battle, had made it such by filling it with Romans transported from Italy. The apostles were now in Europe, and this was their first contact with a community of Romans. The remark that Philippi was "the first city of the district," can not mean that it was the most important city of one of the four parts into which Macedonia was divided; for Amphipolis occupied this distinction in the part to which Philippi belonged: but it refers to a smaller district, and the comparison is to the small cities and villages not far away.

Vv. 13–15. On entering this strange city the apostles found no Jewish synagogue in which they might be invited to speak "a word of exhortation to the people;" and they were doubtless no little perplexed as to how they should introduce the gospel to the heathen population. The way in which the problem was solved is stated in the next words of our text: (13) **And on the Sabbath day we went forth without the gate by a river side, where we supposed there was a place of prayer; and we sat down and spoke to the women who were** come together. (14) And a certain woman named Lydia, a seller of purple, of the city of Thyatira, one that worshiped God, heard us; whose heart the Lord opened, to give heed unto the things which were spoken by Paul. (15) And when she was baptized, and her household, she besought us, saying, If ye have judged me to be faithful to the Lord, come into my house, and abide there. And she constrained us. From this it seems that they remained until the Sabbath before they decided how and where to begin their work. Had they met with Lydia and her household sooner, it might have been different. The cause of their thinking that there was a place of prayer on the bank of the river may have been that they saw something indicative of it as they crossed the river in approaching the town, or it may have been that, in the course of inquiry as to the presence of Jews in the city, they had heard of some women being accustomed to go out to this place for some purpose every seventh day.

Thyatira, the home of Lydia, was a city of proconsular Asia (Rev. i. 11), situated on its northern border; and Paul's company, in " passing by Mysia " on their way to Troas, had probably passed near it. It was noted for the excellence of its purple dyes,[1] and it is still a pleasantly situated town of about ten thousand inhabitants.[2] As purple was a very costly dye, it was used on none but costly goods; and the fact that Lydia was a dealer in these implies that, while she was not above the necessity of labor, she was in comparatively easy cir-

---

[1] Citations to this effect are made from Homer's Odyssey, i. 14; iii. 9; and from Strabo, xiii. 4–14.

[2] For a description of its present condition and appearance, see the author's Lands of the Bible, 585.

cumstances. The same is implied in the fact that she had a house called her own, which was large enough to entertain Paul and his three companions, and that her household included a plurality of women (13 *cf.* 15). Her character is indicated, not only by the statement that she was "one that worshiped God," but by the considerations that in this heathen city, where the Sabbath was unknown to the inhabitants, she was faithful in observing it; that while the other dealers in purple goods were busy on that day, she closed her shop regardless of the demands of competition; and that, although there was no synagogue in which to worship, and no male Jews to conduct the accustomed worship, she and her employés habitually left the noisy city, and spent the holy day in prayer on the bank of the river. Such fidelity to God, under circumstances so unfavorable, is not often witnessed in our own more favored times. It was observed from on high, and it met its reward.

We can now begin to see the design of God in turning Paul back from Asia, and back from Bithynia, when he desired to go to these countries; in leading him across Mysia to Troas; in sending him the vision by night in that city, and in bringing him and his company by so singular a chain of providences to this Roman colony. These women had been wont to repair to this river bank on the Sabbath day for prayer. God had heard their prayers, as in the case of Cornelius, and he chose this mysterious way of bringing to them the preachers through whose words they might believe in Christ and learn the way of salvation. He had directed the journey of Paul by land and sea, and had timed the motion of the ship with reference to that weekly prayer-meeting, as he had once directed the flight of an angel

from heaven, and timed the steps of Philip with reference to movements of the eunuch's chariot.   Now, as in
those instances, he answers the prayers of the uncon-
verted, not by direct operations of his Spirit within
them, but by bringing to them the gospel on the lips of
a living preacher ; and it is quite a singular circumstance,
as noted by Alford, that though Paul had been forbidden
to preach in Asia, his first converts in Philippi were
Asiatics.

The statement that the Lord opened Lydia's heart
implies that previously her heart was in some way closed.
It was certainly not closed by the hardness of a sinful
life, or by inherited depravity ; for such a supposition is
forbidden by the steadfastness with which, under great
temptation, she had previously clung to the worship
of God.   It was closed in the sense in which the pious
and earnest heart of a Jewish worshiper might be closed.
Every Jew, and every Jewish proselyte, was at that
time so wedded to the belief that the coming Christ
would establish an earthly kingdom, as to have the heart
very tightly closed against the conception of a crucified
Christ, whose reign as a king is purely spiritual.   It was
this that had caused the mass of the Jews to reject the
Christ while he was still on earth, and it continued to be
their "stumbling block" (Jno. v. 44; I. Cor. i. 23).
Whether Lydia was a Jewess or a proselyte, this was
"the hope of Israel" in which she had been instructed,
and for which she had been taught to devoutly pray ;
and if the natural effect of it had not been removed from
her heart, she must have rejected the gospel, as did the
mass of those who had been her teachers.   The statement then that the Lord "opened her heart" means that
he removed this mistaken conception which would have

prevented her from receiving the Christ. The effect of
the opening was precisely that which was aimed at ; it
led her " to give heed to the things which were spoken
by Paul." The Greek verb here rendered " to give
heed " means, in some connections, to fix the mind upon
a matter, and in others, to put something in practice.[1]
Here it can not mean the former, for Lydia had already
fixed her mind upon the preaching, as is declared in the
words, " a certain woman named Lydia *heard* us." She
first heard, then the Lord opened her heart, and then she
gave heed to the things which Paul had spoken. The
meaning is, that she put in practice the things spoken by
Paul. What these things were, Luke has told us so
often that he does not reiterate them here, but he indirectly shows that baptism is one of them by the way in
which he mentions her observance of that ordinance.
He says, " and when she was baptized," implying that
this was one of the things that she gave heed to. We
know that in preaching to such persons Paul always
directed them to believe the gospel, to repent of their
sins, and to be baptized ; and if Lydia gave heed to the
things which he spoke, she did these three things.

We have yet to notice, from another point of view,
the statement nowhere else found in connection with a
case of conversion, that the Lord opened Lydia's heart.

---

[1] The word is προσέχειν. It is used in the sense of fixing the
attention, in such expressions as these : " *Take heed* that ye do
not your alms before men ?" (Matt. vi. 1) ; " *Beware* of false
prophets " (vii. 15) ; " *Take heed* to yourselves " (Luke xvii. 3) ;
" Neither *give heed* to fables and endless genealogies " (I. Tim. i. 4) ;
et al. It has the other sense in these clauses : " Not *given* to much
wine " (I. Tim. iii. 8) ; " *Give heed* to reading, to exhortation, to
teaching " (iv. 13) ; " From which no man hath *given attendance* at
the altar " (Heb. vii. 13).

We have seen what the opening was, and what were its effects; we now inquire in what way it was done by the Lord. It is too common to understand such expressions as this in the sense of immediate actions of God or of his Holy Spirit, and to ignore the secondary agencies or instrumentalities employed. In this instance we are likely to jump to the conclusion that the Lord opened Lydia's heart by a direct operation of his Spirit, and thus to ignore a very different method clearly indicated by the context. In order to see this, we must put ourselves in the place of our author, and inquire what led him to make a remark in regard to Lydia, which he has not made in regard to any other person whose conversion he has described. It can not be because God did for Lydia something which he omitted in other cases; for in the case of every Jew and proselyte the same process was necessary. The difference is only in the phraseology employed. This is accounted for by the fact that Luke, together with Paul and all his company, had been very much puzzled for weeks past, as to what God was doing and intending to do, by turning them away from fields of labor which appeared to them the most promising, and leading them on, they knew not whither, until he had brought them to this heathen city where there appeared to be no opening for a ready introduction of the gospel. In the very midst of their perplexity they unexpectedly met with these women; and though they had never met them before, and though they might have expected, under the circumstances, a long and ardent struggle to overcome their natural repugnance to a crucified Messiah, they are surprised to find Lydia's heart immediately opened, and they see at once what the Lord has done and has been doing since they were first forbidden to go into Asia. Had not the Lord interfered, Paul would now have been in Asia or Bithynia, and these simple hearted women would have still prayed on in ignorance of the salvation which had been provided for them. It was so strikingly the Lord's doing, that Luke was moved to this mode of expressing it. The Lord opened Lydia's heart, as he did that of the eunuch, by bringing from afar, at the proper juncture, the living preacher through whose word the end was accomplished.

The fact that Lydia's household were baptized with her has been taken by some Pædobaptist scholars as presumptive evidence in favor of infant baptism. Albert Barnes argues as follows: "The case is one that affords a strong presumptive proof that this was an instance of *household* or infant baptism. For (1) *her* believing is particularly mentioned. (2) It is not intimated that *they* believed. On the contrary, it is strongly implied that they did not. (3) It is manifestly implied that *they* were baptized because *she* believed." It would be difficult to find an instance of more fallacious reasoning. In the expression, "household or infant baptism," it is tacitly assumed that the two are identical, the very thing to be proved. The statement that "her belief is particularly mentioned" is misleading; for her belief is not mentioned at all; it is only implied. Finally, the assumed implication that "*they* did not believe," and that "*they* were baptized because *she* believed," has not the slightest support in a word of the text. It was read into the text from Mr. Barnes' imagination. Dr. Alexander states the case thus: "The real strength of the argument lies not in any one case, but in the repeated mention of whole households as baptized;"

and in thus stating it, he follows the oft quoted demand
of Bengel: "Who can believe that in so many families
there was not an infant?" The answer is, that there are
only four whole households mentioned in the New Testament as being baptized, and that there is positive proof
that in three of these there was not an infant. In that
of Cornelius there was none, for they all spoke in tongues
and believed (x. 46; xv. 9); none in that of the jailer,
for they all believed and rejoiced in the Lord (xvi. 34);
and none in that of Stephanas, for "they set themselves
to minister to the saints" (I. Cor. i. 16; xvi. 15). The
inference, therefore, in reference to the household of
Lydia is reversed; for, inasmuch as one peculiarity of
all the households baptized, of which the facts are
known, is the absence of infants, we are justified in the
conclusion, no evidence to the contrary appearing, that
this was also a peculiarity of the household of Lydia.
If the number of whole households baptized were much
greater than it is, the argument would remain the same;
and it should not be forgotten that it is an every day
occurrence now, among the large number of evangelists
who are constantly baptizing multitudes in our western
states, to baptize whole households without an infant in
them. Almost any active evangelist can relate many
such instances within his own experience. The ablest of
Pædobaptist commentators are more candid on this subject; thus Alford, commenting on the case of Lydia,
says: "It may be that no inference for infant baptism is
hence deducible." Gloag says: "Evidently the passage
in itself can not be adduced as a proof either for or
against infant baptism; there is in it no indication
whether there were or were not infants in the household
of Lydia." Meyer says that of the baptism of infants

" no trace is found in the New Testament ;" and Dean Plumptre expresses himself in these words: " The statement that her household were baptized has often been urged as evidence that infant baptism was the practice of the apostolic age. It must be admitted, however, that this is to read a great deal between the lines, and the utmost that can be said is that the language of the writer does not exclude infants. In this instance, moreover, there is no evidence that she had children, or even that she was married. The household may well have consisted of female slaves and freed-women whom she employed, and who made up her *familia.*" In this last remark this acute and candid writer hits upon the explanation really given in the text; for when Paul reached the river bank he "spoke to the women who were come together" (13) ; and when, in the second verse after this, the writer speaks of Lydia's household, he evidently means to identify those women as the household. It is entirely within the range of probability, as Plumptre also suggests, that among these women were Euodia and Syntyche, who subsequently labored with Paul in the gospel, and whose alienation from each other at a still later period became a subject of deep solicitude to the apostle (Phil. iv. 2, 3).

The baptism of this whole family opened to the apostle and his companions a lodging place far more congenial than that in some heathen household, which they had hitherto endured ; and yet a proper feeling of delicacy forbade him to accept Lydia's hospitality, until her plea showed clearly that she would regard a final refusal as evidence that she was not fully trusted as " faithful to the Lord." By this plea, Luke says, " she constrained us."

5. PAUL AND SILAS ARE SCOURGED AND IMPRIS-
ONED, 16–24.

Vv. 16–18. We are next introduced to an incident
which led to the first persecution experienced by the
apostles at the instigation of Gentiles. (16) And it
came to pass, as we were going to the place of prayer,
that a certain maid having a spirit of divination met
us, who brought her masters much gain by sooth-
saying. (17) The same following after Paul and us
cried out, saying, These men are servants of the most
high God, who proclaim unto you the way of salvation.
(18) And this she did for many days. But Paul, being
sore troubled, turned and said to the spirit, I charge thee
in the name of Jesus Christ to come out of her. And it
came out that very hour. Literally translated, it was a
Python spirit by which the maid was possessed, the word
Python identifying its manifestations with those of the
women who gave out the oracles at Delphi in Greece;
and who were supposed by the heathen to be inspired
by the serpent called Python, to whose wisdom these
oracles were accredited. Luke's language can not be
regarded as an indorsement of this supposed inspiration;
but he distinctly recognizes a real spirit in the maid, and
styles it a Python spirit for the reason given. The case
was undoubtedly one of demon possession, such as so frequently occur in our gospel narratives, and with which
Luke's readers were presumed to have become acquainted through his former narrative. It is worthy of remark,
too, that the title " most high God," which is used by
this spirit, is the same that was used by " the legion "
in Gadara (Mark v. 7).

As the maid was proclaiming the truth to a people who had some confidence in her utterances, and the very truth which Paul was most solicitous that they should accept, why did he reject her coöperation, and shut the mouth of an apparent friend? The answer can only be, that to have accepted demons as witnesses to the gospel would have convinced the people that there was an alliance between them and the apostles; and thus all the good repute of the apostles would have been reflected on the demons, and all the evil repute of the demons would likewise have been reflected on the apostles. To guard against this double evil both Jesus and the apostles invariably cast out all demons who ventured to speak in their favor. Paul was "sore troubled" in this instance, and delayed for many days the act which at last became unavoidable, because he knew that the money value of the slave would be greatly reduced by the expulsion of the demon, and he dreaded the consequences of appearing in this heathen city to interfere with the rights of property. That the maid followed the preachers to the place of prayer many days before the demon was expelled, indicates that the place of prayer was chosen as their daily place of preaching. It is highly improbable that they could find so suitable a place inside the city. What became of the maid thus miraculously relieved of demon possession, we are not informed; but gratitude for so great a deliverance should have thrown her under the influence of Paul and of the good women who were now actively coöperating with him, and who would be naturally interested in her behalf.

Vv. 19–21. The consequences which had troubled Paul in anticipation (18) were soon realized. (19) **But** when her masters saw that the hope of their gain was gone,[1] they laid hold on Paul and Silas, and dragged them into the marketplace before the rulers, (20) and when they had brought them unto the magistrates, they said, These men, being Jews, do exceedingly trouble our city, (21) and set forth customs which it is not lawful for us to receive, or to observe, being Romans. The officers here called magistrates were styled in Latin *duumviri*,[2] two men in whom was lodged the supreme power in a Roman colony. It seems that the apostles were first brought before rulers of a lower rank in the agora, the open square improperly called " market place " in our version, and that by these officers they were referred to the two chief rulers. The real cause of complaint was suppressed, and a false one preferred, because, in the first place, to have stated the fact in the case would have reflected credit on Paul in the eyes of the magistrates; and in the second place, it was easy in a heathen city like this to get up an outcry against Jews on almost any pretence. When Paul reached Corinth on his present tour all Jews had but recently been expelled from Rome by order of the emperor (xviii. 2), and perhaps this had already taken place. If so, the circumstance could but intensify in the minds of all loyal Romans the common hatred of this persecuted race.

Vv. 22–24. The hypocritical outcry of the slave owners had the effect aimed at on the heathen rabble, and on the magistrates. (22) And the multitude rose up

----

[1] Luke here makes a somewhat humorous play upon a word, which is lost to the English reader. He says that when the evil spirit ἐξῆλθεν " went out," the masters saw that the hope of their gain ἐξῆλθεν " went out."

[2] The Greek word employed is στρατηγοὶ, the equivalent of the Latin, prætors.

together against them : and the magistrates rent their
garments off them, and commanded to beat them with rods.
(23) And when they had laid many stripes upon them,
they cast them into prison, charging the jailer to keep
them safely : (24) who, having received such a charge,
cast them into the inner prison, and made their feet fast
in the stocks. Here we have an example of that same
truckling to the clamor of a mob which has made infamous the name of Pontius Pilate; for the magistrates
gave the prisoners no opportunity to defend themselves,
so that even the forms of justice were disregarded. The
rods with which the apostles were beaten were those
habitually borne in a bundle by the lictors, who always
attended Roman prætors; and in order that the beating
might be effectually applied, the victims were doubtless
strapped, as usual, to the whipping post. The jailer
entered fully into the spirit of the mob, and carried out
the order to " keep them safely " with the utmost rigor.
Locking them up in the inner prison would have kept
them safely ; but to safe keeping he added torture by
means of the stocks. With their legs locked in these
clamps, and their feet projecting beyond them, they
could neither lie down nor sit up without pain, nor could
they find relief by a change of position. The pain grew
more intense continually, and no one who has never experienced it can imagine how intense it was.

6. The Jailer and his Family are Baptized,
25–34.

Vv. 25, 26. The condition of the two prisoners as
night drew on was piteous in the extreme. Besides the
physical pain of sitting in a dark dungeon with their
backs bleeding from the scourge, and their legs cramped

in the stocks, they were racked in mind by a sense of the cruel injustice which they had suffered at the hands of men whom they came to bless; and their faith was heroic indeed if some painful questioning did not intrude as to why God allowed them to receive such a reward for their faithful service. The historian leaves all this to our imagination as respects the first half of the night. (25) But about midnight Paul and Silas were praying and singing hymns unto God, and the prisoners were listening to them; (26) and suddenly there was a great earthquake, so that the foundations of the prison-house were shaken: and immediately all the doors were opened; and every one's bands were loosed. Men do not pray when they are enraged, or sing when they are in deep distress. That these men prayed at midnight is therefore proof that ere this the tempest of their feelings, which at the whipping post, and when first thrust within the dungeon and fastened in the stocks, made them almost wild, had now subsided. The cheerfulness necessary to singing must have been a consequence of their prayer; and thus Paul was learning by experience the lesson which he afterward taught the disciples in this very city, saying: "In nothing be anxious; but in everything by prayer and supplication with thanksgiving let your requests be made known unto God. And the peace of God, which passeth all understanding, shall guard your hearts and your thoughts in Christ Jesus" (Phil. iv. 6, 7). That singing was a strange sound to the criminals in the prison; and when, as they listened attentively, they suddenly felt the rocking of the earthquake, heard the slamming of the prison doors, and felt their own fetters slipping off their limbs, they instinctively connected these frightful phenomena with the singers, and with the God whose praises they sang. The effect was paralyzing.

Vv. 27, 28. The jailer seems not to have heard the singing. He was awakened by the motion of the earthquake, and he doubtless heard the slamming of the doors, and the clanking of the fetters as they fell on the stone floor. (27) **And the jailer being roused out of sleep, and seeing the prison doors open, drew his sword, and was about to kill himself, supposing that the prisoners had escaped. (28) But Paul cried with a loud voice, saying, Do thyself no harm : for we are all here.** Knowing that death was the penalty for allowing prisoners to escape, he was about to act upon the Roman code of honor, which required a man to die by his own hand if necessary to escape that of an enemy or an executioner. It is not likely that he rushed to this desperate resort without some outcries which indicated his purpose, and which were caught by the quick ear of Paul, whose loud voice snatched him back, in the very nick of time, from the brink of eternity.

Vv. 29, 30. As soon as the jailer could collect his senses he remembered that the speaker who had called to him had been preaching salvation in the name of the God of Israel, and he instantly perceived that the earthquake, the opening of the doors, and the unlocking of the fetters were connected with him, and were the work of his God. Seizing this thought, and glancing into the black eternity from which he had just been rescued, his own salvation, rather than the security of his prisoners, at once absorbed his thoughts. (29) **And he called for lights, and sprang in, and, trembling for fear, fell down before Paul and Silas, (30) and brought them out, and said, Sirs, what must I do to be saved ?**

At sunset, when coldly thrusting the apostles into the
dungeon, he cared nothing for them, or for the salvation
which he knew they had been preaching ; for then he was
in the midst of life and health, and all went well with
him ; but at midnight, when he had been within an inch
of death, a change as sudden as the earthquake passes over
him, and he falls trembling at the feet of his prisoners.
The other prisoners are forgotten ; and even Luke is so
absorbed in the excitement of the jailer that he fails to
tell us what became of them.   We may infer that they
were so paralyzed with fear that they remained quiet
in their places until Paul and Silas were led out, and
the outer door was locked.

Vv. 31–34.   Leading the apostles into his family
apartment, he received at once a full and satisfactory
answer to his questions. (31) And they said, Believe on the
Lord Jesus, and thou shalt be saved, thou and thy house.
(32) And they spake the word of the Lord unto him,
with all that were in his house.   (33) And he took them
the same hour of the night, and washed their stripes ;
and was baptized, he and all his, immediately.   (34) And
he brought them up into his house, and set meat [1] before
them, and rejoiced greatly, with all his house, having
believed in God.   The jailer had not previously listened
to Paul very attentively, if at all, or he would have
known what to do to be saved ; for the apostles, unlike
many modern preachers, never left their hearers in doubt
on that supreme question.   The first part of Paul's
answer would have been vain without the remainder.
Had he stopped with the words, " Believe on the
Lord Jesus," the jailer might have answered, as did the

---

[1] Literally, *set a table before them* (παρέθηκε τράπεζον), equivalent
to our household phrase, *set the table.*

man born blind (Jno. ix. 36), "Who is he, sir, that I
may believe on him?" For this reason the preachers
"spake the word of the Lord unto him." As Plumptre
happily expresses it: "The very title of Christ; the acts
and words that showed that Jesus was the Christ; his
life and death and resurrection; the truths of forgiveness
of sins and communion with him, and the outward signs
which he had appointed as witnesses of these truths; all
this must have been included in the word of the Lord
which was preached to that congregation so strangely
assembled between the hours of midnight and dawn."
All this was included in the answer to the question,
" What must I do to be saved;" and the words, " Believe
on the Lord Jesus, and thou shalt be saved, and thy
house," are but the beginning of it. Those therefore
who catch at these words of Paul, and draw the conclusion that salvation is by faith alone, leave the jail too
soon. They should remain till they hear all—till they
hear Paul tell the man to repent and be baptized; till
the design of baptism is explained to him; till he is baptized; till he is found rejoicing greatly immediately after
his baptism. It would not require a long delay; for it
was all done " the same hour of the night." If we compare Paul's answer with those given by Peter and
Ananias when the same question was propounded, we
find that Ananias said, " Arise and be baptized, and wash
away thy sins;" for the questioner in that case had
already believed and repented; that Peter said, " Repent
and be baptized;" for his questioners had already believed; while Paul says to his questioner, who had done
neither of the three, " Believe on the Lord Jesus,"
and then added the other two commands. Thus the
three inspired oracles perfectly agree. The conse-

quence of faith, " and thou shalt be saved, and thy house," is stated in connection with the command to believe, not because salvation would follow faith unattended by repentance and baptism; but because the right degree of faith always wrought repentance, and, in the apostolic practice, was always promptly followed by baptism. In other words, belief, in such connections, was put for the whole process which it constantly superinduced.

While some Pædobaptist writers are candid enough to admit that the baptism of the jailer and his family furnishes no evidence for infant baptism,[1] others have tried to show that it favors both this practice and affusion. In support of the latter it is assumed that the babtism took place in the prison, and it is claimed that facilities for immersion could scarcely have been found there. But it is clearly stated that the jailer " brought them out of the prison " (30) before they preached " unto him, with all that were in his house." It is made equally clear that he " took them " somewhere to wash their stripes and to be baptized (33); and then it is said (34) that after the baptism " he brought them up into his house." It follows that the baptism occurred neither in the prison nor in the house, but in the place to which " he took them." Whether this was in the court of the prison, if it had a court, or in the river in which Lydia was baptized, we have no certain means of deciding; but in either case

---

[1] Thus Plumptre, in commenting on the passage, remarks: " What has been said above (see note on verse 15) as to the bearing of the narratives on the question of infant baptism, applies here also, with the additional fact that those who are said to have been baptized are obviously identical with those whom St. Paul addressed (the word " all " is used in each case), and must, therefore, have been of an age to receive instruction together with the gaoler himself." (*Commentary in loco*).

there is nothing unfavorable to the practice of immersion. The idea advanced by the English translator of Lechler's Acts is worthy of notice here, because it presents this issue from the point of view held by some extreme controversialists. He demands: " If Paul had stealthily gone forth during the night, in order to immerse the jailer in a neighboring stream, how could he, as an honest man, have on the next day declared that, after being ignominiously conducted within the prison walls he would not leave them until the magistrates personally led him forth?" To this it is answered, that it is very absurd to represent Paul as going forth "stealthily," if he went to administer a solemn ordinance of the Lord which he had reason to believe he would not be permitted to administer the next day; and this, too, when God had himself opened the prison doors and prepared the way for this baptism. It would be equally absurd to suppose, as others have done, that the jailer would have scruples about going out for this purpose with his prisoners; for he did so in obedience to manifestations of divine power and authority. As to Paul's honesty in doing this, and then refusing to leave the prison the next morning until escorted by the magistrates, the question of honesty has no place in the matter; for the demands of duty to God in the salvation of his converts required the former, while the protection of his own reputation, as we shall see below, required the latter. The supposition that there is here evidence for infant baptism is not only unfounded, but it is precluded by the facts; for Paul spake the word of the Lord to all the household, and in common with the head of the house they all rejoiced, and all believed in God. There were certainly no infants in the family.

7. The Prisoners are Released, 35–40.

Vv. 35, 36. When the magistrates ordered Paul
and Silas to prison, we would naturally suppose that they
intended to make some further inquiry into the charges
preferred against them. **(35) But when it was day, the
magistrates sent the serjeants, saying, Let those men
go. (36) And the jailer reported the words to Paul, saying, The magistrates have sent to let you go : now therefore come forth, and go in peace.** This order was issued
without knowledge of what had taken place in the night,
so far as we are informed. As for the earthquake, by
which some scholars suppose that the magistrates had
been alarmed, as it was undoubtedly a miraculous and
not a natural one, there is no ground for supposing that
it extended beyond the prison. The order for release
is most naturally accounted for by the fact that, as the
scourging and imprisonment had been inflicted only to
silence the clamor of the mob, there was now no need of
protracting the imprisonment. It was thought that the
prisoners, released thus early in the morning, would be
glad to escape from the city, and no further agitation of
the multitude would occur. The magistrates little knew
the kind of men they were dealing with.

Vv. 37–39. To be thus released from prison, as
though they had merely suffered punishment which they
deserved, would be injurious to the apostles, if a report
of it should follow them to other cities; and fortunately
the means of escaping it were at hand. **(37) But Paul
said unto them, They have beaten us publicly, uncondemned, men that are Romans, and have cast us into
prison; and do they now cast us out privily ? nay,
verily ; but let them come themselves and bring us out.**

(38) And the serjeants reported these words unto the
magistrates : and they feared, when they heard that they
were Romans; (39) and they came and besought them ;
and when they had brought them out, they asked them to
go away from the city. The word serjeants is a modern
English title improperly used here in our version for
lictors, the real title of these officers. They habitually
attended Roman prætors with bundles of rods in their
hands, and by them the " many stripes " had been laid
on Paul and Silas the day before. The purpose of Paul's
demand is obvious ; if now the fact of his having been
scourged and released should follow him to other cities,
there would also follow the fact that the rulers by whose
order it was done had made amends for it, while the victims had spared their persecutors deserved punishment.

As it was a crime under Roman law to scourge a Roman citizen,[1] the apostles might have avenged themselves for the outrage perpetrated upon them, but Paul
taught his brethren not to avenge themselves (Rom. xii.
19), and he acted according to his own precepts. The
incident justifies Christians in appealing to the civil law
for protection ; but not for the punishment of their
enemies.

Baur attempts to discredit this whole story by arguing that if the apostles had really asserted their citizenship they would have done so before the scourging, as
Paul did on a subsequent occasion (xxii. 25) ; and that,
if they allowed themselves to be scourged when they

---

[1] The " Porcian law," enacted B. C. 300, forbade absolutely the
scourging of a Roman citizen (Livy, x. 9). A climax used by
Cicero, in pleading against Verres for a violation of this law, is
often quoted : ": It is a misdeed to bind a Roman citizen—a crime
to scourge him—almost parricide to put him to death."

could so easily have prevented it, they had themselves alone to blame for it (*Paul*, i. 154). But how does Baur know that they did not assert it before the scourging? Certainly the silence of the historian does not furnish this information, and it is highly improbable in itself. Much more probable is it that, as these men were arraigned under the guise of Jews who exceedingly troubled the city by introducing unlawful customs, their claim of Roman citizenship, though proclaimed by them, was disbelieved and scoffed at in the excitement of the moment; but that, when repeated the next morning in connection with a refusal to leave the prison without an apology from the magistrates, it was believed and respected.

VER. 40. When the prisoners were discharged they took their own time to comply with the request of the magistrates, and they did so with becoming dignity. **(40) And they went out of the prison, and entered into the house of Lydia : and when they had seen the brethren, they comforted them, and departed.** The brethren here mentioned were doubtless those who had been baptized during the "many days" (18) which the apostles had spent in the city before their imprisonment. Luke and Timothy, as we shall see farther along (xvii. 1), were also among the number. These, together with the jailer's family, constituted the church now planted in Philippi, and Paul has learned more fully the divine purpose in bringing him thither instead of permitting him to go to Asia or to Bithynia.

8. Preaching and Persecution in Thessalonica,
xvii. 1–9.

Vv. 1–3.   The pronoun of the third person which
Luke now resumes, after using that of the second person
since the apostolic company left Troas, implies that he
himself remained at Philippi; and as the pronoun used
refers grammatically to Paul and Silas, it is implied that
Timothy also remained with Luke, to still further instruct and organize the church.   We find this church at
a later period fully equipped with officers (Phil. i. 1);
and the appointment of these was doubtless the work of
these two brethren.   Leaving the cause thus guarded in
their rear, Paul and Silas advance to another field of
labor.   (1) **Now when they had passed through Amphipolis and Apollonia, they came to Thessalonica, where
was a synagogue of the Jews: (2) and Paul, as his custom was, went in unto them, and for three Sabbath days
reasoned with them from the Scriptures, (3) opening and
alleging, that it behoved the Christ to suffer, and to rise
again from the dead; and that this Jesus whom I proclaim to you, is the Christ.**   The distance from Philippi
to Thessalonica is about one hundred miles.   It was doubtless the synagogue in this city which drew the apostles on
without stopping to preach in Amphipolis or Apollonia,
for a synagogue in a city indicated the presence of a considerable Jewish population, with a nucleus of Gentile
proselytes about it, and furnished an open avenue for the
introduction of the gospel.   Thessalonica, on account of
its commercial importance, was then, and continues to be,
under its modern name Salonica, a great resort for Jews.
    The course of argument followed by Paul on these
three Sabbath days was substantially the same as his

own in Antioch of Pisidia, and Peter's on Pentecost;
and doubtless, if we had reports of his sermons preached
to Jews elsewhere, we would find them very much the
same. It was the course dictated by the state of mind
of the hearers. The preaching of the Christ as one
who had been crucified was to the mass of the Jews a
scandal, because it appeared to them totally inconsistent
with the glorious reign of the Christ as they read it in
the prophets. Until they could be made to see that in
this particular they misread the prophets, it was impossible to convince them that the crucified Jesus could be
their Christ; so to this end Paul first addressed his remarks, and when he had proved according to the
prophets "that it behoved the Christ to suffer, and to
rise again from the dead," it was a very easy task to show
that "this Jesus whom I preach to you is the Christ."
It was well known that he had suffered death; and Paul
had abundant means of proving that he had risen. This
latter proof was not limited to the testimony of the
original witnesses, but he gave ocular demonstration of
the living and divine power of Jesus, by working miracles in his name. This we learn from the first epistle to
the church which he established here, in which he says:
" Our gospel came not to you in word only, but also in
power, and in the Holy Spirit, and in much assurance;
even as ye know what manner of men we showed ourselves toward you for your sake" (I. Thess. i. 5). The
power of the Holy Spirit working miracles before them
gave an assurance of the resurrection and glorification of
him in whose name they were wrought, which " the word
only " of all the men on earth could not give. Without such attestation the word of man in reference to
the affairs of heaven has no claim on our confidence;

but with it, it has a claim which none can honestly reject.

During the two weeks intervening between the three Sabbaths mentioned, the two brethren carefully avoided everything which might raise a suspicion of selfish motives. They would not burden any one by even asking for their daily bread; and although they received some contributions from the church at Philippi, the amount was so scanty as to leave them to the necessity of "laboring night and day" (I. Thess. ii. 9; Phil. iv. 15, 16).

VER. 4. Such arguments and demonstrations, accompanied by such a life, could not fail of good results. **(4) And some of them were persuaded, and consorted with Paul and Silas ; and of the devout Greeks a great multitude, and of the chief women not a few.** It seems from this statement that the largest class of the converts were "devout Greeks," that is, Gentiles who had learned to worship God according to the example of the Jews. Next to these were the chief women, also Gentile proselytes; and least of all, Jews. The great majority, then, were Gentiles; and Paul, on account of this preponderance, could afterward write to them, "Ye turned unto God from idols, to serve a living and true God" (I. Thess. i. 9).

Vv. 5–9. Such a movement among the devout Gentiles, whose presence in the synagogue was a source of pride to the Jews, was exceedingly mortifying to those Jews who remained in unbelief, and they were able, by their number and their influence with the rabble of the city, to give serious trouble to Paul and Silas, which they were not slow to do. **(5) But the Jews, being moved with jealousy, took unto them certain vile fellows of the rabble, and gathering a crowd, set the city on an** uproar; and assaulting the house of Jason, they sought to bring them forth to the people. (6) And when they found them not, they dragged Jason and certain brethren before the rulers of the city, crying, These that have turned the world upside down are come hither also; (7) whom Jason hath received: and these all act contrary to the decrees of Cæsar, saying that there is another king, one Jesus. (8) And they troubled the multitude and the rulers of the city, when they heard these things. (9) And when they had taken security from Jason and the rest, they let them go. The Jews seem not to have had the same influence with the chief men of the city as in Antioch of Pisidia (xiii. 50); so they stirred up the rabble, and through them brought the affair before the rulers. Knowing that Paul and Silas lodged in the house of Jason, "they sought to bring them forth to the people," with the evident purpose of subjecting them to mob violence; but failing to find them, their proceedings with Jason himself were more orderly—they dragged him and some of the other disciples before the officers, styled in the Greek politarchs (city-rulers). The charge of turning the world "upside down" was based on the mob violence which had attended their labors in other cities, of which these Jews of Thessalonica had evidently heard a great deal, and for which they unjustly laid the blame on the apostles, while they were themselves repeating the wicked procedure of other mobs. The other charge was true in a proper sense, for they had preached Jesus as a king; but the charge was a perversion, deliberate and intentional, on the part of the Jews, though not detected as such by the rabble. The people and the rulers were troubled, because they feared the consequences of permitting treasonable plots against Cæsar to

be propagated in the city. If Paul and Silas had themselves been brought before the politarchs, it is not certain that they would have fared better than at the hands
of the prætors of Philippi ; but as the only accusation
against Jason was that he had entertained the preachers,
he was released after giving bond to keep the peace.

The title politarch, which Luke here applies to the
chief magistrates of Thessalonica, is nowhere else found
as an official title in all Greek literature ; and it is easy
to see what a clamor the enemies of the faith would
have made over this use of the term, but for the fact that
an ancient triumphal arch of marble until recently
spanned the principal street of the city, with an inscription in which this very title is applied, and the names of
seven of the politarchs are preserved. When the arch
was torn down, the slabs containing the inscription were
secured by the British consul then at Thessalonica, and
they are now kept in the British Museum. Three of the
names are Sosipater, Secundus and Gaius, the names of
three well known fellow laborers of Paul (xix. 29 ;
xx. 4).

9. Success in Berœa, 10–15.

VER. 10. Although Paul and Silas suffered less in
Thessalonica than in Philippi, their departure from the
former was more humilating than from the latter. When
they heard the result of the attempt to seize them, they
saw at once that their further continuance in the city
would be likely to involve Jason and the others in a for-
feiture of their bond, and would bring personal violence
to themselves ; so they sought safety for all in flight.
(10) **And the brethren immediately sent away Paul and
Silas by night unto Berœa : who when they were come**

thither went into the synagogue of the Jews. This
flight by night must have reminded Paul of that from
Damascus in the beginning of his apostolic career ; and
it may have been effected by a similar method of escape.

From Philippi to Thessalonica, Paul and Silas had
followed one of those splendid military roads constructed
by the Romans for the passage of armies at all seasons of
the year, which were properly graded, and then paved
with flag-stones. Remnants of them are still found in
almost every country then included in the empire ;
and this one, called the Via Egnatia, connecting the
Hellespont with the Adriatic sea, was the great thoroughfare across the peninsula of Macedonia toward the distant East. On leaving Thessalonica in the night they
did not have to grope their way ; for they still followed
the same highway westward till, probably after daylight,
they left it and turned more to the southwest in order to
reach Berœa. Their route all the way lay across a level
country traversed by historic streams ; and Berœa itself,
about sixty miles from Thessalonica, is thus described :
" Berœa, like Edessa, is on the eastern slope of the
Olympian range, and commands an extensive view of
the plain which is watered by the Haliacmon and the
Axius. It has many natural advantages, and is now
considered one of the most agreeable towns of Rumili.
Plane trees spread a grateful shade over its gardens.
Streams of water are in every street. Its ancient name
is said to have been derived from the abudance of its
waters ; and the name still survives in the modern
Verria, or Kara-Verria." [1] It is still a walled city with
a population of between fifteen and twenty thousand

---

[1] Conybeare and Howson, following the description of the
traveler Leake.

Here again the apostle found a synagogue, and made it the starting point of his labors.

Vv. 11, 12.　We now have the pleasure of seeing one Jewish community listen to the truth and examine it like rational beings.　(11) Now these were more noble than those in Thessalonica, in that they received the word with all readiness of mind, examining the Scriptures daily, whether these things were so.　(12) Many of them therefore believed; also of the Greek women of honorable estate, and of men, not a few.　The conduct of these Jews can not be too highly commended, or too closely imitated.　A common sin of men is a refusal to examine candidly and patiently the claims of the gospel.　The Jews, having fallen into error by their traditions, resisted with passion and uproar every attempt to give them the true light; and their folly has been imitated ever since by both unbelievers and the partisans of religious error.　If such persons live and die in ignorance of the truth, and in consequent neglect of duty, their ignorance, instead of excusing them, will be one of their chief sins.　There is scarcely a greater sin than to stop our ears when God speaks, or to close our eyes to truth which he brings before us.　All who profess to be disciples of Christ should search the Scriptures upon the presentation of everything offering a decent claim to be God's truth, and see " whether these things are so."　To follow implicitly wherever the word of God leads can never be unacceptable to its Author.　As a consequence of the noble conduct of the Berœan Jews, the result was not, as in Thessalonica, that *some* of them believed, and a *great multitude* of the Greeks, but *many* of them believed, and *not a few* of the Greeks.　Let us not fail to notice, too, that their believing is ascribed by Luke expressly to the fact that they searched the Scriptures, whether these things were so; again showing that faith comes by hearing the word of God.

Vv. 13, 14.   There seems to have been no serious obstacle to the gospel in Berœa, and the disciples may have begun to flatter themselves with the hope of turning the whole city to the Lord, when an unexpected foe assailed them from the rear.   (13) **But when the Jews of Thessalonica had knowledge that the word of God was proclaimed by Paul at Berœa also, they came thither likewise, stirring up and troubling the multitudes.   (14) And then immediately the brethren sent forth Paul to go as far as to the sea: and Silas and Timothy abode there still.   (15) But they who conducted Paul brought him as far as Athens: and receiving a commandment unto Silas and Timothy that they should come to him with all speed, they departed.**

Here is an exhibition of that same malevolent zeal which characterized the Jews of Antioch and Iconium when they pursued Paul to Lystra (xiv. 19), showing that the Jews were the same the world over.   Again it was the heathen population that they stirred up, and one of their pleas, no doubt, as in the case at Lystra, was that these men had been compelled to fly from the city of Thessalonica.   Thus one persecution was made the plea for another.

When Paul left Berœa, it seems from the expressions used, that he had formed his plans only so far as to go to the sea, which was about sixteen miles distant at the nearest point; but on going that far it was determined that he should sail to Athens, and this determination made it necessary for him to send back word to Silas and Timothy. The obvious purpose of leaving these two brethren behind, at some risk no doubt to their personal safety, was to still further instruct and encourage the newly baptized disciples ere they were left to their own resources for edification. As Timothy had been left with Luke at Philippi (xvi. 40), and now first appears again in the narrative, it is uncertain whether or not he overtook Paul in Thessalonica. In leaving Macedonia Paul left behind him three churches, planted at radiating points, from which the gospel could be successfully spread throughout the province, if the disciples proved faithful and zealous. Thessalonica occupied the central position, with Philippi one hundred miles to the northeast, and Berœa sixty miles to the southwest. We have the testimony of Paul that from at least one of these the light shone with great brilliancy ; for he afterward wrote to the Thessalonians : "From you hath sounded forth the word of the Lord, not only in Macedonia and Achaia, but in every place your faith to Godward is gone forth ; so that we need not to speak anything" (I. Thess. i. 8). There was no need of Paul's voice at any but central points when he could leave such congregations behind him. No doubt much of their zeal and fidelity was due to the fostering care of Luke, Timothy and Silas, who alternately lingered behind the apostle for this purpose.

10. PAUL IN ATHENS, 16–21.

Vv. 16, 17. In the ancient world there were two distinct varieties of civilization, which had reached their culmination in the days of the apostles. One was the result of human philosophy ; the other, of a divine revelation. The chief center of the former was the city of

Athens; of the latter, the city of Jerusalem. If we compare them with respect either to the moral character of
the peoples brought under their influence respectively,
or with reference to their preparation for the perfect
religion of Christ, we shall find the advantage in favor
of the latter. Fifteen hundred years before, God had
placed the Jews under the influence of revelation, and
left the other nations of the earth to " walk in their own
ways." By a severe discipline, continued through many
centuries, the former had been lifted out of the idolatry
in which they were sunk at the beginning, and which
still prevailed over all other nations. As a consequence
they presented an example of purity in private morals
which stands unrivaled in ancient history previous to
the advent of Christ. On the other hand, the most ele-
gant of the heathen nations were now exhausting in their
social life, as Paul testifies in the first chapter of his
epistle to the Romans, the catalogue of base and beastly
practices of which men and women can be guilty. In
Athens itself, where flourished the most profound philosophy, the most glowing eloquence, the most exquisite
poetry, and the most refined creative art which the
world has ever seen, there was the most complete and
studied abandonment to every vice which passion could
prompt or imagination invent. In the center of Jewish
civilization the gospel had now been preached, and
many thousands who had embraced it had attained to an
excellence in human virtue not known before since the
fall of man. In surrounding countries, and in distant
lands, wherever the Jewish synagogue was found, devout
and honorable men and women by the thousands had
done the same; but nowhere had this blessed light
penetrated far into the darkness of heathenism. The

struggle now about to take place in Athens is to demonstrate still further, by contrast, how successful a "schoolmaster to bring us to Christ" had been the law and the prophets. Paul knew well the reputation of Athens, but he could not have realized, until he saw it, the extent to which it was given to idolatry. (16) Now while Paul waited for them at Athens, his spirit was provoked within him, as he beheld the city full of idols. (17) So he reasoned in the synagogue with the Jews and the devout persons, and in the market place daily with them that met with him. Though a lonely stranger, who might have been awed into silence by the magnificence with which sin had fortified itself in this great city, his soul was stirred to make a mighty struggle for the triumph of the gospel even here. His first effort, as usual, was in the Jewish synagogue; but the Jews and proselytes were so completely under the spell of the gilded iniquity around them, that his efforts were unsuccessful. Having access to no other formal assembly, he next goes upon the streets, and the places of public concourse, and discourses with "them that met with him."

VER. 18. By persistent efforts Paul succeeded in attracting some attention from the idle throng, but it was of a character at first not at all flattering. (18) And certain also of the Epicurean and Stoic philosophers encountered him. And some said, What would this babbler say? Other some, He seemeth to be a setter forth of foreign demons:[1] because he preached Jesus and the

---

[1] Instead of "strange gods," as in our version, the more correct rendering is "foreign demons." Our English translators have dealt very strangely with the term δαιμόνιον. In every other place they have rendered it *devils*, though there is but one devil, and

resurrection. The persistency with which he pressed
his message on every one he met suggested the epithet
babbler, while the prominence which he gave to the
name of Jesus, a man who had died and risen again,
suggested the idea of demon-worship, because the demons
worshiped by the Greeks were dead men deified.

The two classes of philosophers which he encountered were the antipodes of each other, and the practical
philosophy of each was antipodal to the doctrine of Paul.
The Stoics taught that the greatest good in life was to be
attained through a total indifference to both the sorrows
and the pleasures of the world; the Epicureans, that it
was to be obtained through the prudent gratification of
every passion and propensity; and they united in denying
conscious existence after death. In opposition to the
former, Paul taught that we should weep with those who
weep, and rejoice with those who rejoice; in opposition

---

here they have most inconsistently rendered it *gods*. But while
demons were worshiped by the Greeks, they were a class of
beings distinct in the minds of Jews from the devil and fallen
angels, and distinct in the minds of Greeks from those gods
which they styled " The Immortals;" and it is inexcusable in a
translator to confound to the minds of his readers things which
are so distinct in the original. A uniform use of the word demon
throughout the N. T., which was insisted upon by the American
Committee of the Revisers, is plainly demanded by fidelity to the
original. The term ζένοι, here rendered *strange* in our version, as
it is everywhere else except in one passage where there is a
necessity for a variation (Rom. xvi. 23), has a more definite meaning than our word strange. It means foreign, in the sense of belonging to another country, or a different system. Here, and in
verse 20, it has specific reference to the origin in a foreign land,
that is, in Judea, of the teaching to which it is applied; and in
verse 21 those called strangers in our version were foreigners, and
not mere strangers to the Athenians, which they might have
been if they were Greeks who had not visited Athens before.

to the latter, that we should deny all ungodliness and worldly lusts ; and in opposition to both, that the final goal of human hopes is a resurrection from the dead to life everlasting.

Vv. 19–21. Notwithstanding the contempt with which Paul was regarded by many, he succeeded at last in arresting the earnest attention of a few. (19) **And they took hold of him, and brought him unto the Areopagus, saying, May we know what this new teaching is, which is spoken by thee ?** (20) **For thou bringest certain foreign things to our ears : we would know therefore what these things mean.** (21) **(Now all the Athenians and the foreigners sojourning there spent their time in nothing else, but either to tell or hear some new thing.)** They " took hold of him " in a familiar way, to lead him from the noisy crowd to a better place of hearing. The agora (inaccurately rendered " market place " in our version), in which Paul was talking to the people, was bounded on the whole northern side by a ridge of coarse marble which rises abruptly to the height of about thirty feet. Toward the west it slopes downward gradually until in the course of about a quarter of a mile it descends to the level of the plain. This is the Areopagus, or, as rendered into English, the hill of Mars—so called because a temple of Mars once stood on its summit. Its summit is reached from the agora by a flight of steps cut in the natural rock, the most of which remain unbroken to the present day; and here in the open air sat the court of the Areopagus, by whose decisions grave questions in religion were settled, and sometimes great criminals were condemned. The informal character of the proceedings on this occasion shows that it was not the court that had summoned Paul; but merely that the philosophers who wished to give him a quiet hearing chose this spot for the purpose. The agora was spread out in full view below, and the hum of its confused sounds could be distinctly heard; but these would not prevent the small audience from hearing the voice of the speaker.

Luke's parenthetical statement, that all the Athenians and the foreigners dwelling there spent their time in nothing but hearing and telling something new, though not true, of course, of the laboring classes and tradesmen, who are evidently not contemplated in the remark, was strictly true of the great mass; for in those days men came to Athens from every nation to extend their education by hearing the numerous lecturers on all topics; and to learn about countries foreign to their own from visitors therefrom; so that every one was both a hearer and a teller of something that was new to others· It was in perfect keeping with this habit that these philosophers desired to hear the foreign teaching which Paul seemed anxious to impart.

11. PAUL'S DISCOURSE ON "THE UNKNOWN GOD," 22-31.

Vv. 22, 23. After his persevering but necessarily disconnected conversations in the agora, Paul was delighted to have now an audience assembled for the express purpose of hearing him. He could not begin by opening the Scriptures, and speaking of the long expected Messiah; for of the Scriptures, and even of the God who gave them, his auditors were profoundly ignorant. Before he could preach to them Jesus as the Son of God, he must make them acquainted with God himself; and for this purpose his observations in the city had supplied him with a most admirable text. (22) **And Paul stood**

in the midst of the Areopagus, and said, Ye men of
Athens, in all things I perceive that ye are very demon-
fearing.[1] (23) For as I passed along, and observed the
objects of your worship, I found also an altar with this
inscription, TO AN UNKNOWN GOD. What therefore
ye worship in ignorance, this set I forth unto you. The
people of Athens were worshipers of demons, or of dead
men deified, and they regarded it as a virtue to be scru-
pulous in all the forms of this worship.[2] Paul's audi-

---

[1] The Greek word here rendered "too superstitious" in the
A. V., and "somewhat superstitious" (margin, "religious") in
the R. V., is δεισιδαιμονεστέρους, the comparative degree of δεισιδαίμων,
which means demon-fearing. It is compounded of δείδω, to fear,
and δαίμων, a demon. As θεοσεβής is properly translated god-fearing,
δεισιδαίμων is with equal propriety rendered demon-fearing. The
comparative degree of the adjective does not institute an explicit
comparison between the Athenians and others in this respect;
for the context furnishes no basis for such a comparison; and
therefore, according to a common rule of Greek grammar, it is to
be construed as indicating an unusual degree of the quality referred to, and should be preceded by the adverb very in the English rendering of it. "Very demon-fearing," then, is the exact
meaning of the word. While the Athenians were, from either a
Jewish or a Christian point of view, "somewhat superstitious,"
"too superstitious," and "somewhat religious," in thus fearing
demons, these expressions fail to translate the term employed by
Paul, and therefore they should not be employed. They really
express an inference of the translators, and therefore have the
nature of a comment, rather than that of a translation. It is as
if one were translating a single word from some foreign tongue
which meant the fear of ghosts, and were to render it too superstitious; or a Chinese word meaning the fear of Joss, and were to
render it somewhat religious. See more on the subject of demon
worship in the next note below, and the note under xxv. 19.

[2] Paul says (I. Cor. x. 20): "The things which the Gentiles
sacrifice they sacrifice to demons, and not to God." He probably
meant to stigmatize all of their deities as demons; or it may be
that he had in mind their own distinction between demons and

tors therefore were complimented by his opening remark. His next remark presented a proof of the first.

---

gods, and meant that not all, but the great mass of their sacrifices were offered to the former, which was true. One of the most
prominent of the complaints brought against the Christians of
the second century by Celsus was based on their refusal to honor
the demons, and in making it he seems to have been in earnest.
He says : " We must either not live, and indeed not come into
this life at all, or we must do so on condition that we give thanks
and first fruits and prayers to demons, who have been set over
the things of this world ; and that we must do as long as we live,
that they may prove good and kind." (*Origen vs. Celsus*, viii. 33).
" The satrap of a Persian or Roman monarch, or ruler, or governor, or general, yea, even those who fill lower offices of trust or
service in the state, would be able to do great injury to those
who despised them, and will the satraps and ministers of earth
and air be insulted with impunity ?" (*ib.* 35). He styles Jesus
the Christian's demon, and says : " Do you not see, good sir,
that even your own demon is not only reviled, but banished from
every land and sea, and you yourself, who are as it were an
image dedicated to him, are bound and led to punishment, and
fastened to the stake, whilst your demon, or, as you call him, the
Son of God, takes no vengeance on the evil-doer ?" (*ib.* 39 ; see
also vii. 67–69). As to the nature of these beings, there was in
the minds of Greek writers some confusion ; but Plato says :
" The poets speak excellently who affirm that when good men
die they obtain great honor and dignity, and become demons "
(*Cratulus*). He also says, " Every demon is a middle between
God and mortal ;" and he shows the ground of the worship of
these good demons by the further statement : " Demons are re-
porters and carriers from men to the gods, and again from the
gods to men, of the supplications and prayers of the one, and of
the injunctions and rewards of devotion from the other " (*Sympos.*
iii. 202, 203). It is not difficult to see here the source of the invocation of saints practiced by Greek and Roman Catholics. But
in the Greek system there were also wicked demons. Plutarch
writes : " It is a very ancient opinion that there are certain wicked and malignant demons, who envy good men, and endeavor to
hinder them in their pursuit of virtue, lest they should be partakers of greater happiness than they enjoy " (*Dion.* i. 958). The

The unknown god, to which the altar mentioned had been erected, could not be one of the immortals, who were all well known, and therefore he must have been a demon not hitherto worshiped by name. After erecting altars and statues to all the known gods, so that a Roman satirist[1] said that it was easier to find a god than a man in Athens, they had shown their zeal for demon-worship by honoring a being whom they did not know. The commentators have suggested many hypotheses to account for the erection of this altar; but there are so many causes which may have led to it,[2] that it is impossible to fix upon any one with much assurance. It is sufficient that it answered Paul's purpose in proving that the Athenians were very demon-fearing, and in introducing to them the only true and living God, as though he were the God whom they thus already worshiped. In this way he avoided the appearance of inviting them to a worship which was foreign to their customs, and which they otherwise might have regarded as unlawful.

Jewish conception was precisely the same, except that they limited their use of the term to the spirits of wicked men. Thus Josephus says: "Demons are no other than the spirits of the wicked, that enter into men that are alive, and kill them, unless they can obtain some help against them" (*Wars*, vii. 6. 3). This being the accepted meaning of the term with both Jews and Greeks, we must understand it when used by Jesus and by Paul in the same sense. Similar information is furnished in a condensed form in the Liddell and Scott Greek Lexicon, under the word δαίμων.

[1] Petronius, Satire 17.

[2] Individuals as well as the state were in the habit of erecting small marble altars to the honor of gods or goddesses from whom they supposed themselves to have received special favors. Some of these, recovered from the ruins, are even now standing, as they did in ancient times, in the court of the Acropolis.

Vv. 24–28. He next introduces the God to whom he refers, by making a series of statements concerning him, every one of which presents him in striking contrast with the gods of the Greeks. (24) **The God that made the world and all things therein, he, being Lord of heaven and earth, dwelleth not in temples made with hands; (25) neither is he served by men's hands, as though he needed anything, seeing he himself giveth to all life, and breath, and all things ; (26) and he made of one every nation of men for to dwell on all the face of the earth, having determined their appointed seasons, and the bounds of their habitation; (27) that they should seek God, if haply they might feel after him, and find him, though he is not far from each one of us : (28) for in him we live, and move, and have our being ; as certain even of your own poets have said, For we are also his offspring.** With Paul's hearers there was no God who " made the world and all things therein ;" so, by this thought he lifted his God above all that they conceived of theirs. As he had made all things, this made him Lord, not of the sea, as Neptune, nor of the sky, as Jupiter, but " Lord of heaven and earth." From this it was easy to see the conclusion, that he dwells not in handmade temples—that these are too small to contain him. Here Paul had allusion to the magnificent marble temples which were in sight all around him, and especially to the Parthenon, the glory of Greek architecture, which towered above the Areopagus just to the east. Both from this consideration, and from another next mentioned, this God is not served by men's hands, as though he needed something which men could supply, seeing that from him, as the final source, men receive their life, their breath, and all that they enjoy. Of no

heathen god had this been said ; for to none of them did
their worshipers ascribe such power. He next shows
that this God, instead of being the god of some single
nation, over whose destiny he presides, while he defends
it against all other nations, actually created every nation,
made them all from one man, to dwell on the face of the
whole earth ; and further, that the seasons of prosperity
and adversity of all these nations, together with their
national boundaries, instead of being regulated, as the
heathen supposed, by separate national gods, were all
controlled by this one God. Finally he shows them
that the purpose of God in all these things was to induce
men to obtain the very knowledge of himself which Paul
was now trying to impart to his hearers. What nobler
pursuit of knowledge than to seek such a God, even
though we have to " feel after him " like blind men.
But such obscure seeking, he lets them know in the same
breath, is not needful, seeing that he is not far away, but
round about us at all times and in all places. One of
their own poets had very nearly expressed this thought,
in saying, " We are also his offspring ;" for God, like an
earthly father, would not leave his children to grope
after him in the dark, and to call him an " unknown
god." By this train of thought, more fully expressed
no doubt than we have it in Luke's epitome, the God
whom they had worshiped without knowing him was
brought before them ; and let it be observed that they
had worshiped him in a closer sense than we are apt to
suppose ; for whatever may have been the benefit received, which had led some one to set up the altar in
question, that benefit had really come from the true God,
and this expression of gratitude had been offered un-
wittingly.

VER. 29. From these reflections, and especially from the last, Paul next draws a logical conclusion inimical to all forms of idol worship. (29) **Being then the offspring of God, we ought not to think that the Godhead is like unto gold, or silver, or stone, graven by art and device of man.** Their own self-respect should forbid them to think of him from whom they derived their being as like these dead works of their own hands, however skillfully and beautifully wrought out.

The statement in verse 26, that God " made of one all the nations of men," is an incidental assertion of the unity of the human race ; and it accords with the Mosaic history. To deny it because we find some difficulty in reconciling it with the present diversities in the types of men, is to deny an assertion of the Scriptures, not because of what we know, but because of what we do not know ; for if we knew the whole history of our race, we should doubtless know the causes of these varieties, and the times in which they came into existence.

Vv. 30, 31. Having now made known the true God to his hearers, Paul next calls upon them to repent of their idolatry ; and he presents, as a motive to this, the solemn fact of the future judgment. (30) **The times of ignorance therefore God overlooked ; but now he commandeth men that they should all everywhere repent:** (31) **inasmuch as he hath appointed a day, in the which he will judge the world in righteousness by the man whom he hath ordained ; whereof he hath given assurance unto all men, in that he hath raised him from the dead.** By saying that God had overlooked the times of ignorance, Paul does not mean that he had excused it; for this would be inconsistent with this call to repentance. He means that God had not hitherto attempted to break it up, as he now does, by sending forth preachers of the truth. True, the message of Jonah to Nineveh, the proclamations concerning the true God forced from the pens of Nebuchadnezzar, Darius and Cyrus, together with many overthrows of heathen armies like that of Sennacherib, were loud voices from heaven reminding heathen nations of the God whom they had forgotten; but these were isolated acts, and not parts of a continuous and systematic call to repentance, such as was sent forth by the mission of the apostles.

The soul-stirring fact that God has "appointed a day in which he will judge the world in righteousness," is a powerful motive to repentance, because a judgment in righteousness must inevitably involve the condemnation of all the unrighteous; and Paul's hearers could now see the unrighteousness of their idolatry. In thus presenting the final judgment as the first and foremost motive to bring men to repentance, Paul was but following the example of Jesus, and proceeding according to the demands of human nature. The terrors of that great day, and of the awful fate awaiting those who shall then be condemned, constitute the heavy artillery of the gospel, by which the fortification that sin has constructed about the hearts of wicked men must be battered down, ere the tenderer motives of the gospel can be brought to bear. The wicked man must be made afraid to continue in sin, before the goodness of God can lead him to repentance; and the preacher of the gospel who neglects to employ the thunders of this heavenly artillery not only fails to preach according to the divine model, but he will preach a feeble gospel that can never work deep seated repentance

It is just at this point in his discourse that Paul first introduces Jesus; and he introduces him first, not as a loving Saviour, but as a universal judge; he introduces him not in his birth of the virgin, or in his baptism by John, or in his healing power, or in his death for the sins of men; but in the closing act of his Messianic reign, the everlasting judgment; and he presents, as the proof that Jesus will thus judge, the fact that God has raised him from the dead. This fact, considered in itself alone, would not furnish this proof; but considered in connection with the statement of Jesus before his death, that all judgment had been given into his hands (Jno. v. 22–29), it does. Of course Paul's hearers did not yet see the force of this; for what is here said about Jesus, even without naming him, was evidently intended by Paul as the mere introduction of a theme which he intended to expand in the remainder of his remarks. Indeed, he had just now reached that which was to be the chief theme of his discourse; and we can see that his plan of discourse was, first, to make these idolaters acquainted with the true God; second, to call on them to repent toward God; and third, to present Christ as he through whom their repentance might be available in enabling them to obtain forgiveness of sins and everlasting life.

Vv. 32, 33. But Paul was not permitted to finish his discourse. Just as he had reached its most vital part he was interrupted. (32) **Now when they heard of the resurrection of the dead, some mocked; but others said, We will hear thee concerning this yet again.** (33) **Thus Paul went out from among them.** From a modern point of view there are two strange features in the conduct of this audience: first, that they listened quietly while Paul was demonstrating the folly of their idolatrous worship, which we should naturally expect them to defend; and second, that they interrupted him when he spoke of a resurrection from the dead, which we should have expected them to welcome as a relief from the gloom that shrouded their thoughts of death. But the former is accounted for by the infidelity which then prevailed among philosophers in reference to the heathen deities, rendering formal and heartless with them the worship which was still observed by the ignorant masses with some devoutness and sincerity; while the latter is explained by their pride of opinion and their party zeal. The two sects of philosophy to which they belonged had long ago proved, by arguments which the Platonists, they fondly thought, could never set aside, that there is no future state, and that therefore the idea of a resurrection from the dead is preposterous. Thus a false philosophy had crushed out of their hearts some of the better instincts of our nature, and caused them to mock at that which is the dearest of all hopes to the chief part of mankind. Still, those who said, " We will hear thee concerning this yet again," began, perhaps, to feel a rekindling of their better instincts; and let us hope that some of these may yet be found among the sons of light.

VER. 34. Although his discourse was broken off by the mockery of a portion of his audience, the apostle's effort was not altogether fruitless. (34) But certain men clave unto him, and believed: among whom also was Dionysius the Areopagite, and a woman named Damaris, and others with them. Among these converts Dionysius is selected for special mention, because, as his title indicates, he was one of the judges of the Areopagus, and therefore a man of high official standing in the city ; and Damaris is made conspicuous because it was unusual for a woman to be found in an audience of philosophers. That she was there, however, proves the freedom of the Greek women of the period, and is quite inconsistent with the notions often expressed by shallow interpreters concerning some of Paul's remarks about women in his epistles.[1]

12. Paul Begins the Work in Corinth, xviii. 1–4.

VER. 1. Paul's comparative failure in Athens aptly illustrates, if it did not suggest, his subsequent remark to the Corinthians, " God made foolish the wisdom of the world. For seeing that in the wisdom of God the world through its wisdom knew not God, it was God's good pleasure through the foolishness of the preaching to save them that believe " (I. Cor. i. 21). Having thus failed in the literary capital of Greece, he next resorts to its political and commercial capital. (1) After these things he departed from Athens, and came to Corinth. This city was situated on the western coast of the isthmus which connects the Peloponnesus with Attica. It was only nine miles distant across the isthmus from Cenchrea at the head of the Saronic gulf, and in this direction it had easy communication with all the great cities of Asia ; and, being at the head of the gulf of Corinth on the west, it enjoyed, through it and the Adriatic sea, close communication with Italy and the west. It was therefore a city of great commercial advantages, and these had drawn into it a large Jewish population.

[1] I. Cor. xiv. 34–37 ; I. Tim. ii. 8–15.

Vv. 2–4. Paul entered this great city alone, a total stranger, and penniless. The little means which he had brought with him from Macedonia was exhausted, and his attention was turned first to the supply of his daily bread. By a combination of providences he found most desirable lodgings, and the means of livelihood. (2) And he found a certain Jew named Aquila, a man of Pontus by race, lately come from Italy, with his wife Priscilla, because Claudius had commanded all the Jews to depart from Rome: and he came unto them; (3) and because he was of the same trade, he abode with them, and they wrought; for by their trade they were tentmakers. (4) And he reasoned in the synagogue every Sabbath, and persuaded Jews and Greeks. To be thus under the necessity of laboring as a journeyman tentmaker, when he was aiming to evangelize a proud and opulent city, was anything but encouraging. From the calm and unimpressive style of Luke's account, we might imagine that Paul's feelings were callous to such considerations; but his own pen, which often reveals emotions unnoticed by Luke, gives a far different representation. Writing to the Corinthians several years afterward, when all transient emotions had been forgotten, he says: "I was with you in weakness, and in fear, and in much trembling" (I. Cor. ii. 3). He was keenly sensitive to the weakness of his situation; he feared a failure similar to that in Athens; and he trembled at the thought that the salvation of so many souls was dependent on so feeble an instrumentality. Whether he found in Aquila and Priscilla immediate Christian fellowship and encouragement, we are not able to determine; for while it is possible that they were among the Jews from Pontus who were present on the

great day of Pentecost (ii. 9); or that they may have
been baptized more recently in Rome by disciples there
who had heard Peter's great sermon (*ib.*); and while
there is nothing said by Luke about their being baptized
by Paul; yet if they were already disciples, it is very
difficult to account for Luke's entire silence in reference
to the fact. At any rate, Paul found them true hearted
worshipers of God, and formed a personal attachment
to them which lasted to the latest day of his life. We
shall meet them again and again in the course of the
narrative, and always to hear of something praiseworthy
in their conduct.

The preaching in the synagogue, which continued
through several Sabbaths, seems to have been slower
than usual in taking effect. Perhaps this was because
the preacher was a tent-maker, as well as a stranger;
and possibly it was due in part to the less aggressive
manner of Paul, superinduced by the weakness and fear
and trembling of which we have just spoken.

13. The Arrival of Silas and Timothy, and a
Breach with the Jews, 5–11.

Vv. 5–7. The loneliness of Paul's situation was at
length relieved, and a change came over his manner of
preaching. (5) But when Silas and Timothy came down
from Macedonia, Paul was constrained by the word,
testifying to the Jews that Jesus was the Christ. (6)
And when they opposed themselves, and blasphemed, he
shook out his raiment, and said unto them, Your blood
be upon your own heads; I am clean: from henceforth I
will go unto the Gentiles. (7) And he departed thence,
and went into the house of a certain man named Titus
Justus, one that worshiped God, whose house joined

hard to the synagogue. It will be remembered by the reader that Silas and Timothy, whose arrival is here mentioned, had tarried in Berœa, that Paul had sent them word to rejoin him as soon as possible, and that he had waited for them in Athens (xvii. 15, 16). Luke is silent as to whether they overtook him at Athens; but we learn from Paul that Timothy did. He writes: " When we could no longer forbear, we thought it good to be left behind at Athens alone, and sent Timothy . . . to establish you and comfort you concerning your faith " (I. Thess. iii. 1, 2). This remark not only shows that Timothy had overtaken Paul at Athens, but that he had been sent back thence to Thessalonica. It also proves the correctness of our judgment as to why Paul had habitually left behind him for a time, with almost every church planted, some one of his fellow laborers—that is, " to establish them and comfort them concerning the faith." Timothy's present arrival in Corinth, as we now see, was not from his original stay in Berœa, but from a recent visit to Thessalonica. Probably Silas had remained until now in Berœa.

The statement that on the arrival of Silas and Timothy Paul was " constrained by the word, testifying to the Jews that Jesus was the Christ," implies, I think, that hitherto he had only argued, as at the beginning in Thessalonica, that according to the Scriptures the Christ must suffer and rise again from the dead, without advancing as yet to the further proposition, that " this Jesus whom I preach to you is the Christ." The former might cause no outbreak; the latter was sure to do so among Jews who had already heard something of Jesus, as the Corinthian Jews almost certainly had. The anticipated crisis came, and the breach followed. Fortu-

nately, one Gentile proselyte, who was a man of means,
was favorably impressed by Paul; and as he had a house
close to the synagogue, he threw it open for the subsequent meetings. Justus was not yet a disciple, but, as
suits the meaning of his name, he desired to see justice
done to the apostle and his cause.

Ver. 8. Although Paul left the synagogue in apparent discomfiture, he was not without fruits of his labor.
(8) And Crispus, the ruler of the synagogue, believed in
the Lord with all his house; and many of the Corinthians, hearing, believed, and were baptized. It was
very seldom that men of high positions in the synagogue
obeyed the gospel; and it is therefore greatly to the
credit of Crispus that he did so, and this at the moment
when the opposition and blasphemy of the other Jews
was at its height. He must have been a man of inde-
pendence and sincerity—the very kind of man to form
the nucleus for a congregation of disciples. His conversion, and that of the other Corinthians here mentioned,
are not so fully described as those of the eunuch, of
Saul, and of Cornelius; yet enough is said to show that
the process was the same. "Hearing, they believed and
were baptized." To hear the gospel preached, to believe
it, and to be baptized, is the whole process briefly
expressed.

Vv. 9, 10. Although his success when leaving the
synagogue must have been a source of comfort to Paul,
we have evidence that he was far from being relieved as
yet from the "weakness, and fear, and much trembling,"
which had oppressed him since his coming to Corinth.
We have now reached the period of his letter-writing,
and we shall henceforth have his epistles as contemporary documents to fill some of the blanks in his personal

history left by Luke. The first epistle to the Thessalonians was written from Corinth soon after the arrival of Silas and Timothy, as is proved by the concurrence of the two facts, that these two brethren overtook Paul in Corinth, and that in the epistle Paul speaks of Timothy's arrival as having just taken place at the time of writing (iii. 6). Several statements in this epistle throw light on the inner experience of Paul at the time. He was racked by uncontrollable anxiety for the brethren in Thessalonica, for whom he would willingly have laid down his life, and who were suffering the severest persecution (ii. 8; 14–16). The good report of their constancy brought to him by Timothy gave him much joy; but it was joy in the midst of distress; for he says: "When Timothy came even now unto us from you, and brought us glad tidings of your faith and love, and that ye have good remembrance of us always, longing to see us, even as we also to see you; for this cause, brethren, we are comforted over you in all our distress and affliction through your faith: for now we live if ye stand fast in the Lord" (iii. 6–8). Undoubtedly a part of this "distress and affliction" was the result of his failure to save those Jews in Corinth who were now reviling him, and who, he well knew, would leave untried no device by which they might hope to drive him from the city. It was just at this crisis that the Lord Jesus, in whose behalf he was suffering, drew aside the intervening veil, and gave a word of cheer. (9) **And the Lord said unto Paul in the night by a vision, Be not afraid, but speak, and hold not thy peace: (10) for I am with thee, and no man shall set on thee to harm thee: for I have much people in this city.** The Lord never broke his accustomed silence to comfort a servant except when comfort was needed. The comfort which he gave on this occasion was not the assurance of personal safety alone, but that which Paul valued far higher, the assurance that his labors and sufferings in Corinth would yet be rewarded by the salvation of many souls.

In the words, " I have much people in this city," the Lord speaks of persons who were as yet unbelievers, and perhaps idolaters. This accords with the Calvinistic idea that God's people are a definite number whom he has individually selected from all eternity ; but it does not prove it ; for the language equally accords with the supposition that he called them his merely because he foresaw that under Paul's preaching they would yet believe. The same style is employed in Revelation, when the angel, announcing the downfall of mystic Babylon, cries, " Come out of her, my people, that ye be not partakers of her sins, and that ye receive not of her plagues " (xviii. 4). God knew that in answer to his call a people would come out of Babylon whom he would accept, and he calls them his people by way of anticipation.

Vv. 11. Supported by the assurance given in the vision, Paul continued his labors long and patiently. (11) **And he dwelt there a year and six months, teaching the word of God among them.** This is longer than he had ever yet stayed in any one city, and the word " teaching," which describes his work, shows that during this long period he was executing chiefly the second part of the apostolic commission, " teaching them to observe all that I have commanded you " (Matt. xxviii. 20). From this we can see that, notwithstanding the many disorders which were afterward found in the Corinthian church, it was probably the best taught of all the churches thus far planted by Paul. If they had been less fully instructed, what might have been their later condition ?

14. Paul Arraigned Before Gallio, 12–17.

Vv. 12, 13. The attempt of the Jews to suppress the preaching, which Paul had been looking for ever since he left the synagogue, came at last, but it came in an unusual form, and with unusual results. (12) **But when Gallio was proconsul of Achaia, the Jews with one accord rose up against Paul, and brought him before the judgment seat, (13) saying, This man persuadeth men to worship God contrary to the law.** The charge preferred was that of law-breaking, as in Philippi and Thessalonica ; but in those instances it was preferred by Gentiles with reference to Roman law, while in this the Jews had the boldness to prefer it in their own name, and with reference to their own law. This indicates a degree of confidence in their own influence which we have not met with in any other Gentile city. They hoped that Gallio would be willing to silence a Jew who was teaching contrary to the law of his own people.

Vv. 14–16. In this instance, however, the Jews had to deal with a man far different from the prætors of Philippi, or the politarchs of Thessalonica. Gallio was a brother of Seneca, the famous Roman moralist, who speaks of him as a man of admirable integrity, amiable and popular.[1] He was true to this representation on the

---

[1] He says: "No mortal man is so sweet to any single person as he is to all mankind." "Even those who love my brother Gallio to the very utmost of their power, yet do love not him enough" (*Quæstiones Naturales*, iv. præf. Secs. 10, 11.) It is a sad comment on the superstition which shrouded their minds, that both the brothers perished by suicide.

present occasion. (14) But when Paul was about to open his mouth, Gallio said to the Jews, If indeed it were a matter of wrong or of wicked villainy, O ye Jews, reason would that I should bear with you: (15) but if they are questions about words and names and your own law, look to it yourselves; I am not minded to be a judge of these matters. (16) And he drove them from the judgment seat. Gallio's phraseology, "words and names and your law," shows that he had a very confused conception of the issue between Paul and the Jews; but he knew enough to justify his decision. This is the only instance in all the experience of Paul in which his accusers were dealt with justly and summarily.

VER. 17. Prompt and energetic vindication of the right nearly always meets the approval of the masses of the people, and it sometimes reverses the tide of popular prejudice. We do not know how the masses of the city stood toward Paul before this decision, but they expressed themselves very vigorously as soon as the decision was rendered. (17) And they all laid hold on Sosthenes, the ruler of the synagogue, and beat him before the judgment seat. And Gallio cared for none of these things. The judgment seat, the chair of state in which the proconsul sat, was not erected inside of a court room, as with us, but in the open air, and usually in the agora, or forum. Consequently, all trials which excited public interest were witnessed by a crowd of spectators made up largely of the idlers on the streets. These are the only parties who could have been tempted to thus lay hands on Sosthenes, who, as the leader of the Jews, had preferred the charge against Paul. With that keen sense of the fitness of things which often characterizes such a crowd, they saw that Sosthenes deserved the beat-

ing which he had laid up for Paul ; and perhaps with a
laugh and a yell they gave it to him.[1]   The reason that
Gallio " cared for none of these things " was because, as
respects the question between Paul and the Jews, he did
not understand it ; and as respects the beating of Sosthenes, he rather enjoyed it, because Sosthenes so richly
deserved it.   The disappointment and rage of the Jews
were unbounded, but they had learned from bitter experience how to choke down such feelings, and to keep
quiet.

Before Paul left Corinth, and perhaps previous to
the arraignment before Gallio, he wrote the second
epistle to the Thessalonians. The indications of time and
place in the epistle are meager, but in the absence of
conflicting evidence they are conclusive.   First, there is
such a connection in thought and subject matter between
it and the first epistle as to indicate that there was no
long interval between them ; and second, Silas joined
with Paul in the salutation (i. 1) ; but Silas was not with
Paul after the latter left Corinth. If we knew just
when the separation from Silas took place, whether on
Paul's departure from Corinth, or at some previous
time, we could come nearer fixing the exact date ; but it
is commonly supposed that it was written within the

---

[1] The grammatical connection points to the term Jews in the
preceding context as the antecedent of " they ; " but this would
make the Jews the party that beat Sosthenes, which is altogether
improbable ; for why should they beat their own synagogue
ruler merely because Gallio had driven both him and them from
the court ? The grammatical connection must then yield, as it
does in xix. 33, and John viii. 33, two parallel cases, to the demands of the context, in determining the meaning. Farrar, who
takes the same view of the meaning, says of it, " I give the view
which seems to me most probable, passing over masses of idle
conjecture " (*Life of Paul,* 323, *n* 4).

same year as the first, and this would fix the date of both in the year 52.[1] The epistle reveals the fact that this church was still suffering severe persecution, but that they were enduring it with marvelous patience, so that Paul could say to them, "We are bound to give thanks to God always for you, brethren, even as it is meet, for that your faith groweth exceedingly, and the love of each one of you all toward one another aboundeth; so that we ourselves glory in you in the churches of God for your patience and faith in all your persecutions and in the afflictions which ye endure" (i. 3, 4). The extreme anxiety which he had felt for them at the time of writing the first epistle, and his diligence both in sending Timothy back to them and in writing to them, had been abundantly rewarded by their perseverance. Paul was moved not only to thanksgiving, but to many tender prayers in their behalf, which he briefly quotes in the epistle.[1] He had heard that "either by spirit, or by word, or by epistle" as from him, they had been troubled concerning the second coming of the Lord (ii. 2); and in order to guard against imposture in the future, he gives them a token by which they may test the genuineness of any epistle claiming to come from him. He says: "The salutation of me Paul with mine own hand, which is the token in every epistle: thus I write" (iii. 17). This shows that he ordinarily employed an amanuensis in writing his epistles (cf. Rom. xvi. 22), but that he wrote the salutation with his own hand as an evidence of genuineness. The employment of a skillful scribe, such as could be found in every city, if he had no companion possessed of this accomplish-

---

[1] See Vol. I. Intro., pages xxxix, xxxiv.   [2] See i. 11, 12; ii. 16, 17; iii. 16.

ment, insured such perfection in the manuscript as to
leave no word illegible, while the autographic salutation
attested the genuineness of the document. As these two
epistles are the earliest of the New Testament books, we
can readily believe that Paul's example, in thus guarding
the inspired documents against liability to misreading or
to imposture, was followed by the other writers.

15. Paul's Return to Antioch, 18–22.

Ver. 18. The last incident which Luke chooses to
mention in Corinth was the arraignment before Gallio,
though Paul continued there yet for a considerable time.
(18) **And Paul, having tarried after this yet many days,
took his leave of the brethren, and sailed thence for
Syria, and with him Priscilla and Aquila ; having shorn
his head in Cenchrea : for he had a vow.** His stay of
eighteen months in Corinth may be taken as an indication of the time which he would have spent with some
other churches had he been permitted to do so. Thanks
to Gallio, this was the only church in Macedonia and
Greece in which he was permitted to remain as long
as he thought proper. We shall hereafter see, however,
that this church, which was free from persecution, was
none the better for it as compared with those in Thessalonica and Philippi.

In aiming to sail to Syria, it was necessary to cross
the isthmus to Cenchrea, where we find a church at a later
period, which had probably been planted during Paul's
stay in Corinth. On arriving at this port, the time of
some vow which he had taken expired. In imitation of
the Nazirite, he had permitted his hair to grow during
the period of the vow, and at its close he resumed the
regular shaving of his head which is customary with

turban-wearing nations.   Many have mistaken this for
the Nazirite vow itself, through failure to remember
that at the close of this vow the hair was to be shaved
off at the temple, and burned in the fire of the altar
(Num. vi. 13–18).

Vv. 19–22.   A vessel sailing from Cenchrea to
Syria could very conveniently touch at Ephesus, which
was the destination of Aquila and Priscilla.   **(19) And
they came to Ephesus, and he left them there: but he
himself entered into the synagogue, and reasoned with
the Jews.   (20) And when they asked him to abide a
longer time, he consented not; (21) but taking his leave
of them, and saying, I will return again unto you, if
God will, he set sail from Ephesus.   (22) And when he
had landed at Cæsarea, he went up and saluted the
church, and went down to Antioch.**   Paul had now
decided that it was time for him to return once more to
Antioch, and report progress, before undertaking the
evangelization of another great city.   Having fixed on
Ephesus as his next point of attack, he feels the pulse,
as it were, of the Jews there, by a few remarks in the
synagogue; and finding it to beat favorably, he leaves
Priscilla and Aquila there for the evident purpose of
preparing the ground as well as they can, and of being
there when he returns, to help him as they had done in
Corinth; then, promising to return, he hurries on.   The
voyage to Cæsarea, and thence to Antioch, is without
recorded incident, except that on landing at the former
city he " went up and saluted the church."   This is the
church which had been planted there by the baptism of
Cornelius and his friends.[1]   On reaching Antioch we

---

[1] The commentators in general, misled by the interpolated
clause in the Textus Receptus, and the old English versions, " I

can not doubt that he once more gladdened the hearts of the brethren who had commended him and Silas to the favor of the Lord, by rehearsing to them all that God had done with him, and how he had opened still wider " the door of faith to the Gentiles." It may be that Silas had preceded him ; if not, he doubtless stated to them, as Luke has not stated to us, the circumstances under which they had separated. As to the changes which may have taken place in Antioch during the three years of Paul's absence, Luke is equally silent ; for he has his eye, as Paul had his, on the contemplated labors in Ephesus, which he hastens to describe.

SEC. IV. PAUL'S THIRD TOUR.

(XVIII. 23—XXI. 16.)

1. Second Visit to Galatia and Phrygia, 23.

Ver. 23. In a single brief sentence Luke disposes of a journey which must have occupied several months at least ; for it covered five or six hundred miles. (23) **And having spent some time there, he departed, and went through the region of Galatia and Phrygia in order, establishing all the disciples.** In order to reach Galatia and Phrygia,

---

must by all means keep this feast that cometh in Jerusalem " (21), assume that the church which Paul went up and saluted was the Jerusalem church; but in the absence of that clause there is nothing to justify this conclusion. He had doubtless landed at Cæsarea because the ship in which he sailed was bound for that harbor, and he had been contented to sail in that ship rather than lose time waiting for another, because it was but a short sail from Cæsarea to Antioch, and coasting vessels for the voyage could be found almost daily.

the only districts in the route that are mentioned, he
must have made the circuit once more from Antioch
around through Syria into Cilicia, and thence by way
of the Gates of Cilicia into the elevated tablelands of
Lycaonia and Pisidia, past Derbe, Lystra, Iconium and
the Pisidian Antioch. This was his third visit to these
communities, and his passage through Galatia and
Phrygia was a second visit to the churches which he had
planted there. If we may judge from the rapidity of
his passage, he found the churches in all the regions in
such a condition that they did not specially need a protracted visit from him, yet his work among them, brief
as it was, consisted in "establishing all the disciples."
He had this work in view, as well as the report in Antioch, when he declined the invitation to stay in Ephesus
(20, 21).

2. Apollos in Ephesus and Achaia, 24-28.

Vv. 24-26. We have expressed the opinion that
Paul's purpose in leaving Aquila and Priscilla in Ephesus was that they might do such preparatory work as
they could during his absence (19); and now Luke gives
us a specimen of the work of this kind which they did.
(24) Now a certain Jew named Apollos, an Alexandrian
by race,[1] a learned man, came to Ephesus; and he was
mighty in the Scriptures. (25) This man had been instructed in the way of the Lord; and being fervent in
spirit, he spake and taught carefully the things concerning Jesus, knowing only the baptism of John: (26)

---

[1] Apollos is here called "an Alexandrian by race," ($\tau\tilde{\omega}$ $\gamma\acute{\epsilon}\nu\epsilon\iota$),
rather than by birth, as in the A. V., to indicate that he was not
only born there, but born of an ancestry native to that city. The
term serves a similar purpose when used of Aquila in xviii. 1.

and he began to speak boldly in the synagogue. But when Priscilla and Aquila heard him, they took him unto them, and expounded unto him the way of the Lord more carefully. The distinguished position which Apollos afterward acquired in the church at Corinth, and the familiarity of his name among the disciples of subsequent ages, make it a matter of interest to observe closely what is here said of him. That he was an Alexandrian accounts in part for his learning, and indicates the character of it; for Alexandria, having been for at least two centuries the chief point of contact between Greek and Hebrew literature, had now become the chief seat of Hebrew learning. This learning included a knowledge of the Greek version of the Old Testament, of the other Greek literature of the later Jewish ages, and to some extent of Greek philosophy. The statement that he was " mighty in the Scriptures " means not merely that he was familiar with them, but that he knew how to handle them in argument and exposition with great effect. In a day when a knowledge of the Scriptures had to be acquired from manuscripts, and in which even the art of reading was acquired by only a few, it was no ordinary accomplishment to be thus familiar with the Scriptures. Such an attainment is rare even in this day of printed Bibles, and even among preachers, who are presumed by those who know no better to devote their whole lives to the study of the Bible. Preachers would be more mighty in preaching, and would have less need to search for might where it can not be found, if they would be more careful to follow the example of Apollos.

But while Apollos was mighty in the Scriptures, and while with a fervent spirit he " taught carefully the things concerning Jesus," Aquila and Priscilla, on hearing him, soon discovered that he did not understand Christian baptism—that he knew "only the baptism of John." They were not so ignorant on this subject as to suppose, with some of our moderns, that there is no difference between the two baptisms; nor so indifferent to it, as a "mere external rite," that they considered the difference of no importance. On the contrary, they took the powerful and zealous preacher to their own home, and taught him the truth on the subject. To his credit as a candid seeker after truth, he appears to have accepted gladly the correction. He learned that, while John's baptism had attached to it no promise of the Holy Spirit, this was one of the distinctive features of Christian baptism; and that while John baptized into no name, the apostles were taught to baptize into the name of the Father, and of the Son, and of the Holy Spirit (ii. 3; Matt. xxviii. 19). The question, whether he was rebaptized, will come before us in connection with xix. 5.

It should be observed that Priscilla took part with her husband in giving more perfect instruction to Apollos, and this illustrates the manner in which certain faithful women were eminent helpers of the apostles and evangelists in the spread of the gospel; yet it can not, without a deceitful handling of the Scriptures, be urged as proof that even the most eminent of the female helpers took part in public preaching.

Vv. 27, 28. For a reason not given, Apollos decided to leave Ephesus, and visit the churches planted by Paul in Achaia. (27) And when he was minded to pass over into Achaia, the brethren encouraged him, and wrote to the disciples to receive him: and when he was come, he helped them much who had believed through grace: (28)

for he powerfully confuted the Jews, and that publicly, showing by the Scriptures that Jesus was the Christ. This is the first mention of letters of commendation given to disciples going from one Christian community to another. They are mentioned at a later period as being in common use (II. Cor. iii. 1, 2). The brethren " encouraged him" to go, because they knew his peculiar power, and they knew that the churches needed it in their controversies with the Jews. Who these brethren were, besides Aquila and Priscilla, Luke does not just here inform us; but we learn a little farther on (xix. 1). Their expectations concerning the labors of Apollos in Achaia were happily realized in the great help which he gave to the disciples, and his successful confutation of the Jews. His special power being in the use of the Scriptures, he was the very man to reach the Jews, and to strengthen the faith of the believers. To confute is not always to convince; but we have evidence that in addition to confuting the Jews, Apollos brought many into the church; for Paul afterward referred to his labors as a watering of the church which he had planted, and then, changing his figure, said, " I laid the foundation, and another buildeth thereon " (I. Cor. iii. 6–10). As Paul had made a comparative failure with the Jews of Corinth, the success of Apollos illustrates the value of a variety of talents and acquirements among preachers, in order to the successful evangelization of the great variety of minds and characters often found in a single community.

3. Paul Reaches Ephesus, and Rebaptizes a Dozen Men, xix. 1-7.

Vv. 1-7. The historian now reaches the point for which he had so hurriedly passed over the voyage of Paul from Ephesus to Antioch, and his land journey thence through Galatia and Phrygia. Paul is permitted at last to begin a work which he had in mind when, on his preceding tour, he was "forbidden by the Holy Spirit to speak the word in Asia" (xvi. 6); and also to fulfill the appointment which he had left here on his journey homeward (xviii. 21). (1) And it came to pass, that, while Apollos was at Corinth, Paul having passed through the upper country came to Ephesus, and found certain disciples: (2) and he said unto them, Did ye receive the Holy Spirit when ye believed? And they said unto him, Nay, we did not so much as hear whether the Holy Spirit was given. (3) And he said, Into what then were ye baptized? And they said, Into John's baptism. (4) And Paul said, John baptized with the baptism of repentance, saying unto the people. that they should believe on him who should come after him, that is, on Jesus. (5) And when they heard this, they were baptized into the name of the Lord Jesus. (6) And when Paul had laid his hands upon them the Holy Spirit came on them; and they spoke with tongues, and prophesied. (7) And they were in all about twelve men. This passage, in connection with what is said in the previous paragraph about Apollos (xviii. 25), shows that John's baptism was still preached and practiced in some places; and it also shows how the apostles dealt with persons thus baptized. These men were introduced to Paul as disciples of Jesus, and they were doubtless "the brethren" who had united with Aquila in giving a letter to Apollos (xviii. 27). Paul's first question, "Did ye receive the Holy Spirit when ye believed?" had reference not to the ordinary indwelling of the Spirit; for this all receive who repent and are baptized (ii. 38), and therefore he could have no ground for doubting that they received this. But some disciples, after baptism, received through imposition of apostolic hands the miraculous gift of the Spirit; and it is of this that Paul inquired, as is proved not only by these considerations, but by the fact that it is this which he conferred upon them at the close of the conversation. When they answered, "We did not so much as hear that the Holy Spirit was given," he saw at once that there was something wrong about their baptism; hence his next question, "Into what then were ye baptized?" He meant not into what baptism, but into what name; for when he hears their answer, he directs them to be baptized "into the *name* of the Lord Jesus," which is but an abbreviation for "into the name of the Father, and of the Son, and of the Holy Spirit," the form of expression employed by Jesus himself (Matt. xxviii. 19). If they had been thus baptized they could not have been ignorant about the Holy Spirit into whose name they were baptized. Moreover, in that case they would already have been told, as Peter told the people on Pentecost, that on being baptized they would receive the Holy Spirit. Having no knowledge of this baptism into a name, and therefore missing the aim of Paul's second question, the men answered, "Into John's baptism;" and thus Paul discovered the cause of their ignorance about the Holy Spirit; for John's baptism had no promise of the Holy Spirit, and he did not baptize into any name. Paul's brief explanation was promptly accepted, and when the men were baptized he bestowed upon them the miraculous gift to which his first inquiry had reference.

As this is an instance of the rebaptism of men who had received John's baptism, it raises the question whether all of John's disciples were rebaptized in order to admission into the church; and if not, why were these? It seems necessary to answer the first part of this inquiry in the negative; for the reason that the apostles, some (if not all) of whom had received John's baptism, and the one hundred and twenty who with the twelve constituted the church before Pentecost, of whom the same is almost certainly true, were not rebaptized;[1] and if these were not, then the same must be true of the rest of John's original disciples. Why then were these at Ephesus baptized again? The most probable answer, and the only one which harmonizes with the facts, is that they had been baptized by Apollos, or by some one teaching as he taught, since John's baptism had ceased to be a valid ordinance. It certainly had not been valid since the baptism of the apostolic commission was introduced on the great day of Pentecost; and no one had rightly administered it since John was shut up in prison.

---

[1] That these were not rebaptized is evident from the statement that those who were baptized on Pentecost "were added unto them" (ii. 41). But if they were not baptized at that time, they must have been previously; and as the only baptism administered previously, even that ministered by the disciples of Jesus (Jno. iv. 1. 2), was John's baptism, it was this which they had received. Furthermore, as Jesus insisted that it was the duty of all to submit to John's baptism (Luke vii. 29, 30), it is in the highest degree improbable that he acknowledged any as his own disciples who had refused to do so. Certainly the five disciples whom he gained at the Jordan shortly after his own baptism were John's disciples before they became his, and had been baptized already (Jno. i. 35–51).

Even Jesus, who administered it for a short time before John's imprisonment, did so no longer. From the very nature of the case it could be no longer accepted as a baptism when it had ceased to be a living ordinance. These twelve were accordingly regarded as not having been baptized at all ; and now for the first time they received real baptism. If Aquila was acquainted with their condition before Paul's arrival in Ephesus, he had evidently awaited Paul's decision in the case, instead of settling the question himself. It is not certain that he felt competent to say what should be done. It is more probable, however, that Paul's question, intended to ascertain whether they had as yet received any miraculous gifts, brought to Aquila at the same moment that it did to Paul a knowledge of the facts. If Apollos was not rebaptized (and the implication is rather that he was not), the reason may be that Aquila did not know what should be done in such cases ; or it may be that Apollos, while on some visit to Judea, had been baptized by John himself.

This incident shows that Paul was in the habit of inspecting the condition of the disciples already found in a place, before adding to their number ; and it is a precedent worthy of careful imitation by modern evangelists.

4. PREACHING IN THE SYNAGOGUE, AND IN THE SCHOOL OF TYRANNUS, 8-12.

Vv. 8, 9. Having corrected what he found wrong in the little band of disciples, Paul next grapples with the Jewish and pagan errors which abounded in the city. (8) And he entered into the synagogue, and spake boldly for the space of three months, reasoning and persuading as to the things concerning the kingdom of God. (9) But when some were hardened and disobedient, speaking

evil of the Way before the multitude, he departed from
them; and separated the disciples, reasoning daily in
the school of Tyrannus. The scene in the synagogue
is quite uniform in its details with others which we have
observed—the same earnest argument and persuasion by
Paul, on the same invariable theme; the same increasing
obstinacy and evil speaking on the part of the unbelieving Jews; and the final separation of Paul and the
believers from the synagogue and the majority that
controlled it. As a private dwelling had been Paul's
refuge in Corinth, the school-room of Tyrannus was his
resort in Ephesus. Such incidents have their counterpart in the history of all men who have attempted to
correct the religious teachings of their contemporaries.

Vv. 10–12. Here once more, as in the case of Paul's
stay in Corinth, Luke gives us a definite note of time. (10)
And this continued for the space of two years; so that all
they who dwelt in Asia heard the word of the Lord, both
Jews and Greeks. (11) And God wrought special miracles by the hands of Paul: (12) insomuch that unto the
sick were carried away from his body handkerchiefs or
aprons, and the diseases departed from them, and the
evil spirits went out. The two years here mentioned,
added to the three months in the synagogue, give us two
years and three months as the length of Paul's stay in
Ephesus—his longest stay in any one city, and mentioned, no doubt, on that account.[1] The miracles mentioned are styled "special," because of their extraordinary
character, reminding us of some witnessed once in the
career of Peter (v. 15), and once in that of the Master

---

[1] When Paul himself afterward spoke of the time as three
years (xx. 31), he followed the uniform Jewish method of counting
a part of a year at the close or the beginning of a period as if it
were a whole year (cf. note under x. 30).

(Mark vi. 56). Such miracles are no more incredible than others. They were brought about by the increasing zeal of the people in seeking the benefit of the healing power. No wonder that "all who dwelt in Asia," by which is meant all in the Roman province of that name, "heard the word of the Lord Jesus, both Jews and Greeks." All who could would naturally come to Ephesus to hear, and all who came would instinctively repeat what they had heard wherever they went. The result was that we read later of "the seven churches of Asia" (Rev. i. 4).

5. Exorcists Exposed, and Books of Magic Burned, 13–20.

Vv. 13–17. It is difficult to imagine how men could witness these miracles, and not acknowledge the presence of divine power. We should suppose that even atheism would be confounded before them, and that the most hardened sinner would tremble. Yet Simon the sorcerer had sought to purchase such power from Peter with money; Barjesus had sought to convince Sergius Paulus that it was a cheat; and a similar display of human depravity, followed by a castigation almost as severe as in the last instance, occurred here in Ephesus. (13) But certain also of the strolling Jews, exorcists, took upon them to name over them who had the evil spirits the name of the Lord Jesus, Saying, I adjure thee by Jesus whom Paul preacheth. (14) And there were seven sons of one Sceva, a Jew, a chief priest, who did this. (15) And the evil spirit answered and said unto them, Jesus I know, and Paul I know; but who are ye? (16) And the man in whom the evil spirit was leaped on them, and mastered both of them, and prevailed against them, so that they fled out of that house naked and wounded. (17) And this became known to all, both Jews and Greeks, that dwelt at Ephesus; and fear fell upon them all, and the name of the Lord Jesus was magnified. These exorcists, as their title indicates, pretended to the power of casting out demons; and they appeared to the people to succeed often enough to keep up some reputation. Doubtless the fact that they were seven brothers added to the mystery of their pretensions, just as a fortune-teller at the present day who is the seventh daughter of the seventh daughter is more highly credited than others of her class. They employed for the purpose incantations over the demoniacs, in which they uttered certain unmeaning words that they claimed to have derived from Solomon,[1] and they naturally supposed that the secret of Paul's power was something of the same kind; so they watched him as he cast out demons, to see if they could discover his talismanic word. They were not long in observing that in every instance he used the name of Jesus; and they concluded that the charm was in that word; so two of them put the matter to a test by getting a demoniac into a room where they would be unobserved if they met with a failure, and intending, if they succeeded, to go before the public as rivals of Paul. The evil spirit seems to have been outraged by the wickedness of the two villains, and the manner in which he exposed them seems like a grim joke. Certainly all Ephesus must have laughed at them as they fled naked and bruised along the street; but when the people took a second thought, and remem-

---

[1] Josephus gives a detailed account of an expulsion of a demon in the presence of Vespasian during the siege of Jerusalem (Ant., viii. 2, 5; Wars.?)

bered that this discomfiture had come from a misuse of the name of Jesus, it was but natural that this name was magnified, and that fear came upon all.

Vv. 18–20. The exposure of the seven exorcists, by the mysterious but very effective way in which it was accomplished, threw discredit on all the pretenders to magic in Ephesus. The visible results were immense and astonishing. **(18) Many also of them that had believed came, confessing, and declaring their deeds. (19) And not a few of them that practiced curious arts brought their books together, and burned them in the sight of all; and they counted the price of them, and found it fifty thousand pieces of silver. (20) So mightily grew the word of the Lord and prevailed.** It is not to be understood that the believers who confessed had continued to practice magic after they became believers; but only that they now confessed and declared the secret processes by which they had formerly deceived the people. Of the book-burners, many, apparently, and possibly all, were not as yet disciples, though they were deeply impressed with the wickedness of their deceptive practices. The fifty thousand pieces of silver were doubtless Attic didrachmas; for Ephesus was a Greek city, and this was the most common silver coin. Its value was about the same as that of the Roman denarius, so often translated "penny" in our version, which equals a little more than sixteen cents of American money. The whole value then of the books was more than $8,000. Their value depended not so much on their number or their size, as on their contents; for they contained plainly written directions for the performance of tricks of jugglery, and the purchaser, by a little practice, could be as skillful a juggler as the original owner. The book, like

the secret in the compound of a patent medicine, which
could be written on a small scrap of paper, was 'he stock
in trade of the juggler, and its value depended upon its
being kept secret.   This wholeaccount fully confirms the
reputation assigned to Ephesus by ancient writers as the
chief center of magical arts in the whole Roman empire.[1]

6. Paul Forms a Plan for Future Journeys, 21, 22.

Vv. 21, 22.   The great triumph of the word of the
Lord which followed the book-burning brought the
affairs of the church to such a point that Paul began to
think of leaving Ephesus.   (21) **Now after these things
were ended, Paul purposed in the spirit, when he had
passed through Macedonia and Achaia, to go to Jerusalem,
saying, After I have been there, I must also see Rome.**
(22) **And having sent into Macedonia two of them who
ministered to him, Timothy and Erastus, he himself
stayed in Asia for a while.**   We shall see hereafter that
this plan of future journeying was carried out to the
letter, but in a way far different from that which Paul
purposed.   The words, "he purposed in the Spirit,"
have been taken by the majority of the commentators to
mean no more than that he formed the purpose ; and our
revisers seem from their use of the small s with the word
spirit, to have understood them in the same way.   But
if this is the meaning of the expression, it is tautologi-
cal, the words " in the spirit " being redundant.   These
writers forget the facts mentioned before by Luke,
which account for the expression.   When Paul first pur-

---

[1] See the citations on this subject in Conybeare and Howson,
ii. 21, and in Farrar's Life of Paul, 358.

posed to come to this very city of Ephesus, as the capital of Asia, he was forbidden by the Holy Spirit to do so; and when he then purposed to go into Bithynia he was likewise forbidden (xvi. 6, 7); and by this experience he had learned to lay out no plans for the future without an expressed allowance for this divine overruling. Even when he promised, on leaving Aquila and Priscilla at Ephesus, to return thither, his words were, "I will return again unto you if God will" (xviii. 21). So now, when forming a purpose concerning journeys which might require years for their accomplishment, he purposes "in the Spirit" to make them. A few interpreters understand the expression as meaning that the Spirit moved him to form the purpose; but in that case we should not find him so uncertain as he afterward was, as to whether they could be carried out (see Rom. xv. 24; 30–32). The real meaning, determined by both his previous and his subsequent experience, is that he formed this purpose subject to the approval of the Holy Spirit, and with a conscious reference to the probability that the Spirit might overrule it. Timothy was sent into Macedonia, that he might go thence to Corinth, and give the brethren there some instruction concerning Paul's ways and teaching (I. Cor. iv. 17); while Erastus was sent because, being the treasurer of Corinth (Rom. xvi. 23), that was his home; and perhaps, also, that he might render assistance to Timothy.

Some scholars have argued with much plausibility that Paul had made a short visit to Corinth before this, and returned to Ephesus, using as evidence certain statements in Second Corinthians. The question is not an important one; and consequently, while I regard the evidence for the position as inconclusive, I will not discuss it. The reader who is curious to investigate it will find the arguments in the affirmative well set forth by Mr. Howson, and those in the negative by Paley.

The first epistle to the Corinthians was written from Ephesus, and at a time of great prosperity in the work there, as appears from the following words in the epistle: "I will tarry at Ephesus until Pentecost; for a great and effectual door is opened to me, and there are many adversaries" (I. Cor. xvi. 8, 9). This language fixes not only the place of writing, but almost exactly its date. The opening of the "great and effectual door" can refer only to the triumph attending the book-burning. The epistle was written, then, about the time that Timothy and Erastus were sent forward into Macedonia, on their way to Corinth, and there can be no reasonable doubt that one of them was the bearer of it.

This is not really the first epistle written by Paul to the church at Corinth; for in it he speaks of another which he wrote previously on the subject of fornication: "I wrote you an epistle not to keep company with fornicators" (v. 9). This single statement contains all we know of this epistle; and perhaps the document was allowed to perish because the contents of it were repeated, and the subject treated more elaborately in the epistle now called the first.

Subsequent to the date of the lost epistle some members of the household of Chloe, a sister in the church at Corinth, had brought Paul information of great disorders and corruption in the church (i. 11), and it was for the purpose of correcting these that the epistle was written. He learned that the congregation was distracted by party strife (i. 12; iii. 1–4); that fornication, and even incest were being tolerated (v. 1–13); that some mem-

bers were engaged in litigation against the brethren in
the civil courts (vi. 1–8); that his own apostolic authority was being called in question (iv. 1–6; 14–21); that
their women, contrary to the prevailing rules of mod-
esty, engaged in the public worship with unveiled faces
(xi. 1–16); that some confusion and jealousy had arisen
in reference to spiritual gifts (xii. xiii. xiv.); that some
among them were even denying the resurrection (xv.
12); and that the Lord's supper was profaned by feast-
ing (xi. 17–34). Besides, he had received a letter from
the church calling for information in reference to marriage and divorce, and the eating of meats offered to
idols (vii. 1; viii. 1). Although the epistle in which these
questions are answered, and all these disorders rebuked,
is calm and severe in its tone, it is not conceivable
that Paul could hear of this state of things in a church
which had cost him so much labor and anxiety, without great pain and sorrow. He suppressed these feelings
as he wrote, but afterward he confessed them, saying,
" Out of much affliction and anguish of heart I wrote to
you with many tears " (II. Cor. ii. 4). It was with a
heart full of anguish, then, in reference to some of the
results of his past labors, but buoyed by the opening of
a wide and effectual door in his present field, that he
sent forward Timothy and Erastus with this epistle,
while he tarried for a season longer in Asia.

7. THE MOB OF THE SILVERSMITHS, 23–41.

Vv. 23–27. By the same stroke of the pen with
which Paul wrote to the Corinthians, " a great and
effectual door is opened unto me," he also wrote, " and
there are **many adversaries** " (I. Cor. xvi. 8, 9); which
shows that he was not unmindful of the power of that

foe over which he had won a great victory. Idolatry and superstition had been crippled in one of their strong holds, but they could not be expected to die without a desperate struggle. Sooner than Paul may have anticipated, the powers of darkness rallied. (23) And about that time there arose no small stir concerning the Way. (24) For a certain man named Demetrius, a silversmith, who made silver shrines for Diana, brought no little business unto the craftsmen; (25) whom he gathered together, with the workmen of like occupation, and said, Sirs, ye know that by this business we have our wealth. (26) And ye see and hear, that not alone at Ephesus, but almost throughout all Asia, this Paul hath persuaded and turned away much people, saying that they be no gods, which are made with hands; (27) and not only is there danger that this our trade come into disrepute; but also that the temple of the great goddess Diana be made of no account, and that she should even be deposed from her magnificence, whom all Asia and the world worshipeth.

This is the most truthful and candid of all the speeches made against Paul by any of his contemporaries. All the charges were strictly true, and the dangers apprehended from his influence were accurately stated. Even the motive actuating the speaker was not disguised. He was not ashamed to acknowledge that his love of gain was that which inspired his zeal. At the same time, he and the craftsmen whom he addressed had reason to know, even better than any one else in Ephesus, that the pieces of silver which they had hammered and polished with their own hands were not gods. His allusion to the temple can be better appreciated when we remember that it was one of the seven wonders of

the ancient world, and the glory of the city of Ephesus.
It was four hundred and twenty-five feet long, and one
hundred and twenty wide. All around this vast space
stood a row of white marble columns sixty feet high,
and less than four feet apart. They were one hundred
and twenty in number, and they supported an entablature
of vast marble slabs which constituted the roof of the
peristyle. The interior was adorned with paintings and
sculptured figures wrought by the most famous artists of
antiquity, and an inner sanctuary contained a rude image
of a many-breasted woman, the symbol of fecundity,
which was believed to have been dropped down from
heaven by Jupiter. Three or four temples like Solomon's could have been placed within the circuit of its
magnificent colonnade. No wonder that the wrath of
the heathen populace was kindled against Paul, when it
appeared that by his preaching this magnificent structure
was to be brought into contempt.[1]

---

[1] The process by which, through a long series of ages, this
temple was brought to utter ruin, is so happily sketched by
Plumptre, that we quote his words entire: " The first real blow
to the worship which had lasted for so many ages was given by
the two years of Paul's work of which we read here. As by the
strange irony of history the next stroke aimed at its magnificence
came from the hand of Nero, who robbed it, as he robbed the
temples of Delphi, and Pergamos, and Athens, not sparing even
villages, of many of its art treasures for the adornment of his golden
house at Rome. Trajan sent its richly sculptured gates as an
offering to a temple at Byzantium. As the Church of Christ advanced, its worship, of course, declined. Priests and priestesses
ministered in deserted shrines. When the empire became Christian the temple of Ephesus, in common with that of Delphi, supplied materials for the church erected by Justinian in honor of
the divine wisdom, which is now the mosque of St. Sophia. When
the Goths devastated Asia Minor, in the reign of Gallienus (A. D.
263), they plundered it with a reckless hand, and the work which

Vv. 28, 29. The artisans were enraged at the prospect of financial ruin, but they were shrewd enough to see that reverence for the temple and the goddess was the better theme on which to cry out before the people. (28) And when they heard this they were filled with wrath, and cried out, saying, Great is Diana of the Ephesians. (29) And the city was filled with the confusion : and they rushed with one accord into the theater, having seized Gaius and Aristarchus, men of Macedonia, Paul's companions in travel. The outcry, and the tone in which it was uttered, awakened the old-time enthusiasm of the idolaters who heard it, suggesting, as it did, some assault on the honor of the goddess. The gathering mob was in a frenzy, and it was a kind providence that Paul was out of their reach. They rushed into the theater because there was not room in the narrow streets common to all Asiatic cities for such a multitude. That theater still remains with its marble seats intact, by far the best preserved ruin on the site of Ephesus.[1] It was capable of seating several thousand spectators.

Vv. 30, 31. When Paul heard that his two companions had been seized by the mob and dragged within the theater, he feared that they would be torn to pieces in his stead, and he instantly resolved that this should not be. (30) And when Paul was minded to enter in unto the people, the disciples suffered him not. (31) And certain also of the chief officers of Asia, being his friends, sent unto him, and besought him not to adven-

they began was completed centuries later by the Turks " (*Commentary in loco*).

[1] When the author visited the spot in 1879 he took a solemn pleasure in standing on one of the highest tiers of marble seats and reciting to his companions the speech of the town clerk which follows below.

ture himself into the theater. The feelings which impelled him were confessed afterward to his brethren in Corinth: "We would not have you ignorant, brethren, concerning our affliction which befell us in Asia, that we were weighed down exceedingly, beyond our power, insomuch that we despaired even of life ; yea, we ourselves have had the answer of death within ourselves, that we should not trust in ourselves, but in God who raiseth the dead : who delivered us out of so great a death, and will deliver " (II. Cor. i. 8–10). Both he and his friends were fully persuaded that to go into the theater was certain death ; and his resolve to go in was a resolve then and there to die. The timely inhibition of his brethren and the friendly officials he regarded as the hand of God delivering him from "so great a death." The words, "chief officers of Asia," represent only the single word Asiarchs in the original, the title of ten men of wealth and reputation, who were chosen annually to preside over the athletic games of the province. That some of these were friends of Paul, is an indication of the extent to which his preaching and his personal character had become known in the highest circles of heathen society in Asia.

Vv. 32–34. After showing what it was that kept Paul out of the theater, and saved his life, Luke next leads us inside that enclosure, to witness the further proceedings of the mob. (32) Some therefore cried one thing and some another : for the assembly was in confusion ; and the more part knew not wherefore they were come together. (33) And they brought Alexander out of the multitude, the Jews putting him forward. And Alexander beckoned with the hand, and would have made a defense unto the people. (34) But when they perceived that he was a Jew, all with one voice about the space of two hours cried out, Great is Diana of the Ephesians. The Jews had good reason to fear the wrath of this mob; for it was well known in Ephesus that they were as much opposed to idolatry as Paul was, and it was also known that Paul himself was a Jew. Fidelity to their own principles should have prompted them to stand by Paul; but if the defense which they wished to make through Alexander had been heard, it would have been an attempt to show that Paul was an apostate from the Jewish faith, and that the Jews must not be held responsible for what he might say. The quick-witted in the crowd saw through the trick at once, and gave it the rebuke which it deserved by drowning Alexander's voice in their yells.

Vv. 35–41. The fury of a mob, when at its height, is always inflamed by opposition, as a fire by fresh fuel; but when it begins to be exhausted a few well chosen words will often restore quiet. Recognizing this, the city authorities did not at first interfere; but when the long continued vociferation of the people had nearly exhausted their strength, the following well timed and well worded speech was addressed to them. (35) And when the town clerk had quieted the multitude, he saith, Ye men of Ephesus, what man is there who knoweth not how that the city of the Ephesians is temple-keeper of the great Diana, and of the image which fell down from Jupiter? (36) Seeing then that these things can not be gainsaid, ye ought to be quiet, and to do nothing rash. (37) For ye have brought hither these men who are neither robbers of temples, nor blasphemers of our goddess. (38) If therefore Demetrius, and the craftsmen who are with him, have a matter against any man, the courts are open, and there are proconsuls : let them accuse one another. (39) But if ye seek anything about other matters, it shall be settled in the regular assembly. (40) For indeed we are in danger to be accused concerning this day's riot, there being no cause for it : and as touching it, we shall not be able to give account of this concourse. (41) And when he had thus spoken, he dismissed the assembly. This is evidently the speech of a man well skilled in the management of excited crowds; and we may suppose that the town clerk was selected for the task by those in authority, because of his known skill in this particular. His assertion that no man could be ignorant of the devotion of Ephesus to the worship of Diana, or of the fact that the image was heaven-descended, was an open espousal of their cause; and the remark, that the unquestionable certainty of these facts ought to make them feel quiet, even though some one should contradict them, was the very remark to bring about the composure at which he aimed. Advancing then to the cause of the disturbance, like a trained advocate he ignores the real charge against the disciples, that of denying that images made with hands are gods, and declares that the men are neither temple-robbers, nor blasphemers of the goddess. Clearing them of this charge appeared to the majority, who "knew not wherefore they had come together," a complete vindication of the prisoners. Then, as for the men who had disturbed the multitude with private matters of their own, their proper recourse was to the proconsular court. This was calculated to turn the feeling of the people against the silversmiths, as having made tools of their neighbors for the benefit of their craft. Finally, the remark about the unlawfulness of the assembly, and their inability to

account for the riot, was a hint of danger from the
Roman authorities in the way of fines which might be
imposed on the whole community; it made every man
of property feel anxious to get away. The formal dismission, as if the assembly had gotten through with its
business, and a motion to adjourn had been adopted,
was the last skillful device of the clerk, and it sent the
people down the streets in perfect quiet. The city authorities congratulated themselves and their clerk that so
fierce a mob had been so easily quelled; and the disciples were very thankful to God that they had escaped so
easily. Even Gaius and Aristarchus, who had doubtless
despaired of life, escaped, and lived to labor and suffer
much longer in the Master's cause.[1]

8. Paul's Second Visit to Macedonia and Greece, xx. 1–6.

VER. 1. (1) **And after the uproar was ceased, Paul
having sent for the disciples and exhorted them, took
leave of them, and departed to go into Macedonia.** Thus
ended the long-continued abode of Paul in Ephesus. The " great and effectual door " which was open
to him but a few weeks previous had been suddenly
closed; and the " many adversaries," for the noble purpose of resisting whom he had resolved to remain in
Ephesus until after Pentecost (I. Cor. xvi. 8, 9), had
prevailed against him. He had accomplished much in
the city and province, but there had come a fearful reaction in favor of the time-honored idolatry, threatening
to crush out the results of his protracted and arduous

---

[1] Both of them traveled with Paul afterward from Corinth to
Jerusalem (xx. 3, 4), and Aristarchus was his fellow prisoner on
his voyage from Jerusalem to Rome (xxvii. 1, 2; Col. iv. 10).

labors. When the disciples, whom he had taught and warned with tears both publicly and from house to house for the space of three years (verse 31), were gathered about him for the last time, and he was about to leave them in a great furnace of affliction, no tongue can tell the bitterness of the farewell. All was dark behind him, and all forbidding before him, as he turned his face toward that shore across the Ægean on which he had been welcomed before with stripes and imprisonment. We have no expression of his feelings until he reached Troas, where he was to embark for Macedonia, and where he expected to meet Titus with news from Corinth. At this point a remark of his own reveals the pent up sorrow of his heart. He writes to the Corinthians: "When I came to Troas for the gospel of Christ, and when a door was open to me in the Lord, I had no relief for my spirit, because I found not Titus my brother; but taking my leave of them, I went forth into Macedonia" (II. Cor. ii. 12, 13). We have followed him through many disheartening scenes, and will yet follow him through many more; but only on this occasion do we find his heart so sinking within him that he can not enter an open door to preach the gospel. He had hoped that the weight of sorrow which was pressing him down, above his strength to bear, would be lightened by the sympathy of Titus, and especially by some good news from the distracted church in Corinth; but the pang of disappointment added the last ounce to the weight that was crushing him, and he rushed on, blinded with tears, in the direction from which Titus was coming. A heart so strong to endure, when once crushed, can not readily resume its wonted buoyancy. Even after the sea was between him and Ephesus, and he was once more among the beloved disciples of Philippi, he was constrained to confess, " When we came into Macedonia, our flesh had no relief, but we were afflicted on every side; without were fightings, within were fears " (II. Cor. vii. 5). Finally, the long-looked-for Titus met him with good news from Corinth, and thus the Lord, who never forgets his servants in their affliction, brought relief to the overburdened heart of Paul, and enabled him to change the tone of his second epistle to the Corinthians, and to say : " Nevertheless he that comforteth the lowly, even God, comforted us by the coming of Titus; and not by his coming only, but also by the comfort wherewith he was comforted in you, while he told us of your longing, your mourning, your zeal for me ; so that I rejoice yet more " (ib. 6, 7). And this shows us that it was not on account of himself, but on account of his children in the gospel, that he had been so distressed. Titus told him of the good effects of the former epistle ; that the majority of the church had repented of their evil practices; that they had excluded the incestuous man (ii. 5-11); and that they were forward in their preparation for a contribution to the poor saints in Judea (ix. 1, 2). But the news was not all of a cheering kind. He also brought word that Paul had some personal enemies in the church who were endeavoring to impair his influence and break down his apostolic authority (x. 1; xi. 13-15). For the purpose of counteracting the machinations of these " ministers of Satan," encouraging the faithful brethren in their renewed zeal, and presenting to all many touching reflections suggested by his own sufferings, he addressed to them another epistle, and forwarded it by the hands of Titus and two other brethren whose names are not given (viii. 16-20). That we are

right in regard to the date of this epistle, is easily
proved ; for first, Paul refers in the epistle to having recently come from Asia into Macedonia (i. 8 ; vii. 5) ;
and this he had just done according to the paragraph of
the history now before us. Second, he wrote from Macedonia when about to start from that province to Corinth
(ix. 3, 4; xii. 14; xiii. 1), which he had not done previous to this, except when there was as yet no church in
Corinth, and which he never did afterward. The time
was the summer of the year 57, the first epistle to the
same church having been written in Ephesus the previous spring.[1]

Vv. 2, 3. The labors of the apostle on this visit to
Macedonia and Greece are summed up in this brief
statement. (2) And when he had gone through those
parts, and had given them much exhortation, he came
into Greece. (3) And when he had spent three months
there, and a plot was laid against him by the Jews as he
was about to set sail for Syria, he determined to return
through Macedonia. Several events of great importance
occurred in the interval thus hurriedly passed over, a
knowledge of which can be gleaned from Paul's epistles.

We remember the promise made by Paul to Peter,
James and John, that while laboring among the Gentiles he would " remember the poor " in Judea (Gal. ii.
6-10). In accordance with this agreement we find that
Paul was now urging a general collection in the churches
of Macedonia and Achaia, as he had done in Galatia,
for this purpose (I. Cor. xvi. 1, 2 ; II. Cor. viii. 1-15).
For prudential considerations, such as prompted him so
often to labor without compensation, he declined to bear
the gift himself, though the churches in Macedonia had

---

[1] See Introduction, Chronology, xxviii·

entreated him to do so (II. Cor. viii. 4). At first indeed
he had not fully intended to go to Jerusalem in connection with it, but had said to the churches, " Whomsoever
ye shall approve by letters, them will I send to carry
your bounty unto Jerusalem : and if it be meet for me
to go also, they shall go with me " (I. Cor. xvi. 3, 4).
The importance of the mission, however, grew as time
advanced, so that he resolved to go himself; and the enterprise assumed a most absorbing interest.

The circumstance which led to this change of purpose was the increasing alienation between the Jews and
the Gentiles within the church. The decree of the apostles, as we have seen, gave great comfort to the church
in Antioch, where the controversy originated, and it had
done good everywhere it had been carried (xv. 31; xvi.
4, 5) ; but other judaizing teachers had renewed the controversy, and were ignoring the decree. They had per-
sisted in their schismatical efforts until there was now a
widespread disaffection between the two sections of the
church. By their influence the churches in Galatia had
become alienated from Paul, for whom they once would
have been willing to pluck out their own eyes, and they
were being rapidly led back under the bondage of the
law (Gal. i. 6 ; iv. 15–20). The church in Rome, at the
western extremity of the territory which had been evangelized, was also disturbed by the controversy, the Jews
insisting that justification was by works of law, and that
the distinction of meats and holy days should be perpet-
uated in the church (Rom., iii., iv., v., xiv.). This state of
affairs filled Paul with inexpressible anxiety, and while
the danger was imminent he bent all his energies to the
task of averting it.

Already engaged in a general collection among Gentile churches for the poor in Judea, and knowing the tendency of kindness to win back alienated affection, he pushed the work forward for this additional consideration, as we see from the following appeal which he made to the Corinthians: " For the ministration of this service not only filleth up the measure of the wants of the saints, but aboundeth also through many thanksgivings unto God; seeing that through the proving of you by this ministration they glorify God for the obedience of your confession unto the gospel of Christ, and for the liberality of your contribution unto them and unto all; while they themselves also, with supplication on your behalf, long after you by reason of the exceeding grace of God in you" (II. Cor. ix. 12–14). So great was his confidence in the good results of the enterprise that he here speaks as if they were already accomplished—as if the Jews were already offering many thanksgivings and prayers for the Gentiles in consideration of their kindness.

Thus Paul felt while he was stimulating the liberality of his brethren; but when the collections had all been made, and he was about to start from Corinth to Jerusalem with the money, he began to fear that the Jews in Palestine would not accept the gift, and that by their refusal the breach which he was trying to close would be opened wider. We know this by the almost painful earnestness with which he besought the brethren in Rome to pray with him that this calamity might be averted. He says: " Now I beseech you, brethren, by our Lord Jesus Christ, and by the love of the Spirit, that ye strive together with me in your prayers to God for me; that I may be delivered from them that are disobedient in Judea, and that my ministration which I have for Jerusalem may be acceptable to the saints ; that I may come unto you in joy through the will of God, and together with you find rest" (Rom. xv. 30–32). If he called thus earnestly for the prayers of the distant church in Rome, how much more must he have enlisted those of the churches in Achaia and Macedonia, who were immediate participants in the enterprise. We have here the spectacle of a man who was regarded with suspicion, if not with positive dislike, by a large portion of his brethren, securing from others, who were involved with him in the same reproach, a self-denying contribution for the temporal wants of the disaffected party ; and then, fearing lest their disaffection was so great as to cause them to reject the gift—a fear which would cause most men to withhold it entirely—he calls upon all the donors to unite in persistent prayer that it might not be rejected. No nobler example of disinterested benevolence can be found in the history of men. The prosecution of the enterprise, as we shall see hereafter, was in keeping with the magnanimity of its inception. But before we consider it further we must notice briefly some kindred facts.

For the same noble purpose which prompted the great collection, Paul wrote, during his three months in Corinth, his epistles to the Galatians and the Romans. This date we have already assumed in referring to them as contemporaneous documents. The most conclusive evidence for assigning them this date may be briefly stated as follows : In the epistle to the Romans Paul expressly states that he was about to start for Jerusalem with a contribution which had been made by the churches in Macedonia and Achaia (xv. 25, 26) ; and

this could have been said only at the close of his present
stay in Corinth. Moreover, Gaius, who lived in Corinth,
was his host at the time of writing (xvi. 23 ; *cf.* I. Cor. i.
14); and Phœbe, of the Corinthian seaport Cenchrea,
was the bearer of the epistle (xvi. 1). As for Galatians,
it contains an allusion to Paul's first visit to Galatia,
implying that he had been there a second time. His
words are : " Ye know that by an infirmity of the flesh
I preached the gospel unto you the first time " (iv. 13).
It was written then, after this second visit, and another remark shows that it was not very long after that visit. He
says, " I marvel that ye are so quickly removing from
him that called you in the grace of Christ unto a different gospel " (i. 6). When at Corinth he had been away
from Galatia only a little more than three years ; and
this was a short time for so great a revolution in sentiment and faith as had occurred in those churches. Finally, the close correspondence in subject matter between
this epistle and that to the Romans, both being devoted
principally to setting forth the doctrine of justification by
faith, in opposition to the scheme of salvation by works
of law which was propagated by the judaizers, indicates
that they were both written under the same condition of
affairs, and therefore about the same time. As in Romans Paul speaks of his departure to Jerusalem as
imminent, it is probable that Galatians had been written
a short time previous. In both the apostle contended by
argument and by authority against the destructive teaching of the judaizers, at the same that he was aiming, by
a noble act of self-denial, to win back their good will
both to himself and the Gentiles whose cause he had
espoused.

Having dispatched these two epistles, and collected about him the messengers of the various churches, the apostle was about to start for Syria by water, which was much the swifter route, when, as the text last quoted affirms, he learned that a plot was laid against him by the Jews, which led him to change his course. This plot probably consisted in a notification to highwaymen to lie in wait for the company in the mountains between Corinth and Cenchrea, and rob them of the money which they were bearing to Jerusalem. By the change of route, the road to Cenchrea could be avoided, and the waiting robbers left in the lurch. A much longer journey was necessitated; but it led Paul once more by the way of churches which he would otherwise have failed to revisit.

Vv. 4, 5. (4) And there accompanied him as far as Asia Sopater of Berœa, the son of Pyrrhus; and of the Thessalonians, Aristarchus and Secundus; and Gaius of Derbe, and Timothy; and of Asia, Tychicus and Trophimus. (5) But these had gone before, and were waiting for us at Troas. These seven brethren were the messengers chosen by the churches, as Paul had directed (I. Cor. xvi. 3), to bear their contributions to Jerusalem. There being no banks or paper currency in those days, the money had to be carried in silver on the persons of the messengers, and it was important that no one should be so loaded as to indicate the fact to the sharp eyes of robbers: hence the necessity for so many messengers to carry it. Sopater (abbreviation of Sosipater) was a kinsman of Paul, one of his converts at Berœa, and had united with him in saluting the church in Rome (Rom. xvi. 21). Aristarchus was doubtless the same Macedonian who was seized by the mob in Ephesus

(xix. 29), but had escaped and reached his home in Thessalonica. Secundus (*second*) was probably so named because he was his father's second son, as were Tertius and Quartus (*third* and *fourth*), because they were the third and fourth sons (Rom. xvi. 22, 23). As they were all three with Paul at Corinth, it is not improbable that they were brothers. Gaius of Derbe was not of course the Macedonian Gaius who had suffered in the silver-smith mob with Aristarchus. His presence here, so far west from his home, implies that he had followed Paul through interest in his labors. Tychicus (*fortunate*) and Trophimus (*foster-child*) are new names among the companions of Paul. As they are of Asia, they had doubtless turned to the Lord while Paul was preaching in Ephesus, and had followed him thence into Greece. Luke's "us," here introduced once more, implies that he too joined the company at Philippi. It was here, on the first tour, that this pronoun was dropped, and the presumption is that Luke had remained at Philippi ever since the departure of Paul and Silas therefrom, six or seven years previous. During this absence from the narrative, many parts of it have been hurried and ellipti-cal; but we shall henceforth find it much more circum-stantial.

VER. 6. If Paul's only purpose in passing through Macedonia was to reach Asia in safety, he would have had no occasion to revisit Philippi, which was at least a day's journey out his way; but the next verse finds him in that city and leaving it for Troas. (6) **And we sailed away from Philippi after the days of unleavened bread, and came unto them to Troas in five days: where we tarried seven days.** The other brethren, in going before unto Troas, had probably set sail from Thessalonica, or

Neapolis, without making the detour northward to Philippi; and their design in going before may have been to get speedily out of the country in which many enemies knew of the money on their persons, while Paul, freed from anxiety on that account, might make another short visit to the church at Philippi, whose honored teacher was to join him in the journey to Jerusalem. It so happened that the days of unleavened bread, the seven days following the paschal supper, had just expired when he and Luke set sail for Troas, and thus we are able to see that nearly a whole year had passed since he left Ephesus; for he left there earlier than he had expected, and therefore earlier than Pentecost the previous year (I. Cor. xvi. 8).

The fact that the voyage from Philippi to Troas occupied five days, whereas on a former occasion they sailed from Troas to Philippi in two days (xvi. 11, 12), is suggestive of adverse winds.

When Paul was last in Troas an effectual door was opened to him by the Lord, but he passed on without entering it (II. Cor. ii. 12). Now at last some of the work then neglected was done; for the seven brethren had preceded him more than five days, and the whole company remained there seven days; and nine such men as these could accomplish much in a town like this in the course of two weeks.

9. A LORD'S DAY MEETING IN TROAS, 7–12.

VER. 7. The stay of seven days in Troas terminated on the Lord's day. (7) **And upon the first day of the week, when we were gathered together to break bread, Paul discoursed with them, intending to depart on the morrow; and prolonged his speech until midnight.**

This passage shows that the first day of the week was the day in which the disciples broke the loaf; and also that the prime purpose of their meeting on that day was to observe this ordinance. Paul's preaching on the occasion was incidental. In the original institution of the Lord's supper, nothing was said as to the frequency with which it was to be observed. The Lord's words are, " This do, as oft as ye drink it, in remembrance of me " (I. Cor. xi. 25). Had nothing more been said, every congregation of believers would have been left to its own judgment as to frequency of observance. But the apostles were afterward guided by the Holy Spirit in this, as in other matters left indefinite by the Lord's personal teaching, and their example is our guide. Little is said on the subject, but that little is decisive in favor of a weekly observance of the ordinance. Here it is represented as furnishing the chief purpose of the Lord's day meeting; and the same appears in the rebuke administered to the Corinthians: " When therefore ye assemble yourselves together, it is not possible to eat the Lord's supper; for in your eating each one taketh before other his own supper " (I. Cor. xi. 20, 21). Such being the purpose of the Lord's day meeting, as surely as the disciples met every Lord's day, they broke the loaf on that day. Slight as this evidence is, when taken in connection with the universal practice of the church in the second century, and for a long period afterward, it has proved sufficient to win universal agreement among biblical scholars, that this was the apostolic custom; and as the example of the apostles acting under the guidance of the Holy Spirit shows plainly the will of the Lord, our custom should be the same, and all the excuses which we ingeniously frame for rejecting this custom are invalid.

It is this ordinance which brings us nearest of all to the sufferings of our Redeemer; and if we commemorate weekly the fact that he arose again for our justification, why should we not as frequently commemorate the fact that he died for our sins?

The extreme length of Paul's discourse on this occasion is accounted for in the remark that he was " intending to depart on the morrow;" and we learn further on, that he expected never to see these disciples again (38); hence his desire to give them all possible instruction and admonition while he was with them.

Vv. 8–10. The long, solemn discourse was broken off at midnight by an incident which caused great alarm and confusion in the audience. (8) **And there were many lights in the upper chamber, where we were gathered together.** (9) **And there sat in the window a certain young man named Eutychus, borne down with deep sleep; and as Paul discoursed yet longer, being borne down by his sleep he fell down from the third story, and was taken up dead.** (10) **And Paul went down, and fell on him, and embracing him said, Make ye no ado; for his life is in him.** This passage shows that the meeting was held in the night, and in the third story of the building. The third story is suggestive of cheap rent, and also of precaution against interruption of the worship by the heathen rabble on the street. If some of the members were slaves, a night meeting was the only one which they could attend, and this hour may have been selected to suit them. It is probable that on account of Paul's presence the room was crowded, and that Eutychus had taken a seat in the window to make room for some older person; and, being most likely a laboring man, unaccustomed to loss of sleep, he found it impossible, even though deeply interested, to keep awake.   It is not always a sin to go to sleep under a sermon.   Eutychus was dead when they picked him up; but when Paul had embraced him his life was in him, and the embrace brought back the life which was extinguished by the fall.   It was a case of resuscitation like that of the daughter of Jairus (Luke viii. 49–55).

VER. 11.   The alarm caused by the fall of Eutychus, the astonishing display of divine power in his restoration, and the stillness of the midnight hour in which it all occurred, could but add to the solemnity which already pervaded the assembly.   They could not think of sleep, and the meeting was still protracted.   They returned to the upper chamber, where the lights were still burning, and where the elements of the Lord's supper were as yet undistributed.   Paul, notwithstanding the length and earnestness of his discourse, was unexhausted.   (11) **And when he was gone up, and had broken the bread, and eaten, and had talked with them a long while, even till break of day, so he departed.**   Thus the whole night was spent in religious discourse and conversation, interrupted at midnight by a death and a resurrection, and this followed by the commemoration of the Lord's death which brings hope of a resurrection far better.   At daybreak the meeting terminated in one of those tender farewells so often spoken among believers, in which the pain of parting and the hope of meeting to part no more struggle so tearfully for the mastery.   It was a night never to be forgotten by those who were there, and in eternity it will be a theme for much conversation.

It is a question of some interest, whether it was on Sunday morning or Monday morning that this parting took place.   The brethren met in the early part of the

night, yet it was "the first day of the week." We have
no evidence that either Jews or Gentiles had yet adopted
the custom of counting the hours of the day from midnight; consequently we must suppose that the night in
question was that belonging to Sunday, as it was then
reckoned, or Saturday night, as we now style it. It was
the night following the Jewish Sabbath, which was still
observed by all Jewish disciples, and the incident shows
that the disciples at Troas were in the habit of meeting
on this night to break bread. Any time after sunset on
that evening would be the Lord's day as they counted
it, and after midnight, which was the time of breaking
the loaf on that occasion, was on the Lord's day as we
count it.

Ver. 12. Recurring again to the case of Eutychus,
Luke next remarks: (12) **And they brought the lad
alive, and were not a little comforted.** This means that
they brought him from the meeting to his home. This
was done in the morning after the separation from Paul
and his company, and four or five hours after the fall
from the window. Having expected to take him home
dead, and to be charged, perhaps, with fault in reference
to his death, they were not a little comforted that they
could bring him home with such a story as they could
now tell to his friends and neighbors.

10. The Voyage from Troas to Miletus, 13–16.

Ver. 13. The brethren of Troas returned to their
homes, while Paul and his companions resumed their
long journey. (13) **But we, going before to the ship, set
sail for Assos, there intending to take in Paul: for so had
he appointed, intending himself to go by land.** Troas
and Assos are on opposite sides of a peninsula which

terminates in Cape Lectum. The distance across from city to city is about twenty miles, while the coast line around is about forty. Paul could easily walk across while the ship was sailing around. But why did Paul choose, after spending a sleepless night in preaching and conversing, to still further tax his power of endurance by this walk of twenty miles? One would suppose that he would have preferred resting upon a hammock in the ship. Nothing short of an excitement which eschews rest for either mind or body can account for it. But Paul had received in every city on his journey prophetic warnings of bonds and imprisonment awaiting him (23); he was agitated by the critical state of the churches everywhere; he was saddened by the final farewells which he was giving to the churches on his way; and he longed for a season of meditation and prayer which could be found only in solitude. Amid the more stirring scenes of the apostle's life, while announcing with oracular authority the will of God, and confirming the word to trembling thousands by signs and wonders following, we are apt to lose our human sympathy for the man in our admiration for the apostle. But when we contemplate him under circumstances like the present, worn down by the sleepless labors of a whole night; burdened in spirit too heavily to enjoy the society of sympathizing friends; and yet, with all his weariness, choosing a long day's journey on foot that he might indulge to satiety the gloom which oppressed him, we are so much reminded of our own seasons of afflictions as to feel the human tie which binds our hearts to his. No ardent toiler in the vineyard of the Lord, ready to sink at times beneath his load of anxiety and disappointment, but finds relief in permitting the excess of his sorrow to waste itself in silence and solitude. In such hours it will do us good to walk with Paul from Troas to Assos, and to remember how much has been endured by greater and better men than ourselves.

Vv. 14–16. The ship and the footman were not far apart in reaching Assos. (14) **And when he met us at Assos, we took him in, and came to Mitylene. (15) And sailing from thence, we came the next day over against Chios ; and the next day we touched at Samos ; and the day after we came to Miletus. (16) For Paul had determined to sail past Ephesus, that he might not have to spend time in Asia ; for he was hastening, if it were possible for him, to be at Jerusalem the day of Pentecost.** The ship was coasting among the islands scattered along the eastern shore of the Ægean Sea, as a glance at the map will show ; and the part of the voyage here described occupied four days. They cast anchor in the harbor of Mitylene the first night. This city, beautifully situated on the northern shore of the island then called Lesbos, but now Mitylene, from the name of the city, is still a handsome town with a considerable trade. On the second night anchorage was found " over against Chios," without entering a harbor. On the third day they crossed the mouth of the bay which leads up to Ephesus, and "touched at Samos," perhaps for business as well as for a safe anchorage at night ; and a short run on the fourth day brought them to the important seaport of Miletus on the main shore. As they passed by Ephesus, and were yet so near to that scene of protracted labor and suffering, Luke felt called upon for the explanation which he gives. If the ship had been under Paul's control, he could have spent at Ephesus the time afterward spent at Miletus (17, 18), without delaying his arrival in Jerusalem ; but as the vessel was going on its way without regard to his wishes, he could visit Ephesus only by running in on some other vessel from Chios, and taking the risk of finding one in good time sailing from Ephesus to Syria. The reason for his anxiety to reach Jerusalem by Pentecost was, that then brethren from every village in Palestine would be in the city, and he could see to the distribution of the alms which his companions bore, without the necessity of visiting all the churches. We will yet see that he made the journey in time for the feast.

11. An Interview with the Elders of the Church at Ephesus, 17–38.

Ver. 17. As Paul's vessel was to lie at anchor in the harbor of Miletus for at least two or three days, he took advantage of the delay to gratify in part his desire to communicate once more with the brethren of Ephesus. **(17) And from Miletus he sent to Ephesus, and called to him the elders of the church.** The distance was about thirty miles. He might have gone to Ephesus instead of sending for the elders, but for some uncertainty as to the time of the ship's departure. If he should miss this vessel, it might defeat his purpose to attend the feast; whereas, if the elders should arrive after his departure, they would suffer only the inconvenience of the short journey.

Vv. 18–21. The interview which Paul now holds with these elders may be regarded as a type of all those which he held with various bodies of disciples on this mournful journey. He begins his remarks to them by a brief review of his labors in their city. **(18) And when they were come to him, he said to them, Ye yourselves** know, from the first day that I set foot in Asia, after what manner I was with you all the time, (19) serving the Lord with all lowliness of mind, and with tears, and with trials which befell me by the plots of the Jews: (20) how that I shrank not from declaring unto you anything that was profitable, and teaching you publicly and from house to house, (21) testifying both to Jews and to Greeks repentance toward God, and faith toward our Lord Jesus Christ. These elders must have been among the first fruits of Paul's preaching in Ephesus, seeing that they knew so perfectly his manner of life from the first day that he set foot in Asia. His remark about the lowliness of mind, and the tears which had characterized him, shows that the great distress which we have seen attendant on the wild proceedings of the silversmith mob, was by no means the beginning of this kind of experience in Ephesus. The reference, too, to trials which befell him by the plots of the Jews, brings out a new feature of his experience there; for in the narrative Luke has mentioned only one indication of the existence of such plots, the attempt to put forward Alexander before the mob in the theater (xix. 33, 34). It was Paul's sad experience to suffer more, throughout his career, from his own countrymen than from the heathen.

The statements, that he had not shrunk from declaring to the brethren anything that was profitable for them, and that he had taught from house to house, as well as publicly, are both worthy of solemn consideration by the preachers of the present age. The former presents Paul in striking contrast with the time-servers so abundant in our modern pulpits, who never rebuke sin except at a long distance; who speak none but smooth words about corruption in the church; and whose whole study is personal popularity. Such men care for souls only as these souls may in some way glorify them. They are too faithful to their own aggrandisement to think of being faithful to God. The second statement places Paul in contrast with another class of modern preachers, who either neglect to go from house to house in their ministrations, and study paltry excuses for the neglect; or who go from house to house, not to teach the people, but to enjoy society and to engage in gossip. Let all such take notice that, in the true apostolic method of evangelizing a community, and of edifying a congregation, earnest work from house to house was on a par with that in the pulpit.

The order in which Paul here mentions repentance toward God and faith in the Lord Jesus Christ, has been an occasion of confusion to some minds, and has furnished a proof text to some who have espoused the position that in the sinner's conversion to Christ repentance precedes faith. It is true that Paul preached repentance toward God before faith in Jesus Christ, and that his aim was to induce men to repent toward God as a preparation for faith in Christ. John the Baptist prepared the people for Christ by preaching repentance toward God; Jesus did the same; and Paul, in addressing the heathen in Athens, first presented to them the true God, then called on them to repent of their idolatries which had dishonored God; and then presented to them the risen Christ (xvii. 29–31). The two themes were not presented in this order because it was impossible for men to believe in Christ before repenting toward God; but because, if they are brought to repentance toward God in whom they already believe, they are in a better frame of mind for hearing the gospel of Christ,

and believing in him.   In general terms, if we repent of
sinning against the light we have, we are better prepared
to receive any new light which God may see fit to give
us; whereas, if we are impenitent in regard to the
former, we will almost certainly despise the latter.   To
sinners of all ages and countries, who know something
of God, but nothing of Christ, this method of preaching
faith and repentance is doubtless the best; but it may
not be so with sinners reared in Christian lands, who
have by tradition the same faith in Christ which they
have in God, and who realize that their past sins are
really sins against Christ.   This method, however, is
very far from supporting the idea that repentance precedes faith in the sense usually attached to that proposition; for this would require men to repent toward God
before they believe in God, and toward Christ before
they believe in Christ—an obvious absurdity.

Vv. 22–27.   After this very brief review of his
labors in Ephesus, the apostle next speaks of his own
future, and reveals to the elders the cause of the gloom
which had shrouded his spirit on this journey.   (22) **And
now, behold, I go bound in the spirit unto Jerusalem, not
knowing the things that shall befall me there:** (23)
**save that the Holy Spirit testifies unto me in every city,
saying that bonds and afflictions abide me.** (24) **But I
hold not my life of any account as dear unto myself, so
that I may accomplish my course, and the ministry
which I received from the Lord Jesus, to testify the gospel of the grace of God.** (25) **And now, behold, I know
that ye all, among whom I went about preaching the
kingdom, shall see my face no more.** (26) **Wherefore I
testify unto you this day, that I am pure from the blood
of all men.** (27) **For I shrank not from declaring unto**

you the whole counsel of God. By the expression,
" bound in the spirit," he has reference to the bonds
that awaited him in Jerusalem, and he means that he
felt in spirit as if the bonds were already upon him.
He was so certain that the predictions of the Holy Spirit
would be fulfilled, that they seemed a present reality.
This testimony of the Spirit had undoubtedly been given
to him through prophets whom he had met in every
city ; for if it had been given to him directly, it would
not have been confined to the cities. This is another
evidence that the prophetic power of the apostles was
not used to foresee their own future, as their healing
power was not used to cure their own diseases. When
he adds, " I know that ye all among whom I went about
preaching the gospel, shall see my face no more," we are
not to understand that the Holy Spirit, who had previously revealed some of his future to him through others,
had now revealed this to him directly ; but rather that
he here expresses a strong conviction, based on these predictions, and also on his own fixed purpose, God willing,
to spend the remnant of his days in new fields of labor
(xix. 21 ; Rom. xv. 23, 24). When therefore we learn
from his first epistle to Timothy (i. 1–3) that he did
afterward revisit Ephesus, the fact should occasion no
great surprise.

In the closing remark of this part of the address
(26, 27), Paul recurs to his fidelity in declaring everything that was profitable to them, and he holds this up
as proof that he is free from every man's blood. " I
am pure from the blood of all men. For I shrank not
from declaring unto you the whole counsel of God." It
is implied that if a religious teacher does shrink, through
any personal or selfish consideration, from declaring the

whole counsel of God to those whom he teaches, in some
sense the blood of those who may be lost through his
neglect will be upon him (*cf.* xviii. 6; Ezek. iii. 16–21).
This is an unspeakably fearful responsibility, and it
should never be lost sight of.

Vv. 28–35. Having spoken of his own past and his
own future, the apostle next speaks of the future of the
elders and their church; and he places his own example
before them for imitation. (28) Take heed unto yourselves, and to all the flock, in the which the Holy Spirit
has made you bishops, to feed the church of God, which
he purchased with his own blood. (29) I know that after
my departing grievous wolves shall enter in among you,
not sparing the flock; (30) and from among your own
selves shall men arise, speaking perverse things, to draw
away the disciples after them. (31) Wherefore watch ye,
remembering that by the space of three years I ceased
not to admonish every one night and day with tears.
(32) And now I commend you to God, and to the word of
his grace, which is able to build you up, and to give you
the inheritance among all them that are sanctified. (33)
I coveted no man's silver, or gold, or apparel. (34) Ye
yourselves know that these hands ministered unto my
necessities, and to them that were with me. (35) In all
things I gave you an example, how that so laboring ye
ought to help the weak, and to remember the words of
the Lord Jesus, how he himself said, It is more blessed
to give than to receive.

Here the apostle styles bishops those whom Luke at
verse 17 calls elders, which shows that the two titles
were applied to the same church officer, and that the bishops of the apostolic church were not diocesan bishops,
such as now rule in episcopal bodies, but officers of sin-

gle congregations. While the word bishop is derived from the original term here used (ἐπίσκοπος), it does not translate it, because the idea commonly attached to the one is quite different from the meaning of the other. The exact English equivalent of the Greek word is over-seer, which is used here in the A. V., and should have been retained by the revisers. In order to impress these brethren more deeply in regard to their responsi-bility, Paul reminds them that they had been made over-seers of the flock in Ephesus by the Holy Spirit. The Holy Spirit had made them overseers by giving them the spiritual qualifications which rendered them eligible to the office, and by guiding the church in selecting them, as well as the apostle in appointing them. They are exhorted, first, to take heed to themselves; second, to take heed to "all the flock;" and third, to be shep-herds to the church; for this is the meaning of the word rendered *to feed.* The first required that personal godli-ness without which no man's ministrations in the church have any value; the second required such watchfulness as would allow nothing in the condition of the church to escape their notice; and the third required them to do for the church all that an eastern shepherd does for his flock. They were reminded that this church was pur-chased by God with his own blood shed in the person of his Son, in order that they might be willing, on account of the price God paid for it, to make all needed sacri-fices for its good. They were warned against two dan-gers which Paul's prophetic vision could foresee: the en-tering in of men from abroad, whom he styles " grievous wolves " who would not " spare the flock;" and the up-rising from among themselves of factionists, who would draw the disciples away from the Lord to follow them.

It would have been useless to tell them of these dangers, if there were no means of guarding against them; so they are told, first, to watch. Watchfulness would enable them to see the first symptoms of coming trouble, and to attack it while it was weak. The shepherd of the church who is not watchful as to the teachers who come from abroad, and as to ambitious men within the congregation, is like the literal shepherd who sleeps until the wolf has entered the fold, or until the flock begins to scatter. Secondly, they are told to remember how he had done in such matters during his stay among them—to remember it that they might imitate it—that is, he had " not ceased to admonish every one night and day with tears." By such admonitions, on the first appearance of trouble from within or from without, they were to keep in safety the flock committed to their care. In leaving them to this great responsibility, he points them to the only source of courage and strength sufficient for them, by commending them to God and to his word, assuring them that the word was able to build them up, and to give them inheritance among the sanctified. After this benediction, which appears as if intended to close the address, he adds still another admonition, which he enforces by both his own example and some treasured words of the Lord Jesus. It has reference to caring for God's poor; and it required them, elders though they were, to labor with their own hands that they might be able to " help the weak." His own example was most graphically and touchingly depicted in the words: " I have coveted no man's silver, or gold, or apparel. Ye yourselves know that these hands [lifting them up] have ministered to my necessities, and to them that were with me;" and the sentence quoted from the Lord Jesus, " It is more blessed to give than to receive," was one of those precious morsels of divine truth, of which many thousands fell from his lips that are not recorded in our brief gospels.

Vv. 36–38. An address so solemn, so tender, so heart-crushing both to speaker and hearers, could be followed with propriety only by prostration before the throne of grace. (36) **And when he had thus spoken, he kneeled down, and prayed with them all. (37) And they all wept sore, and fell on Paul's neck, and kissed him, (38) sorrowing most of all for the word which he had spoken, that they should behold his face no more. And they brought him on his way unto the ship.** Luke records not a word of that prayer. There are some prayers that are so broken with emotion, so interrupted by weeping, that though they leave a holy benediction on the soul, no connected words in them are remembered. The tears of women and of children are sometimes shallow; but when full grown men like these, men of gray hairs, who have been hardened to endurance by years of danger and suffering, are seen to weep like children, and to fall upon one another's necks, the depth of their grief can not be questioned. When the man of the world is thus overcome with grief, his heart often grows harder while it is breaking; but the sorrow of the man of faith is softening and purifying; it binds the afflicted more closely to one another and to God, while it is sanctified by prayer. It is a sorrow which we are willing to feel again, and which we love to remember. The pathway of the church is strewn with scenes like this. When the paths of many pilgrims meet, and for a few days they mingle together their prayers, their songs of praise, their counsels, and their tears, the hour of parting is often a repetition of this scene on the sea shore at Miletus. Tears and heavings of the breast, which tell of grief and love and hope struggling within, the parting hand, the fond embrace, the blessing of God invoked, and the sad turning away to duties which the soul feels for the moment too weak to attempt—these are all familiar to the toiling servants of God.

If Paul had been parting from these brethren under cheerful anticipations for himself and them, the parting would have been painful; but added to the pain of a final parting was the gloom of their own uncertain future, and of the undefined afflictions which certainly awaited him. He had already, twelve months before this, recounted a catalogue of sufferings more abundant than had fallen to the lot of any other man. He had been often in prison, and often on the verge of death. From the Jews he had five times received forty stripes save one, and three times he had been beaten with rods. Once he was stoned, and left on the ground, supposed to be dead. He had been shipwrecked three times, and had spent a day and a night in the waters of the great deep. In his many journeys he had been exposed to perils by water, by robbers, by his own countrymen, by the heathen; in the city, in the wilderness, in the sea, and among false brethren. He had suffered from weariness and painfulness and wakefulness. He had endured hunger and thirst, and he had suffered from cold for want of sufficient clothing. Throughout all he had borne, and was still bearing, that which was little less painful, the care of all the churches. At the same time there was a thorn in his flesh, a messenger of Satan to buffet him, which was so irritating and humiliating that he had three times prayed the Lord to take it from him.

He had been constrained to write to the brethren in
Galatia, " From henceforth let no man trouble me:
for I bear branded on my body the marks of the Lord
Jesus."[1]   Most men would have said, I have suffered
enough : the success of my present enterprise is doubtful
at best, and it is certain to bring me once more into prison,
and into untold afflictions : I will therefore remain where
I am, amid brethren who love me, and let my companions
complete this work of benevolence which I have undertaken.   But no such thoughts were entertained ; and
when the Ephesian elders were parting from such a man,
well might they weep, and stand mute upon the shore
till the sails of his vessel grew dim in the distance, ere
they turned in loneliness to the toils and dangers which
they now knew they must encounter without the presence or the counsel of their great teacher.   We are not
permitted to return with them to Ephesus, or to hear
their sorrowful conversation by the way ; for we must
follow the receding vessel, and witness the bonds and
afflictions which await its most noted passenger.

12. The Journey from Miletus to Cæsarea, XXI. 1–9.

Vv. 1–3.   The vessel proceeded for a time on its
coasting voyage along the shore of Asia Minor, and then
struck out into the open sea.   (1) **And when it came to
pass that we were parted from them, and had set sail, we
came with a straight course unto Cos, and the next day
unto Rhodes, and from thence unto Patara ; (2) and having
found a ship crossing over unto Phœnicia, we went aboard,
and set sail.   (3) And when we had come in sight of
Cyprus, leaving it on the left hand, we sailed unto Syria,**

---

[1] II. Cor. xi. 21–28 ; xii. 7–10 ; Gal. vi. 17.

and landed at Tyre : for there the ship was to unlade her burden. That they sailed with a " straight course " from Miletus to the island of Cos, implies a favorable wind on the first day. At the city of Rhodes, on the island of the same name, they cast anchor for the night in the harbor, the mouth of which had once been ornamented by a colossus which was one of the seven wonders of the world. It was a brazen statue of Helios, one hundred and five feet in height. It was prostrated by an earthquake, 224 B. C. ; but its fragments were still on the spot at the time of Paul's visit. Patara, where they changed vessels, is on the southern coast of Lycia. They made the change because the new vessel was going directly to the port of Tyre, nearly in the exact direction in which they desired to sail ; and this implies either that the vessel which they left was going no farther than Patara, or that it was intending still to hug the shore of Asia Minor. On passing in sight of Cyprus, Paul must have been reminded of his early experience in that island, when he and Barnabas had preached there on his first missionary tour (xiii. 4–12). The ship's run from Patara to Tyre was one of several days and nights in the open sea, without casting anchor as they had done every night since leaving Troas. Such a run the ships of that day never made, except when they could hope for the light of the moon or stars at night ; and it is a singular circumstance that we are able to determine the phase of the moon at the time of this run. Paul left Philippi seven days after the full moon ; and he was five days reaching Troas, where he spent seven days (xx. 6). This makes nineteen days after the full moon. Leaving Troas, they reached Miletus in four days, and from Miletus they sailed to Patara in three days (xx. 13–15 ; xxi. 1).

These seven days added to the nineteen make twenty-six; and if they spent three days in Miletus, these would make the aggregate twenty-nine since the last full moon, when it would be full moon again. Any traveler who has sailed by moonlight in the summer time on the Mediterranean Sea, when the water was smooth, remembers it as a delightful experience, and it must have helped to soothe the troubled spirits of Paul and his companions.

Ver. 4. The time employed by the sailors in putting out freight, and perhaps in taking in a fresh cargo, gave another opportunity for communing with brethren on shore. (4) **And having found the disciples, we tarried there seven days : and these said to Paul through the Spirit, that he should not set foot in Jerusalem.** The words, "having found the disciples," imply that some search had to be made for them ; and this followed from the fact that Paul had not been there before since the church was established, and his companions, being all of foreign birth, were total strangers in the city. But a church was at any rate found in Tyre, verifying the words of our Lord addressed to cities of Galilee : " If the mighty works had been done in Tyre and Sidon which were done in you, they would have repented long ago in sackcloth and ashes " (Matt. xi. 21). We are not to understand that the entreaties of these Tyrian brethren were dictated by the Holy Spirit; for this would have made it Paul's duty to comply with them, and he certainly would have done so ; but we are to understand that the Holy Spirit revealed to some of them, as he had done in other cities, what awaited Paul in Jerusalem, while they of their own accord entreated him not to go thither. Their entreaties show that although they had not been evangelized by Paul, they knew and appreciated his worth to the cause of Christ.

Vv. 5, 6. When the seven days were past, including, as they must, a Lord's day in which the disciples came together to break bread, another scene of painful parting occurred like that at Miletus. (5) **And when it came to pass that we had accomplished the days, we departed and went on our journey ; and they all, with wives and children, brought us on our way, till we were out of the city : and kneeling down on the beach, we prayed, (6) and bade each other farewell ; and we went on board the ship, but they returned home again.** Here the parting scene was even more tender than that at Miletus ; for the sobs of women and children were mingled with those of the men. All, however, were sanctified by a prayer which must have soothed every heart, and have remained in blessed remembrance with the saints at Tyre.

VER. 7. The rest of the journey by water was completed in a single day ; for the distance is not more than a day's journey by land. (7) **And when we had finished the voyage from Tyre, we arrived at Ptolemais ; and we saluted the brethren, and abode with them one day.** Ptolemais was the name at that time of the modern city of Acre. Its original name, Accho, which it bore while in possession of the Canaanites, had been changed to Ptolemais by one of the Ptolemies of Egypt, in honor of himself ; but, as is the case with many cities of Palestine whose names were changed by its Greek and Roman conquerors, when the conquering power passed away the original name in a slightly different form was restored. That Paul found brethren here as well as in Tyre, is proof of the thoroughness with which this region had been evangelized. Acre was situated in the territory formerly occupied by the tribe of Asher, but it had become a Greek city in the interval since the captivity.

Vv. 8, 9. The single day spent with the brethren in Ptolemais was sufficient for the admonitions which Paul was leaving with all the churches, and for another painful farewell. (8) And on the morrow we departed, and came unto Cæsarea: and entering into the house of Philip the evangelist, who was one of the seven, we abode with him. (9) Now this man had four daughters, virgins, who did prophesy. From Ptolemais the road leads around the Bay of Acre, almost in a semicircle, along a smooth beach, to the sea end of Mt. Carmel, whence it leads in a direct line almost due south along the Mediterranean shore to Cæsarea. The distance is about thirty-five miles, and it must have occupied the greater part of two days.

The designation of Philip the evangelist, as " one of the seven," clearly identifies him as the Philip whose early labors are recounted in the eighth chapter. At the close of that account he is said to have preached in all the cities from Azotus to Cæsarea (viii. 39, 40), and now we find him residing in the latter city. His four maiden daughters who had the gift of prophecy had been well trained no doubt by their godly father, and were therefore suitable in character for the distinction conferred upon them by the Holy Spirit. His house must have been a capacious one, as it enabled him to entertain the nine men who made up Paul's company.

13. Agabus Predicts the Imprisonment of Paul, 10–14.

Vv. 10–14. During the time spent with the family of Philip, another, and the last, of the prophetic warnings which Paul met with on this journey was given, and it caused a scene similar to those at Miletus and Tyre. (10) And as we tarried there many days, there came down from Judea a certain prophet, named Agabus. (11) And coming to us, and taking Paul's girdle, he bound his own feet and hands, and said, Thus saith the Holy Spirit, So shall the Jews at Jerusalem bind the man that owneth this girdle, and shall deliver him into the hands of the Gentiles. (12) And when we heard these things, both we and they of that place besought him not to go up to Jerusalem. (13) Then Paul answered, What do ye, weeping and breaking my heart? for I am ready not to be bound only, but also to die at Jerusalem for the name of the Lord Jesus. (14) And when he would not be persuaded, we ceased, saying, The will of the Lord be done. Although Luke here introduces Agabus as if he had not been mentioned before, he is doubtless the same prophet who predicted in Antioch the famine which led to the first mission of Paul and Barnabas from Antioch to Jerusalem (xi. 27–29). The dramatic manner in which the prediction was delivered, in imitation of some of the Old Testament prophets,[1] made it the more impressive, while the words uttered gave Paul a more distinct conception of the affliction which awaited him. If his traveling companions had hitherto been silent when brethren were entreating him not to go up to Jerusalem, their courage now failed them, and they joined in the

---

[1] See Jer. xxvii. 1–11; xxviii. 1-17; Zech. xi. 7–14.

entreaties of the brethren in Cæsarea. The prospect
was sufficiently trying while he enjoyed the silent sympathy of his brave fellow-laborers ; but when they threw
the weight of their own entreaties on the heavy burden
he was already bearing, the effect was crushing to his
heart, though the steadfastness of his purpose was not
shaken.   Whatever he might suffer would be for the
name of Jesus, because it was for the church which upheld the honor of that name among men ; and to serve this
high purpose was paramount to all personal considerations.   Men of less faith in divine providence than were
his companions, when they found all their entreaties
were in vain, might have reproached him for his self-
will ; but these men saw in this very fixedness of purpose
the guiding hand of God, and hence their exclamation,
" The will of the Lord be done."

14. The Journey From Cæsarea to Jerusalem,
15, 16.

Vv. 15, 16.   It seems that the prediction by Agabus
was uttered about the close of the time which Paul's company spent in Cæsarea ; and though we may believe that
the first part of that stay was rich in religious communion to the saints gathered there from the east and
the west, it had a sorrowful termination.   (15) **And after
these days we took up our baggage, and went up to
Jerusalem.   (16) And there went with us also certain of
the disciples from Cæsarea, bringing with them one
Mnason of Cyprus, an early disciple, with whom we
should lodge.**   The journey had been completed in time
for the Pentecost : for to the twenty-nine days which we
have already counted between the previous Passover
and the arrival at Patara (see under 3), we have to add,

say three days from Patara to Tyre, seven days at Tyre, and four in passing thence to Cæsarea, which make an aggregate of forty-three out of the fifty between the Passover and the Pentecost, leaving six for the stay in Cæsarea. But it is almost certain that in this count some pieces of days are counted as whole days, and that the time in Cæsarea was more than six days. This last stay is styled "many days" by Luke, not because it was many compared with other stops on this journey, but because it was many for men going to Jerusalem on an important mission, and now within two short days' journey of the Holy City. Naturally, they would have been expected to hasten to their journey's end. The fact that Mnason of Cyprus had a house in Jerusalem in which all of Paul's company could lodge, implies that he was a man of means, if not of wealth, who, besides his home in Cyprus, kept one also in Jerusalem. He is styled "an early disciple," because he had become one in the early history of the church.

COMMENTARY ON ACTS.

---o---

PART FOURTH.

PAUL'S FIVE YEARS' IMPRISONMENT.

(*XXI. 17.—XXVIII. 31.*)

---o---

SEC. I.—HIS IMPRISONMENT IN JERUSALEM.

(XXI. 17 —XXIII. 30.)

1. HIS RECEPTION BY THE ELDERS, AND THEIR ADVICE, 17–25.

VER. 17. The hour which had been looked forward to for months with prayerful anxiety had now come, and Paul was to know, without further delay, whether the service which he had for Jerusalem would be accepted by the saints (Rom. xv. 31). The historian was able to say: (17) **And when we were come to Jerusalem, the brethren received us gladly.** If Luke had said anything at all about the contribution which Paul brought, we should have expected him to say something more definite about its reception than is implied in this remark. But as he saw fit to omit all mention of the enterprise, we are at liberty to infer from the glad reception of the messengers the grateful reception also of their gift. The main purpose of Paul's visit, and of his prayers, was now accomplished. He had finished this part of his course and of his ministry with joy, and whether the Lord would deliver him from the disobedient in Jerusalem was to him a matter of minor importance.

Ver. 18-26. After the general statement that they were gladly received by the brethren, Luke states more in detail what followed. (18) And the day following Paul went in with us unto James; and all the elders were present. (19) And when he had saluted them, he rehearsed one by one the things which God wrought among the Gentiles by his ministry. (20) And they, when they heard it, glorified God; and they said unto him, Thou seest, brother, how many thousands there are among the Jews of them who have believed; and they are all zealous for the law: (21) and they have been informed concerning thee, that thou teachest all the Jews who are among the Gentiles to forsake Moses, telling them not to circumcise their children, neither to walk after the customs. (22) What is it therefore? they will certainly hear that thou art come. (23) Do therefore this that we say to thee: We have four men who have a vow on them: (24) these take, and purify thyself with them, and be at charges for them, that they may shave their heads: and all shall know that there is no truth in the things whereof they have been informed concerning thee; but that thou thyself also walkest orderly, keeping the law. (25) But as touching the Gentiles who have believed, we wrote, giving judgment that they should keep themselves from things sacrificed to idols, and from blood, and from what is strangled, and from fornication. (26) Then Paul took the men, and the next day purifying himself with them went into the temple, declaring the fulfillment of the days of purification, until the offering was offered for every one of them.

In verse 18 a distinction is made between James and the elders, which indicates that he did not bear the latter title. In a later age, when the organization of the church had been changed by uninspired men, it became customary, as it still is among episcopalian bodies, to call him bishop of the church in Jerusalem, because he seems here to have had precedence over the elders. But nowhere in the New Testament is the title bishop thus used; and consequently this custom reads into the inspired record most improperly an unauthorized conception of a later age. As we have seen before (Vol. I. 189), James ranked as an apostle of the secondary class, and this fully accounts for his position at the head of the Jerusalem church, when none of the twelve was present. Paul's minute rehearsal, "one by one," of the things which God had wrought by his ministry, most probably went back no farther than the time of the conference described in the fifteenth chapter; for then he had rehearsed to James and others all that had preceded that date (xv. 4). The fact that when they heard it all "they glorified God," shows plainly enough that they were in full accord with Paul in his teaching and practice, and contradicts flatly the modern assumption of rationalists, that there was antagonism between Paul and the leading men of the Jerusalem church.

The remarks addressed to Paul by these brethren, doubtless through James as their spokesman, show very plainly the position held by the Jerusalem church as to the law and circumcision, and also the exact ground of the prejudice entertained against Paul by members who were laboring under false information concerning him. They show, first, that these disciples were " zealous for the law " (20) ; second, that they continued to circumcise

their children (21) ; third, that the purifications of the
law, though they involved in some instances the offering
of sacrifices, were still regarded as proper for Christians
(23, 24) ; and fourth, that they imposed none of these observances on the Gentile brethren, but still adhered to the
decision which had been issued in the name of the whole
church at the time of the conference (25). The ground
of prejudice against Paul on the part of the multitude
is stated with equal clearness. It was that he had
taught the Jews who were among the Gentiles to forsake
Moses ; and there were two specifications under this general charge : first, that he taught them not to circumcise
their children ; second, that he taught them not " to walk
after the customs "—an expression for those observances
which had acquired the force of law in the Jewish conscience, although they were not specified in the law itself
(21). The advice given in the address, having in view
the specific purpose of proving to the multitude that
there was no truth in these things, and that Paul did
walk orderly, keeping the law (24), shows that James
and the elders understood that these reports were false ;
while Paul's agreement to do as they advised shows that
they certainly were false. He had not taught the Jews
not to circumcise their children ; on the contrary, he
had with his own hand circumcised Timothy, who
was one-half a Jew. He had not taught them to forsake
the customs ; on the contrary, he had written to the Corinthians more than a year previous, that he had been a
Jew to the Jew, that he might win the Jew ; and as to
the law in general, he had been " as under the law," that
he might gain them who considered themselves still
bound to keep the law (I. Cor. ix. 20, 21) In order to
reconcile this position with Paul's teaching in those

epistles written previous to this time, we have only
to observe the distinction which he never lost sight of,
between that which we are at liberty to do for the sake
of others, and that which we are bound to do in order
to obey God. He had taught that the law had been
"our tutor to bring us to Christ;" and that since faith
is come "we are no longer under a tutor" (Gal. iii.
24–25); that the Jews had been made "dead to the law
through the body of Christ" (Rom. vii. 4); and that in
Christ neither circumcision availeth anything, nor uncircumcision (Gal. v. 6; vi. 15; I. Cor. vii. 19). But
while teaching thus, he had found no fault with the
Jews who continued the observances of the law; he had
only tried to convince them that the observance was no
longer binding on their consciences. The only difference between him and the most extreme Judaizers, of
whom there were doubtless some in the multitude of
believers to whom James referred, was that the latter
held these observances to be matters of duty, while
he held them to be matters of indifference.

The device of uniting himself with the four disciples
who had a vow, in order to convince the multitude that
they had been misinformed, sets the whole subject of
Paul's relation to the law in a still stronger light.
These four, as a comparison of what is said of them
with the law of Nazirite clearly shows, were under the
Nazirite vow, and had become unclean from a dead body
before the termination of the time included in the vow
(23, 24, 26, *cf.* Num. vi. 2–12). This necessitated their
purification, which required seven days for its completion, the shaving of their heads at the altar, the
sacrifice of a sin offering and a burnt offering for each
of them, and the loss of the time passed under the vow.

Paul's part with them was, first, "to be at charges for them," meaning that he paid part or all the expenses of the victims which they had to offer ; and second, to go into the temple and notify the priests when their days of purification would be fulfilled, so that a priest might be prepared to sacrifice their offerings (23, 26). The last they could not do themselves, because the law shut them out of the Jewish court during their uncleanness; but as Paul was unclean not from contact with a dead body, but from some of the many other causes mentioned in the law, he could purify himself in a single day by washing his clothes and bathing his flesh and remaining unclean until evening (Lev. xv. 1–30, *et al.*). That which renders this proceeding a more striking exhibition of Paul's present attitude toward the law is the fact that in it he participated in the offering of sacrifices, which seems to be inconsistent with his repeated declaration of the all-sufficiency of the blood of Christ as an atonement for sin. I think it must be admitted that subsequent to the writing of the epistle to the Ephesians, and more especially that to the Hebrews, he could not consistently have done this ; for in those epistles it is clearly taught, that in the death of Christ God has broken down and abolished "the law of commandments contained in ordinances," which he styles "the middle wall of partition" (Eph. ii. 13–15) ; that the Aaronic priesthood had been abolished (Heb. vii., viii.) ; and that the sacrifice of Christ had completely superseded that of dumb animals (ix., x.). But in Paul's earlier epistles, though some things had been written which, carried to their logical consequences, involved all this, these points had not yet been clearly revealed to his mind, and much less to the minds of the other disciples ; for it pleased God to make Paul the chief instrument for the revelation of this part of his will. His mind, and those of all the brethren, were as yet in much the same condition on this question that those of the early disciples had been in before the conversion of Cornelius in reference to the salvation of the Gentiles. If Peter, by the revelation made to him in connection with Cornelius, was made to understand better his own words uttered on Pentecost (ii. 39), it should cause no surprise that Paul in his early writings uttered sentiments the full import of which he did not apprehend until later revelations made them plain. That it was so, is but another illustration of the fact that the Holy Spirit guided the apostles into all the truth, not at one bound, but step by step. In the wisdom of God the epistle to the Hebrews, the special value of which lies in its clear revelations on the distinction between the sacrifices and priesthood under Moses and those under Christ, was written but a few years previous to the destruction of the Jewish temple, and the compulsory abrogation of all the sacrifices of the law; and that thus any Jewish Christian, whose natural reverence for ancestral and divinely appointed customs may have prevented him from seeing the truth on this subject, might have his eyes opened in spite of himself.

2. Paul is Assailed by the Mob, and Arrested by the Chief Captain, 27–36.

Vv. 27–30. Thus far Paul's reception in Jerusalem was gratifying, and to all human foresight his prospect for escaping personal violence was good; and so it continued for several days. (27) And when the seven days were almost completed, the Jews from Asia, when they saw him in the temple, stirred up all the multitude, and

laid hands on him, (28) crying out, Men of Israel,
help : This is the man, that teacheth all men everywhere
against the people, and the law, and this place : and
moreover he brought Greeks also into the temple, and
hath defiled this holy place. (29) For they had before
seen with him in the city Trophimus the Ephesian,
whom they supposed that Paul had brought into the
temple. (30) And all the city was moved, and the people ran together : and they laid hold on Paul, and
dragged him out of the temple : and straightway the
doors were shut. The " Jews from Asia " who raised
this outcry were a portion of those from whose plots
Paul had suffered so much in Ephesus (xx. 19). Their
false accusation as to what he had taught everywhere
was that, the report of which had excited the prejudices
of his own Jewish brethren, as stated by James (21).
They had no reason whatever to believe that Paul had
brought Trophimus into the temple ; but, having recognized Trophimus with him in the city, it occurred to
them to bring this accusation as the quickest way to excite the wrath of the multitude. Perhaps the success of
Demetrius in rousing the heathen population of their own
city by the outcry concerning the temple of Diana, suggested the device (xix. 23–28). The part of the temple
which they charged him with defiling was the Jewish
court ; for Gentiles were admitted within the outer court ;
and so, when it is said that they dragged him out of the
temple, its meaning is that they dragged him out of the
Jewish into the Gentile court. Outside the latter court,
which now includes thirty-five acres of ground, there was
no room in the narrow streets for such a mob to move.

Vv. 31–34. For the second time in his life a Roman
officer rescued Paul from the hands of his countrymen,

the first having occurred in Corinth. (31) And as they were seeking to kill him, tidings came up to the chief captain of the band, that all Jerusalem was in confusion. (32) And forthwith he took soldiers and centurions, and ran down upon them: and they, when they saw the chief captain and the soldiers, left off beating Paul. (33) Then the chief captain came near, and laid hold on him, and commanded him to be bound with two chains; and inquired who he was, and what he had done. (34) And some shouted one thing, some another, among the crowd: and when he could not know the certainty for the uproar, he commanded him to brought into the castle. The expression, "chief captain of the band," should be chiliarch of the cohort; for such is the exact meaning of the original. The Roman legions were divided into cohorts of a thousand men each, and the commander of the cohort was called chiliarch, leader of a thousand, just as the commander of one hundred was entitled centurion, leader of a hundred.

That he took centurions, in the plural number, each of course accompanied by his command, shows that he came at the head of several hundred men. A smaller number might have been overpowered by the furious mob. The expression, "ran down upon them," is the language of an eye-witness; for the tower of Antonia, the fortress in which the Roman garrison was quartered, stood at the northwestern angle of the temple court; its foundations were laid on solid rock which rises about twenty feet above the level of the court; and a flight of stone steps descended from its door to the floor of the court which is here the natural rock.[1] The chiliarch saw at a glance that the man whom they were beating

---

[1] For a full description, see Lands of the Bible, 177.

was in some way the occasion of the disturbance; and jumping to the conclusion that he was a criminal on whom the Jews were inflicting summary vengeance, he had him chained for safe keeping, and demanded who he was, and what he had done, so that he might know how to deal with him. But the majority of the mob did not know who he was or what he had done, and the confused answers in their outcries made it plain to the chiliarch that he must wait and seek the information in some other way; hence the order to take him into the castle.

Vv. 35, 36. The soldiers very promptly and vigorously obeyed the order of their commander. (35) **And when he came upon the stairs, so it was that he was borne of the soldiers for the violence of the crowd; (36) for the multitude of the people followed after, crying out, Away with him.** Paul was so stunned by the beating, or so reluctant to running from the face of his foes, that he did not move fast enough to suit the soldiers, so two of them lifted him in their arms, or threw him across their shoulders, and thus hurried him along. As the pursuers could not get hold of him, they affected to acquiesce in what was being done, by the outcry, " Away with him."

3. PAUL OBTAINS PERMISSION TO ADDRESS THE MOB, 37–40.

Vv. 37–40. Though Paul was suffering from many a bruise, which, together with mental distress, would have prevented any other man from wishing to make a speech, when he saw those prison doors about to shut him out from his enraged countrymen, and leave them a prey to passion aroused by falsehood, he conceived the thought of at once attempting to appease them. (37) **And as Paul was about to be brought into the castle, he saith**

unto the chief captain, May I say something unto thee ?
And he said, Dost thou know Greek ? (38) Art thou not
then the Egyptian, who before these days stirred up to
sedition and led out into the wilderness the four thousand men of the Assassins ? (39) But Paul said, I am a
Jew, of Tarsus in Cilicia, a citizen of no mean city : and
I beseech thee, give me leave to speak unto the people.
(40) And when he had given him leave, Paul, standing
on the stairs, beckoned with the hand unto the people ;
and when there was made a great silence, he spake
unto them in the Hebrew language, saying,

This brief conversation shows how utterly the chiliarch, in the excitement of the moment, had misconceived
his prisoner. The Egyptian for whom he mistook him
is doubtless the one mentioned by Josephus, but whom
the latter represents as leading thirty thousand men instead of four thousand.[1] He was the only man the chiliarch could think of at the moment against whom the
Jews could feel such violent hatred. When he learned
that Paul was a Jew, and a citizen of such a city as Tarsus, his wonder as to the cause of the trouble was greatly
increased, and he at once concluded that by allowing him
to speak as requested he could learn from the speech the
real charges laid against him ; for he expected of course
that Paul would speak of them explicitly. When permission was given, the soldiers placed him on his feet,
and they appear to have released at least one of his arms

---

[1] He claimed to be a prophet, and promised his dupes that
they should take Jerusalem from the Romans, as a proof of
which he declared that when he reached the top of the Mount
of Olives he would cause the walls of the city to fall by his
miraculous power. Josephus is somewhat inconsistent with
himself in regard to the numbers that were captured and slain.
(Ant. xx. 8, 6 ; Wars, ii. 13, 5).

from the chains ; for he " beckoned with his hand to the
people," using his habitual gesture,[1] to secure silence.
It was the same that had been used in vain by Alexander in the mob at Ephesus (xix. 23). The silence which
followed is probably called " great " because it was difficult to obtain any silence at all in such a multitude. It
was still greater when they heard him speaking in the
native tongue (xxii. 2).

4. PAUL'S ADDRESS TO THE MOB, XXII. 1–21.

I. AN ACCOUNT OF HIMSELF BEFORE HIS CONVERSION,
1–5.

Vv. 1–5. Seeing that the chiliarch had so misconceived his personality, and knowing from the outcries of
the people in answer to the chiliarch's inquiry, that
many of them were equally ignorant of him, Paul begins
his speech with an account of himself. (1) **Brethren
and fathers, hear ye the defense which I now make unto
you.**

(2) **And when they heard that he spake unto them in
the Hebrew language, they were the more quiet: and he
saith,**

(3) **I am a Jew, born in Tarsus of Cilicia, but brought
up in this city, at the feet of Gamaliel, instructed according to the strict manner of the law of our fathers, being
zealous for God, even as ye all are this day: (4) and I
persecuted this Way unto the death, binding and delivering into prisons both men and women. (5) As also the high
priest doth bear me witness, and all the estate of the
elders : from whom also I received letters unto the breth-**

---

[1] In addition to the instance above, we see it noted by Luke in
the opening of the address in Antioch of Pisidia, and in the one
before king Agrippa (xiii. 16 ; xxvi. 1).

ren, and journeyed to Damascus, to bring them also who
were there unto Jerusalem in bonds for to be punished.
Some in the audience, Paul's old companions in persecution, and his subsequent enemies, knew all the facts here
recited, but they were unknown to the majority of the
crowd; and his evident purpose in reciting them was,
first, to disabuse the minds of any who may have made
similar mistakes to that of the chiliarch, and secondly, to
awaken some sympathy toward himself as having once
stood in the same attitude with themselves toward the
Christian Way.

II. AN ACCOUNT OF HIS CONVERSION, 6–16.

Vv. 6–16. The preceding division of the speech,
which is its introduction, was calculated not only to
awaken sympathy toward the speaker, but while it
presented him as once a persecutor like his hearers, it
awakened at the same moment a desire to know what
could have turned him from that position to the one he
now occupied; and this desire he next proceeds to
gratify. (6) And it came to pass, that, as I made my
journey, and drew nigh unto Damascus, about noon,
suddenly there shone from heaven a great light round
about me. (7) And I fell unto the ground, and heard a
voice say unto me, Saul, Saul, why persecutest thou me?
(8) And I answered, Who art thou, Lord ? And he said
unto me, I am Jesus of Nazareth, whom thou persecutest. (9) And they that were with me beheld indeed
the light, but they heard not the voice of him that spake
to me. (10) And I said, What shall I do, Lord? And
the Lord said unto me, Arise, and go into Damascus ; and
there it shall be told thee of all things which are appointed for thee to do. (11) And when I could not see for the

glory of that light, being led by the hand of them that were with me, I came into Damascus. (12) And one Ananias, a devout man according to the law, well reported of by all the Jews that dwelt there, (13) came unto me, and standing by me said unto me, Brother Saul, receive thy sight. And in that very hour I looked up on him. (14) And he said, the God of our fathers hath appointed thee to know his will, and to see the Righteous One, and to hear a voice from his mouth. (15) For thou shalt be a witness for him unto all men of what thou hast seen and heard. (16) And now, why tarriest thou? arise, and be baptized, and wash away thy sins, calling on his name. This account furnishes several interesting details omitted by Luke in his brief narrative (ix. 3–8).[1] It informs us that the light from heaven flashed around him "about noon;" that his companions, though they heard the voice, did not hear it, that is, so as to catch the words that were spoken; and that the command to go into Damascus, where he should be told what to do, was given in answer to his inquiry, "What shall I do,

---

[1] The statement of Luke that they heard the voice (ix. 7), and this of Paul that they heard it not, have long been treated by un_ friendly critics as contradictory, notwithstanding the well known fact that it is common among all classes of men to say, I did not hear, when they mean that they did not hear the words spoken, though they did hear the sound of the speaker's voice. Paul himself furnishes another instance of the usage when, writing about the employment of unknown tongues in the congregation, he says: "For he that speaketh in a tongue speaketh not unto men, but unto God; for no man heareth" (I. Cor. xiv. 2). Here our translators have obscured the usage by rendering the word "understand," instead of "hear." If they had taken the same liberty in the passage before us, the question of a contradiction would never have been raised, at least by an English reader; and the idea of Paul would have been expressed, but not in his way of expressing it.

Lord?" On the other hand, Paul does not state the
duration of his blindness; he says nothing of the fasting
and praying; and instead of telling what the Lord said
to Ananias, he speaks of the good reputation which the
latter enjoyed among the Jews of Damascus. He told
this in order to reflect respectability in the minds of his
hearers on the proceedings connected with his baptism.
He also omits the words of Ananias quoted by Luke,
and mentions others. The whole speech of Ananias is
to be obtained by putting together these two pieces of it.
The miracle wrought upon him by Ananias was mentioned, not merely to show how his eyesight was restored, but more especially to show that God's approval
attended his baptism. The words, " why tarriest thou?"
were suggested by the unusual delay of baptism after
believing, a delay of which Ananias did not then know
the cause. In the expression, " wash away thy sins,"
there is undoubtedly a reference to the forgiveness of
sins which takes place in baptism, and the metaphor in
the term wash away (ἀπόλουσαι) was suggested by the
washing of the body which takes place in baptism. He
was to wash his sins away, by undergoing that washing
in which God forgives them. He was to do this, " calling
on his name," because it is through the name of Jesus
that we now receive every blessing, and especially the
forgiveness of sins.

The evident purpose of this division of the speech
was to win the Jews to a favorable consideration of his
cause, by showing them that he had been turned from
the position of a persecutor like themselves, to that of a
believer and advocate of the claims of Jesus, by miraculous evidence from heaven which could not be miscon-
strued, and which, according to all the maxims of the

fathers, made it his indispensable duty to do as he had done ; and at the same time he accomplished the additional purpose of furnishing his hearers evidence of the resurrection and glorification of Jesus, which ought to convince them as it had him. He was aiming to defend himself by winning his accusers over to his own position.

III. HIS MISSION TO THE GENTILES, 17–21.

Vv. 17–21. Paul's next step was to show that the divine authority which had changed him from a persecutor into an advocate of the Way had determined for him the peculiar field of labor which distinguished him from the other apostles. (17) **And it came to pass, that, when I had returned to Jerusalem, and while I prayed in the temple, I fell into a trance, (18) and saw him saying unto me, Make haste, and get thee quickly out of Jerusalem : because they will not receive of thee testimony concerning me. (19) And I said, Lord, they themselves know that I imprisoned and beat in every synagogue them that believed on thee : (20) and when the blood of Stephen thy witness was shed, I also was standing by, and consenting, and keeping the garments of them that slew him. (21) And he said unto me, Depart : for I will send thee forth far hence unto the Gentiles.** Paul here reveals to us the interesting fact, omitted by Luke in the previous narrative, that when the brethren sent him away from Jerusalem to Tarsus (ix. 28–30), he did not consent to go until commanded by the Lord ; and that even when thus commanded he mildly remonstrated with the Lord for so commanding him. His plea for wishing to remain was based on the belief that as the Jews knew of his connection with the death of Stephen, and the dispersion of the church, he was now the very man to bring them over to the truth. He was forgetting the intense malice always felt by partisans toward a man whom they can stigmatise as a deserter, or as a traitor to their cause. That he had urged this plea when the Jews were just then laying plots to kill him, is at once proof of his courage, and of his willingness to die, if need be, on the very spot where he had witnessed the death of Stephen.

5. THE IMMEDIATE EFFECTS OF THE SPEECH, 22–29.

Vv. 22–24. The unbelieving Jews had learned by this time to endure the preaching of Christ among the circumcised, but they still had the greatest abhorrence for the admission of the uncircumcised into religious fellowship with Jews; consequently it was Paul's position as the apostle to the Gentiles which excited their especial animosity toward him. This mob had now listened in perfect silence to his vindication of his position as a Christian, and had heard for the first time in their lives Paul's peculiar testimony to the resurrection and glorification of Jesus; and if he had concluded his remarks at that point, they might have gone away with favorable impressions; but when he claimed that his going to the Gentiles, which they looked upon as a shameful procedure, was due to an express command from heaven overriding his own preferences, and was about, as they supposed, to justify all the charges which they had heard against him, they could listen no longer. (22) And they gave him audience unto this word; and they lifted up their voice, and said, Away with such a fellow from the earth: for it is not fit that he should live. (23) And as they cried out, and threw off their garments, and cast dust into the air, (24) the chief captain commanded him to be brought into the castle, bidding that he should be examined by scourging, that he might know for what cause they so shouted against him. They did not dare to throw stones at him, lest they should strike the soldiers: so they vented their rage like maddened brutes by throwing dust into the air. What the rest of his speech would have been but for this interruption, we can judge only by what had already been said. It certainly would have been a still farther attempt to convince his hearers of the divine authority under which he had ever acted; for he sought no vindication for himself that did not involve the vindication of the cause to which he had committed his life. Whether Lysias understood the Hebrew tongue in which Paul spoke, or had his words repeated by an interpreter, he was certainly disappointed in his hope of learning from the speech what the charges were which the Jews held against Paul, so he immediately determined on the more direct method of extorting the desired information from Paul himself. It was quite a common practice among Roman provincial rulers to scourge into a confession of their crimes men whom they held as criminals, and against whom suitable evidence was not at hand.

Vv. 25-29. When Paul was led within the castle, the executioner, under the direction of a centurion, made immediate preparation for the cruel task. (25) **And when they had tied him up with the thongs, Paul said unto the centurion that stood by, Is it lawful for you to scourge a man that is a Roman, and uncondemned? (26) And when the centurion heard it, he went to the chief captain, and told him, saying, What art thou about to do? for this man is a Roman. (27) And the chief captain came, and said unto him, Tell me, art thou a**

Roman? (28) And he said, Yea. And the chief captain
answered, With a great sum obtained I this citizenship.
And Paul said, But I am a Roman born. (29) They then
who were about to examine him straightway departed
from him: and the chief captain also was afraid, when
he knew that he was a Roman, and because he had
bound him. Previous to applying the scourge the victim
was bent forward upon a reclining post, and bound to
it by leather thongs. It was this binding which alarmed
the chiliarch, and not the previous binding with chains.
The latter was legal, and Paul continued to be thus
bound (30; xxvi. 29.) Paul gave no evidence but his
own word that he was a citizen; but the lofty manner in
which he had declared himself a citizen by birth, while
Lysias had to acknowledge that he had obtained the
same distinction by bribery,[1] together with the impressive
deportment of Paul before the mob, left no room to
doubt the truth of his claim; so it was respected, and the
executioners did not wait to be told to depart from him.
Thus a second time Paul saved himself from ignominy,
and this time from incalculable suffering, by the quiet
proclamation of his rights as a Roman citizen. We can
but admire the majesty of the law, which, in a remote
province, and within the walls of a prison, could thus

---

[1] Citizenship was lawfully obtained in three different ways.
It was conferred by the senate for meritorious conduct; it was inherited from a father who was a citizen; and it was the birthright
of one who was born in a free city; that is, a city which, for
some especial service to the empire, was rewarded by granting
citizenship to all born within its limits. It was unlawfully obtained by the use of money in the absence of meritorious conduct. In the reign of Claudius, this distinction had become such
an article of merchandise that Messalina, the wife of the emperor,
is said to have openly sold it, at first for a large sum, and at last
for a trifle.

dash to the ground the uplifted instruments of torture
under the simple declaration, " I am a Roman citizen."

6. Paul is Brought Before the Sanhedrin,
xxii. 30—xxiii. 10.

Ver. 30. The chiliarch was disposed to do his duty
by the prisoner thrown fortuitously into his hands, but
he was puzzled to know what his duty was. He had
first inquired of the mob ; then he had listened to a
speech from Paul; then he had gone as far as he dared
toward the trial by scourging; yet he knew nothing
more about the charges than he did at first. He determined to make one more effort. (30) **But on the morrow, desiring to know the certainty, wherefore he was
accused of the Jews, he loosed him, and commanded the
chief priests and all the council to come together, and
brought Paul down, and set him before them.** This
meeting was held in the Gentile court, if anywhere about
the temple ; for Lysias and his soldiers would not have
been admitted within the Jewish court; and to this agree
the words " he brought Paul down," seeing that the
tower of Antonia, in which the soldiers were quartered,
stood at a higher elevation than this court (see under
xxi. 31–34).

Vv. 1, 2. No sooner had the prisoner and his accusers met face to face than the chiliarch must have suspected another disappointment ; for, instead of preferring
formal charges against Paul, they required him to speak
first. (1) **And Paul, looking steadfastly on the council,
said, Brethren, I have lived before God in all good conscience until this day. (2) And the high priest Ananias
commanded them that stood by him to smite him on the
mouth.** No doubt the blow was as prompt as the word.

Ananias affected to regard it as an insult to the council
for a man who was arraigned before them as a criminal
of the deepest dye to proudly declare that he had lived
in all good conscience before God. To smite him in the
mouth for it, was much easier than to disprove it. To
us Paul's remark is most credible, and the only question
is, Did he intend it to cover the period before his conversion, when he was persecuting the church, or only the
period within which the Jews condemned him? It certainly covered the latter; and a later statement, that he
verily thought he ought to do many things contrary to
the name of Jesus (xxvi. 9), makes it probable that he
had the former also in mind.

Vv. 3–5. The interruption, so unexpected and so
exasperating, called forth from Paul a burst of indignation similar to that with which he had long ago denounced Bar-jesus in the presence of Sergius Paulus
(xiii. 10). (3) **Then said Paul unto him, God shall smite
thee, thou whited wall: and sittest thou to judge me according to the law, and commandest me to be smitten
contrary to the law?** (4) **And they that stood by said,
Revilest thou God's high priest?** (5) **And Paul said, I
knew not, brethren, that he was high priest: for it is
written, Thou shalt not speak evil of a ruler of thy people.**
This remark was not an outburst of improper passion.
It was rather an angry expression of a righteous judgment
as to how God would deal with a man so unjust and
hypocritical. It was an incident like that in the experience of our Lord, when he looked around " with anger "
on a similar set of men, and then immediately did the
act which they held to be a sin (Mark iii. 5). It was, in
Paul's own phraseology, to " be angry, and sin not "
(Eph. iv. 26). When told, however, that it was the high

priest whom he had thus denounced, Paul at once admitted, not that the rebuke was unjust, but that it would have been improper to so address this dignitary, had he known who he was. And here is a proper distinction. A rebuke which is perfectly just and right in itself may be improper on account of the official relations of the person addressed. Had Paul known that Ananias was the high priest, and had he been left to himself without the guidance of the Holy Spirit promised for such occasions (Matt. x. 17–20), he would have withheld the rebuke; and the world would have been the loser; for rebukes like this help to strengthen the moral sense of men. He knew not Ananias personally, for he was not the Ananias of the Gospels, but a new usurper of the high priesthood; and it is certain that on this occasion he wore no robe or badge to indicate his office, or Paul could not have failed to know his position. The fact that he presided on this occasion did not show it, because the high priest was not always present at meetings of the sanhedrim, and especially at meetings called unexpectedly, as this one was. This Ananias was one of the worst men who ever wore the robes of a high priest. His career of crime and extortion, fully set forth in various chapters of Josephus, finally ended in assassination.

Vv. 6–10. The presence in which Paul stood was not unfamiliar to him. He doubtless remembered the faces of many in the council, and he was intimately acquainted with the party feuds which often distracted their deliberations. He knew that the chief instigators of the persecution were the Sadducees, as they had been at the beginning; and he determined to enlist, if possible, the Pharisees in his own behalf; so we read: (6) **But when Paul perceived that the one part were Sad-**

ducees, and the other Pharisees, he cried out in the
council, Brethren, I am a Pharisee, a son of Pharisees:
touching the hope and resurrection of the dead, I am
called in question. (7) And when he had so said, there
arose a dissension between the Pharisees and the Sadducees : and the assembly was divided. (8) For the Sadducees say that there is no resurrection, neither angel,
nor spirit; but the Pharisees confess both. (9) And there
arose a great clamor : and some of the scribes of the
Pharisees' part stood up, and strove, saying, We find no
evil in this man: and what if a spirit hath spoken to
him, or an angel ? (10) And when there arose a great
dissension, the chief captain, fearing lest Paul should be
torn in pieces by them, commanded the soldiers to go
down and take him by force from among them, and bring
him into the castle. Paul's declaration that he was a
Pharisee has been treated by some writers as deceptive;
and he has been censured for stirring up such a row
among his enemies. The charge is unfounded;[1] for while
it is true that he was not in every particular a Pharisee,
he was one in the sense attached to his remark by his
hearers. All present knew that he was a Christian, and
consequently they knew that he claimed to be a Pharisee only in the sense of agreeing with that party in their

---

[1] Farrar indulges in this censure. He says: "His belief in
the risen Messiah was *not* the point on which he was mainly being called in question." "Did not then the words of the apostle
suggest a false issue ?" "Had he a right to inflame an existing
animosity ? And could he worthily say, I am a Pharisee ?"
"Was there not the least little touch of a *suggestio falsi* in what
he said ?" These insinuations are sufficiently answered above;
and it is worthy of note that Farrar does not repeat them in connection with the same declarations of Paul made before king
Agrippa (xxvi. 6–8), and before the unbelieving Jews in Rome
(xxviii. 20).

points of antagonism with the Sadducees. His statement, that it was touching the hope of the resurrection
that he was called in question, must be understood with
the same qualification.   All knew that this was not the
immediate cause of his arrest; but all knew equally well
that this was the ultimate ground of the hatred of him
by the Sadducees.   Both remarks were strictly true in
the sense attached to them, and this sense was distinctly
perceived by both parties.   As to the row which followed, there is no evidence that Paul aimed at or expected such violence.   He aimed at enlisting the sympathy
of the Pharisees, in the hope of securing a more just consideration of his own cause; and he doubtless desired a
more peaceable procedure; but for the violence which
followed he was not responsible.   And even if he had
anticipated all that followed, it would seem too great a
refinement of moral distinctions to blame him: as well
blame a man for putting two bulldogs at each other's
ears to keep them from devouring him.

The more surprising circumstance in the proceedings
is that some of the Pharisees (not all) were so quickly
turned in Paul's favor.   But the whole council were in
an awkward predicament.   They were called together by
the chiliarch, to show cause why they and their followers
had clamored so for the death of Paul, and they knew
themselves utterly unable to render a reason that would
appear even plausible to the mind of this heathen officer.
It was for this cause that, instead of preferring charges
against Paul at the beginning of the proceedings, they
had required him to speak first.   All must have felt
anxious for some turn in the affair which would relieve
them of their embarrassment; and when Paul boldly proclaimed that he was a Pharisee, the shrewder men of that

party saw at once that this was their chance to slip out
and leave the Sadducees in the mire. The latter were
exasperated by the trick, and thus the row came on. The
trick was the more exasperating, because the speaker for
the Pharisees pointed his arrow with the intimation that
Paul may have heard the voice of an angel or a spirit,
the very existence of whom the Sadducees denied. It is
not necessary to suppose that the Pharisees thought it
probable that an angel or a spirit had spoken to Paul;
for if they were known as not believing any such thing,
this only poisoned with irony the shaft which they
hurled at the Sadducees.

In Luke's remark, that while the Sadducees say there
is no resurrection, neither angel nor spirit, the Pharisees confess both, we should naturally expect him to
say all three, instead of both; but he doubtless included
in the thought of angels and spirits the single idea of
beings without fleshly bodies.

Lysias was once more disappointed in his efforts
to learn the truth about Paul's case; but he certainly
learned that his enemies had no charge against him
which they were willing to formulate.

7. PAUL IS ENCOURAGED BY A VISION, 11.

VER. 11. If we had an epistle from Paul's pen
written at this time, it would probably speak of great
distress and despondency; for such a state of mind is
clearly implied in the incident next mentioned. (11)
**And the night following the Lord stood by him, and said,
Be of good cheer: for as thou hast testified concerning me
at Jerusalem, so must thou bear witness also at Rome.**
Such words of cheer from the Lord himself are not
spoken except when they are greatly needed; and this

makes it certain that Paul was sorely troubled in spirit
that night. Well he might be. The bonds and affliction
which had been predicted all along his journey from Corinth to Jerusalem had now befallen him, and it was not
apparent whether the earnest prayers which he and
others in his behalf had offered to God, that he might be
delivered from those who were disobedient in Jerusalem,
were to be granted. Outside the prison he could hope
for nothing but death, and inside there was no field of
usefulness. In whatever direction he could look, prison
walls or a bloody death confronted him, and hedged his
way. At this opportune moment he was cheered by the
first ray of light in regard to his future; and though
it was impossible for him to conjecture as yet how it was
to be brought about, he had the assurance that in the
Lord's own way and time he should yet escape the
present danger, and preach the gospel in Rome.

8. A Conspiracy Formed and Exposed, 12–22.

Vv. 12–16. Notwithstanding the gleam of hope
granted to Paul in the night, his prospects grew darker
than ever the next morning. (12) And when it was day,
the Jews banded together, and bound themselves under a
curse, saying that they would neither eat nor drink until
they had killed Paul. (13) And they were more than
forty who made this conspiracy. (14) And they came to
the chief priests and the elders, and said, We have bound
ourselves under a great curse, to taste nothing until
we have killed Paul. (15) Now therefore do ye with
the council signify to the chief captain that he bring him
down unto you, as though ye would judge of his case
more exactly: and we, or ever he come near, are ready
to slay him. (16) But Paul's sister's son heard of their

lying in wait, and he came and entered into the castle, and told Paul. (17) And Paul called unto him one of the centurions, and said, Bring this young man unto the chief captain : for he hath something to tell him. (18) So he took him and brought him to the chief captain, and saith, Paul the prisoner called me unto him, and asked me to bring this young man unto thee, who hath something to say to thee. (19) And the chief captain took him by the hand, and going aside asked him privately, What is that thou hast to tell me ? (20) And he said, The Jews have agreed to ask thee to bring down Paul to-morrow unto the council, as though thou wouldst inquire somewhat more exactly concerning him. (21) Do not thou therefore yield unto them : for there lie in wait for him of them more than forty men, who have bound themselves under a curse, neither to eat nor drink till they have slain him : and now are they ready, looking for the promise from thee. (22) So the chief captain let the young man go, charging him, Tell no man that thou hast signified these things to me. It is difficult to imagine the malignity which animated these conspirators, both the prime movers in it, and the priests and elders who gave it their sanction. The latter classes were of course Sadducees who had been enraged by the proceedings of the previous day, whilst the former were desperate roughs of the city. Their scheme, if left unexposed, would almost certainly have been successful ; for Lysias, in his perplexity, would have gladly complied with their request ; and as the prisoner was led along the narrow street, or along the pavement of the great court, it would have been easy for forty desperate men, having chosen their position in advance, to have rushed in among the unsuspecting soldiers, and slain Paul before a blow could have

been struck in his defense. But a conspiracy so desperate, known to so many persons, and aimed against a man
concerning whom the whole community was excited to a
white heat, could not well be kept secret. It leaked into
the ears of some of Paul's friends, and this nephew, who
for some unknown cause was in the city, was charged with
the hazardous task of revealing it to Paul and to the
chiliarch. The young man trembled no doubt when he
was ushered into the presence of the Roman officer; but
Lysias, with kindly consideration, reassured him by taking his hand and leading him aside, that he might deliver
his message in secret. Then, fearing for the young
man's life if his act should become known, and desiring to keep hid from the conspirators the cause of the
move on which he at once determined, he dismissed him
with a charge of the strictest secresy.

9. PAUL IS REMOVED TO CÆSAREA, 23–30.

Vv. 23–30. On receiving this information, Lysias
had at least three lines of policy between which to choose.
Had he been disposed to gratify the Jews, he might have
permitted them to carry out their plot without probability of being known to his superiors as accessory to the
murder. Had he preferred to defy their power and display his own, he might have sent Paul down under a
guard so strong and so instructed that they would have
slain the conspirators. Or if he desired to protect Paul,
and to avoid offense to the Jews and bloodshed, he might
send him away that night before their request had been
laid before him. It reflects credit on his military skill,
and on his character as a man, that he chose the course
which both justice and prudence dictated. (23) **And he
called unto him two of the centurions, and said, Make**

ready two hundred soldiers to go as far as Cæsarea, and horsemen three score and ten, and spearmen two hundred, at the third hour of the night : (24) and he bade them provide beasts, that they might set Paul thereon and bring him safe unto Felix the governor. (25) And he wrote a letter after this form :

(26) Claudius Lysias, unto the most excellent governor Felix, greeting. (27) This man was seized by the Jews, and was about to be slain by them, when I came upon them with the soldiers, and rescued him, having learned that he was a Roman. (28) And desiring to know the cause wherefore they accused him, I brought him down unto their council : (29) whom I found to be accused about questions of their law, but to have nothing laid to his charge worthy of death or of bonds. (30) And when it was shown to me that there would be a plot against the man, I sent him to thee forthwith, charging his accusers also to speak against him before thee. But for one slight misrepresentation in this letter, there would be nothing in the whole procedure of Lysias discreditable to him. He had acted like a just and prudent man ; but in reporting to his superior he so stated the facts as to give himself credit for rescuing Paul because he was a Roman citizen ; whereas he had only learned this fact when he was about to scourge him. The statement that he had commanded Paul's accusers to appear before Felix, though not absolutely true at the moment it was written, he intended to make true before the letter could be read ; consequently it was not intended to deceive. The letter also shows that, although he did not understand the nature of the charge against Paul, he had learned enough to know that he was not accused of anything criminal. Under this conviction, he would soon

have released him but for the plot of the Jews, and so, as they must have learned afterward, the conspiracy over-reached itself, and really caused their intended victim to slip out of their hands. The sound judgment and pru-dence of Lysias was still farther shown by the fact of his sending so strong a body of troops with Paul as to prevent bloodshed even had his movement been discov-ered by the Jews, because the guard was too formidable to be attacked by an unarmed mob.

10. PAUL IS DELIVERED TO FELIX, 31–35.

Vv. 31-35. The centurion in command executed his commission with judgment and fidelity. (31) **So the soldiers, as it was commanded them, took Paul, and brought him by night to Antipatris. (32) But on the morrow they left the horsemen to go with him, and re-turned to the castle: (33) and they, when they came to Cæsarea, and delivered the letter to the governor, pre-sented Paul also before him. (34) And when he had read it, he asked of what province he was; and when he un-derstood that he was of Cilicia, (35) I will hear thy cause, said he, when thine accusers also are come: and he com-manded him to be kept in Herod's palace.** Antipatris was reached after decending from the mountains of Ephraim into the plain of Sharon, where its ruins have been identified at the source of the river Aujeh.[1] It was

---

[1] The place is called *Ras el Ain* (*Promontory of the Spring*), from the large body of water which rises out of the ground under its northern and western sides and forms the river Aujeh. The top of the hill is crowned with the ruins of a large castle built by the crusaders, and the place is known to represent Antipatris, be-cause the latter is represented by Josephus to be in the plain, close to the hills, with a river encompassing it (*Antiq* xvi. 5. 2), and this is the only ruin answering to the description. It is

about half way between Jerusalem and Cæsarea, and about thirty miles from either place. As the rapid march through the night had brought the little army beyond all possible danger of attack from Jerusalem, the seventy horsemen were a sufficient guard the rest of the way. To Paul, unaccustomed to riding on horseback, this long and rapid ride through a whole night was doubtless very fatiguing It is not quite certain for what reason Felix inquired as to Paul's province. It may have been from natural curiosity ; or it may have been with the purpose of sending him to the governor of his province, if it should be one near by ; but when he learned that it was Cilicia, accessible only by sea, he did not hesitate to keep him in his own hands. It seems that Herod's palace, more properly prætorium, in which Paul was now kept under guard, had a guard-room in it for the confinement of such prisoners.

SEC. II.   PAUL'S IMPRISONMENT IN CÆSAREA.

(XXIV. 1—XXVI. 32.)

1. He is Accused Before Felix, 1–9.

Ver. 1. When the Jews of Jerusalem were commanded by Lysias to present their accusations against Paul before Felix, though they had been bitterly disappointed by the miscarriage of their plot, they still hoped

----

11½ miles from Lydda, and 30¼ from Cæsarea. " From it," says Conder (Tent-Work in Palestine), " the stream flows rapidly away westward, burrowing between deep banks, and rolling to the sea, a yellow, turbid, sandy volume of water, unfordable in winter, and never dry, even in summer."

to secure his death, and they followed up the prosecution without delay. (1) **And after five days the high priest Ananias came down with certain elders, and with an orator, one Tertullus; and they informed the governor against Paul.** It is most natural, in counting these five days, to suppose that they extended from the next day after Paul left Jerusalem, which was the day on which they received notice from Lysias, till their arrival in Cæsarea. Tertullus was a Roman, as his name indicates, and they brought him, as a paid attorney, because they now had to appear in a regular Roman court, and they must have a man familiar with the proceedings in such a court to represent them.

Vv. 2-9. The formal proceedings were opened, very much as in our modern courts, by a speech from the prosecuting attorney, presenting the accusation; and this was followed by the testimony of the witnesses for the plaintiff. (2) **And when he was called, Tertullus began to accuse him, saying,**

Seeing that by thee we enjoy much peace, and that by thy providence evils are corrected for this nation, (3) we accept it in all ways, and in all places, most excellent Felix, with all thankfulness. (4) But that I be not further tedious unto thee, I intreat thee to hear us of thy clemency a few words. (5) For we have found this man a pestilent fellow, and a mover of insurrection among all the Jews throughout the world, and a ringleader of the sect of the Nazarenes: (6) who moreover assayed to profane the temple; on whom also we laid hold: (8) from whom thou wilt be able, by examining him thyself, to take knowledge of all these things, whereof we accuse him. (9) And the Jews also joined in the charge, affirming that these things were so. While Felix was guilty of much corruption in his administration of affairs, the complimentary words with which Tertullus opened his speech were not undeserved; for he had restored tranquility to the country when it was disturbed, first, by bands of robbers; second, by organized assassins; and lastly, by that Egyptian for whom Lysias at first mistook Paul (xxi. 38).

The accusation against Paul was the general one of being a " pestilent fellow," and the specifications under this charge were three; first, that he had excited the Jews in many places to insurrections; second, that he was a ringleader of the sect of the Nazarenes; and third, that he had attempted to profane the temple. Any one of these specifications, sustained, would sustain the charge; and Tertullus closed by affirming that Felix could find proof of them all by examining Paul himself —a hint of the examination by scourging, which Paul had escaped, Tertullus knew not how, at the hands of Lysias. The witnesses supported the charges by affirming that these things were so.

2. PAUL'S DEFENSE, 10–21.

Vv. 10–21. Paul was now required, without previous notification of the charges, and without a moment for premeditation, to make his defense against an accusation which, if sustained in the judgment of the court, would have cost him his life. Without a single witness to support his representations, he could rely only upon the self-evident truthfulness of what he might say; but he had the support of the words of Jesus: "Settle it therefore in your hearts, not to meditate beforehand how to answer: for I will give you a mouth and wisdom, which all your adversaries shall not be able to withstand or

gainsay " (Luke xxi. 15). On this assurance he could
and did rely. (10) And when the governor had beckoned
unto him to speak, Paul answered,

Forasmuch as I know that thou hast been of many
years a judge unto this nation,[1] I do cheerfully make
my defense: (11) seeing that thou canst take knowledge, that it is not more than twelve days since I
went up to worship at Jerusalem: (12) and neither in
the temple did they find me disputing with any man,
or stirring up a crowd, nor in the synagogues, nor in the
city. (13) Neither can they prove to thee the things
whereof they now accuse me. (14) But this I confess
unto thee, that after the Way which they call a sect, so
serve I the God of our fathers, believing all things which
are according to the law, and which are written in the
prophets: (15) having hope toward God, which these also
themselves look for, that there shall be a resurrection
both of the just and unjust. (16) Herein do I also exercise myself to have a conscience void of offense toward
God and men alway. (17) Now after many years[2] I
came to bring alms to my nation, and offerings: (18)
amidst which they found me purified in the temple, with
no crowd, nor yet with tumult: but there were certain
Jews from Asia (19) who ought to have been here before
thee, and to make accusation, if they had aught against
me. (20) Or else let these men themselves say what
wrong-doing they found, when I stood before the council,

---

[1] He was now in the seventh year of his procuratorship of
Judea. This was " many years," in comparison with those of his
predecessors in the same office.

[2] If we omit, as we have done, the visit supposed by many to
be referred to in xviii. 22, he had not been in the city since
the visit of chapter xv., which was eight years previous. See
Chronology, Intr. xxvii, xxix.

(21) except it be for this one voice, that I cried standing among them, Touching the resurrection of the dead I am called in question before you this day.

This speech contains a direct reply to every specification made by Tertullus. The statement that it was only twelve days since he went up to Jerusalem, answers the charge of stirring up sedition, at least in that city; for as he had been away from there five days, and was in prison there one, this left only six, which were insufficient for such movements. Moreover, he had not engaged in disputation with any one, in the temple, in the synagogues, or in any part of the city. As to being a ringleader of the sect of the Nazarenes, without alluding to the title ringleader he admits that he belongs to the sect so-called, yet he believes all the law and the prophets, hopes for a resurrection of the dead, and leads a conscientious life. Finally, the statement that, when found in the temple by certain Jews from Asia, he was purified as the law required, and that he was engaged about almsgiving and the offerings of the temple, refuted the charge of profaning the temple (xxi. 28), now changed into *attempting* to profane it (6). In conclusion, he notes the significant fact, that those who first seized him, and who were the only personal witnesses of what he did in the temple, were not present to testify; and then he calls upon Ananias and the elders, who witnessed only what was done in the Sanhedrin, to testify as to any wrong doing there, unless it was that remark in reference to being a Pharisee, which had set Ananias and his friends in a fierce quarrel with the rest of the elders. He makes this last reference, not because he was conscious of wrong in the matter, but in order to taunt his

Sadducee accusers, and to show Felix that they were moved against him by party jealousy.

3. The Case Continued, 22, 23.

Vv. 22, 23. As Paul's defense consisted in nothing but his own statements, it was doubtless a surprise to both him and his accusers, that Felix virtually decided in his favor. **(22) But Felix, having more exact knowledge concerning the Way, deferred them, saying, When Lysias the chief captain shall come down, I will determine your matter. (23) And he gave order to the centurion that he should be kept in charge, and should have indulgence; and not to forbid any of his friends to minister unto him.** This decision is ascribed to his having more accurate knowledge of the Way, by which we are to understand, not that he had just acquired such knowledge from Paul's speech, for it contained very little information on this point, but that Felix had already more exact knowledge than to be deceived by the representations of the Sadducees. Having been in Judea now for six years more, he had been compelled, whether willing or not, to become acquainted with the religious parties into which his subjects were divided, and he well knew the jealousies which existed among them. The reason which he gave for postponing a decision in the case was a mere subterfuge, as must have been apparent to the Sadducees. Paul's confinement was now the least irksome that was consistent with safe keeping.

4. Paul Preaches to Felix and Drusilla, 24–27.

Ver. 24. The freedom which Paul enjoyed of receiving his friends not only left open to him the fraternal visits of Philip and other brethren who lived in Cæsarea, but also gave him opportunity to preach the gospel to any unbelievers who might be induced to hear him. It may have been his activity in this work that led to the incident next related. (24) **But after certain days Felix came with Drusilla, his wife, who was a Jewess, and sent for Paul, and heard him concerning the faith in Christ Jesus.** The word "came" indicates either that he had been absent from the city and returned to it, or that he came from his usual place of residence to an apartment in Herod's prætorium where Paul was kept. Drusilla, as we learn from Josephus, was a daughter of Herod Agrippa, who murdered the apostle James, and miserably perished soon afterward (xii. 1, 2; 20–23). She was but six years old when her father perished, and as that was in the year 44, and her present appearance in our narrative was in 58, she was now only twenty. She had been given in marriage at an early age to Aziz, king of Emesa; but Felix, having seen her and become enamored of her beauty, had, through the machinations of a sorcerer named Simon, induced her to abandon her husband and come to him, so she was now living in open adultery with Felix.[1] Concerning Felix it is asserted by Tacitus, one of the most judicious and fair-minded of Roman historians, that "with every kind of cruelty and lust, he exercised the authority of a king with the temper of a slave."[2] He and his brother Pallas had actually been slaves in the household of Agrippina, the mother of the emperor Claudius, and by the latter he had been sent from the position of a slave to that of ruler over a province.

---

[1] Josephus, *Antiquities*, xx. 7. 2.

[2] "Antonius Felix, per omnem sævitiam et libidinem, jus regium servili ingenio exercuit" (History, v. 9).

VER. 25. Under the summons to speak concerning the faith in Christ, Paul was at liberty to choose for himself the special topic of discourse, and he did so with direct reference to the spiritual wants of his hearers. (25) **And as he reasoned of righteousness, and temperance, and the judgment to come, Felix was terrified, and answered, Go thy way, for this time ; and when I have a convenient season, I will call thee unto me.** Nothing could be more terrifying than to speak of righteousness to a man of such iniquity ; of temperance in all things to a man of such unbridled lust ; or to drive home what was said on these topics by depicting the judgment to come. I here adopt the burning words of Farrar : " As he glanced back over the stained and guilty past, he was afraid. He had been a slave in the vilest of all positions, at the vilest of all epochs, in the vilest of all cities. He had crept with his brother Pallas into the position of a courtier at the most morally degraded of all courts. He had been an officer of those auxiliaries who were the worst of all troops. What secrets of lust and blood lay hidden in his earlier life we do not know ; but ample and indisputable testimony, Jewish and Pagan, sacred and secular, reveals to us what he had been—how greedy, how savage, how treacherous, how unjust, how steeped in the blood of private murder and public massacre— during the eight years which he had now spent in the government, first of Samaria, then of Palestine. There were footsteps behind him ; he began to feel as though 'the earth were made of glass'" (Life of Paul, 550). The terror which seized him was the beginning necessary to a change of life ; but lust and ambition smothered the kindling fires of conscience, and he made the common excuse of alarmed but impenitent sinners to get rid of his too faithful monitor. The "convenient season" to which he deferred the matter, never came, and it never could come: for how could it ever be convenient for a man to put away a beautiful woman with whom he was living in sin, and to radically revolutionize the whole course of his previous life? This change must be made at a sacrifice of much convenience and much pride by every wicked man who makes it. How Drusilla was affected we are not told; but it is scarcely possible that she was more composed than the hardened Felix.

Vv. 26, 27. Felix maintained the character in which Tacitus paints him to the very last. (26) He hoped, withal, that money would be given him of Paul: wherefore also he sent for him the oftener, and communed with him. (27) But when two years were fulfilled, Felix was succeeded by Porcius Festus; and desiring to gain favor with the Jews, Felix left Paul in bonds. From having incidentally learned, through Paul's speech at his trial, that he had been up to Jerusalem to bear alms from distant churches, and knowing, besides, the general liberality of the disciples toward one another in distress, he had not a doubt that Paul could raise a large sum to secure his release from imprisonment, and that it would be forthcoming on the merest hint that it would be accepted. Undoubtedly, had Paul thought it right to obtain release in this way, the money would have been in hand soon; for what would not his brethren have given to relieve him from the ignominy of imprisonment, and to set him free in apostolic usefulness. But bribe-giving is next in turpitude to bribe-taking, and Paul could be no party to a crime.

The removal of Felix was brought about by accusations of misgovernment preferred against him by the

Jews. He was called to Rome by Nero to answer for
his crimes, and, barely escaping execution, he was banished into Gaul, where he died. Drusilla clung to him
in his failing fortunes; but a son whom she bore to him,
and who was named Agrippa, after her brother, perished
in the eruption of Mt. Vesuvius, which engulfed the
cities of Pompeii and Herculaneum.[1]

These two years of imprisonment in Cæsarea, if we
may judge from the silence of history, were the most inactive of Paul's career. There are no epistles which
bear this date; and though his brethren and others had
free access to him, we have no recorded effects of their
interviews with him. The only moments in which he
emerges into view are those in which he appears before his judges.

5. Paul's Trial before Festus, xxv. 1–12.

Vv. 1–5. The long imprisonment of Paul seems
not in the least to have moderated the hatred of his
enemies; so, on the change of governors, they renewed
their efforts for his destruction. (1) Festus therefore,
having come into the province, after three days, went
up to Jerusalem from Cæsarea. (2) And the chief priests
and the principal men of the Jews informed him against
Paul; (3) and they besought him, asking favor against
him, that he would send for him to Jerusalem; laying
wait to kill him on the way. (4) Howbeit Festus
answered, that Paul was kept in charge at Cæsarea, and
that he himself was about to depart thither shortly. (5)
Let them therefore, saith he, who are of power among
you, go down with me, and if there is anything amiss
in the man, let them accuse him. He also told them, as

---

[1] Josephus, *Ant.* xx. 7. 2.

we learn from a later speech (16), that it was contrary to Roman law to condemn a man before he had an opportunity for defense, face to face with his accusers. All this shows that Festus was disposed to act justly. He of course knew nothing then of the plot to waylay Paul.

Vv. 6-8. He made no delay in granting them the promised hearing. (6) **And when he had tarried among them not more than eight or ten days, he went down unto Cæsarea ; and on the morrow he sat on the judgment-seat, and commanded Paul to be brought.** (7) **And when he was come, the Jews who had come down from Jerusalem stood round about him, bringing against him many and grievous charges, which they could not prove ;** (8) **while Paul said in his defense, Neither against the law of the Jews, nor against the temple, nor against Cæsar, have I sinned at all.** The specifications which Paul makes in his defense are the same as in his defense against the charges preferred by Tertullus before Felix (xxiv. 10–21), showing that the charges were also the same. Being a "ringleader of the sect of the Nazarenes" was his sin against the law ; attempting to profane the temple, his sin against the holy place ; and the incitement of insurrections among the Jews, his sin against Cæsar. In the last specification, reference was had to the mobs which the Jews were in the habit of stirring up against him, whose crimes were thus charged upon him.

VER. 9. As the accusers were not able to prove their charges (7), and the prisoner pleaded "not guilty" to every one of them, he should have been unconditionally released ; but Festus, at this point, allowed his sense of justice to be biased by his desire for popularity. (9) **But Festus, desiring to gain favor with the Jews, answered Paul, and said, Wilt thou go up to Jerusalem, and there** be judged of these things before me ? As Cæsarea was the seat of government for the province, he had no right to order the trial of a citizen elsewhere ; hence the inquiry whether Paul was willing to be tried in Jerusalem. It is probable that he knew nothing of the plot mentioned in verse 3, but he must have known that the petition of the Jews that Paul be carried to Jerusalem for trial, was prompted by some sinister motive, and he should have rejected it without hesitation.

Vv. 10–12. The purpose of the Jews was well understood by Paul. He had not forgotten the vow of the forty conspirators, and, although they must have broken their vow in breaking their fast before this time (xxiii. 12, 13), this made them only the more determined to kill him, if they could. Fortunately, his very imprisonment, which exposed him to this new danger, furnished him the means of escaping it, and in the resolution which he instantly formed he saw a glimpse, at last, of Rome. (10) But Paul said, I am standing before Cæsar's judgment-seat, where I ought to be judged ; to the Jews have I done no wrong, as thou also very well knowest. (11) If, then, I am a wrong-doer, and have committed anything worthy of death, I refuse not to die ; but if none of those things is true, whereof these accuse me, no man can give me up unto them. I appeal unto Cæsar. (12) Then Festus, when he had conferred with the council, answered, Thou hast appealed unto Cæsar ; unto Cæsar shalt thou go. The statement, " I stand at Cæsar's judgment-seat, where I ought to be judged," was his protest against being sent to Jerusalem ; and his declaration that Festus knew that he had done the Jews no wrong, was based upon the developments of the trial. The appeal to Cæsar, which was the right of every Roman

citizen, required the judge before whom the appeal was
made to instantly suspend proceedings in the case, and
to send the prisoner, together with his accusers, to Rome,
that the case might be adjudged by the imperial court.
In Paul's case, this appeal was not a call upon a military
power by a free man for protection, but a demand made
upon the military power which held him in unjust confinement, not to add to this injustice that of exposing
him to assassination. The answer of Festus betrays
some bitterness of feeling, the natural effect of the reproach implied in the appeal, and at the same time it
hints at the inconvenience to which Paul would himself
be subjected by it. It subjected him to being sent to
Rome as a prisoner under a military guard, and to all the
delay which might attend the coming of the witnesses to
testify against him, as well as that often resulting from the
dilatoriness of the imperial court itself. This inconvenience deterred citizens from making the appeal except
in extreme cases.

6. Paul's Case Stated to King Agrippa, 13–22.

VER. 13. The custom among princes of extending
congratulations to those of like rank who are newly appointed in neighboring provinces, led to the next recorded incident of Paul's confinement. (13) Now when
certain days were passed, Agrippa the king and Bernice
arrived at Cæsarea, and saluted Festus. This Agrippa
was the only son of the Herod who had murdered the
apostle James (xii. 1, 2). He was only seventeen years
old when his father died, and, being thought too young
for the government of his father's dominions, he was
made by the emperor king of Chalcis, a small district
east of the Jordan. He was now thirty-one years of

age. Bernice was his sister, and like the younger sister, Drusilla, she was remarkable for her beauty. She had been the wife of her own uncle, the former king of Chalcis, but she was now a widow, and living with her brother.[1]

Vv. 14–21. Festus knew that the charges against Paul had reference to the Jewish law, but he was still very much in the dark as to their exact nature; and as he was now under the necessity of sending a statement of them to the emperor, he determined to seek for light by appealing to Agrippa's more intimate knowledge of Jewish affairs. (14) And as they tarried there many days, Festus laid Paul's case before the king, saying, There is a certain man left a prisoner by Felix; (15) about whom, when I was at Jerusalem, the chief priests and the elders of the Jews informed me, asking for sentence against him. (16) To whom I answered, that it is not the custom of the Romans to give up any man before that the accused have the accusers face to face, and have had opportunity to make his defense concerning the matter laid against him. (17) When, therefore, they were come together here, I made no delay, but on the next day sat down on the judgment seat, and commanded the man to be brought. (18) Concerning whom, when the accusers stood up, they brought no charge of such evil things as I supposed; (19) but had certain questions against him of their own demon-worship,[2] and of one Jesus, who was dead, whom Paul affirmed to be alive. (20) And I, being perplexed how to inquire concerning these things, asked whether he would go to Jerusalem,

---

[1] Josephus, *Ant.* **xx.** 7. 3.

[2] For a justification of this rendering, see remarks under xvii. **18. 23.**

and there be judged of these matters. (21) But when
Paul had appealed to be kept for the decision of the emperor, I commanded him to be kept till I should send him
to Cæsar. From this speech we learn the exact conception which Festus had thus far formed of Paul's case.
He had discovered that Paul contended for the worship,
with divine honors, of Jesus, a man who was dead; and
as this, to the mind of a Greek or a Roman, was demon-
worship, he so styles it here. He supposed that the
Jews, like other nations, were accustomed to such worship, and consequently that the dispute between them
and Paul was over the question whether they should
worship Jesus in common with other demons. His ignorance of the religious ideas of the Jews, and his still
more susprising ignorance about Jesus, whom he styles
" one Jesus," as though he had never heard of him before, shows that, like most politicians in that day as in
our own, he had made no study of religious questions.
Agrippa must have smiled at his ignorance.

VER. 22. This could not have been the first time
that Agrippa had heard of either Paul or Jesus. Being
the son of the Herod who tried to suppress the Christian
faith by killing the apostle James, and imprisoning
Peter with the purpose of killing him; a nephew of the
Herod who had killed John the Baptist, and mocked
Jesus on the day of his crucifixion; and a great grandson of the one who attempted to kill Jesus in his cradle
at Bethlehem, the names of Jesus and his apostles had
been household words in his family for generations back.
The name of Paul was doubtless less familiar than those
of the original apostles, but of him he could not have
been ignorant. He would not have deigned, as would
none of his ancestors, to visit a congregation for the

purpose of hearing an apostle ; but in the privacy of the pretorium in which Paul was a prisoner he could gratify his curiosity by hearing him, and at the same time render some assistance to Festus. (22) **And Agrippa said unto Festus, I also could wish to hear the man myself. To-morrow, saith he, thou shalt hear him.** The proposal pleased Festus, because of the information which he hoped to obtain, and also, perhaps, because it provided another day's entertainment for his royal guests.

8. Paul's Case Publicly Stated, 23–27.

VER. 23. Without intending to honor Paul, but rather to suitably entertain his royal guests, Festus provided for Paul the most magnificent audience, from a worldly point of view, that he had ever been permitted to address. (23) **So on the morrow, when Agrippa was come, and Bernice, with great pomp, and they were entered into the place of hearing, with the chief captains, and the principal men of the city, at the command of Festus Paul was brought in.** If the officer who was sent for Paul had told him that king Agrippa wanted him brought out that he might behead him, as his father had beheaded James, he would probably have been but little surprised. But who can imagine his surprise when told that this scion of the Herod family desired to hear him preach? Could it be true that the gulf between Christ and this bloodiest of all the families which had stood against him since the beginning, was so nearly bridged over that one of them, and he a king, really desired to hear the gospel? This question must have flashed upon Paul's mind, as he made hasty preparation to appear before the splendid audience awaiting him. The bare possibility of winning a Herod over to the

cause of Christ must have thrilled his soul, and stirred
him up to an effort worthy of the auspicious occasion.
He began to feel almost repaid for two years of confinement, by the privilege now afforded him. For the first
time, and perhaps the last, an apostle stood face to face
with a Herod, unless James had enjoyed that privilege
just before he was beheaded.

Vv. 24–27. The proceedings were conducted with
all the dignity and formality suited to so august an audience. (24) And Festus saith, King Agrippa, and
all men who are here present with us, ye behold this
man, about whom all the multitude of the Jews made suit
to me, both at Jerusalem and here, crying that he ought
not to live any longer. (25) But I found that he had
committed nothing worthy of death ; and as he himself
appealed to the emperor, I determined to send him. (26)
Of whom I have no certain thing to write unto my Lord.
Wherefore I have brought him forth before you, and especially before thee, king Agrippa, that, after examination had, I may have somewhat to write. (27) For it
seemeth to me unreasonable, in sending a prisoner, not
withal to signify the charges against him. This was a
very candid confession, before a brilliant audience, of his
heathenish ignorance concerning a faith which had been
propagated in every part of the Roman empire, and had
established itself even in the imperial city of Rome.
There were probably many in the audience besides
Agrippa who were surprised at such ignorance ; for it is
scarcely possible that the " chief men of the city " who
were present, and even some of the chiliarchs under his
own command, did not understand the position of Paul.
But all could see that Festus was in a bad predicament,
in having held as a prisoner a man who was entitled to

his liberty, until, now that he had appealed to Cæsar, there was no chance to get rid of him.

8. Paul's Defense before Agrippa, xxvi. 1–29.

1. HIS INTRODUCTION, 1-3.

Vv. 1–3. When Festus took his seat, Agrippa assumed control of the proceedings. (1) **And Agrippa said unto Paul, Thou art permitted to speak for thyself. Then Paul stretched forth his hand, and made his defense :**

(2) **I think myself happy, king Agrippa, that I am to make my defense before thee this day touching all the things whereof I am accused by the Jews ; (3) especially because thou art expert in all customs and questions which are among the Jews : wherefore I beseech thee to hear me patiently.** This was a sincere expression of his happiness on the occasion. He was happy for a reason which it would have been unwise for him to express—the hope of winning the young king to Jesus; and for the especial reason, that now he had an opportunity to speak before one who, unlike Lysias, Felix, and Festus, being familiar with Jewish questions and customs, would be able to understand the case. Agrippa had been brought up in the Jewish faith, and on this account had been entrusted by the emperor with the oversight of religious affairs in Jerusalem, while Judea was under Roman procurators.[1]

2. HIS POSITION TOWARD JEWISH PARTIES, 4-8.

Vv. 4–8. After the exordium he proceeds to declare that he had been reared a Pharisee, and that he still adhered to the hope peculiar to that party. (4) **My**

---

[1] Josephus, *Ant.* xx. i. 3.

manner of life then from my youth up, which was from
the beginning among mine own nation, and at Jerusalem,
know all the Jews ; (5) having knowledge of me from the
first, if they be willing to testify, how that after the
straitest sect of our religion I lived a Pharisee. (6)
And now I stand here to be judged for the hope of the
promise made of God unto our fathers ; (7) unto which
promise our twelve tribes, earnestly serving God night
and day, hope to attain. And concerning this hope
I am accused by the Jews, O king ! (8) Why is it
judged incredible with you, if God doth raise the dead?
His purpose in these statements was not to defend himself against any charge ; for they meet no charge which
had been preferred ; but to awaken within the heart of
the king a chord of sympathy with himself, and thus to
open the way for more serious impressions which he
hoped to make. To this end also he emphasized the
fact that he had spent his youth among his own nation,
and in Jerusalem ; for, had he spent it among foreigners,
he might have been indifferent to Jewish hopes and interests. His declaration that he was brought into judgment because of the hope of the resurrection, is to be understood here, as in xxiii. 6, and xxiv. 21. He means
that his persecution by the Sadducees, the real authors of
his present imprisonment, was instigated chiefly by his
preaching the resurrection, and preaching it through the
risen Jesus. In the demand, "Why is it judged incredible with you, if God doth raise the dead ?" he turned, as
the plural number of the pronoun shows, from Agrippa,
whom he had addressed exclusively before, to the rest of
the assembly, who were, including Festus, unbelievers
in the resurrection. The purpose of the demand was to
challenge them to produce in their own minds a reason

for their incredulity. It was calculated also to strengthen the hold on Agrippa which he may have gained by his previous remarks.

3. HIS FORMER POSITION TOWARD JESUS, 9-11.

Vv. 9–11. In the next division of the speech, Paul makes another and more obvious attempt to enlist the sympathy of the king. (9) I verily thought with myself, that I ought to do many things contrary to the name of Jesus of Nazareth. (10) And this I also did in Jerusalem; and I both shut up many of the saints in prisons, having received authority from the chief priests, and when they were put to death, I gave my vote [1] against them. (11) And punishing them oftentimes in all the synagogues, I strove to make them blaspheme; [2] and being exceedingly mad against them, I persecuted them even unto foreign cities. This brief review of his career as a persecutor, which, brief as it is, adds several new items of information to those given by Luke (viii. 1–3; ix. 1, 2), must have caused Agrippa to say within himself: Why, the man was once on the same side with my family, and he showed the same zeal to suppress the cause of the Nazarene as did my father, my uncle, and my grandfather. It was intended to have this effect, and also to start within the astonished young

---

[1] This remark shows that Paul had a vote in deciding who among the victims of persecution should be slain. This is usually construed as proving that he was a member of the Sanhedrin; but it may be that his vote was cast as a member of a commission appointed by the Sanhedrin to conduct the persecution, and that he had reference to this when he said that he had received "authority and commission" from the chief priests (xxvi. 12.)

[2] Not blaspheme the name of God, which he would not desire them to do · but the name of Jesus.

man the question : ~~How did this persecutor come to un-~~
~~dergo so great a change ?~~

4. HIS INTERVIEW WITH JESUS, 12-18.

Vv. 12–18.   As if to answer the question which he
had raised in the mind of Agrippa, Paul next gives the
cause of his change from a bloody persecutor to an ardent
advocate of the cause of Jesus.   (12) **Whereupon, as I
journeyed to Damascus with the authority and commission of the chief priests, (13) at midday O king, I saw on
the way a light from heaven, above the brightness of the
sun, shining round about me and them that journeyed
with me.   (14) And when we were all fallen to the earth,
I heard a voice saying unto me in the Hebrew language,
Saul, Saul, why persecutest thou me ?   It is hard for
thee to kick against the goad.   (15) And I said, Who
art thou, Lord ?   And the Lord said, I am Jesus
whom thou persecutest.   (16) But arise, and stand upon thy feet ; for to this end have I appeared unto thee,
to appoint thee a minister and a witness both of the
things wherein thou hast seen me, and of the things
wherein I will appear unto thee ;   (17) delivering thee
from the people, and from the Gentiles, unto whom I
send thee, (18) to open their eyes, that they may turn
from darkness to light, and from the power of Satan unto God, that they may receive remission of sins, and an
inheritance among them that are sanctified by faith in
me.**   On the supposition that Paul told the truth,
Agrippa must have seen in these statements enough evidence of the resurrection and glorification of Jesus to
convince him as well as Paul ; and it was probably new
evidence to him ; for, although he must have heard long
before something about the testimony of the original

witnesses of the resurrection, he may never before have heard of Paul's. The evidence conveyed with it proof also that Paul had been like an unruly ox, kicking when goaded, and thereby adding to his own pain while he persecuted the church; and this had doubtless been the experience of Agrippa's ancestors; for no man can persecute unto death unresisting men and women without many pangs of regret, even when he thinks, as Paul did, that he was doing God a service (*cf.* 9).[1]   Furthermore, Agrippa learned from this portion of the discourse that Paul had a commission from heaven, even from the glorified Jesus, to pursue the very course in life which he was now pursuing.

5. WHY HE WAS NOW IN BONDS, 19-27.

Vv. 19, 20.   Having received such a commission, the speaker next tells the king how he had executed it. (19) **Wherefore, O king Agrippa, I was not disobedient unto the heavenly vision; (20) but declared both to them of Damascus first, and at Jerusalem, and throughout all the country of Judea,[2] and also to the Gentiles, that they should repent and turn to God, doing works worthy of repentance.**   Did not the king respond within himself, You are right, Paul; if you saw what you say

---

[1] The fact that he thought he was doing God service must prevent us from interpreting the remark about kicking against the goad as referring to the goadings of conscience.

[2] By construing Paul's language here as if he were aiming to mention the countries which he evangelized in the order in which he visited them, and comparing it with the previous record in Acts, he has been made to contradict Luke. But he uses no expression to indicate that he is following such an order. He follows the order of place instead of the order of time, and therefore there is no contradiction. This statement is to be understood in the light of the preceding narrative.

you did, you were right to obey the heavenly vision, and our people have done wrong in opposing you.

Vv. 22, 23. To show still further that his enemies were in the wrong, he proceeds to tell how they had acted. (21) For this cause the Jews seized me in the temple, and assayed to kill me. (22) Having therefore obtained the help that is from God, I stand unto this day testifying both to small and great, saying nothing but what the prophets and Moses did say should come ; (23) how that the Christ must suffer, and how that he first by the resurrection of the dead should proclaim light both to the people and to the Gentiles. Unless Paul was insincere in these statements of what he had done and taught, Agrippa had no alternative but to acknowledge that he had been unjustly dealt with by the Jews ; and he could certainly see no ground for doubting Paul's sincerity. Furthermore, while claiming that he had taught nothing contrary to the law and the prophets, Paul very ingeniously wove into his argument the claim that the essential feature of his preaching, the resurrection of the Christ from the dead, was itself a matter of inspired prediction. Indeed, he shows that according to prophecy the Christ by his own resurrection was to throw clear and unmistakable light on that very hope of resurrection which had been the glory of Israel, and especially of the Pharisees. All of this was calculated to very deeply impress the mind of the king.

6. AN INTERRUPTION, AND THE CONCLUSION, 24-29.

VER. 24. At this point in the speech Paul was interrupted by Festus. In the ears of that benighted heathen the speech was a very strange one. It presented to him a man who from his youth had lived in a faith

whose chief tenet was belief in the resurrection of the
dead ; who had once persecuted to the death his present
friends, but had been led to change his course by a
vision from heaven ; and who, from the moment of that
change, had been enduring stripes, imprisonment, and
constant exposure to death, in his efforts to inspire
others with his own hope of a resurrection. Such a
career, on the part of a man of great learning and talent,
he could not reconcile with those maxims of ease or of
ambition which he regarded as the highest rule of lif .
Moreover, he saw this strange man, when called to
answer the accusations of his enemies, appear to forget
himself in his zeal to convert his judges. There was a
magnanimity in both the past and the present of his
career, which rose above the comprehension of the sen-
suous politician, and which he knew not how to reconcile with soundness of mind. He seems to have forgotten the proprieties of the occasion, so deeply was he
absorbed in listening to and thinking of Paul. (24) **And
as he thus made his defense, Festus saith with a loud
voice, Paul, thou art mad; thy much learning doth turn
thee to madness.** How darkened the mind that could
regard in this light the life which has been the admiration
of enlightened men, both believers and unbelievers, in
every subsequent age !

VER. 25. Paul saw from the tone and manner of
Festus, as well as from the admission of his own great
learning, that the charge of madness was not intended as
an insult, but was rather the sudden outburst of an excited
and puzzled brain; so his answer was respectful, and
even courteous. (25) **But Paul saith, I am not mad,
most excellent Festus ; but speak forth words of truth
and soberness.** This reply is the only remark in the

whole speech expressly intended for Festus. Paul knew
before, and the charge of madness was only an additional
proof of it, that Festus was beyond the reach of the
gospel; so he seems to have had no thought of him while
he was reaching after king Agrippa.

Vv. 26, 27. In Agrippa Paul had a very different
hearer. His Jewish education enabled him to appreciate
Paul's arguments, and to see repeated in that noble life
of self-sacrifice, which was an enigma to Festus, the
heroism of the old prophets. As Paul turned his eyes
away from Festus and fixed them again on the king, he
saw the hold which he had obtained on the latter, and he
pressed the advantage to the utmost. (26) **For the king
knoweth of these things, unto whom also I speak freely;
for I am pursuaded that none of these things is hidden
from him; for this hath not been done in a corner.
(27) King Agrippa, believest thou the prophets? I
know that thou believest.** He could speak thus confidently of Agrippa's knowledge and of his belief, because
he knew his past history. He knew that the name of
Jesus and his apostles had been household words in the
family of Agrippa for generations, and that the questions
between them and the unbelieving Jews had been discussed in his presence from his childhood, though always
from the view of the enemies of the faith. The remark
that "this hath not been done in a corner" was intended
for Festus, to let him know that his ignorance of the
matter was no proof of its obscurity.

Ver. 28. With matchless skill the apostle had
brought his evidences to bear upon his principal hearer,
and with the boldness which only those orators can feel
who are determined upon success, he pressed this personal appeal so unexpectedly that the king, like Festus,

was surprised into an open expression of his thoughts.
(28) **And Agrippa said unto Paul, With but little
pursuasion thou wouldst fain make me a Christian.**[1]
The remark shows that Agrippa saw very clearly the
aim of the apostle. It is to his credit, being a Herod,
that he did not take offense at an obvious attempt
of the kind. It was evidently embarrassing to him;
but while he turned it off in this cool manner, he
evidently regarded Paul with a respect far beyond that
ever entertained for an apostle by any of his ancestors.
This was a great gain for the gospel; for it showed that
by the patient endurance of persecution, and the continuous pressing of the gospel's claims upon men, the later
generations of its bloodiest foes had been made willing
to give it a respectful hearing.

VER. 29. Paul's reply was never excelled for propriety of diction and magnanimity of sentiment. (29) **And
Paul said, I would to God, that whether with little, or
with much, not thou only, but also all that hear me this
day, might become such as I am, except these bonds.** It
was not till he came to express a good wish for his hearers
and his jailers, a wish for that blessedness which he himself
enjoyed in Christ, that he seems to have thought again
of himself, and to have remembered that he was in chains.

9. THE IMMEDIATE RESULT OF THE SPEECH, 30–32.

Vv. 30–32. The heart that beats beneath a royal
robe is too deeply absorbed in worldly cares to often or

---

[1] Except for the needless introduction of the obsolete word
"fain," this rendering is sustained by the scholarship of this age,
the expression ἐν ὀλίγῳ, on which the whole meaning turns,
never having the meaning "almost," which is given it in the
rendering of A. V.

seriously entertain the claims of the religion of Jesus.
A corrupted Christianity, which shifts its demands to
suit the rank of its hearers, has been acceptable to the
great men of the nations, because it helps to soothe an
aching conscience, and it is often useful in controlling
the ignorant masses; but men of rank and power are
seldom willing to become altogether such as the apostle
Paul. They turn away from a close pressure of the
truth, as did Paul's royal auditor. (30) **And the king rose
up, and the governor, and Bernice, and they that sat
with them : (31) and when they had withdrawn, they
spake one to another, saying, This man doeth nothing
worthy of death or of bonds. (32) And Agrippa said
unto Festus, This man might have been set at liberty if
he had not appealed unto Cæsar.** The decision of those
who had not heard Paul before, that he was not worthy
of death, or even of bonds, was based on nothing but
the speech to which they had listened ; and in that there
was no attempt to state the charges, or to make a formal
reply to them. The decision then was evidently the result of the tone of honesty and sincerity which breathed
all through the speech, and which could not be feigned
so as to deceive these experienced men of the world.
As Agrippa coincided with the rest, Festus was led to
regret that he had not released Paul before he made his
appeal to Cæsar ; for now he is in the same predicament
precisely as when he first stated the case to the audience.
He was under the painful necessity of sending to the emperor a prisoner, the charges against whom he was not
able to express in writing, and of whom he would be
compelled to say, that he had done nothing worthy of
being sent at all. The fact that he did send such a statement (*elogeum* was its official title) must have much to

do with the mildness of Paul's imprisonment when he
reached Rome (xxviii. 16, 30, 31), and with his subsequent release.

SEC. III.   PAUL'S VOYAGE TO ROME.

(XXVII 1–XXVIII. 16.)

1. FROM CÆSAREA TO FAIR HAVENS, 1–8.

Vv. 1, 2.   Very soon after the speech before Agrippa,
Paul found himself about to begin the long expected
voyage to Rome.   The answer to his prayers was about
to be realized (Rom. xv. 30–32), and the promise made
by night in the prison of Claudius Lysias, that he should
yet testify of Jesus in Rome, was about to be fulfilled.
This was brought about, not by any miraculous interposition, but by a providential combination of circumstances.   The machinations of the Jews, the avarice of
Felix, the indecision of Festus, the prudence of Paul,
and the Roman statute for the protection of citizens, had
very strangely, yet very naturally, combined to fulfill
a promise of God made in answer to prayer.   (1) **And
when it was determined that he should sail for Italy,
they delivered Paul and certain other prisoners to a centurion named Julius, of the Augustan band.   (2) And
embarking in a ship of Adramyttium which was about
to sail unto the places on the coast of Asia, we put to sea,
Aristarchus, a Macedonian of Thessalonica, being with
us.**   Here once more we see the significant "we" of
Luke, showing that he was in Paul's company at this
time, and started with him to Rome.   As he had come
with Paul to Jerusalem (xxi. 17, 18), the probability is

that he had been close to him during his imprisonment. This stay of more than two years in Palestine gave Luke the opportunity, if he had not enjoyed one before, to gather up all the information contained in his gospel; and it is highly probable that he also composed his gospel at this interval of comparative inactivity.[1] Aristarchus had also come up with Paul to Jerusalem (xx. 4), and as Paul, in an epistle written after his arrival in Rome, styles him his fellow-prisoner (Col. iv. 10), it is probable that, for some cause not mentioned in the text, he also had been arrested in Judea, and was sent to Rome on an appeal to Cæsar.[2]

The Augustan band (cohort), in which Julius was a centurion, was so called in honor of the emperor. As the ship was of Adramyttium, a city on the western coast of Mysia, it was homeward bound; and it was not expected to convey the soldiers and their prisoners to Rome. The centurion started out with the expectation, afterward realized, of falling in with some vessel sailing to Italy, into which he could transfer his prisoners and soldiers.

VER. 3. Luke's account of the voyage on which Paul and his company are now embarked is the only

---

[1] If the book of Acts was completed, as I have argued in the Introduction (xxiii. *ff.*), during the Roman imprisonment, Luke's gospel, which certainly was written earlier (Acts i. 1), was probably written during the first part of the same imprisonment, or during that in Cæsarea; for there was probably no earlier interval in which he had the leisure and the opportunity to gather all the information which he claims in his introduction (i. 1–4).

[2] This is held in doubt by Alford and Gloag (see their commentaries), who suppose that the term "fellow prisoner" is used figuratively when applied to Aristarchus; but there is no fact noted by either of them to justify the figurative interpretation of the term.

narrative of the kind in the Bible, and it is full of interest from beginning to end. **(3) And the next day we touched at Sidon ; and Julius treated Paul kindly, and gave him leave to go unto his friends and refresh himself.** The friends found in Sidon were doubtless brethren in Christ; and from this we infer that Sidon, as well as Tyre, had received the gospel (*cf.* xxi. 3–6). With the brethren in the latter place Paul had spent a week on his sad voyage to Jerusalem, and now, on his voyage to Rome, he is cheered by the hospitality of those in the former. That he needed refreshing the next day after he had set sail is best accounted for by supposing that he was subject to seasickness, and the side wind them prevailing (4), which caused the ship to rock, accounts for the seasickness. A few hours on shore afforded great relief, although it was but temporary.

Vv. 4–6. The vessel continued to sail northward for a time, and avoided striking out into the open sea. **(4) And putting to sea from thence, we sailed under the lee of Cyprus, because the winds were contrary. (5) And when we had sailed across the sea which is off Cilicia and Pamphylia, we came to Myra, a city of Lycia. (6) And there the centurion found a ship of Alexandria sailing for Italy; and he put us therein.** As the proper course of the ship was westward, the lee of Cyprus must have been its eastern end, whereas the southern coast would have been chosen had the wind been favorable. Another reason for passing into the waters north of Cyprus and south of Cilicia may have been that sailors then knew, as they do now, that a sea current there runs to the westward, by the aid of which they could make better headway in tacking against a contrary wind. The ship from Alexandria, which they met according to their expectation, must also have encountered the prevailing westerly winds, and was therefore far to the east of the direct line from Alexandria to Italy. She had a cargo of wheat (38) brought from the granaries of Egypt, and she was a vessel of the largest size, accommodating, after her new passengers were taken aboard, two-hundred and seventy-six souls, including the crew (37).

Vv. 7, 8. When they left Myra in the new ship the wind was still contrary. (7) **And when we had sailed slowly many days, and were come with difficulty over against Cnidus, the wind not further suffering us, we sailed under the lee of Crete, over against Salmone ; (8) and with difficulty coasting along it we came unto a certain place called Fair Havens ; nigh whereunto was the city of Lasea.** The distance from Myra to the Island of Cnidus is only about one hundred and thirty miles, and as they were "many days" making that distance, the sailing must have been slow indeed. From that island to Cape Salmone, the eastern extremity of Crete, the direction is nearly due south ; and this run was therefore made at a right angle to the wind. The purpose of this tack was to avoid the open sea west of Cnidus, and also to take advantage of the lee shore of Crete, by which they could make about one hundred miles toward their destination before reaching the open sea again. In the meantime they were hoping every day for a change of the wind. The difficulty of sailing along the coast of Crete grew out of the unfavorable course of the wind, which constantly threatened to drive them out to sea, and compelled them to make short tacks, as the headlands, causing counter currents in the wind, afforded them opportunity. Good seamanship was required for this, as it had been all the way.

Fair Havens was about halfway the length of the island.

2. Discussion about Continuing the Voyage, 9–12.

Vv. 9–12. The voyage had thus far been so tedious that winter was now approaching, and it was deemed unsafe to attempt to complete it before spring. It was a question, however, whether they should spend the winter where they were, or try to reach a more desirable winter haven. (9) **And when much time was spent, and the voyage was now dangerous, because the Fast was now already gone by, Paul admonished them, (10) and said unto them, Sirs, I perceive that the voyage will be with injury and much loss, not only of the lading and the ship, but also of our lives. (11) But the centurion gave more heed to the master and to the owner of the ship, than to those things which were spoken by Paul. (12) And because the haven was not commodious to winter in, the more part advised to put to sea from thence, if by any means they could reach Phœnix, and winter there ; which is a haven of Crete, looking north-east and south-east.** The fast here mentioned is the Jewish fast on the day of atonement, which was the tenth day of the seventh Jewish month (Lev. xxiii. 26, 27), and it occurs usually within our month of October. Paul's advice was the beginning of an activity on his part which forms the chief matter of interest in the remainder of the voyage. He spoke from experience, and not from inspiration (see under 21–26), but his words, as we shall see, came very near being fulfilled. It was quite natural that the centurion credited the judgment of the sailing master and the owner of the ship, rather than that of Paul, of whose nautical experience he knew nothing. The centurion had control of the ship, notwithstanding the presence on board of the owner, because he had taken it into the service of the emperor. As the harbor of Phœnix looked (seaward) to the north-east and the south-east, being open in those directions, and closed in others, it was well adapted to protecting vessels from such winds as had been prevailing. It was westward of Fair Havens on the southern coast of Crete, and only thirty-four miles distant.

3. A VAIN ATTEMPT TO REACH PHŒNIX, 13–20.

VER. 13. The harbor called Fair Havens lay on the east side of Cape Matala, which the sailors would have to double in order to reach Phœnix, and this they could not do in the face of a west or northwest wind ; so they waited for the wind to change. (13) **And when the south wind blew softly, supposing that they had obtained their purpose, they weighed anchor and sailed along Crete, close in shore.** The words, " thinking they had gained their purpose," express the thought that they were " as good as there" when they started with this soft wind from the south, the very wind for which they had waited. It was a deceitful lull, the prelude to a fearful change.

Vv. 14–20. The ship sailed smoothly for awhile over an unruffled sea, with its boat hanging astern ready for the debarkation at Phœnix. (14) **But after no long time there beat down from it a tempestuous wind, which is called Euraquilo ; (15) and when the ship was caught, and could not face the wind, we gave way to it, and were driven. (16) And running under the lee of a small island called Cauda, we were able, with difficulty, to secure the boat ; (17) and when they had** hoisted it up, they used helps, undergirding the ship; and, fearing lest they should be cast upon the Syrtis, they lowered the gear, and so were driven. (18) And as we labored exceedingly with the storm, the next day they began to throw the freight overboard; (19) and the third day they cast out with their own hands the tackling of the ship. (20) And when neither sun nor stars shone upon us for many days, and no small tempest lay on us, all hope that we should be saved was now taken away. The name Euraquilo, given to this wind, is equivalent to North-easter, and it indicates the direction from which it blew. It rushed down suddenly from the mountain tops of Crete, and struck the vessel when she was within but a few hours of her destination. Under the lee of Cauda the water was not so rough, and this enabled the sailors, before getting out into the rough water again, to take the three precautions here mentioned. They got the boat on board to prevent it from being dashed to pieces against the side of the vessel. The undergirding consisted in passing cables around the hull of the vessel, and drawing them tight by the capstan, so as to add their strength to that of the vessel's hull, and prevent her timbers from parting. The gear, or rigging, was lowered, all except sail sufficient for steering the vessel, in order to impede her progress toward the dreaded Syrtis, the great banks of quicksand near the coast of Africa, toward which the wind was driving them. The vessel was lightened on the following day by tossing overboard a part of the freight, that in consequence of drawing less water, the waves might strike her sides with less force. The tackling was thrown overboard the next day for the same purpose; and it consisted in the spars, planks, cordage, and so forth, which were carried for the purpose of making repairs. As the mariners of the age were dependent on the sun and the stars exclusively for a knowledge of the direction in which they were sailing, when they had seen neither for many days, and the storm was unabated, they had no definite idea as to where they were, and hence their despair of being saved.

Vv. 21–26. The owner of the ship, the master, the centurion, and all on board had formed by this time a better estimate of Paul's judgment, and they were prepared to listen with respect when he addressed to them the following speech :   (21) **And when they had been long without food, then Paul stood forth in the midst of them, and said, Sirs, ye should have hearkened unto me, and not have set sail from Crete, and have gotten this injury and loss.   (22) And now I exhort you to be of good cheer ; for there shall be no loss of life among you, but only of the ship.   (23) for there stood by me this night an angel of the God whose I am, whom also I serve, (24) saying, Fear not, Paul; thou must stand before Cæsar ; and lo, God hath granted thee all them that sail with thee.   (25) Wherefore, sirs, be of good cheer ; for I believe God, that it shall be even so as it hath been spoken unto me.   (26) Howbeit we must be cast upon a certain island.**   Paul's former prediction had come so near being fulfilled, that his hearers were not disposed to be captious about the apparent discrepancy between that and what he now says; and when they heard him now predict their safety on the ground of a direct revelation from heaven, which he had not claimed before, they could see clearly that the former prediction was only his judgment. Moreover, the words of the angel, " I have granted thee all them that sail with thee," conveyed the idea that but for this grant they all would have perished, and that this grant was made in answer to his prayers in their behalf. Let it be noted, too, that foremost of all in this answer to Paul's prayers is the assurance that he "must stand before Cæsar;" for with Paul the chief ground of wishing to escape the present danger was that he might at last see Rome, answer before Cæsar as he had before Agrippa, and then, being set free, preach to the Jews and the Gentiles in the "eternal city."

4. The Ship at Anchor, and Paul on the Watch, 27–32.

Vv. 27–32. Notwithstanding the assurance of safety given by Paul, the peril for a time became more imminent. (27) But when the fourteenth night was come, as we were driven to and fro in the sea of Adria, about midnight the sailors surmised that they were drawing near to some country; (28) and they sounded, and found twenty fathoms; and after a little space, they sounded again, and found fifteen fathoms. (29) And fearing lest haply we should be cast ashore on rocky ground, they let go four anchors from the stern, and wished for day. (30) And as the sailors were seeking to flee out of the ship, and had lowered the boat into the sea, under color as though they would lay out anchors from the foreship, (31) Paul said to the centurion and to the soldiers, Except these abide in the ship, ye can not be saved. (32) Then the soldiers cut away the ropes of the boat, and let her fall off. The ship was nearing the island now called Malta, which is farther south than that portion of the sea now called the Adriatic, so this name covered a greater space in geography then than now. The ground of the surmise among the sailors, that they were nearing land, must have been the roar of breakers on the rocky shore, at first so indistinct that they could not be certain what it was. The sounding tested the surmise, the rapidly decreasing depth proving that land was near. To run ashore in such a storm, and on such a coast, would be certain destruction to the ship and all on board. To cast out all the anchors at hand would be in all probability to wreck the vessel where she was by attempting to hold her stiff against the rushing waves, even if the cables did not part and leave her to drift upon the rocks. The sailors felt so sure that the one fate or the other would befall the ship before morning, that they resolved to risk their own lives in an attempt to get ashore, notwithstanding the darkness and the rocks. They easily deceived the landsmen by their pretense of putting another anchor out at the bow, where it could not possibly be of any service; but Paul was too much of a seafaring man to be so deceived, and his watchfulness saved the lives of all the passengers. Although he had assurance from God, which he implicitly believed, that not a life on board would be lost, he remembered that the promise was, "God hath granted thee all them that sail with thee," and so he was just as watchful to save those committed to his care as if no promise of their escape had been given. Indeed he goes so far as to tell the soldiers that none would be saved if the sailors were allowed to leave the ship. This was because none but skillful sailors could run the vessel safe ashore in such a wind and on such a coast. From this we gather the lesson, that when God makes us any promise the realization of which can in any part be promoted by our own exertion, such exertion is an understood condition of the promise. The rule has many applications in matters both temporal and spiritual, which we can not pause to specify. In decreeing that a thing shall be done, or predicting that it will be done, God anticipates the voluntary actions of the parties concerned, and interferes directly only when the purpose would otherwise fail ; and in our dealings with God we are therefore to be as active and laborious as though we had no promise of his help, and yet as confident of help as though all were to be done by God alone.

5. Paul Comforts the Crew, and the Ship is Lightened, 33–38.

Vv. 33-36. When the treacherous attempt of the sailors had been frustrated, there seemed to be nothing to do but to trust to the anchors and wait for day. The deck was swept from stem to stern by every large wave, so doubtless the hatchways were closed, and all descended below. In moments of supreme terror like this, when the stoutest heart is apt to quail, a man who maintains complete self-possession is instinctively leaned upon by the rest. Paul was this man. By outwitting the sailors he had impressed both them and the soldiers with a sense of his coolness and watchfulness, and this at once made him the leading spirit in the whole ship's company ; and now, while they were swinging at anchor, and had nothing to do except to keep themselves from rolling about on the floor, he imparted to them all a portion of his own cheerfulness and strength. (33) **And while the day was coming on, Paul besought them to take some food, saying, This day is the fourteenth day that ye wait and continue fasting, having taken nothing. (34) Wherefore I beseech you to take some food, for this is for your safety ; for there shall not a hair perish from the head of any of you. (35) And when he had said this, and had**

taken bread, he gave thanks to God in the presence of
all, and he brake it, and began to eat. (36) Then were
they all of good cheer, and themselves also took food.
Paul knew that there is nothing so cheering to tired and
hungry men as a good meal ; and he knew that in order
to safely reach the shore, there was exertion yet to be
required of them for which they were not capable in
their present enfeebled condition. His statement that
they had taken no food for fourteen days, if taken literally, would not be incredible to those who are familiar
with the famous fast of forty days by Dr. Tanner, of
Philadelphia; but in rightly judging it we are to remember that this is not Luke's statement to his readers,
but Paul's to his hearers ; and that if they had taken
any food at all, they knew how to interpret his remark
accordingly. When a kind hostess in these days asserts
that her guests have eaten nothing at all, and insists that
they shall take a little more, no one misunderstands her,
or charges her with misrepresentation. It is a colloquial
exaggeration which is common and admissible. Those
addressed by Paul had certainly eaten but little; those
of them who were much given to seasickness had scarcely
raised their heads from their couches during the time ;
and those who had suffered the least had not been able to
sit down in quiet to eat. Certainly no cooking could
have been done on the vessel. The free and easy way in
which Paul spoke of the matter was in itself cheering,
and the statement that the eating which he advised was
for their safety, still further exhibits his conviction that
the promised escape of every one was dependent in part
on their own exertions (cf. note under 31).

Vv. 37, 38. The assembling of the whole ship's
company at the time of this meal seems to have suggested

the mention of the number of persons on board; and
perhaps it was at this moment that a count was first
made, in order that, by another count when they landed,
it should be known whether any perished, and if so, how
many. (37) **And we were in all in the ship two hundred
three score and sixteen souls. (38) And when they had
eaten enough, they lightened the ship, throwing out the
wheat into the sea.** This further lightening of the ship
was for the purpose of enabling her to run nearer in
shore than she otherwise could, ere she would strike bottom. It was no easy task to raise the sacks of grain from
the hold of the vessel and get them overboard when she
was pitching and rolling as she must have been. They
needed for it all the renewed strength imparted by the
food they had taken.

6. THE SHIP IS STRANDED, BUT THE MEN ESCAPE, 39–44.

Vv. 39–41. All was now done that could be until
daylight should reveal the exact nature of the breakers
ahead, and of the shore beyond. (39) **And when it was
day, they knew not the land; but they perceived a certain bay with a beach, and they took counsel whether
they could drive the ship upon it. (40) And casting off
the anchors, they left them in the sea, at the same time
loosing the bands of the rudders; and hoisting up the
foresail to the wind, they made for the beach. (41) But
lighting upon a place where two seas met, they ran the
vessel aground; and the foreship struck and remained
unmovable, but the stern began to break up by the violence of the waves.** It seems, from the consultation of the
sailors, that they thought it barely possible to so guide
the ship as to strike the only smooth spot on the

shore ; and the difficulty was occasioned by the intervening rocks between which the ship must be safely
steered. This revealed to the passengers the wisdom of
Paul in keeping the sailors on board when they tried to
leave the ship the night before. The anchors were left
in the sea, both because they would be of no further use
to the ship, and because, if ever so much needed, they
could not have been recovered. The rudders were only
paddle-rudders, one at each corner of the stern, and
while the ship was riding at anchor their handles were
pressed down on deck, and fastened there, so that their
paddle ends would be lifted out of the water, and saved
from being broken by the waves. These were now
loosed that they might be used in steering, and at the
same moment the foresail was hoisted to give the vessel
the forward movement through the water without which
the rudders would have little effect. By skillful use of
both sail and rudders, the ship was steered clear of the
rocks, and landed at or near the point aimed at. The
impetus with which wind and wave sent her forward
caused her bow to plow its way deep into the sand, so
that she was held fast. Two heavy waves (in sailor's
phraseology, " two seas"), coming from different directions around the rocks, alternately struck the immovable
stern like two immense hammers in the hands of giants,
and the timbers, which had already been greatly strained
by swinging at the cables all night, immediately began
to give way. If the persons on board were to escape,
there was now no time to be lost in leaving the vessel.

Vv. 42–44. At this critical juncture the soldiers
proved themselves as unfeeling as the sailors had in
the night. They could now see plainly that they owed
their lives to Paul, yet they had no sense of gratitude

for it. (42) And the soldiers' counsel was to kill the prisoners, lest any of them should swim out and escape. (43) But the centurion desiring to save Paul, stayed them from their purpose ; and commanded that they who could swim should cast themselves overboard, and get first to the land : (44) and the rest, some on planks, and some on other things from the ship. And so it came to pass that they all escaped safe to the land. The centurion, who showed himself a kind and discreet man throughout the voyage, seems to have been the only soldier on board who had the right sense of gratitude to Paul for his invaluable services, and yet for the other prisoners he seems to have had little or no concern, seeing that it was for Paul's sake that he saved them. The necessity for swimming, even after the vessel struck, grew partly out of the fact that she was still in water too deep for wading; for a ship of her size draws not less than eight or ten feet when she is light; and partly because large waves were rolling in from the deep and sweeping high up on the shore. It was no easy task to reach the shore, and the escape of all was truly remarkable, the more so in that it had been predicted by Paul.

7. Paul Escapes Another Peril, xxviii. 1–6.

Vv. 1, 2. Fortunately for the shipwrecked voyagers, they struck a hospitable shore, and one that was well populated. Doubtless as soon as daylight appeared the inhabitants along the coast saw the distressed vessel, and watched with eagerness her perilous run ashore. They were at the spot in crowds when the vessel stranded. (1) And when we were escaped, then we knew that the island was called Melita. (2) And the barbarians showed us no common kindness ; for they kindled a fire, and re-

ceived us all because of the present rain, and because of the
cold. They knew the name of the island (now Malta) by
what the islanders told them. Luke calls the islanders
barbarians because thus the Greeks and Romans styled
all people except themselves. The term bore less of reproach then than it does with us. These barbarians were
very far from being savages. It was with no little labor
that they kindled a fire in the rain, and a fire so large
that two hundred and seventy-six men could get near it.
These men were already drenched from swimming ashore,
and the rain that was falling prevented them from getting dry ; but still the warmth of a large brush fire made
them much less uncomfortable. The rain was one of
those chilling October or November drizzles, which are
sometimes more disagreeable than a colder rain in the
middle of winter.

Vv. 3–6. Paul was not a preacher after the style of
a modern clergyman, who is particular not to soil his
hands with menial labor, and who expects everybody to
be ready to serve him, while he preserves his dignity and
looks on. He did not stand by the fire which others
had kindled, and allow others without his help to keep
it burning : but he took a hand in the disagreeable job
with the barbarians and the sailors. (3) But when Paul
had gathered a bundle of sticks, and laid them on the
fire, a viper came out by reason of the heat, and fastened
on his hand. (4) And when the barbarians saw the
beast hanging from his hand, they said one to another,
No doubt this man is a murderer, whom, though he has
escaped from the sea, yet Justice hath not suffered to
live. (5) Howbeit he shook off the beast into the fire,
and took no harm. (6) But they expected that he would
have swollen, or fallen down dead suddenly; but when

they were long in expectation, and beheld nothing amiss
come to him, they changed their minds, and said that he
was a god. This is Lystra reversed. There Paul was
first taken for a god, and afterward stoned. Here he
was first taken for a murderer, and then for a god. The
bad opinion of him was not based on the naked fact that
he had been bitten by the viper; for they knew that
good men were liable to that; but by the occurrence of
this fatality in so close connection with his escape from
an apparently hopeless shipwreck. If they had discovered that he was a prisoner, this contributed to their
conclusion. They ascribed his punishment to the god-
dess of justice, ($\delta i \varkappa \eta$) who appeared to be determined
that he should not escape her hands. But when they
discovered that the bite, the fatality of which they knew
so well, had no effect on him, their conclusion that he
was a god was as natural to them as the previous conclusion that he was a murderer. The miracle was
wrought by the direct power of God, and it was intended
to make the very impression on the islanders that it did
—a temporary impression which must have been followed
before many days by a true conception of Paul's person
and office.[0]

8. Paul's Usefulness in Melita, 7–10.

Vv. 7–10. The voyagers were fortunate in the place
at which they landed, not only in its being inhabited,
but in the character of its principal inhabitants. (7)
Now in the neighborhood of that place were lands be-

---

[1] For the nautical information connected with this voyage,
not found in the text, I am largely indebted to Mr. Howson's ex-
haustive treatise on the subject in Life and Epistles of Paul, vol.
ii. chap. xxiii.

longing to the chief of the island named Publius, who
received us, and entertained us three days courteously.
(8) And it was so, that the father of Publius lay sick of
**fever and dysentery ; unto whom Paul entered in, and
prayed, and laying his hands on him healed him.** (9)
**And when this was done, the rest also who had diseases
in the island came and were cured : (10) who also honored us with many honors : and when we sailed, they
put on board such things as we needed.** The title here
given to Publius, " the chief man of the island," is am-
biguous ; but the Greek words so translated ($ὅ\ πρῶτος\ τῆς$
$νήσου$) have been found on inscriptions in the island, as
the title of the Roman ruler, and this justifies the conclusion that Publius held this office. If by " us," in
verse 7, Luke means the whole ship's company, which is
the most natural reference, the hospitality of Publius in
entertaining with food and lodging two hundred and seventy-six men was worthy of all commendation. Perhaps he placed some of them in the houses of his tenants
on the estate, but they were provided for at his expense
for three days, after which some other arrangement
seems to have been made. He was well rewarded however by Paul in the healing of his father, whose disease,
even in our own days of medical skill, is considered a
very dangerous one. It is probable, too, that the ship's
company found accommodations in the homes of the
others in the island whose sick were healed in the same
manner. In this way Paul, who at the beginning of the
voyage was one of the most unobserved of all the passengers, at last became the mainstay of the whole company, and exercised an ascendancy over every mind. It
was gratitude to him that caused the islanders at last to
supply the ship's company with all the comforts needed

for the remainder of their voyage. By this time the soldiers were doubtless glad that they had not killed him before they left the ship (xxvii. 42).

We can not suppose that Paul healed diseases among the islanders so generally without mentioning the name of Jesus. On the contrary, though Luke makes no mention of it, we must think that from the palace of the governor to the remotest hamlet of the island the name and power of Jesus were fully made known during the three months of his stay.

9. THE JOURNEY COMPLETED, 11–16.

Vv. 11–14. It was the winter months which were spent in the island ; and so soon as navigation was considered safe in the early spring, the voyage was resumed. (11) And after three months we set sail in a ship of Alexandria, which had wintered in the island, whose sign was The Twin Brothers. (12) And touching at Syracuse, we tarried there three days. (13) And from thence we made a circuit, and arrived at Rhegium : and after one day a south wind sprang up, and on the second day we came to Puteoli ; (14) where we found brethren and were intreated to tarry with them seven days ; and so we came to Rome. This ship of Alexandria, like the one that had been wrecked, was doubtless loaded with wheat for the Italian market ; and it had been checked in its course the previous fall by the same tempest which had wrecked the other ship. It was kept in port three months or more when it was within three or four days' sail of its destination. The Twin Brothers, whose wooden images, standing at the bow or the stern, constituted her sign, or, as we would say in modern phraseology, her name, were Castor and Pollux, the two fabled sons of Jupiter who were the special guardians of sailors. Thus the emblems of heathenism were kept constantly before the eyes of the early Christians. The stay at Syracuse, the famous city of ancient Sicily, may have been occasioned either by contrary winds, or by the discharge of freight. It is distant from Malta something less than one hundred miles, and the run was made in less than twenty-four hours. Rhegium, the next port at which they touched, was at the southern extremity of Italy, and not far from the mouth of the straits of Massena. It is now called Reggio. The circuitous sail in reaching it was doubtless the result of unfavorable winds. The south wind which sprang up after they left Rhegium was directly in their favor, and the run of one hundred and eighty miles thence to Puteoli, in a single day, was a swift one. Puteoli, the ruins of which are still visited by travelers, was situated on the northern shore of the bay to which Naples afterward gave its name. The latter city, which was then a mere hamlet, superseded Puteoli in the course of time as the seaport of that portion of Italy, while the latter gradually sank into decay. That Paul found brethren in Puteoli, is proof of the extent to which the gospel had already been preached in Italy ; and that he obtained permission from the centurion to remain with them seven days, is proof additional of the respect with which Julius had come to regard him. The seven days included a Lord's day, in which Paul and his companions had the privilege of breaking the loaf with these newly found brethren.

Vv. 15, 16. The journey from Puteoli was over a paved road, which was a branch of the famous Appian Way that led from Rome to Brundusium, the modern Brindisi. The space is now traversed by a railroad.

This main road was reached at Capua, thirty-three miles
from Puteoli, whence the route lay along this road to
Rome, the whole distance by land being about one hundred and fifty miles. The reason that the ship had
landed so far from Rome, was that Puteoli had the nearest harbor that would admit vessels of the deepest draft.
The delay at Puteoli. and the long journey by land, had
given time for the brethren in Rome to hear that Paul
was coming. (15) And from thence the brethren, when
they heard of us, came to meet us as far as the Market
of Appius, and the Three Taverns : whom when Paul
saw, he thanked God, and took courage. (16) And when
we entered into Rome, Paul was suffered to abide by
himself with the soldier who guarded him. The market
(more properly forum) of Appius, was a town on the
Appian Way forty-three miles from Rome; and the
place called Three Taverns was a village ten miles farther toward the city. The group of brethren who met
Paul at the latter place started later, no doubt, than the
others. That Paul thanked God and took courage when
he met them, implies that he had until then experienced
some fear as to his reception by these brethren. As he
was coming to this proud city a prisoner in chains, they
might have felt that the reputation of the cause in Rome
forbade their recognition of him as one of their great
men; and if the brethren in the city should thus stand
aloof from him, it would be vain to hope to accomplish
any great good there while a prisoner, or even after securing his freedom. When, however, the brethren
showed themselves so true in Christian sympathy as to
ignore time-serving considerations, and to come as
though they were meeting a man who would reflect hon-
or upon them, all gloomy doubts were dissipated. and

courageous hope took their place. Among those brethren we may suppose that he recognized some, at least, of
that noble band whose names he had mentioned with
high encomiums in the last chapter of his epistle to their
church, and who had passed with him through trials of
the faith in years gone by. He had a thrilling story to
tell these faithful brethren about his voyage, and it was certainly a matter of delight to them to find that, although he
was a prisoner, he had won the esteem and confidence of the
centurion who had him in charge, and as we may safely
suppose, of all the soldiers who had once thought of
killing him to prevent the possibility of his escape. They
witnessed, too, on the arrival in Rome, the extension to
him of the further and unusual courtesy of permitting
him, instead of being placed in the common military prison, to dwell by himself, with no restraint other than that
of having a single soldier to guard him. This favor was
the result of the representation made by Festus, that he
had done nothing worthy of death or of bonds, and also
of the representation made by the centurion Julius of his
conduct on the journey. Like Joseph when a slave in
the house of Potiphar, and a prisoner in the king's
prison, he had so conducted himself as to win the implicit confidence of those who had him in charge, from
the beginning to the end of his confinement. So it must
ever be with him who maintains under all circumstances
a strictly Christian deportment.

SEC. IV. PAUL'S PRISON LABORS IN ROME,

(XXVIII. 17-31.)

1. HE OBTAINS AN INTERVIEW WITH THE LEADING JEWS, 17-22.

Vv. 17-20. Paul had now completed a journey which
he had contemplated for many years, and he had met
with some brethren whom he had requested more than
three years before to strive together with him in prayer
to God, that he might come to them with joy, and with
them find rest (Rom xv. 24 ; 30–32). But how different
his entrance into the imperial city from that for which
he had hoped. Instead of coming a free man, to appear
in the synagogue and the forum for the name of Jesus,
he had been marched in between files of soldiers, presented to the authorities as a prisoner sent up for trial,
and was being kept under a military guard night and
day. How dismal his prospect for preaching the gospel
to those who were in Rome! If Paul the tent-maker,
a stranger and penniless, had commenced his labors in
the commercial emporium of Greece, " in weakness and
in fear and in much trembling " (I. Cor. ii. 3), how
must Paul the chained prisoner have felt when he began
a similar work in the capital city of the whole world ?
The prospect was sufficiently disheartening ; but he had
one ground of encouragement which he did not enjoy in
Corinth ; he was supported by a band of tried lieutenants,
both men and women, as brave and true as ever executed
the orders of a great leader ; and every one of these was
a hand which he could stretch out to lead interested
hearers to his place of confinement. He made no delay
in beginning his work, and his first movement was to

call the principal unbelieving Jews of the city to a fraternal interview. (17) And it came to pass, that after
three days he called together those that were the chief
of the Jews; and when they were come together, he said
to them, I, brethren, though I had done nothing against
the people, or the customs of our fathers, yet was delivered prisoner from Jerusalem into the hands of the Romans; (18) who, when they had examined me, desired to
set me at liberty, because there was no cause of death in
me. (19) But when the Jews spake against it, I was
constrained to appeal unto Cæsar; not that I had aught
to accuse my nation of. (20) For this cause therefore did
I intreat you to see and to speak with me; for because
of the hope of Israel I am bound with this chain. Paul's
wisdom in seeking this interview, and in making these
particular statements, is quite obvious. It would naturally have been supposed, from the fact that he was accused by his own countrymen in Judea, that he had
committed some crime; and from his appeal to Cæsar,
that he intended to prefer grave charges against his accusers. The statement that the Romans would have released him but for the opposition of the Jews, was much
in his favor on the first point; and on the latter, his own
disavowal was sufficient. His closing remark, that it
was for the hope of Israel that he was bound with a
chain, which is to be understood in the same sense as
when made on two previous occasions (xxiii. 6; xxvi.
67), was calculated to enlist their sympathies, because it
was no uncommon thing for Jews to be persecuted, and
because it gave them assurance that he still cherished the
fondest hope of the pious Jew.

Vv. 21, 22. The response of the Jews was candid
and becoming. (21) And they said unto him, We nei-

ther received letters from Judea concerning thee, nor did
any of the brethren come hither and report or speak any
harm of thee. (22) But we desire to hear of thee what
thou thinkest: for as concerning this sect, it is known
to us that everywhere it is spoken against. It is rather
surprising that they had heard nothing from Judea concerning Paul; but it often happens that events pass
almost unnoticed by a living generation, which become
afterward the important events of history. By hearing
nothing they had heard " no harm " of him, though they
had heard much prejudicial to the " sect " which he re-
represented. If they had acted as many do now, they
would have refused to hear him at all because of the evil
report of his sect: but the fact that the latter was everywhere spoken against was the very reason they wished
to hear Paul in reference to it. Perhaps they had themselves refused to hear the preachers that preceded Paul
in Rome ; but the courteous manner in which he had invited them to his lodging, and the conciliatory manner
of his address to them, had won them to a better feeling.
Had they always felt as they now did, they would doubtless have heard of him before, and most favorably,
through the epistle which he had written to the church
in their city more than three years previous.

2. A SECOND INTERVIEW WITH THE JEWS, 23-28.

Vv. 23, 24. Before the Jews took leave of Paul
they made an appointment to come again and give him
a formal hearing. (23) And when they had appointed
him a day, they came to him into his lodging in great
number: to whom he expounded the matter, testifying
the kingdom of God, and persuading them concerning
Jesus, both from the law of Moses and from the prophets,

from morning till evening. (24) And some believed the things which were spoken, and some disbelieved. The discourse was a long one, occupying sufficient time to place the whole subject before them, and to support every separate proposition with adequate evidence; but the result was the one always experienced in a congregation of Jews.

Vv. 25–28. From what follows we have reason to suppose that the disbelieving party gave some unbecoming expression to their sentiments. (25) And when they agreed not among themselves, they departed, after that Paul had spoken one word, Well spake the Holy Spirit by Isaiah the prophet unto your fathers, (26) saying,

Go thou unto this people and say,

By hearing ye shall hear, and shall in no wise understand ;

And seeing ye shall see, and shall in nowise perceive :

(27) For this people's heart is waxed gross,

And their ears are dull of hearing,

And their eyes they have closed ;

Lest haply they should perceive with their eyes,

And hear with their ears,

And understand with their heart,

And should turn again,

And I should heal them.

—(28) Be it known therefore unto you, that this salvation of God is sent unto the Gentiles : they will also hear. So skillful a preacher as Paul would not have closed his discourse with a warning like this, had he not seen or heard something in his audience to call forth these burning words from the sixth chapter of Isaiah. The passage had been quoted before by Jesus, and ap-

plied to the unbelieving Jews of Galilee (Matt. xiii. 14,
15); and it was after this used by the apostle John in
explaining the unbelief of those who heard Jesus in Jerusalem (Jno. xii. 40). It furnishes the true explanation
of the failure of the gospel to win some who hear it fully
proclaimed; and the explanation is contradictory to the
once popular doctrine, that the Holy Spirit must regen-
erate the soul by an immediate exercise of its power before the gospel can be received. According to this doctrine, the reason why some of Paul's hearers went away
unbelievers was that a divine influence was withheld
from them which was granted to the others. But according to the view expressed in this passage, the Lord had
done as much for the one class as he had for the other;
and the reason some were believers and the others not,
was because the latter were " dull of hearing, and their
eyes were closed." Their eyes and ears were not closed
by some power above themselves; for they are expressly
charged with closing them. As they closed them voluntarily, they had the power to keep them open; and it is
implied that, had they done so, the result would have
been reversed—that they would have seen the truth,
that they would have heard it favorably, that they would
have understood it, and that they would have turned to
the Lord and been healed. This was precisely the experience of the party who believed. They had themselves been gross of heart and dull of hearing, and had
closed their eyes against the previous preachers in Rome;
but now they opened their eyes and ears to what Paul
presented, and as a consequence they understood with
their hearts, they turned, and were healed. In this order of things there is no respect of persons with God,
neither can any man ascribe his final ruin to a with-

holding of saving influences on the part of the Holy Spirit.

3. Duration of the Imprisonment, and Continued Labors, 30, 31.

Vv. 30, 31. The narrative is now brought abruptly to a close. (30) **And he abode two whole years in his own hired dwelling, and received all that went in unto him, (31) preaching the kingdom of God, and teaching the things concerning the Lord Jesus Christ with all boldness, none forbidding him.** This hired dwelling is the one alluded to in verse 16, where it is said that " Paul was suffered to abide by himself with the soldier that guarded him." This soldier, as we see in the remark, " I am bound with this chain," (20) was chained to him day and night. The guard was changed according to uniform custom every three hours, unless an exception was made of the sleeping hours in this particular case. In this way it became the privilege of not less than five or six different soldiers to be present and hear his preaching and teaching every day. As this continued for two whole years, it is by no means surprising to hear Paul say in his epistle to the Philippians, " My bonds became manifest in Christ throughout the whole prætorian guard, and to all the rest" (i. 13). The prætorian guard was a body of soldiers kept at Rome, in a camp outside the city, for the purpose of guarding the emperor, and keeping prisoners awaiting trial in the imperial court. As each soldier returned to the camp from guarding Paul, he had a strange story to pour into the ears of his companions, and so it spread from lip to lip. It even reached some of the household of Cæsar, perhaps by means of the guards about the palace (*ib.* iv. 22).

The remark, that " he received all that went in unto him," implies many visitors. These were in part drawn together by the increasing fame of the imprisoned preacher ; but chiefly we may assume by the activity of Paul's brethren in the city, who would naturally busy themselves in this way. By the zeal of the same brethren the rent of his hired dwelling was paid; but such was their own poverty, that when a contribution was forwarded to him by the distant church in Philippi, it relieved a felt want (Phil. iv. 10, 11, 18).

Preaching and teaching are here distinguished, as they are throughout the book of Acts, the former being addressed to the unbelievers, and the latter to the believers. That he did both shows that both believers and unbelievers were drawn to his lodging. His activity was unforbidden, because, being limited to those who voluntarily sought him in his private dwelling, it could cause no such outbreak, as it had in other cities. The results of these labors Luke does not see fit to enumerate, neither does he gratify the natural curiosity of the reader by telling us the result of Paul's appeal to Cæsar. This last circumstance can be accounted for, as we have argued in the Introduction (xxiii.–xxvi.) only by the supposition that the last sentence of the book was written just at the end of the two years, and previous to the trial. But with the exception of this omission, the leading purpose of the narrative suggests this as a fitting close. Having started out to show the manner in which the apostles executed their commission in turning sinners to the Lord, the writer has now led us from Jerusalem through Judea, Samaria, the provinces of Asia Minor, the islands of the Mediterranean, Macedonia, and Achaia, to the imperial city of Rome; and leaving the principal laborer here, still " preaching the kingdom of God, and teaching the things concerning the Lord Jesus Christ," his main purpose is accomplished, and the narrative closes.

A commentary on Acts, strictly confined to the text, would here be brought to a close; but as it has been a part of our plan to give more fullness to the narrative by drawing from other inspired sources, we have yet a few paragraphs to pen. The desire inspired in the thought_ful reader by the closing chapters, to trace a little farther the career of Paul, may in some degree be gratified. This desire has reference especially to the two questions, what were the results to the cause of Christ of his long imprisonment? and what was the issue of his appeal to Cæsar?

In reference to the first question, we have already remarked that his entrance into Rome was so different from that which he had hoped for, that his prospect for doing good there must have been very gloomy. But as he was permitted without interruption to teach and preach for two whole years in his hired dwelling, we can not doubt that he accomplished much, notwithstanding his confinement as a prisoner. We learn something of the results from epistles written during the time. Ephesians, Colossians, and Philemon were the earliest of these epistles. They were all written at one time, and forwarded, the first two by Tychicus, and the last by Onesimus, the two messengers traveling together.[1] In the

---

[1] As he sent Onesimus back to Philemon, and had to send the epistle by some messenger, we conclude that he sent it by him (8–12); and as he sent Tychicus to the brethren to whom the two other epistles were directed, we likewise conclude that he sent those epistles by him (Eph. vi. 21, 22; Col. iv. 7, 8); and it is stated expressly that Onesimus was sent with Tychicus (Col. iv. 8, 9).

two former he shows a sense of the embarrassments of
his situation, by exhorting the brethren to pray for him,
that a " door of utterance " might be opened to him, and
that he might have boldness to speak the gospel as it
ought to be spoken. The last reveals the fact that at
the same time he had already accomplished something.
Out of the very dregs of the dissolute society of the
metropolis, a runaway Greek slave had been induced to
visit the apostle, and hear the gospel. It proved the
power of God to free him from a bondage far worse than
that from which he had fled. After he became a disciple
Paul found him " profitable to him for the ministry," being of service, no doubt, in bringing within the sound of
the gospel many of his former companions. His master
was Philemon, a convert of Paul's residing in Colosse.
Paul desired to retain him in his service ; but out of respect to the legal rights of Philemon he sent him home
with an epistle in which he delicately intimates the propriety of setting free a slave capable of such usefulness ;
and thinking it probable that Onesimus had defrauded
his master in some way, promises to pay the sum, whatever it might be (Philemon, 8–21). His preaching had
begun to take effect on the most hopeless class of the
city's population, at the time when he was urging distant
brethren to pray that God would open to him a door of
utterance (Eph. vi. 18–20; Col. iv. 2, 3). But eventu-
ally a door of utterance was opened far wider than he
had dared to expect. In the epistle to the Philippians,
written at a later period, when he was expecting his
trial and release, he says : " Now I would have you
know, brethren, that the things which have happened to
me have fallen out rather unto the progress of the gospel ;
so that my bonds became manifest in Christ through-

out the whole prætorian guard, and to all the rest; and that most of the brethren in the Lord, being confident through my bonds, are more abundantly bold to speak the word of God without fear" (i. 12–14). He also says, near the close of the same epistle, "All the saints salute you, especially they that are of Cæsar's household" (iv. 22). These results, as we have stated before, sprang most naturally from the word carried into the barracks of the prætorian guard by the many soldiers who alternately guarded Paul, and heard what he taught and preached to his visitors; for the soldiers of the guard, and the employés about the palace of Cæsar, would naturally be among the very last to visit the apostle's lodging for the purpose of hearing him.

During these arduous and embarrassing labors, Paul enjoyed the coöperation not only of the true and brave men and women whom he found in the church at Rome, but also of other fellow-laborers who had toiled with him in other fields, and who came to him from a distance. Timothy, last mentioned before in the journey from Corinth to Jerusalem, united with him in the salutations of Colossians, Philemon, and Philippians. Aristarchus and Epaphras were his fellow prisoners (Col. iv. 10; Philemon 23); Mark, who once forsook him, and went not with him and Barnabas to the work, was now with him, and about to go on a distant journey at his request (Col. iv. 10); Demas, who afterward forsook him and went to Thessalonica, "having loved this present world," was as yet by his side (Col. iv. 14; II. Tim. iv. 10); and Luke, the beloved physician, who shared the perils of his voyage from Cæsarea, was his constant companion (Col. iv. 14).

In reference to Paul's appeal to Cæsar nothing is said expressly in the New Testament; yet there is conclusive inferential ground for the belief that it was successful in securing his release. This evidence is found in the events and journeys described in the epistles to Timothy and Titus, for which no place can be found in the period covered by Acts. Among these are his leaving Timothy in Ephesus to counteract the influence of certain teachers, while he went into Macedonia (I Tim. i. 3); his leaving Titus in Crete to set in order the things that were wanting there (Titus i. 5.); his visit to Miletus when he left Trophimus there sick (II. Tim. iv. 20); and his journey toward Nicopolis to spend the winter (Tit. iii. 12.)

It would be interesting, were it not going beyond the limits of a commentary on Acts, to follow in the details of these labors till the curtain of authentic history drops and shuts out from our view his departure to be with Christ. When he obtained a hearing under the appeal which brought him to Rome, his enemies could have nothing to say against him worse than they had said before Felix and Festus; and his defense before them, together with that before King Agrippa, suggests the line in matter and method of that which he most probably laid before the emperor and his council. We shall not tax our imagination in an attempt to depict the scene. We bid him adieu till the resurrection morning, well pleased that the course of the narrative on which we have commented has kept us for so long a time in his company.

INDEX.